JOHN TURNER

JOHN TURNER

An Intimate Biography of
Canada's 17th Prime Minister

STEVE PAIKIN

sh.

**SUTHERLAND
HOUSE**

TORONTO, 2022

Sutherland House
416 Moore Ave., Suite 205
Toronto, ON M4G 1C9

Sutherland House and logo are registered trademarks of The Sutherland House Inc.

First edition, October 2022

If you are interested in inviting one of our authors to a live event or media appearance, please contact sranasinghe@sutherlandhousebooks.com and visit our website at sutherlandhousebooks.com for more information about our authors and their schedules.

We acknowledge the support of the Government of Canada.

Manufactured in China
Cover designed by Lena Yang

Library and Archives Canada Cataloguing in Publication
Title: John Turner : an intimate biography of Canada's 17th prime minister / Steve Paikin
Names: Paikin, Steve, 1960- author.
Identifiers: Canadiana 20220234469 | ISBN 9781989555835 (hardcover)
Subjects: LCSH: Turner, John N. | LCSH: Prime ministers—Canada—Biography. | LCGFT: Biographies.
Classification: LCC FC626.T87 P35 2022 | DDC 971.064/6092—dc23

ISBN 978-1-989555-83-5

To my dear friend Arthur Milnes,
Whom I first met at John Turner's birthday party,
And who truly loved Canada's 17th Prime Minister.
Thanks for your friendship and legendary stories.

Table of Contents

Introduction

S T. MICHAEL'S CATHEDRAL BASILICA IN downtown Toronto should have been the perfect place to pay tribute to one of the most significant figures in Canadian political history. Spectacularly beautiful inside and out, the 175-year-old church has capacity for 1,600 souls. Under normal circumstances, even that would have been inadequate to accommodate all the people wanting to gather on October 6, 2020, to pay their respects to the deceased. Of that man, former prime minister John George Diefenbaker once said: "He was a person who could walk down the main street of most cities and towns in Canada and meet people he knew by name."

Even John Turner himself (who once famously saved Diefenbaker from drowning) used to break into a big grin thinking about the range of his contacts. "The only boast I've ever made," he'd say, "is that I know more Canadians by their first names than any other Canadian alive." There is no way to prove him right but few doubted him.

John Napier Turner started September 19, 2020, at breakfast with his wife, Geills. Ninety-one years old and in failing health, he died around noon. His long career in Canadian public life and wide acquaintance called for a massive send-off at St. Michael's. It was not to be.

The world was in its sixth month of one of the worst pandemics ever, formally known as SARS-CoV-2. What that meant on October 6 was that fewer than 180 people would be permitted to gather at the basilica. They arrived at designated times, wearing masks, and sitting far from one another. Hymn singing was

1

forbidden. Many people who wanted to be there could not be accommodated on the slimmed-down invitation list, and many who were invited wouldn't come for fear of catching the virus, including Turner's only surviving sibling, Brenda Norris, his Liberal disciple, former federal cabinet minister Lloyd Axworthy, and his long-time friend, the environmental watchdog Monte Hummel, founder of the World Wildlife Fund, who was supposed to deliver one of the eulogies. Precious few Canadians had yet been vaccinated. Thousands were dying and the elderly, in particular, were terrified to gather indoors.

The impression conveyed by Canada's all-news networks, which covered the funeral live, was that a small portion of Turner's friends and family had wanted to be there that day. It was not true by a long shot, and it was not the only indignity the Turner family would suffer after the patriarch's death. Canada's national newspaper, *The Globe and Mail*, announced in its banner headline: "Former Prime Minister John Turner, who was in office for just 11 weeks, dies aged 91."

"I thought it was stupid and dishonorable," says former Turner staffer Marc Kealey, speaking for many of the deceased's fans. They were furious that a lifetime of accomplishment and public service was ignored by the headline in favour of what, in fact, was one of the less important parts of Turner's life, his brief time at 24 Sussex.

"Seventy-nine days is your whole legacy?" Kealey asks incredulously. "Not balancing the budget as finance minister? Supporting Meech Lake against his party? The fight of his life, the Free Trade Agreement? His championing of democracy? He was a prophet on all of that."

Bob Rae, Canada's newly appointed ambassador to the United Nations, dropped his diplomatic guard on Twitter, referring to the *Globe* headline as a "cheap shot. John Turner was a man of great achievement and public spirit."

"I was so sad he didn't get the send-off he deserved," says John Baird, who despite being a former Conservative cabinet minister both federally and in Ontario, had a long-standing friendship with Turner, and admiration for him. "He was a good man I think he's one of the truly great Canadians of his generation."

Politicians, like good dramas, often have three acts to their lives. There's life before politics, life in politics, and life after politics. For many, the middle period is the central feature of their narrative, and sometimes the whole of their reputation and accomplishments.

The extraordinary thing about John Turner is that three acts aren't nearly enough to capture the ebb and flow of fortune, political or otherwise, in his life. His early years in England were tragic with the death of his father and brother, neither of whom he knew. He was lucky to have a mother who somehow overcame those tragedies and put him, her only surviving son, on a path to a life of consequence. He was an Olympic-level athlete, a world traveller, a successful lawyer, and a parliamentarian for the first time at age thirty-three, just eighteen months after John F. Kennedy became president of the United States. The comparisons to JFK in terms of ambition, lifestyle, and handsome appearance would follow Turner for decades.

He was *the* star in Prime Minister Pierre Elliott Trudeau's star-studded cabinets of the late 1960s and 1970s, carrying both the justice and finance portfolios. He then shocked the country by quitting politics to become a Bay Street rainmaker at the tender age of forty-six. Despite Turner's spending nearly a decade on the sidelines, Liberals embraced his return to public life in 1984 when he succeeded Trudeau as party leader and became prime minister. As *The Globe* reminded us, it didn't last long. He would have the shortest tenure of any Canadian prime minister save for Sir Charles Tupper, whose sixty-eight days in 1896 remain the fewest.

His six years as leader of Her Majesty's loyal opposition were punctuated by internecine warfare within the Liberal ranks, disloyalty on a shocking level, and self-inflicted wounds of such significance that when he left politics again in 1990 many of his former colleagues on Bay Street lost his phone number, thinking he was damaged goods. It is odd but accurate to say that becoming the prime minister of Canada did not crack the list of Turner's most significant accomplishments. But it is what many, especially in the media, remembered of him. Turner rarely complained about his predicament. He had always known that his return to politics in 1984 could be spectacular or disastrous. It was both. The rejection he experienced wounded him deeply.

Kealey left Turner's office in 1990 but kept in touch. "We spoke every day," he recalls. Turner loved the telephone, and much preferred it to the impersonal nature of emails. He'd spend hours every day calling his vast network of friends and associates and, especially, Kealey, his unofficial aide-de-camp. Every former Canadian prime minister seems to have someone who takes it upon themselves to become his or her unofficial contact with the rest of the world. In Turner's case, Kealey wanted the job. The two men loved one another and enjoyed shooting the breeze, and Kealey appreciated that his old boss needed the emotional support of someone in his corner from his political days reminding him that he was still relevant. Almost all ex-politicians, never mind former prime ministers, suffer a kind of depression on exiting political life. They know that no future position will provide the sense of purpose offered by high public office. The phone often stops ringing and without some new mission to snap you out of your funk, the days can be excruciatingly long and lonely.

That must have been what was pre-occupying Turner one day in 1992 as he spoke with Kealey, who was now vice-president of planning and development at Whitby General Hospital, an hour east of Toronto. It was likely extremely difficult for someone of his generation, a man who took pride in his toughness and resiliency, to raise the matter he wanted to discuss. The former prime minister seemed to be *persona non grata* in a federal Liberal Party now led in opposition by Jean Chrétien, Turner's most despised intra-party rival. Turner was ensconced at a good law firm, Miller Thomson LLP in Toronto, but it was second-tier, not one of the famed "Seven Sisters" such as Stikeman Elliott where he'd begun his legal career. The hurting sixty-two-year-old ex-politician eventually got to the point.

"Marc, I need your help rehabilitating my reputation," he said.

At this same time, another Turner protégé, Richard Mahoney, was practicing law on his own in Ottawa. Mahoney (pronounced MA-hunny) had been president of the Young Liberals in the mid-1980s when Turner was leader. After graduating from the University of Ottawa faculty of law in 1985, he worked in Turner's office on Parliament Hill. "We'd come of age politically in the Liberal Party because of him," Mahoney says. "We loved him, admired him. We were all star-struck by him. Then I got to know him. He made our careers in the Liberal Party."

On leaving Turner's office, Mahoney had run a monthly cigar club for former Turner staffers. They would invite guest speakers, gather for dinner and a stogie, and enjoy reminiscing. (The club fizzled out once it became illegal to smoke in restaurants.) Around the same time Turner made his request of Kealey, Mahoney had been thinking it might be fun to have Turner join his group in a friendly, low-key setting. It wasn't about redemption so much as an opportunity to fete a man he admired. Mahoney called Kealey with the idea. Maybe because the proposed event wasn't ambitious enough, Kealey steered their conversation to a larger celebration of Turner's birthday, something that would appropriately honour his legacy.

Mahoney suggested the bash take place at his favourite restaurant, Les Fougères, a highly acclaimed Quebec dining spot just over the Ontario–Quebec border in the Gatineau Hills' town of Chelsea. They decided to invite several dozen of Turner's colleagues from over the years, taking over the entire restaurant for the night and charging each invitee enough to cover the costs.

On the assigned day, Turner and a posse of his former staffers including Mahoney, Kealey, Al Pace, and John Webster, flew to Ottawa, rented a car, and drove to the cottage of former Turner chief-of-staff Peter Connolly on Meech Lake in Quebec. The group would hang out at the cottage before heading to the restaurant and then crash at Connolly's overnight. Knowing his former boss, Mahoney brought along a bottle of Scotch for Turner to give to Connolly as a thank-you. Nearly a decade after doing it for real, Mahoney was still "staffing" Turner.

They pulled up at a Meech Lake marina in the rental car. Kealey honked the horn to the beat of "shave and a haircut, two bits," the signal for Connolly's pontoon to pick them up and make for his island cottage. Turner presented his host with the bottle of Scotch: "This is for you, and it's not a fucking souvenir!" The group polished it off on Connolly's dock before heading to Les Fougères.

On arriving at the restaurant, everyone noticed something strange. A car was parked off to the side with two men inside, one of them Derek Lee, member of Parliament for Scarborough–Rouge River. It was odd because Lee hadn't been invited to the event. When pressed to explain himself, Lee confessed that he'd been ordered to "take names" of who was attending and report back to someone in the prime minister's office of Jean Chrétien. Apparently, Liberal MPs were told attending the Turner soirée was forbidden. (Thunder Bay–Nipigon MP Joe Comuzzi said "screw it" and went anyway; veteran MP Herb Gray, interim party leader between Turner's departure and Chrétien's takeover in 1990, followed orders.) Clearly, some in the PMO thought attendees were up to no good. They also thought the choice of restaurant, so close to Meech Lake, signalled a poke at Chrétien (Turner had supported the so-called Meech Lake constitutional accord while Chrétien had not).

"None of this was anti-Chrétien," Mahoney insists. "We just wanted to celebrate a man who was so good to us." That may have been the case, but Chrétien loyalists took the dinner as evidence that the Turner–Chrétien feud was alive and well, never mind that Turner's political career was long over.

The surroundings were ideal for a night of reminiscing. Les Fougères, according to restaurant critic Joanne Kates, was then the second-best restaurant in the country. The setting was bucolic, a wood structure with a screened-in porch and a garden where the proprietors grew their own vegetables. Drinks were served in the garden, after which guests took their seats according to a seating plan personally reviewed and approved by Turner. Jeff King gave the invocation. He had been a Turner supporter for decades. The former Ottawa city councillor and president of the Ontario Liberal Party was a member of the famed "195 Club," a reference to the 195 delegates at the 1968 Liberal leadership convention who stuck with Turner until he fell off the ballot. King, like Turner, was also a serious Roman Catholic. (He quit the law to become a priest in 1999 and died in May 2020, several months before Turner.)

After dinner, David Lockhart rose to speak. An adviser during Turner's time as leader of the opposition, Lockhart is renowned for his fantastic impression of his boss, usually performed in his absence. For this occasion, he chose to perform by heart his impression of JFK's presidential inaugural, a tribute to his and Turner's mutual admiration for the Kennedy clan. Asked how a normally shy man managed to recite the entire inaugural before a demanding audience, Lockhart shrugs: "I had been drinking."

Later in the evening, Kealey welcomed the assembled guests and introduced Mahoney who ad-libbed his introduction of the guest of honour. Turner took the floor and, always cognizant of not overstaying his welcome, spoke for 12 minutes. "He never liked it when people went on too long," Mahoney says.

Turner spoke about one of the great passions of his life: the importance of participating in politics, and his firm contention that one person *can* make a difference. He reminded the audience of the paper he presented on legal reforms at the 1960 Kingston Conference, a meeting designed to start Liberals thinking about new policies after two straight election defeats. Two years later, Turner was a member of Parliament and six years after that he was the justice minister who implemented the tenets of his paper, designed to give all Canadians greater access to their justice system.

"He was proof that one person could have an impact on society," Mahoney says. "It was just a great story."

At the conclusion of his remarks, the guests rose and gave Turner a standing ovation. Tears flowed and menus specially printed for the occasion were passed around for his autograph. He signed them all with his favourite slogan: "Keep the faith."

Many days later when word of the party leaked, some considerable unhappiness about it surfaced. Jan Innes, a long-time Liberal adviser who spent two decades as a vice-president at Rogers Communications, learned not only that she hadn't been invited, but that no women were.

"Jan gave me total shit," Kealey admits. "It was a total oversight not to invite women. We just didn't think of it."

While it's accurate to say that Turner gave many young women their first big break in politics, it's also fair to point out that keeping up with evolving social norms regarding women wasn't his strongest suit. The party may have been an example of that.

"Mr. Turner wanted to swear and drink so he preferred it that way," Kealey explains. "Then we went back to the [Connolly] compound after for the greatest after-party ever."

Ahh yes, the after-party. If the event at Les Fougères put everyone in a boozy, ribald mood, it paled in comparison to what transpired later at Connolly's Meech Lake hideaway. A bunch of guests continued to reminisce and drink into the early morning. It might have been 3 a.m. before everyone finally went to sleep, well aware that many of them had to be up in a few hours to catch a flight back to Toronto. Kealey knocked on Turner's bedroom door over and over in hopes of waking him. All he heard in return was a shouted, "Yeah, fuck you." Eventually, everyone who needed to get up and get dressed did so. They gathered on the dock ready to pontoon back to civilization. Turner, despite almost no sleep, looked sharp in a business suit when a woman in her sixties came paddling by in a canoe. The lake was calm. The sun was glinting off it, a scene of serenity.

"Good morning, Mr. Turner," she said. "Quite the party you had last night."

The seventeenth prime minister of Canada, the Rt. Hon. John N. Turner, looked back at another citizen of this great country and responded: "Lady, you have no fucking idea."

* * *

What was intended as a one-time birthday celebration for Turner became a turning point in his life. Tales of the legendary evening swept through Liberal political circles and his birthday parties became an annual affair, drawing bigger crowds in larger venues. As he got older and politics got harsher, Turner's message of nurturing and participating in democracy seemed to gain import. It was more than quaint advice from a voice of yesteryear. It was an urgent *cri de coeur* from someone who himself had made huge personal and financial sacrifices to serve the public.

I was invited to attend Turner's seventy-ninth birthday in 2008 at the home of Al Pace and Kristin Morch in Toronto, and his eightieth birthday party at the

Fairmont Château Laurier in Ottawa, emceed by former CTV News anchor Lloyd Robertson. Not long after that, Turner, Kealey, and I would gather for lunch every June, having realized that our birthdays were within three days of one another. It all culminated in 2019 with an extravaganza in Ottawa for Turner's ninetieth birthday, at which hundreds showed up to pay tribute to him, as columnist Andrew Cohen said, "with levity, sentimentality, and generosity." Every living prime minister contributed, most with in-person speeches, a few by videotape. Turner had now become one of only four Canadian prime ministers to live into his nineties. He was no longer seen as the leader who'd led the Liberals to their worst drubbing ever (that dubious distinction now belonged to Michael Ignatieff's third place showing in 2011). Rather, he was honoured by a roomful of political friends and one-time adversaries for being one of the country's greatest living champions of democracy, and the media coverage was extraordinarily positive. Physically, Turner was in rough shape. He needed a walker to get into the Sir John A. Macdonald Ballroom on Wellington Street, and ample assistance to mount the few steps to get onstage. But even Chrétien, his one-time nemesis, got into the spirit of the evening. Recalling the night he (or someone in his office) sent spies to "take names" at Les Fougères at the inaugural birthday bash, Chrétien leaned down to whisper in Turner's ear: "And John, we won't be taking names tonight." Turner laughed.

The reputational redemption tour was complete: mission more than accomplished.

A year later on June 7, I called to wish Turner a happy birthday and we spoke on the phone for several minutes. He was now too infirm to attend our annual lunch. While he sounded fine, I did wonder how many more times we might speak. As it turned out, it was the last time.

After Turner's death, some of his former political colleagues approached me with the idea of writing a biography of him. Turner never wrote his memoirs, telling friends that he was "never a kiss-and-tell kind of guy." When I pointed out that Carleton University historian Paul Litt had written a Turner biography only a decade earlier, Turner's friends made some strong points.

Much had happened in the former PM's life since the Litt book's publication. More importantly, it was suggested that the previous book was a fine "official" version of Turner's life, but because the subject was still alive at the time, many of the insightful and intimate details of Turner's life had not been disclosed. It was also the case that Turner's family had occasionally awful relations with reporters, and their voice was missing not only from the Litt book but previous ones as well. Finally, it was suggested that my personal knowledge of Turner (and my acquaintanceship with his son David, who used to live across the road and just up the street from me in midtown Toronto) might contribute to a different take.

Having just finished a nearly 600-page biography on one of Canada's greatest premiers, Bill Davis, I was in no rush to write another book. Yet the lure of John Turner's unique story proved to be too enticing to ignore. His was not a typical three-act political play of entry, accomplishments/failures, and exit. It was far more intriguing with stunning contrasts and multiple twists and turns. Despite his tragic start in life, he was our John Kennedy, with everything going for him: good looks, intelligence, connections, a love of country, and an old-fashioned duty to serve. He was also insecure, lacking confidence, needlessly temperamental with those he worked with, and more comfortable with the political world of Mackenzie King, St. Laurent, and Pearson than the era of hyperventilating 24/7 news coverage that dawned in the 1980s. As Conrad Black put it in his memoir *A Life in Progress*: "John went almost overnight from tomorrow's man to yesterday's without ever enjoying the day in which he actually lived."

I was a twenty-four-year-old boy reporter for CHFI and CFTR News on the occasion of Turner's 1984 Liberal leadership convention triumph. I'd had numerous interactions with him subsequently, and we enjoyed each other's company immensely. At the end of every get-together, he'd say "stay in touch" in just such a way that you knew he meant it, and so I did. When something unexpectedly awful happened in my life some years ago, he was one of the first people to call me to offer emotional support.

None of that means this book will be overly laudatory or ignore the myriad personal failings and pitfalls in Turner's life. But maybe his friends were correct that my relationship with him gave me license to go where previous books had not. I was granted unprecedented access by his family to Turner's private papers at Library and Archives Canada. I perused literally thousands of documents stored in the archives. Happily, Turner and his staff kept absolutely everything from his time in politics, including confidential letters and memos circulated among the leader and his staff and advisers during his return to public life from 1984 to 1993. This material is gold to a biographer. I have made ample use of it in these pages, and it has helped me tell Turner's story in much richer and more intimate detail than it has ever been told before.

Steve Paikin
Manitoulin Island, Ontario and Toronto, Canada
2021–2022.

CHAPTER ONE

The Early Years

T HE PEOPLE WHO WERE FORTUNATE enough to attend John Turner's funeral learned something quite surprising about him. We had never known his real name. The late prime minister was born John Napier Wyndham Turner. He dropped Wyndham in his early twenties. The name came from his father, whose full name was Leonard Hugh Wyndham Turner. That Turner had a second middle name was a revelation to everyone who had known him over the years as "JNT."

Turner's mother was the brilliant Mary Phyllis Gregory, the daughter of a miner, born on June 28, 1904, in Rossland, B.C. She earned a bachelor's degree at the University of British Columbia, a masters at Bryn Mawr, and pursued a PhD at the London School of Economics. There is mystery surrounding Leonard, John's father and Phyllis' husband. Some say he was a journalist at the *Manchester Guardian*. There were rumours (almost certainly untrue) that he was a gunrunner in the Great War.

John Turner's wife, Geills, a self-described "family-tree nut," has discovered information about her husband's parents that even he didn't know, for example, that Leonard was born on July 2, 1904, four days after his future wife, in France, because Leonard's father had business in France. "John could have had a French passport, too," says Geills, noting that he had both Canadian and British passports.

Leonard was said to have been a student at Oxford, but his family has been unable to find record of his having enrolled there. When John himself was a student at Oxford, he would visit relatives in search of more information about his father but mostly struck out. "He'd get bits and pieces and insinuations and he could never figure out why that was," says Elizabeth. "My grandfather's family was secretive."

Phyllis and Leonard Turner met, presumably in England, married, and had three children in relatively short order: John, born June 7, 1929, in Richmond, Surrey, England; Michael, born in July 1930 somewhere in Surrey; and Brenda, born August 20, 1931, in Dorking, Surrey. This part of the Turner family history is not only murky but also tragic. There were complications during Michael's birth that required significant medical attention be given to Phyllis. Because of her distress, the mucus wasn't properly suctioned from Michael's nose after he was born and he died shortly thereafter.

Following their loss, the couple seemed to want a fresh start. They agreed to move to Phyllis' native British Columbia. Close to their departure date, Leonard took ill and required thyroid surgery. Phyllis urged her husband to have the procedure done in Canada. Michael's death had left her deeply suspicious of the British health care system. But it would have been too expensive to cancel their travel plans then purchase new tickets for the trans-Atlantic boat trip, so the plan was for Phyllis and the two children to keep their scheduled departure date, with Leonard joining them in Canada after what was expected to be a relatively simple operation. Leonard's operation was botched and he died from complications on November 18, 1932. He was twenty-eight. His son, John, was three.

It often happens after family tragedy that the past is buried. The two surviving Turner children, John and Brenda, would learn little of their family history. Neither knew where their father was buried. Neither knew their parents' wedding date, giving rise to speculation that Phyllis had been pregnant with John by the time the couple married. Their mother was an intensely private person, and those questions either weren't asked or, if they were, remained unanswered. The historian Robert Bothwell was a great friend of Turner but says "I could never get John to talk about his father."

After a very hopeful start to life, Phyllis, with more educational credentials than all but a few women of her day, now found herself home in Rossland, a widow and mother of two children, living with her parents, and trying to figure out how to start over. Her PhD thesis would go unfinished. In 1934, she wrote directly to Prime Minister R.B. Bennett, applying for a job in the federal public service. His office urged her to come to Ottawa without her family to see what might be available. Phyllis went to Ottawa with her kids. "That was kind of gutsy on her part," says granddaughter Elizabeth.

Appointed to the Canadian Tariff Board, Phyllis moved permanently to Ottawa with her children. She eventually moved to the Dominion Trade and Industry Commission, and then the Wartime Prices and Trade Board. She worked her way up to chief economist to the minister of finance during World War II and was the highest-ranking female civil servant in the country, earning the cover of *Maclean's* magazine. "My mother was an extraordinary woman," Brenda says. "She was much smarter than either John or me."

Phyllis was also a demanding mother, insisting her children apply themselves in school. Only A's were acceptable and any mark of B or lower was greeted with, "What's this for?" She was also compassionate. Brenda remembers that when she contracted polio as a child of two or three, her mother took time off from work to massage her legs every hour on the hour for two straight weeks, per the medical advice she received. Other children she knew who did not receive the same treatment, says Brenda, wound up with permanent leg braces. "But thanks to my mother, sports became a huge part of my life. I could have been in an iron lung."

Although they wouldn't have used the term then, the Turner kids grew up in a world of privilege. John would take the family's English Springer Spaniel, Blue, for a walk in the same exclusive Sandy Hill neighbourhood where William Lyon Mackenzie King, who replaced Bennett as prime minister, lived at nearby Laurier House. As devout Catholics, the kids would attend mass every Sunday at St. Joseph's Parish before lunching at the Château Laurier with their mother, who would be meeting other high-ranking officials. After lunch, John and Brenda would head to the pool for a swim. The Turner family's summer cottage at Kirk's Ferry in the Gatineau Hills was next door to that of diplomat and future prime minister Lester Pearson. The Mackenzie King government's minister of everything, C.D. Howe, would drop by the Turner cottage for visits.

Phyllis was an attractive as well as an accomplished woman and very much in demand in Ottawa's social whirl. She would often attend events on the arm of the bachelor prime minister and, later, opposition leader R.B. Bennett. He would frequently send her a dozen roses. Lord Tweedsmuir, the governor general, was always excited to see her. She also accompanied another bachelor prime minister, Mackenzie King, to events. Carl Goldenberg, a prominent constitutional adviser and future senator, once took Phyllis out on a date but nothing came of it. "There was this awful brat hanging around," he said, referring to John. "I thought he needed a good spanking." Phyllis clearly had opportunities but she was unwilling to start another relationship with her children still young and a war to be won.

"It was a happy childhood," says Brenda. "There were just the three of us so we were all very close. John and I fought and argued all the time but he was my idol. I adored him."

The absence of Leonard was not as devastating as it might have been at other times. "We all grew up without fathers," Brenda stresses. "You have to remember during the war, all our friends had fathers serving overseas. We never felt deprived. All our friends were in the same situation."

Young John may have led a privileged life but his family wasn't rich and he resented being told that he was. He started his education at a public Catholic elementary school, Holy Cross Convent in Sandy Hill, where one of his best friends was Douglas Roche. The boys were born seven days apart (Turner was older).

"I've known him longer than anyone else alive except for his sister," says Roche, now ninety-two and living in Edmonton. The two would ride their bikes around Ottawa. As a demonstration of how small Canada was in these years, Turner and Roche would eventually serve as MPs during the same three-year stretch in the early 1970s. Roche would be succeeded in his Edmonton–Strathcona seat in 1979 by David Kilgour, Turner's brother-in-law.

When he turned eleven, Turner enrolled at the exclusive Ashbury College independent school, but eventually reunited with Roche at St. Patrick's College school in the Roman Catholic board when Ashbury's fees got too high. By the time they were both sixteen, Turner was two years ahead of Roche in school. "He was a genius," Roche says.

Turner was the editor of *The Patrician*, the St. Patrick's school newspaper, and Roche was one of the reporters Turner assigned to cover junior football games. "I found him rather intimidating," Roche recalls. "He was very smart and a real track star. The whole school watched him in competition. He was a big man on campus. People thought the sun rose and set on him. It was clear this was a guy going places."

Two things happened to Turner at the age of sixteen. He finished high school and decided to follow in his mother's footsteps at UBC, living at the Beta Theta Pi fraternity house. He enrolled in a general arts program and continued to pursue his journalistic interests, writing a sports column called "Chalk Talk" for the campus newspaper, *The Ubyssey*. He was now going by the byline "Chick" Turner.

Secondly, his mother remarried and moved to Vancouver, becoming Mrs. Frank Ross, the wife of a wealthy industrialist who was one of the

"Dollar-a-Year Men" performing war-time service in Ottawa. Ross was a friend of C.D. Howe's and owner of the Saint John Shipyard and Dry Dock Co. Ltd. in New Brunswick. He and Phyllis moved in the same elite circles. The couple flourished in British Columbia, with Ross appointed lieutenant-governor of the province in 1955, and Phyllis serving two terms as chancellor of UBC starting in 1961.

If Turner was the big man on campus during high school, he was doubly so at UBC. He joined the swim team and was captain of the track-and-field team. (When Catherine Clark, daughter of Canada's sixteenth prime minister, interviewed him in 2013 and prefaced a question with, "You were one of the fastest sprinters in the country," Turner raised his index finger to interrupt: "I was *the* fastest sprinter in the country: 9.6 seconds for the 100-yard dash.") Turner routinely competed against the best track stars from universities on America's West Coast. He ran at a 1948 pre-Olympic meet at the Los Angeles Memorial Coliseum, site of the 1932 (and future 1984) Summer Olympic Games, before a crowd of 100,000 onlookers. He placed a highly respectable third in one race, losing to Mel Patten, who won two gold medals at that year's XIV Olympiad in London. Turner made to the Canadian Olympic team but suffered a knee injury in a car accident, putting an end to his career. "We got bounced off by a train," he said. "But I always took what happened to me as God's will. That's what happens in life. Sometimes you're lucky and you win, sometimes you're unlucky and you lose. It doesn't mean you don't get to the starting gate."

By the end of his time at UBC, Turner had been voted the university's most popular student. He beat out forty-nine others for a Rhodes scholarship to Oxford, which also had a good track team. Roger Bannister, the world's first ever four-minute miler, was its captain. "We had a great team," Turner said. "We were European champions. We went over and beat the hell out of Harvard and Yale."

In 1951, Brenda went overseas to visit her brother and the two took a tour of Europe in John's Austin Mini. "We ended up spending most of the time visiting his girlfriends," recalls Brenda, who is still in touch with one of them. "Denise Jolivet. She lived in Lausanne, Switzerland. She was hot and heavy with him," Brenda laughs.

It was at this point in his life that Turner was truly hearing two competing siren calls. On the one hand, he loved living in Europe, prepping for the bar exams in London in 1952, then moving to Paris in 1953 to study international law and learn French. On the other hand, Turner was a Catholic who seriously considered entering the priesthood. That competition for Turner's heart and soul would last for most of the rest of his life.

While studying in Paris, Turner was an activist with the so-called "Committee of Seven." He dealt with government officials on behalf of international students, at one point negotiating with France's interior minister and future president François Mitterrand.

Although Turner and his stepfather didn't have a particularly close relationship, Frank Ross did occasionally intercede in his stepson's life when he thought he could do him some good. When Turner returned to Canada, settling in Montreal in 1955, Ross made a call to his friend, lawyer Heward Stikeman, to see if he could guide his stepson through the Quebec bar. Turner thus became an articling student at the three-year-old firm Stikeman Elliott, which today is a legal powerhouse with offices in eight cities in four different countries. It took little time for Turner to become a big-time player on Montreal's legal, political, and social scene. Again, thanks to his stepfather's influence, he was asked to work with members of the Kennedy family on matters related to the Ross rail business. That began an association with the Kennedys that increased Turner's lustre for years to come (although how close he truly was to Jack, Bobby, and Teddy is a subject we'll come back to).

Turner was soon arguing cases before the Tax Court of Canada, the Court of the Exchequer, and the Supreme Court of Canada. He gained increasing insight into the country's two competing visions: pan-Canadianism versus provinces (particularly Quebec) increasingly flexing their muscles. Perhaps because he grew up fatherless, he was often drawn to older father figures such as Quebec premier Maurice Duplessis, nearly thirty years his senior, with whom Turner became good friends. They once went to a Montreal Canadiens game together. He also had dinner once a month with Cardinal Paul-Émile Léger, who was twenty-five years his senior.

Despite his connections, Turner was occasionally reminded that he was at the bottom of the law firm's food chain. When the firm's co-founder, Fraser Elliott, needed a favour, Turner asked why one of the firm's secretaries couldn't handle it. Elliott shot back: "Because their time is much more precious than yours."

Among the more interesting cases Turner handled in these years was one involving a group of Mennonites from Lethbridge, Alberta. They approached him, clad in their traditional black hats and clothes, and explained that the Ministry of National Revenue was contesting their tax-exempt status. They needed legal help. Turner asked the group members if they were a genuine religion; they assured him they were. He asked why they didn't approach an Alberta firm and was told none could be retained because the case was politically hot. One of them then presented Turner with a large stack of cash and assured him they would pay whatever it took to be well represented. "All of a sudden this interested me a great deal," Turner told Richard W. Pound for *Stikeman Elliott: The First Fifty Years.* He took the case all the way to the Supreme Court where he won a unanimous decision for the Mennonites.

It was during this pre-politics life that Turner met a fellow lawyer who would become both a great friend and nemesis. He and his colleague Jim Robb took up-and-coming Montreal lawyer Donald Johnston to lunch in hopes of recruiting him to Stikeman Elliott. Johnson instantly surveyed the situation and came to a conclusion. "I remember being aware that everyone assumed Turner would one day be Prime Minister," he wrote in his memoir *Up the Hill.* "I sensed he knew it, too."

Turner lived in an apartment near the intersection of Guy and Sherbrooke. Christmas receptions were held at his place when Elliott's apartment proved too small. In fact, Turner introduced Elliott to the woman who would become his wife, Elizabeth Ann McNicoll, at one of his soirées. He may have been the youngest lawyer at the firm, but he was the unofficial social convenor and made sure everyone was invited. "They put their livers in peril" is how those parties are described in Pound's book.

Turner also proved to be trustworthy when it came to delicate personal matters. He once saw a prominent Canadian business executive out to dinner "in gallant company," as it would have been described more than six decades ago. Turner and the executive got to know each other, and the young lawyer made sure not to spill the beans to anyone, particularly his stepfather, who knew the executive. When the same businessman brought some significant legal work to the firm, insisting Turner was the man to do it, Elliott wondered how Turner managed to score the business. Mum was the word.

While Turner was putting down valuable roots in Montreal, his sister was studying political science and history at McGill. Her favourite teaching assistant was a Polish émigré named Zbigniew Brzezinski, whom she dated. Brzezinski would go on to become President Jimmy Carter's national security adviser, and the father of Mika Brzezinski, co-host of MSNBC's "Morning Joe." She went on to do a master's degree in Grenoble at Sciences Po. She found herself neck deep in a romantic relationship with someone in Paris, and her mother sent John to rescue her. "My mother was desperately worried," Brenda recalls. "So John came over. But he did nothing. He had a great time and got his trip to Europe financed out of it."

Turner would later look back at his early years in law as one of the happiest times of his life. There was great camaraderie among the firm's many young lawyers as they were building what would turn out to be one of the country's great law firms from the ground up. In 1960, Turner became president of the Young Bar Association of Quebec, an impressive achievement for an upstart at a young firm. He recruited some impressive talent to Stikeman Elliott, as well, most notably Stanley Hartt, president of Liberal McGill, the university's student club for Liberal Party supporters. Hartt would go on to become a deputy minister of finance and chief-of-staff to Turner's successor as prime minister, Brian Mulroney.

It was also in these years that Turner discovered his zest for politics. He found his way into the orbit of Montreal mayor Jean Drapeau, who won the job in 1954 at age thirty-seven. In 1957, Turner was an "Anglophone organizer" in Drapeau's unsuccessful re-election bid. Despite the loss, Turner stuck with his man and in 1960 Drapeau returned to city hall where he would remain as mayor until his retirement in 1986.

While his political activities brought him a certain profile, it was a 1958 party hosted by his stepfather that made John Turner a national sensation. As British Columbia's lieutenant-governor, Ross was responsible for entertaining Queen Elizabeth's younger sister, Princess Margaret, the Countess of Snowdon, on her visit to the West Coast. He asked Turner to chaperone the princess at a ball on Vancouver's Deadman's Island. They danced three songs before retiring to a small table on the lawn outside the ballroom where they sipped drinks, smoked cigarettes, and talked for an hour and seven minutes, according to a precise news report of the event. Margaret refused four separate invitations to return indoors for supper. Their dalliance had tongues wagging from coast to coast to coast. He was twenty-nine, and she was twenty-seven. *The Toronto Telegram* reported: "Princess Margaret sat in the moonlight last night in an intimate tete-a-tete with a young bachelor-lawyer."

For the rest of his life, Turner would be asked to clarify the exact nature of his relationship with the princess, but he was always discreet. A subsequent news report had him joining her later in her trip at a ball at Government House in Ottawa where he "monopolized" her attentions. It was said that Buckingham Palace disapproved of him as a commoner and a Catholic. Turner would see Margaret again over the years, and every now and then something would hit the news to make people wonder anew how close they really were. That Turner was the only non-official Canadian guest invited to her wedding to Antony Armstrong-Jones in 1960 did nothing to squelch the rumours.

More than half a century later, letters written by Princess Margaret to her friend, the American socialite Sharman Douglas, became public. On May 16,

1966, the princess wrote from Kensington Palace: "John Turner is here, and we meet on Thursday. It will seem so funny as we haven't met since I nearly married him and he's bringing his wife!" That suggests the relationship was much closer than Turner ever let on. "We had a lot of laughs together, and she enjoys a martini, as her mother does," was typically all he'd say. "We hit it off and we had a lot of fun."

Turner had a more indirect brush with celebrity several years later in Ottawa. He and his legal junior, Donald Johnston, were arguing a case in the courtroom of the Board of Transport Commissioners (in what is now the Ottawa Convention Centre). As they looked out the window, they had a perfect view of U.S. President John F. Kennedy and Prime Minister John Diefenbaker laying a wreath at the Ottawa war memorial. Later that day, May 16, 1961, Turner went to watch Kennedy plant a tree at Governor-General Georges Vanier's residence. The event has gone down in history as one of Kennedy's most despised foreign trips because he wrenched his already damaged back trying to plant the tree. As a result, the president had to wear a corset which prevented him from bending over for the rest of his life.

While his career was flourishing and he always gave the impression of a young man who knew how to enjoy himself, Turner's reality in these years was more complicated. He felt enormous pressure to make something of himself, to be of service to his fellow man in some regard, and at the same time he doubted his ability to do it. It was a contradiction that went to the core of his being: he enjoyed success and privilege, yet he was wracked with insecurity, and a certain fragility, as well. "Fear of failing his mother was the overriding motivation in his life," says historian Elizabeth McIninch, who knew him well (Turner would hire her in 1989 to organize his personal and political papers for Library and Archives Canada).

Long-time Turner friend Sean Conway, who would serve as an MPP at Queen's Park for nearly three decades, has a clear recollection of the pressure he was under: "From the first time I heard of him, I'd hear people say, 'That man will be prime minister someday.' There was just a strong sense of needing to fulfil his mother's dreams for him, as if she said to him, 'You've been blessed with good genes and intellect and you've got some responsibility you're expected to meet.'"

The line, perhaps apocryphal but nevertheless attributed to Turner's mother, was: "If he can't be prime minister, he can always be the pope."

CHAPTER TWO

The Run for Parliament

THERE WAS NEVER A DOUBT that John Turner would run for Parliament. It was a question of when. Prime Minister John Diefenbaker answered for him by calling an election for June 18, 1962.

Dief had shocked the country four years and three months earlier, when he captured the biggest majority government in Canadian history: 208 seats, winning 53.67 per cent of the total vote. But relations with the United States were terrible, as the Diefenbaker cabinet was badly split on whether to accept Bomarc nuclear missiles from our closest ally. In addition, his cancellation of the Avro-Arrow fighter jet, considered the finest of its kind in the world, enraged many. The Diefenbaker years were too often tumultuous and his PC Party was vulnerable.

John Turner would be only thirty-three years old on election day. But the time was right.

Not that he needed it, but plenty of people were encouraging Turner to run. Based on his strong performance at the Kingston Conference and his prominence as head of the Quebec junior bar (not to mention dancing with Princess Margaret), party veterans such as Paul Martin Sr. and Allan MacEachen urged him to seek a seat.

"John Turner was unbelievably charismatic," says Sharon Sholzberg-Gray, who knew Turner from her days as a McGill student from 1959 to 1966. "He was the best speaker anywhere. And the best-looking guy anywhere, too."

Canada's two major party leaders at the time were Diefenbaker, age sixty-six, and Lester B. Pearson, a couple of months shy of sixty-five. The previous year, the United States swore in John F. Kennedy as its new president. The contrast could not have been starker. But unlike "The Chief" and "Mike," Turner was an equal to JFK in every way.

"He was such a star," recalls Phil Lind, a McGill undergrad at the time, who would go on to become Ted Rogers' right-hand man at Rogers Cable. "Even then, people said, John's going all the way. He personified the Kennedy appeal in Canada."

Interestingly, others may have made the comparisons to JFK, but Turner never did. "He was *way* too humble to make that kind of comparison or utter it in public," says Marc Kealey. "He was aware that he had as he called it 'a hallowed position' in life and that he was privileged, but he never, ever, ever flaunted that."

Turner decided to run in St. Lawrence–St. George, a Montreal riding in which McGill University was located and once held by Defense Minister Brooke Claxton. In fact, Claxton's son John signed up to be Turner's campaign manager. The riding was currently held by the Tories' Egan Chambers, who had failed to win it three times before finally tasting success in the Dief sweep of '58. Chambers was a parliamentary secretary to two ministers of national defence, and his brother-in-law was the highly respected McGill political philosopher Charles Taylor.

But he was no John Turner.

As a member of McGill's Progressive Conservative student federation, it was in Lind's interests to keep an eye on Turner, and he did. He couldn't help but marvel at the Turner campaign and some of its clever antics. The Liberals set up a tent adjacent to McGill, calling it the Big Chamber of Horrors. Inside, there were cartoons of a buffoonish-looking Diefenbaker.

"It was so clever and so much fun," says Lind. "I thought, this is really smart. John looked like he had all the answers and would be a successful political campaigner. Politics really ran through his blood. He was on top of his game." Turner talked like a jock with the guys and flirted respectfully with the women. He was irresistible. When asked why he wanted to seek political office, he replied: "We wanted to change the world." It was, after all, the 1960s and Turner represented a new generation that wanted to turn the page on the previous decade's decision makers. Youth needed to be served.

The campaign office was at Peel and Sherbrooke Streets and got off to a bizarre start when Pearson visited. The outside of the headquarters was festooned with balloons and when someone cut them to signal the beginning of the campaign, word is they had to stop all the flights at Dorval Airport for safety reasons.

Besides the candidate, there were two other things that made Turner's campaign different from so many others. First, there were the multitudes of young women, most of them McGill students, who signed on. When asked why, one organizer said: "Because every damn one of them would rather be Mrs. John Turner than a B.A." By today's standards, such a response sounds hopelessly chauvinistic. But feminism had not quite made it to Canada yet, and the fact was many women at this time went to university in hopes of meeting their future husbands.

One of those women (who actually *wasn't* looking for a husband) was 19-year-old Sharon Sholzberg. One of her classmates was Diana Drury, whose father Charles "Bud" Drury was a once-and-future Liberal cabinet minister. Diana asked Sharon to come to a meeting of the Young Liberals at McGill and a year later, Sharon was president. (She went on in 1965 to become the first woman to run for student council at McGill.)

The second thing the Turner campaign had was state-of-the-art computer technology. And that happened because of another young female volunteer named Geills Kilgour. It's not an exaggeration to say there may have been no other woman like Geills Kilgour around politics in Canada at this time. Geills (originally pronounced "Jeels," but whom everyone referred to as "Jill") was both beautiful and brilliant. Originally from Winnipeg, her paternal grandfather was a Manitoba judge. Her maternal great grandfather was originally from Prince Edward Island and was the first PEI graduate of the Dalhousie law school, who eventually moved west to Manitoba and married the sister of John McRae, who wrote the immortal *In Flanders Fields* poem. That great grandfather became chief justice of Manitoba, and was replaced on the lower court by Geills' paternal grandfather, in another example of how small a place Canada was back then.

Geills attended the University of Manitoba for two years, but got hooked on business and decided she wanted to attend a different university. So, she did her third and fourth years at McGill University in Montreal, getting her degree in maths and physics. Lest it need saying, this was not the typical path for a woman born in Manitoba in 1937.

Geills' interest in business and science next led her to Radcliffe in Cambridge, Massachusetts, the women's college affiliated with Harvard University where women still weren't permitted. "It was the same professors, the same classes, the same lectures, the same exams, the same clubs," Geills recalls. "It was part of the Harvard Business School, but not really." Geills' timing was just off. The following year, Harvard would accept women, who would graduate with a Harvard degree.

Geills finished the one-year course, then waited to get headhunted. She interviewed with Morgan Stanley and First National City Bank, but neither company was in the market to hire a woman. So, she accepted entry into a sales training program at IBM.

Geills loved working for IBM and living in New York City. She worked with something called the unit record equipment, which was the precursor to the huge mainframe computers. This computer allowed companies to store customer numbers, employee numbers, and salary levels, all automatically processed on to IBM cards. She went to work every day in the standard IBM grey suit and high heels, and then dealt with the usual crap women of her generation dealt with on the job.

"I'd get on the subway thinking, I look pretty cool," Geills recalls. "Then some man would put his hand on your bum. I'd take my five-inch heels and grind them into his foot and never even look at him. He backed off fairly quickly after that."

Another time, a taxi driver delivered her to a client in the garment district. "If I were your mother I wouldn't let you out here," the driver told her. "But you're not my mother, so I'm getting out," Geills responded. She lived with two female roommates at 61st Street and Lexington Avenue in Manhattan and life was good. But in 1961, when her boyfriend left her for someone else, Geills moved back to Montreal to work for IBM there. Almost immediately, she entered the orbit of a well-known Montreal lawyer.

One night, her date suggested the two stop in to visit his friend John Turner. "Everyone knew John Turner," Geills says. "He'd danced with Princess Margaret!"

It would be the first time Geills and John met.

"I'd like to work on your campaign," Geills told him. "I think we can do your polling."

Using the same computer system she worked with at IBM, Geills went door to door in St. Lawrence–St. George, recording where people lived and whether they would be supportive on election day. All the information was stored on file cards which could be instantly retrieved when loaded into the computer. "We were dead on with our polling," Geills now says.

It was an advantage other campaigns didn't have. On election night, June 18, 1962, after the votes were counted, the Diefenbaker government was barely clinging to power, having entered the contest with the biggest majority ever. The PCs received just a quarter of a percentage point more of the total vote than the Liberals. They lost 89 seats, settling for a 116-seat minority government, compared to the Liberals' 100 seats. Social Credit (30 seats) and the New Democrats (19 seats) held the rest. And in St. Lawrence–St. George, Montrealers elected a new MP.

At thirty-three, Turner wasn't the youngest MP in the twenty-fifth Parliament of Canada. In fact, there were 18 members younger than him, including fellow Liberals Donald S. Macdonald, Richard Cashin, and John Munro. But, including the prime minister and opposition leader, there were 31 MPs born in the previous century. Turner was clearly the one to watch among the young Turks in the new Parliament. Everyone knew it, including the assistant to Agriculture Minister Alvin Hamilton, who spotted Turner across the parliamentary dining room one afternoon. Brian Mulroney, a decade younger than Turner, urged his lunch companion to introduce themselves to the newly minted MP from Montreal. "What for?" came the response. "He's a Liberal."

"I don't care," the twenty-three-year-old Mulroney responded. "He's going to be prime minister someday."

Nearly six decades after that first encounter, Mulroney speaks fondly of the man whom he would eventually defeat twice in general elections.

"We were nice friendly acquaintances," Canada's 18th prime minister recalls of their days together practicing law in Montreal, Mulroney at Ogilvie Renault and Turner at Stikeman Elliott. After Mulroney's father died in 1965, he moved his mother to Montreal where he's convinced she voted for Turner.

"She was enthralled with him as they all were in Montreal," he says.

"I used to get Brian dates when he was a bachelor," recalls Geills Turner. "He'd come to Ottawa and I'd get him dates. This was prior to his meeting Mila. I've always liked Brian."

Apparently the feeling is mutual. "I'd known Geills since Montreal," says Mulroney. "She was very attractive, very bright, and very much an asset for John."

Once Turner even secured Mulroney a front-row seat to one of the juiciest scandals in Canadian political history, in which the attractive German national, Gerda Munsinger, was rumoured to be having an affair with Canada's associate minister of defence. Demands for investigations into whether national security had been breached dominated Parliament and the media, and Mulroney was desperate to watch the action in the House.

"John met us and escorted us up to the government visitors' gallery," Mulroney says. "Dief was at the height of his oratorical powers. John got us seats and saw us afterwards for coffee."

But it was another incident that taught Turner one of his most important political lessons. The new MP received a call at his Ottawa office from one Pamela Ambrose, who ran a *maison de debauche* on Stanley Street in Montreal. Apparently, the city of Montreal had installed signs prohibiting parking in front of her establishment.

Turner tried explaining that he was an MP, not a city councillor, and suggested she appeal to her local representative at Montreal City Hall. Ambrose didn't care for the response and told Turner to "Call [Mayor] Drapeau and solve it." Turner, suitably chastened, did just that. An hour later the signs were gone, and the rookie politician learned his first lesson: never let political jurisdiction interfere with fixing a problem.

Turner became quite the sought-after speaker after winning his election. At the University of Toronto, the debating team invited him to participate in one of their events. Up for debate: whether Canada should join the United States. Turner accepted and argued against the resolution.

"We knew from the papers he had dated Princess Margaret, but we wondered, who is this guy?" recalls one of the debate organizers, seventeen-year-old Ian Waddell, who like Turner, started university preternaturally young. "He was really good." (Two decades later, Turner and Waddell would be MPs in neighbouring ridings in British Columbia.)

It was also at this time that Turner met a young party activist who'd read all his speeches and was taking quite an interest. When they met, this president of the Young Liberals asked the new MP: "Are you as good as you look? 'Cuz I think you can do better than that.'"

Turner laughed. "What do you mean?"

"You could be better," said Jerahmiel "Jerry" Grafstein, twenty-seven years old at the time and destined to become the longest-serving member of the Standing Senate Committee on Foreign Affairs and International Trade. Grafstein had no inhibitions telling the star MP, five-and-a-half years his senior, how he could improve his oratorical prowess.

"Well, why don't you send me some stuff?" responded Turner, beginning what would become a more than six-decade-long friendship between the two. From that moment on, Grafstein sent Turner frequent memos replete with policy ideas, speaking tips, and other suggestions.

The 1962 Parliament didn't last long. The governing Tories were neck-deep in massive intraparty difficulties, and Dief's leadership was falling apart, highlighted by his unwillingness to allow the United States to station nuclear Bomarc missiles on Canadian soil to deter the Soviet nuclear threat. At first, Defence Minister Douglas Harkness resigned over the matter, but then it became apparent that half the cabinet was prepared to do likewise. Even Dief temporarily threatened to resign the prime ministership.

The situation was clearly untenable, and the Tories lost a confidence vote in the House, sending Canadians back to the polls for a general election on April 8, 1963. The Liberal campaign, promising "60 Days of Decision," saying yes to the U.S. missile request, a new flag, Medicare, and enhanced old age pensions, carried the day. Oddly enough, however, despite capturing 41 per cent of the total votes and besting the Tories by almost nine points, the Liberals ended up five seats short of a majority (129 to the PCs' 95; the Socreds with 24 and NDP with 17 held the balance of power). In St. Lawrence–St. George, Turner more than doubled his margin of victory, once again over Egan Chambers, from 2,258 votes in 1962 to 4,756 votes in 1963.

Something else was going on in Turner's life at this time, although almost no one knew about it. Geills and John had become a couple, but very secretly.

"We really had to keep it under cover because the '63 election had been called and most of his workers were women who worked for him because they thought they might go out with him," Geills laughs, recalling those times. "We had to be quite strategic."

Given how absent-minded Turner could be, it's a minor miracle the couple ended up together. One day, Turner invited Geills to come over to his place and use his apartment to do whatever work she needed to do; he'd return later and cook dinner for the two of them. Geills arrived at the appointed hour. No Turner. No keys. He'd completely forgotten. Eventually, he showed up, hours late, and profusely apologized, but the future Mrs. Turner was not amused.

Turner didn't save an occasional lack of consideration only for his girlfriend. Sometimes, his sister Brenda would host a party in Montreal and invite her well-known brother to attend. Suddenly, perhaps only an hour into the festivities, Turner would look at his watch then tell his sister: "Well, this has been great, but I'm heading home now. I'll leave you all to have a good time."

John and Geills became engaged over Christmas, travelled to Winnipeg to break the news to the Kilgours, and headed to Vancouver to tell Turner's mother and stepfather. The initial reaction from the Kilgours was not good.

"My mother, when she heard I was marrying a Catholic, burst into tears," Geills recalls. "This was serious stuff. She loved John but this was her initial reaction before she knew him."

Turner was adamant about having a Catholic wedding in a Catholic church. Geills was Anglican and had no intention of converting. "In the early days, this kind of thing mattered a lot," says Geills. "You didn't speak to people in other churches."

The wedding took place on May 11, 1963, at St. Ignatius Parish in Winnipeg. Turner was thirty-three years old ("the age at which Christ was crucified," he often joked), while she was twenty-five. There were a couple of hundred people in attendance, but no political VIPs from Turner's Ottawa life. Geills' paternal aunt, Margaret Gardiner Maitland, travelled from England for the occasion. She met Turner's mother, Phyllis Ross, and the two discovered they had actually been the only two Canadians at Vassar together four decades earlier.

"The coincidences," Geills marvels. "It's crazy."

* * *

If Turner thought his high-profile and lifelong acquaintanceship with Pearson would hasten his entry into cabinet, the new prime minister was happy to disabuse him of the notion. Many may have been dazzled by Turner, but Pearson thought he needed more time on the backbenches and he saw that he got it. However, the PM did make Turner parliamentary secretary to the minister of northern affairs and natural resources, which suited Turner just fine. He embraced the job and began a love affair with Northern Canada that would last the remainder of his life.

Turner also began to think more about another issue that would captivate him into his nineties. He spoke at McGill in 1964 about his concern that the House of Commons was being bypassed as the country's most important forum for debating issues. Instead, Turner feared, the real battlefield of politics was inside the party councils.

"Democracy has become invisible," he said in the speech. "How long can it remain invisible and hidden from public scrutiny and still remain a democracy?" For the next six decades, no Parliamentarian, current or former, would speak more often and more passionately about the state of Canadian democracy than John Turner.

Turner rarely passed an opportunity to urge people he knew to run for office. Often, he even encouraged those he didn't know. In 1963, Montreal-born lawyer

Ian Binnie received a handwritten note of congratulations from Turner for becoming the first Canadian elected president of the Cambridge Union debating society in the United Kingdom.

"He hoped I would enter politics as a Liberal after returning to Canada," Binnie says. "The lesson I took was that as a successful politician you probably have to write hundreds of such letters each year to people you don't know, and the experience probably helped put me off politics for life!" Binnie instead made his name by spending nearly fourteen years as a justice on the Supreme Court of Canada.

One of Turner's most significant acts at this time almost escaped the history books entirely. On December 15, 1964, the Liberal government invoked closure, bringing an end to one of the most acrimonious debates in history. The subject: whether to replace the country's Red Ensign with a uniquely Canadian flag. On February 15, 1965, the red bannered flag with the distinctive red maple leaf in the middle flew above Parliament Hill for the first time. Former Prime Minister Diefenbaker refused even to look at the new flag, and even though he and Turner were great friends, Turner found Dief's act disrespectful.

The next day, Turner and Geills flew to the Caribbean country of Tobago for a winter getaway. As they emerged from their hotel in their bathing suits and walked to the beach, to their surprise the first person they saw was John Diefenbaker. Later during the trip, Geills noticed a man in the ocean losing a battle to the undertow. The man was clearly in distress and on the verge of drowning. Turner, the champion swimmer from his days at UBC, dashed out and grabbed the man by his swimming trunks, then dragged him into shore.

That man, too, was John Diefenbaker.

The incident would have gone unreported had the Tory chieftain not mentioned it in passing to his one-time executive assistant and fellow Progressive Conservative MP Sean O'Sullivan, who was elected in 1972, two months shy of his twenty-first birthday. O'Sullivan famously left politics for the priesthood and described the incident in his memoir, *My Two Houses*, before tragically succumbing to leukemia at age 37. Both Turner and O'Sullivan were hugely influenced by St. Augustine's admonition, as Turner described it: "He to whom God has given some talent has a duty to share it. That's been my motivation. If you've had some advantages in life, share it with your fellow citizens. That means the priesthood or public life." In O'Sullivan's case, it was both. Turner's Catholicity would always play a huge part in his life too, but the priesthood was simply a bridge too far.

"[O'Sullivan] mentioned it," Turner once said of his saving Dief's life. "That's how it became public. I never mentioned it." Remarkably, despite their friendship and numerous future encounters on Parliament Hill, neither Diefenbaker nor Turner ever spoke again of the Liberal MP's derring-do.

Canadian politics was rarely as unstable as it was in the 1960s. Elections in 1962 and 1963 failed to secure a majority for either of the two major parties, and on November 8, 1965, Canadians returned to the polls yet again. One of the highlights of the campaign for Turner took place when Paul Martin Sr. was unable to give a planned speech in Orillia, Ontario, a couple of hours' drive north of Toronto. Turner was pressed into duty as Martin's substitute and he insisted Grafstein come with him to the airport, where the two hopped on a small private plane in hopes of making the event on time. Almost instantly after takeoff, a huge storm began to brew, buffeting the small plane. Grafstein feared they were all going down and was morose. But he looked over at Turner to find the young MP casually reviewing his speaking notes, apparently without a care in the world.

There was another memorable dust up during the '65 election. While speaking at a Liberal nominating meeting in Toronto, Turner took direct aim at the PC party leader: "If Mr. Diefenbaker were to become prime minister again, it would mean one-man government, palace revolutions, economic jingoism, anti-Americanism, and a new wave of French separatism." That prompted a rebuttal from Turner's friend from his Montreal lawyering days.

"It's unfortunate that Mr. Turner ran out of breath when things were just getting exciting," teased Brian Mulroney. "As his hindsight is, no doubt, just as well developed as his great capacity for prophecy, I am sure he would have wanted to tell his fellow Grits just how Mr. Diefenbaker stabbed Julius Caesar, started the War of 1812, and caused the Irish Potato Famine."

The Liberals were convinced they could grab the brass ring in the '65 election yet once again they fell an agonizing two-seats short of a majority government. Turner held his seat, albeit by a slightly smaller margin of 4,272 votes. But the big news for him was Pearson's decision that he'd cooled his heels on the backbenches long enough. The PM appointed him to cabinet, although in a modest role. As minister without portfolio, Turner would report to Transport Minister Jack Pickersgill, twenty-four years his senior, and yet another father figure in his life. (To ensure no potential conflicts of interest, Turner resigned his position at Stikeman Elliott.) There's an expression in politics: "There are no bad seats at the cabinet table." But at this party, Turner's was about as close to the kitchen as possible.

A couple of days after the swearing-in, Turner went to Toronto on a mission to get Jerry Grafstein to come to Ottawa as his executive assistant, in what today would be called the chief-of-staff position. Grafstein was flattered, but he was also married with two kids, close to becoming a partner at the law firm where he worked, and had already turned down offers to work for the Liberals' campaign "Rainmaker" Keith Davey and Finance Minister Walter Gordon.

"Why would I go with you?" he asked Turner.

"Because we'd have fun," the new minister responded. "And we'd make a difference."

Grafstein liked the answer, but he had another problem. His wife Carole despised politics. Her husband had spent too many nights away from home organizing events for the Liberals and had had enough of politics intruding into their lives. "You go talk to Carole about it," Turner told Grafstein.

When Grafstein raised the subject with Carole, he was gobsmacked by her response.

"Oh yes, John already came by for tea," she told her husband. "He said if I don't let you go to Ottawa, you'll never be happy and will always feel unfulfilled. So, John and I have arranged for you to go, and we made a deal." The deal was: one year only, and home every other Wednesday and every Friday for the week-end. The parties had an agreement.

Turner and Grafstein became a great team because they complemented each other's strengths and weaknesses. Turner was the dashing, bright, hail-fellow-well-met politician with a British pedigree, penetrating blue eyes, and an ambition to go places. Grafstein was nobody's idea of a matinee idol: short, alternatively socially awkward or a bulldog, and Jewish in a capital city where there were hardly any Jews. But he had an enormous capacity for hard work and, most of all, was determined to see that Turner made it to the top of the country's political mountain. Turner presented so well in front of the cameras, but he came to depend on Grafstein's behind-the-scenes efforts for his success. Because Grafstein wasn't much of a party-type, you could find him up at both 6 a.m. and 11 p.m. reading cabinet documents. Every document was divided into one of three files: red, orange, or green. Grafstein told Turner to forget about the red files; he didn't need to know that stuff. The orange ones were of longer-range interest. The green files constituted urgent business, and these Turner devoured.

Turner admitted to a tight circle of friends that he wanted to be the minister of justice and attorney-general of Canada. It was a logical ambition for any up-and-coming lawyer. But Pearson had other ideas. He'd courted a dazzling Quebec intellectual named Pierre Elliott Trudeau, ten years Turner's senior, to join the Liberal Party, no doubt with a view to being the PM's eventual replacement. The Liberals would come to be known as Canada's so-called natural governing party in part because of their tremendous success at election time, but also because of an unofficial policy of alternating leaders from English and French Canada. Alexander Mackenzie was followed by Wilfrid Laurier, who was succeeded by Mackenzie King, after whom came St. Laurent and then Pearson. The formula worked and with the exception of the Dief sweep in 1958, Quebec was always good to the Liberals. So, on April 4, 1967, Pearson appointed Trudeau, who had been parliamentary secretary to the PM, as his justice minister. Turner, too, got a promotion: registrar general of Canada with the potential of turning that role into a full-fledged cabinet department.

While Turner's promotion may not have been as memorable as Trudeau's, there was an unforgettable moment after the swearing-in ceremony, an unprecedented shot of Prime Minister Pearson and three of his ministers, all of whom would become future prime ministers: Trudeau, Turner, and a new minister without portfolio who barely spoke any English, Jean Chrétien.

Turner and Grafstein got to work. The registrar general's job was all about patents, but both men had an eye to turning it into something bigger. In the mid-1960s, consumer rights were becoming a big deal. The passionate American consumer advocate Ralph Nader was capturing the public's attention, particularly in 1965 with the publication of his book *Unsafe at Any Speed*, chronicling the appalling safety deficiencies of the American auto industry. Turner wanted to turn the registrar general's job into a full-fledged department for consumer safety, but a lot was standing in his way. First, the more conservative side of the Liberal cabinet was content to let Turner sound as though he was on the side of consumers as long as he didn't scare the heck out of business. And second, Turner's deputy minister, who was a patents expert, was seriously opposed to expanding the R-G's mandate.

"We weren't going to be able to move our legislation through with this guy in place," Grafstein recalls. "So, we came up with a scheme to send him to Europe to an international patents convention. We knew his wife would love the trip, too."

With the deputy away, Turner and Grafstein drafted legislation to create a new department of consumer and corporate affairs, thought to be the first of any government in the Western world, to bring some of the efforts of what would become "Nader's Raiders" to Canada. However, their proposal went to cabinet. Both the department of finance and the privy council office opposed the plan, fearing the new department would spook businesses.

But Grafstein had an ace in the hole. He discovered a royal commission report from the Great Depression that argued the need to create a consumer and commercial affairs department. The secretary of that commission had been none other than Lester B. Pearson. Grafstein urged Turner to hand the PM a copy of the report before going into the next cabinet meeting, which he did. When opposition to the plan surfaced during the meeting, Pearson looked at Turner, nodded, and smiled. The PM was onside, and on December 21, 1967, Turner became Canada's first ever minister for consumer and corporate affairs.

Was Turner a good minister? Apparently, a future governor-general of Canada thought so. In the late 1960s, David Johnston was a young law professor at Queen's University and research counsel to the Ontario Securities Commission. His mission was to help establish a national securities regulator, a consensus for which emerged from Ontario Premier John Robarts' Confederation of Tomorrow Conference in November 1967. Johnston's job was to present the details to Turner.

"Within two minutes, he grasped it," Johnston recalls in an email. Turner liked Johnston's pragmatic solution to a national problem. Alas, Johnston adds, "he couldn't get it through the bureaucracy," which no minister since Turner has been able to do, either, mostly because Quebec has always refused to sign on to a national securities regulator.

* * *

As Turner's political career progressed, so did his family life. Geills and John discovered that trying to live in two different cities, even two as close as Ottawa and Montreal, was difficult, particularly after children came along. So, despite representing a Montreal riding, Turner and his family moved to Ottawa in 1964, first taking an apartment, then a house in Rockcliffe.

The couple's first child was Elizabeth Ross Turner, born in 1964. Complications surrounding the birth necessitated a caesarean section, which would affect Geills' subsequent deliveries. A year later, she became pregnant with John Michael Turner. ("Michael," which is what everyone has always called him, was a tribute to John's brother who had died as a newborn.) Geills asked whether she could deliver Michael naturally but was advised by her obstetrician that strong contractions could cause the previous incision to open up, sending her into shock and risking the life of the baby. So Geills had a second caesarean delivery with her original doctor in Montreal at the Royal Victoria Hospital, despite now living in Ottawa. John and her mother went out for dinner together during the birth.

There would be two more children, and two more caesarean births in Montreal. In 1968, David Russell Turner was born and, in 1971, James Andrew (always known as Andrew) became the last Turner child.

Did John Turner change diapers?

"I think he did, but probably not happily," Geills says. "And badly. He wasn't very ept."

* * *

The year 1967 was a terrifically exciting one for politics in Canada. July 1 marked the country's centennial, and the celebrations at Expo 67 in Montreal brought Canadians together as never before. (It was a far cry from the comparatively muted 150th anniversary celebrations in 2017, by which point more Canadians understood that not everyone shared the same rosy interpretation of the country's progress, which had been particularly debilitating to Indigenous communities.) In 1967, people danced to the omnipresent tune "Ca-na-da," sung by Bobby Gimby and backed by a children's choir, without much soul-searching.

In the winter of 1967, Turner needed to travel to Western Canada for a series of announcements and photo opportunities, some of which were centennial-related. He wanted Grafstein to come with him, but his EA had the mumps and insisted he couldn't go. The minister was equally adamant. He promised Carole Grafstein he'd take good care of her husband and with that, the pair were off to Saskatoon.

They arrived to find Saskatoon mayor Sidney Buckwold waiting in front of a perfect Saskatchewan backdrop for a photo op: a snowy ski hill on a riverbank. Because Turner had promised to carry Grafstein's bags due to his aide's weakened condition, Grafstein arrived on the scene first, with Turner bringing up the rear and carrying the luggage. Mayor Buckwold, who didn't know Turner, extended his hand to Grafstein and said, "Welcome to Saskatoon, Mr. Minister."

"Sorry, but the minister is behind me. I'm his EA," Grafstein replied, shaking the mayor's hand, as the three of them burst into laughter.

As the year progressed, rumours coming out of 24 Sussex Drive suggested the seventy-year-old prime minister was thinking of leaving public life. On December 14, after nearly two decades as the member for Algoma East and a decade as party leader, but less than five years as prime minister, Pearson announced his intention to resign and called a leadership convention for the following April.

For John Turner, it was the culmination of a momentous year in which he finally made cabinet, finally got a department to run, and finally had more pull around the cabinet table. All of that would lead to an inevitable decision: he wanted to be the next leader of the Liberal Party and prime minister of Canada.

CHAPTER THREE

The Run for Leader

JOHN TURNER HAD A PROBLEM. A few, actually.

He'd already started putting together his leadership campaign team well before Pearson's official announcement in mid-December. But at age thirty-eight, he also knew too many Liberals would think him too young to be leader. In fact, when all nine candidates vying to replace Pearson eventually entered the fray, Turner was the only one in his thirties. That said, as Keith Davey observed in Christina McCall-Newman's epic history of the Liberal Party, *Grits*, "If Turner had been nothing more than the pretty boy the backbiters said he was, he would have buckled in the early 1960s. But he didn't buckle. He learned how to be a politician, how to roll and punch and roll again, how to be a winner."

But how would Turner handle the alternation issue? It wasn't official Liberal Party policy, but for a century the party had made a point of switching between anglophone and francophone leaders, and the results much more often than not were positive. Every Liberal leader from Alexander Mackenzie in 1873 to Lester Pearson in 1967 eventually became prime minister (with the lone exception of Edward Blake, who led the party between Mackenzie and Laurier). Turner was an anglophone trying to replace an anglophone. But he hoped his being a fluently bilingual MP representing a riding in Quebec would blunt what seemed to be a big built-in advantage for Trudeau.

Then there was the Jerry Grafstein problem. As promised, Grafstein left Turner's office as his executive assistant after a year and was now back at his law firm in Toronto, about to make partner. He was adamant that Turner run for leader but equally insistent that he couldn't be pressed into duty to run the campaign.

"Talk to Carole," Turner said.

Grafstein did and once again, the Turner magic worked. "With your big mouth, how dare you tell him to run and not do something about it?" Carole told her husband. Grafstein was in as campaign manager, joining a team of young advisers who would go on to have their own prominent careers in politics, including future cabinet ministers David Smith, Lloyd Axworthy, and Irwin Cotler.

On January 17, 1968, Turner was the first candidate to throw his hat into the ring, aggressively pledging to be the voice of a new generation with new ideas. "I'm a reformer," he said. "There has to be a willingness to upset the apple cart." Then, perhaps referring to Trudeau's well-established cool intellectualism, he added that problems aren't solved by logic and intellect alone, "but by the heart and gut, because that is what Canada's all about."

Trudeau may have been the justice minister, but Turner wasn't about to cede that ground to the prospective candidate. He wanted a significant revamping on how the justice system worked, including ditching the old pork-barrel system of appointing judges, plus reforms to bail, arrest, expropriation, wiretapping, and legal aid. Turner was making an impression, as evidenced by a jealous backbencher who said: "The guy has been programmed to be prime minister since he was twelve."

More than half a century later, Trudeau's victory at the 1968 convention may have seemed pre-ordained. That was not the case. Trudeau played the reluctant candidate to the hilt in hopes of building momentum for his leadership bid. Turner never bought it and thought it was all an act.

Trudeau was a polarizing candidate in a way the others weren't. "What's this guy got, anyway?" Turner once asked, not buying the rookie MP's humble intellectualism which was making so many Canadians sit up and take notice. Furthermore, the other candidates weren't pleased that Pearson was pretty clearly putting his thumb on the scale for Trudeau by pointing out he wanted a francophone candidate in the race. He also secretly let Trudeau know that he'd have the outgoing PM's blessing should he enter the race. Beyond that, Pearson adviser Marc Lalonde convinced the PM to send his justice minister across the country to meet with the premiers to discuss constitutional matters, which gave Trudeau an enormous amount of media coverage and ultimately some future leadership endorsements.

Pearson also asked his acting secretary to the cabinet to pass along a message to Turner: "It's a francophone's turn. Don't push too hard against Trudeau."

Turner didn't take the brushback pitch well. "They can go stuff that idea," he told colleagues. "I'm out to win."

Despite being clear rivals, first for the justice portfolio and then for the leadership, Turner and Trudeau shared a mutual respect. They were different in many ways: Turner the conventionally handsome, married-with-kids, back-slapping-but-intelligent jock; Trudeau the unconventionally good-looking, single, cerebral loner. Turner loved to solve problems over drinks, Trudeau after studying all sides of an issue. However, they did have some significant things in common. Both were fluently bilingual Montreal lawyers representing Montreal ridings; both had lost their fathers too soon; and both had studied at elite European universities.

Turner clearly had the youth vote wrapped up. He constantly interacted with young Liberals, who would become the prime base of support for his campaign. He wasn't yet sure who his main challenger would be, but Grafstein did. Despite Trudeau's coy approach to the job, Grafstein knew the justice minister was ambitious for the crown; he was deeply impressed when he saw Trudeau give a barnburner of a speech, making the case for "One Canada, with Quebec." In fact, after the speech, Trudeau asked Grafstein to come to his suite at the Bonaventure Hotel in Montreal to talk. Grafstein did so, with Turner's approval, but when he arrived, there was a lineup down the corridor to get in. At the front of the line was the finance minister, Mitchell Sharp, who himself was thinking of standing for leader. Trudeau emerged from his suite, asked Sharp if he wouldn't mind waiting a little longer, then invited Grafstein to join him. That served to irritate Sharp and make Grafstein nervous. (Sharp eventually declined to run for leader and backed Trudeau.)

Nevertheless, Trudeau employed his Jesuitical technique of asking Grafstein, "What do you think? What's the question?"

"There's only one question," Grafstein told him. "If you run, will you win?"

Trudeau was expected to be the lone francophone candidate but at this moment, it was no slam dunk that he was going to join in. Turner had good support in Quebec and surprisingly, Trudeau didn't. He'd been in Liberal politics for only a few years and when Pearson managed to convince him to enter the race, Trudeau ran in the anglophone Jewish riding of Mount Royal, rather than a more francophone riding.

Grafstein told him, "Quebec respects power. They just want to know you can win. If you can win, they'll support you, because blood is thicker than tomato juice."

Trudeau laughed and then Grafstein tried to make a deal with him. He wanted Trudeau's commitment that if Turner was ahead on the ballot, Trudeau would back Turner, and pledged to do likewise if Trudeau was ahead. Grafstein was adamant that the party not fall into the hands of the more conservative elements, represented by Trade and Commerce Minister Robert Winters, who'd come from the private sector. Trudeau listened to Grafstein's pitch, but he never agreed to it one way or another. One month after Turner's entry, Trudeau officially joined the race. Turner was no longer the "It" candidate.

As the campaign progressed, all the candidates gathered at St. Lawrence Hall in downtown Toronto to press the flesh with prospective supporters. Among the audience that night was a young Richard Alway, who'd become one of Turner's best friends and a future warden at the University of Toronto's Hart House.

"I remember being impressed at how young yet polished he was," Alway says of Turner. "I thought, 'He's going to make it at some point, obviously.'"

However, the big draw that night was the exciting new entrant from Quebec, whose presence had the police blocking off neighbouring streets to traffic because of the overflow crowds. It was the same story in Lethbridge, Alberta, in the second week of March. Turner and fellow cabinet minister and leadership candidate Paul Hellyer met with delegates and drew typically modest crowds. Then the MP from Mount Royal showed up and so did 600 others. Trudeaumania had begun.

Turner's efforts to recruit attractive candidates for the Liberals manifested itself one morning in Prince Rupert, B.C. He did a campaign interview with radio host Iona Campagnolo on CHTK. The interview itself wasn't particularly memorable, but the hour-long discussion after the microphones were turned off was. Turner pitched Campagnolo on the importance of public life, and she listened carefully. Six years later, Campagnolo became one of just nine female MPs in a 264-member House of Commons after the 1974 election.

As the delegate selection meetings took place across the country, Turner's network sprang into action. In Burnaby, B.C., a former UBC frat house brother of Turner's, Jim Clark, who was also president of the local riding association, organized the selection process so well, the entire slate would go to the convention backing Turner. The meeting took place in Clark's home, despite the considerable ruckus caused by the youngest of his four children, three-year-old daughter Christina. Jim Clark would back Turner's political efforts for decades to come, including as a voting delegate at the 1968 convention. (His daughter would become the thirty-fifth premier of British Columbia in 2011, using the more familiar "Christy" as her first name.)

Paul Martin Sr. was thought by some to have a chance this time. At sixty-three, he was the oldest candidate in the race and had a senior statesman vibe about him. He'd run for leader twice before, in 1948 and 1958, but lost to St. Laurent and Pearson. Would 1968 be his year?

Three years earlier, in the run-up to the 1965 election, Turner had introduced the party's new star candidate to Sharon Sholzberg. "Sharon, this is Pierre Trudeau," Turner said. "He's our new candidate in Westmount."

"I know you," Trudeau said to Sholzberg. "You're the head of the student union. You're kowtowing to the separatists too much." Now, three years later, Trudeau's entry into the race proved fatal to Martin Sr.'s chances. Forty members of the Liberal caucus initially backed Martin. After Trudeau entered the race, thirty-seven abandoned him. Only three stayed and one of them was Herb Gray, his fellow Windsorite.

On February 9, one of the most bizarre exchanges took place between any leadership candidate and prospective supporter. Turner received a handwritten letter from his wife's brother, David Kilgour. Kilgour explained that while it might normally make sense for him to support a family member, in this case, he couldn't. But he went further. He bluntly told his brother-in-law that he wouldn't be supporting him for leader "because I think Robert Stanfield would be a better prime minister at this time than any of the Liberal candidates for the job, including John."

If Turner was insulted by Kilgour's note, he didn't indicate this in his reply. "We quite agree with you that it would be a little awkward for you to help me at this stage," he replied. "You are, after all, a Stanfield supporter and that's nothing to be ashamed of." Kilgour would run unsuccessfully for the PCs in a Vancouver riding later that year.

Six weeks before convention day, senior adviser John deBurgh Payne (always referred to as John "deB." Payne) wrote Turner a private and confidential memo outlining his concerns at the state of play. First and foremost, Payne told Turner he'd have to start generating considerably more ink because, "some, in the heat of their love-in for Pierre, have written you off.... Others have soured on you, claiming that you have done nothing and that you are shallow." While Turner's movie-star good looks earned him plenty of attention, that attention came with the typical prejudice that he couldn't possibly be smart as well. Payne concluded his memo urging that "Everything you do and say must show that you have depth, are a serious person, and have the competency to do the job."

Another adviser, W.R. Wright, also offered his advice in a private note and it was much tougher. "You are glib," he told Turner. "I found you quite candid, but the glibness rather tends to distort or cancel this out. Somehow or other, you don't seem quite real, even to me."

Wright's letter also reflected an occasional phenomenon among Turner's advisers, namely a jockeying for position to be the candidate's favourite. About Jerry Grafstein, Wright wrote: "He suffers from thinking he knows more than he does and makes rulings in the communications area that are occasionally beyond his competence."

Wright also said Turner needed 500 votes on the first ballot to win. He signed the note, "with kindest personal regards".

Turner, true to his nature, responded by calling the note "brutal and frank, but I appreciated it." He then demonstrated an impressive level of self-awareness about his speaking style, which would become a significant issue in future years, admitting his rat-a-tat speech patterns are "probably accentuated by the fact that now we are living in a cool age, accentuated by T.V.," and that "Trudeau is setting a style of detachment with which I do not fit."

On April 5, delegates gathered to hear the nine Liberal leadership candidates give their official addresses. Trudeau and Turner spoke back-to-back, Trudeau first. One of the delegates at the convention was twenty-seven-year-old Darryl Raymaker from Alberta. He'd met Turner a couple of years earlier in Calgary at a reception and got the JNT treatment: "A hearty handshake and some jock talk," the now octogenarian Raymaker says. "It was typical Turner. He was handsome as hell." But Raymaker was now one of almost 2,400 delegates at the Ottawa Civic Centre, elected as a Trudeau supporter, but keeping his eye on Turner as well.

"I am restless for Canada," Turner said during his speech. "I am restless to close the gap between the rich and the poor. I am restless to bring our young people into the mainstream of our life. I am restless to reach out and touch, reach out to the disenchanted and the dispossessed."

Turner then used a line that would follow him for the rest of his life because it was just so eerily prescient. He needed to address the elephant in the room that, as the youngest candidate in the race, he actually didn't burn to win this time out. "I'm not here for some next time," he assured the delegates. "I'm not bidding now for your consideration at some vague convention in 1984 when I've mellowed a bit. My time is now and now is no time for mellow men."

The conventional wisdom of the day was that the forty-seven-year-old Agriculture Minister Joe Greene gave the best speech that night. Trudeau had also performed well. But Raymaker saw something else that night.

"Turner's performance," he thought, "together with his telegenic good looks would keep him in delegates' minds as Trudeau's natural successor for years to come."

With the speeches out of the way, it was time to vote. As expected, Trudeau led on the first ballot, but his level of support was underwhelming. The justice minister captured just 31.5 per cent of the tally. A group of four candidates was clustered close together, but well behind Trudeau: Hellyer at 13.8 per cent; Winters at 12.3 per cent; and both Martin and Turner tied for third with 11.6 per cent. Greene, Alan MacEachen, Eric Kierans, and Harold Lloyd Henderson were all well back. The last two dropped off the ballot, as did Martin Sr., heartbroken at his weak showing, and declining to endorse any of the other candidates.

Turner's task at this point was to try to emerge from the pack of three behind the justice minister and become the champion of the anti-Trudeau vote. It was the mission of another future prime minister to ensure that didn't happen: Jean Chrétien sought out Grafstein in an attempt to solicit Turner's support for Trudeau, in advance of the second ballot. But Grafstein told him no dice, suggesting there was still a path to victory for his candidate.

The second ballot clearly established Trudeau as the front-runner and eventual winner unless something dramatic were to occur. Trudeau jumped to 40.5 per cent support, Winters passed Hellyer for second place with 20 per cent of the delegates, while Hellyer came third, just eight votes behind, with 19.5 per cent support. Turner had to accept the disappointing news that his support had barely grown at all: he'd picked up 70 delegates for 14.6 per cent support. Greene and MacEachen were well back but only MacEachen dropped off the ballot.

Again, Chrétien sought out Grafstein, telling him Trudeau was getting quite miffed that Turner had not yet dropped out to support him. But the result was the same. Turner was staying put.

When the cameras caught what has turned out to be the most enduring moment from this convention, one can well understand Trudeau's nervousness. Judy LaMarsh, the first ever female cabinet minister for the Liberals, was furiously trying to convince her candidate, Hellyer, to drop off the ballot and support Winters, who had emerged as the anti-Trudeau champion. CBC-TV's live coverage of the convention caught LaMarsh telling Hellyer: "Come on Paul, you've got to go to Winters. You're forty-four, and we've still got lots of time. Don't let that bastard win it, Paul. He isn't even a Liberal." Hellyer declined to take LaMarsh's advice and in hindsight, missed the best chance the delegates had to defeat Trudeau.

The third ballot results made two things abundantly clear. With 44.2 per cent of the delegates, Trudeau was now a stone's throw away from victory on the ensuing ballot. In addition, had Hellyer and Turner wanted to influence the outcome by backing another candidate, they'd missed their moment. Winters was now the undisputed challenger to Trudeau with 26.1 per cent support; Hellyer was in third having dropped to 16 per cent; similarly, Turner lost almost everything he'd gained on the previous ballot, falling to fourth spot and 11.7 per cent.

Hellyer now dropped off the ballot and endorsed Winters, while Greene departed with just 1.2 per cent support and went to Trudeau. All eyes were now on Turner, the potential kingmaker, whose next move would likely decide the convention. To the surprise of many, Turner declined to back either Trudeau or Winters. He stayed on for the fourth and final ballot, knowing he had no hope of winning, but wanting to convey the image of a guy who wasn't a quitter.

"Turner always told me, 'I'm going right to the end,' and I said, 'Fine,'" Grafstein says more than half a century after the fact. "I thought it would set him up for next time. He was young enough to have a second kick at it. We talked for endless hours game-playing this out."

By staying on for the fourth ballot, Turner deprived Winters of the votes the MP for York West needed to have any chance of passing Trudeau, and the Turner campaign was just fine with that.

"If there had been any danger of Winters winning, we'd have flipped to Trudeau," Grafstein says. "But there wasn't." The Turner campaign was remarkably sure of its position, given the closeness of the outcome.

The final count: Trudeau with 1,203 delegates (50.9 per cent); Winters 954 delegates (40.3 per cent), and Turner 195 delegates (8.2 per cent). Trudeau had won but just barely. Winters would quit politics and be dead a year-and-a-half later at just fifty-nine. But for Turner, a legend began. Who were these 195 delegates who were so loyal to him that they stuck with him to the bitter end, declining to vote for a candidate who actually had a chance to win? Jim Clark was one of them, and his daughter still has a Turner-for-Leader delegate package from that day as a souvenir.

"If John Turner had become the leader in '68, we'd have done a lot better," Christy Clark now says.

Turner's mother, Phyllis, was the highest-ranking female civil servant in Ottawa. Her story made the cover of *Maclean's*. Leonard Turner barely knew his son. He died of a botched operation when John was only three years old.

Phyllis Gregory was a loving but demanding single mother to her son, John, and daughter, Brenda. She expected good marks from both of her children through-out their years in school. Meanwhile, John was an Olympic-level sprinter and the fastest man in Canada in the mid-1940s.

Expect Margaret to Dance Third Time With Montreal Lawyer

Keeps Margaret Gay
John Turner To See Her
Once More in Montreal

Russian Warships
Off Newfoundland
Said 'Power Show'

49 Canadians Drown

Turner was often described as Canada's most eligible and handsome bachelor. He was the big man on campus at the Beta Theta Pi fraternity house at UBC. And his very public dancing with Princess Margaret at a reception in British Columbia made for instant gossip.

Eventually, it was Geills Kilgour, originally from Winnipeg, who won Turner's heart. They met in Montreal and married in 1963. Almost immediately, the couple began having children. Elizabeth, David, and Michael are on their bikes, while Andrew looks on from his mother's arms.

Two remarkable, iconic pictures: Turner with New York Senator and future presidential candidate Robert F. Kennedy; and Prime Minister Lester B. Pearson with three of his cabinet ministers, all of whom would go on to become prime ministers themselves: Pierre Trudeau, Turner, and Jean Chretien. (Calgary Herald)

Turner lost his bid for the Liberal leadership at the 1968 convention (top) to Pierre Trudeau, who would later welcome his rival into his first cabinet. Turner, Trudeau, and cabinet colleagues (bottom). (UPI)

This photo, inscribed by Pierre Trudeau to John Turner, was taken in the House of Commons at 1:06 a.m. on the morning of October 18, 1970, shortly after the announcement that Pierre La Porte, the deputy premier of the province of Quebec, had been murdered by members of the Front de libération du Québec.

The Turner-Trudeau relationship ended on September 10, 1975, when Turner shocked the country by resigning as finance minister. His departure from politics allowed him to take several unforgettable family canoe trips to some of Canada's northernmost destinations. (CP PHOTO/Chuck Mitchell)

Despite enjoying a great and financially rewarding life in the private sector, Turner heard the siren call of the Liberal Party, demanding he return to public life. Here, he prepares to take the stage for his speech at the 1984 leadership convention in Ottawa. (CP Photo/Ron Poling)

The June 16, 1984 Liberal leadership convention victory was the high point of Turner's return to politics after nearly a decade on the sidelines. He's seen here celebrating with son Michael, wife Geills, and daughter Elizabeth.

Turner took part in two of the most consequential election leaders' debates in Canadian history. In 1984, his "I had no option" line contributed to the worst Liberal collapse in history. But four years later, he brought Liberals back to the precipice of victory with a bravura performance in a rematch with Prime Minister Brian Mulroney. (CBC)

Turner's supporters always thought he deserved to be in the pantheon of great leaders such as U.S. President Ronald Reagan and British prime minister Margaret Thatcher. But his ultra-short prime ministership prevented such comparisons.

Turner and Princess Margaret maintained a lifelong friendship. In private letters published a few years ago, Margaret confessed she "almost married" Turner. Meanwhile, Liberal Party President Iona Campagnolo publicly scolded Turner for patting her derrière in public. It raised numerous questions about whether Turner's attitudes towards women were out of date. (Bottom: CBC)

Although devoted to his business and political activities, Turner loved nothing more than escaping to his wife's family cottage in Lake of the Woods, Ontario. He gave his House of Commons chair to Kingston historian and friend Arthur Milnes "because you'll value it." A plaque on the back says: The Right Honourable John N. Turner, A House of Commons Man, 1962–76, 1984–93.

Turner died at home on September 19, 2020 during the height of a COVID-19 lockdown. As a result, strict protocols allowed for only a sparsely attended funeral service at the huge St. Michael's Cathedral in Toronto. (Alamy)

Turner was never happier than when on the water, behind the wheel of a boat, experiencing the magnificent outdoors of the country he so profoundly loved.

"The 195 Club" would prove to be Turner's lifelong support base which would frequently keep his name in the news and his political prospects close to their heads and hearts. With Trudeau now about to take the reins of government, Turner had his best chance to get the mission he always wanted.

The day after Trudeau's victory, Turner invited to his home for breakfast the family of the man whose convention experience was certainly one of the most disheartening of his life: Paul Martin Sr. His son and future prime minister, then twenty-nine-year-old Paul Jr., called Turner's invitation "a gesture I have never forgotten."

When the two candidates gathered, the issue of the convention didn't come up at all.

After the convention dust had settled, Turner's campaign people wrote a blunt post-mortem on the candidate's performance and prospects. Perhaps surprisingly, its immediate strategy was to assume that Trudeau would not be Liberal leader for much more than four years, "and we have this period of time to wipe out [Turner's] unfortunate 'lightweight' image among individual newsmen and the wire and TV people." Campaign advisers felt Turner was distrustful of the media, something he'd need to overcome, and they recommended a full court press to court the press. "Make a point of dropping into the press club twice a month at noon or six for a drink or lunch so those who want to can nail you personally instead of in print," one memo said.

Turner was also advised not "to touch all of the bases each time you come to bat. One main base at a time." That was a reference to the candidate's predilection to drown his interviewers in detail, rather than have a punchy summation of what he wanted to say at the ready.

The campaign stood by Turner's decision not to back either candidate on the final ballot, saying "He had much to lose by making the wrong deal," and that "he was never in a position to be the king-maker. His vote would have split." Finally, advisers felt Turner emerged from the experience "as a man of character and principle. The electors will remember this in days to come."

In fact, Alastair Gillespie, a future member of Trudeau's cabinet, wrote Turner after the convention to praise his decision, as it helped "to reconcile the antagonisms of pro and anti-Trudeau positions, whatever their origins. It helped to de-fuse [sic] the bitterness."

Lloyd Axworthy wrote a thorough, confidential assessment for Turner, saying "other than winning the top job, this campaign was a success for you." Axworthy noted that Turner's stature within the party grew, his strong stands on issues led people to consider him as more than "the man who danced with Princess Margaret," and his making no deals with either Trudeau or Winters reflected "a tough, decisive person who doesn't buckle under pressure."

Axworthy then urged Turner to build "an independent position within the Liberal Party," not in opposition to Trudeau, "but the maintenance of a healthy tension between."

He concluded with a line that seems odd, given that he would eventually spend four years in Trudeau's cabinet in senior roles: "The convention result was, I believe, a mistake. Planning should begin now to ensure the next convention is free of error."

CHAPTER FOUR

The Justice Minister

TWO WEEKS AFTER WINNING THE Liberal leadership, Pierre Elliott Trudeau was sworn in as Canada's 15ᵗʰ prime minister on April 20, 1968, and he gave his colleague John Turner a promotion to Solicitor General of Canada. Again, not the justice portfolio, but a lot closer to it.

As an example of how different official Ottawa was back in the day, on Trudeau's first official day on the job as prime minister, he was walking from 24 Sussex Drive to the prime minister's office when who should drive by? Geills Turner. She asked the new prime minister if he wanted a lift to work and he said, sure.

"He and I were buddies," Geills says. "I drove him to Parliament Hill."

Tradition holds that a new prime minister would likely want to bring the House back into session for at least a couple of reasons. First, the new leader usually wants the country to see him acting prime ministerially in a parliamentary setting. And second, it's an opportunity for the former leader to give his farewell speech in Parliament, something recorded for all time by Hansard. For Lester Pearson, who'd been an MP since 1948, it was a moment he surely wanted to experience.

But Trudeau had been an MP for only two-and-a-half years. Parliamentary tradition was not necessarily his thing. And so, the new prime minister did *not* recall the House, thus depriving Pearson of his final day in the sun. Instead, the new PM called a snap election for June 25 to take advantage of the Trudeaumania sweeping the nation. Pearson loyalists were aghast at the breach of tradition and sad for their former leader. However, with the Liberals having successfully rebranded themselves with an exciting new leader, the question became, why wait?

In 1968, Canadians experienced not only a first election campaign for Trudeau but also the country's first ever election leaders' debate. The United States had already staged its historic four debates between John F. Kennedy and Richard Nixon in 1960. Canada's leaders had only one debate, and while it was hardly a barnburner, it did attempt to tackle some of the most controversial issues of the day.

Trudeau may have been new to federal politics, but he had already uttered a statement that was of such historical significance, it's still frequently quoted today. As justice minister, Trudeau had attempted to bring in new laws that would liberalize the rules around abortion (in some circumstances), homosexuality, and divorce. When asked why, Trudeau said: "There's no place for the state in the bedrooms of the nation. What's done in private between adults doesn't concern the criminal code. When it becomes public, it's a different matter."

While Trudeau may have been ahead of his time when it came to these matters, the fact is he was operating in a minority Parliament. His lack of political experience, combined with the political reality of the day, meant that he simply couldn't get the Criminal Code amendments he wanted through the House. The bill died on the order paper when the election was called.

But on June 9 at the leaders' debate, his proposed changes did cause some moments of friction. While Trudeau quietly and calmly defended his bill, Créditiste leader Réal Caouette opposed the changes around homosexuality, saying: "It could lead to a mature adult man marrying another mature adult man. It would cause problems for the children born out of such groups."

NDP leader Tommy Douglas, a Baptist minister before he was elected an MP in 1935, was open to abortion under strict circumstances, adding: "Persons opposed need not avail themselves of it." But the leader's comments about homosexuality, which he no doubt considered progressive at the time, do not stand up well today.

"Instead of treating it as a crime and driving it underground, we ought to recognize it for what it is: it's a mental illness," said Douglas. "It's a psychiatric condition, which ought to be treated sympathetically, which ought to be treated by psychiatrists and social workers. We're not going to do this by throwing people into jail." Douglas has been worshipped by millions of Canadians for decades, in large measure because of his important role as Premier of Saskatchewan in creating North America's first single-payer Medicare plan. In 2004, the CBC ran a contest in which Douglas was voted the greatest Canadian ever. His 1968 leaders' debate comments were clearly either not known or forgotten by the show's voters.

On election day, Trudeaumania prevailed. The Liberals took more than 45 per cent of the vote for a 155-seat majority government. It provided Trudeau with a twenty-two-seat cushion over the opposition. While our neighbours to the south were mired in seemingly constant upheaval (the Vietnam War protests, the assassinations of Martin Luther King Jr. and Robert F. Kennedy, and President Lyndon B. Johnson declining to seek re-election) much of Canada seemed enamoured with its new head of government. The PM's snap election call had paid off, and John Turner filed that fact away in his memory bank, for a time when he hoped he might find himself in a similarly opportune moment.

The election was also significant for Turner because his St. Lawrence–St. George seat had disappeared due to redistricting, so he contested the riding of Ottawa–Carleton instead. That came as extremely disappointing news to Ken Binks, the PC candidate, who'd been beating the bushes in that riding for the previous three years, hoping to end his losing streak. He'd lost his two previous attempts to get into the House. On election night, Turner crushed Binks by more than 17,000 votes.

"My dad just sat nursing a bottle of Scotch in our living room and enquiring of the assembled mob if he should ask for a recount," recalls Georgie Binks, the candidate's daughter. "Then they went off into fits of laughter every time he said it." (Binks would eventually win a seat in 1979, but alas, lost again in 1980.)

On July 6, when the new cabinet was sworn in, Trudeau gave Turner the mission he'd always wanted, minister of justice and attorney-general of Canada. At this writing, there have been fifty-two Canadian justice ministers/attorneys-general. Only four got the job in their thirties and Turner was one of them. Turner also couldn't help but notice that two previous prime ministers, Trudeau and Louis St. Laurent, became PM with the justice portfolio on their resumés (as would two other future prime ministers, Jean Chrétien and Kim Campbell).

There were other notables in Trudeau's first cabinet, including Turner's future leadership rivals Chrétien (Minister of Indian and Northern Affairs) and John Munro (Health and Amateur Sport); 1968 leadership rivals Paul Hellyer (Transport), Joe Greene (Energy, Mines, and Resources), and Eric Kierans (Postmaster General); plus future players Donald S. Macdonald (president of the privy council), and Otto Lang (without portfolio).

Lang was a rookie MP from Saskatchewan, relatively newly married to Adrian Merchant, whose brother Tony would be a future MLA in Regina (her daughter, the future broadcast journalist Amanda Lang, would be born two years later). Both Adrian and Geills Turner had young children and would often carpool together. But one evening, when both couples were at the Argentine ambassador's residence for dinner, Adrian and John Turner had a moment alone. Adrian was concerned something was amiss with Turner's wife.

"What have I done to offend Geills?" she asked.

Turner gave her a lesson in Ottawa politics. "You're new here," he told her. "One day, I'll be running against your husband for the leadership of the party. So, we're just not going to be friends."

Adrian Lang was shocked but said nothing. For the next several decades, the two families' social and political circles often intersected, particularly after Adrian and Otto divorced and she married widower (and Lang's cabinet colleague) Donald Macdonald. But the friendship was an inch deep. (A future indication of the Turner–Lang rivalry would come in February 1972, when Lang would replace Turner in the justice portfolio. Lang sent Turner a personal note criticizing Turner for his intention to speak to the Canadian Bar Association later that month. "It seems to me not to be desirable or reasonable to make a formal public speech almost as though one were still Minister of Justice after ceasing to be," Lang scolded Turner in the note, going on to call Turner's plan to speak "unacceptable," before imploring him to "understand the justification for my feelings in this regard.")

Turner truly became a national star in Justice, in part because of his approach to getting things done. Typically, he'd invite his opposition critics to dinner and share some informal ideas about what he had in mind on a particular bill. By building consensus in that way, "By the time I put the bill forward, it was as good as passed because the opposition was on board."

The notable exception to this approach was Trudeau's old bill dealing with Criminal Code changes to abortion, homosexuality, and divorce, which was now on Turner's desk and simply too controversial for easy passage, even with a majority government.

The first thing the Liberals had to figure out was whether to handle all of the different changes being proposed in one fell swoop with an omnibus bill or break up the bill into several constituent parts. Turner preferred the latter approach because it empowered individual MPs to have a different and greater say, depending on the issue. Opposition leader Robert Stanfield also preferred the Turner approach and promised his caucus a free vote on each matter.

But Trudeau overruled his justice minister and insisted on one giant bill, covering numerous aspects of Criminal Code reform, all at once. And so, on December 19, 1968, Turner introduced the most far-reaching and controversial legal reforms since Confederation.

"There is nothing in the bill which would condone homosexuality, promote it, endorse it, advertise it, popularize it in any way whatsoever," Turner said. "There are areas of private behavior, however repugnant and immoral, if they do not directly involve public order, should not properly be within the criminal law of Canada."

In introducing the bill for first reading in the House, Turner gave credit to Trudeau and his "indelible imprint" on the bill, even as he disapproved of the prime minister's omnibus approach and Trudeau's inability to get the bill through the previous House: "It was he who had the courage to assemble it, to introduce it into Parliament and to defend it across the land under the sharp scrutiny of a general election," Turner said.

He also made an appeal for civilized disagreement: "Our tolerance to this bill will depend upon our tolerance and our understanding of the needs of a pluralist society where everyone must strive to reconcile his opinions and personal beliefs, including the ones closest to his heart, with those of his neighbours, who are also earnest and sincere."

But Turner could find few supporters on the other side of the House. The Tories' justice critic Eldon Woolliams spoke for many when he said he was content to take homosexuality out of the Criminal Code. But his subsequent statements don't pass the test of time.

"Send these people to centres so they can be rehabilitated," said the MP for Calgary North. "I don't want to encourage homosexuality. I abhor it. It's a tendency by environment. If you give them the proper scientific training, you can relieve the pressure created by environment."

Bellechasse MP Adrien Lambert said: "It is generally recognized that homosexuality is a disease, and sometimes a vice." Lambert went on to compare being gay to having tuberculosis, a once rampant disease, eventually brought under control through a public health education campaign. "The cure for homosexuality is not legalization but rather recourse to preventive measures such as a skillful and objective information campaign among the public, and to curative methods applying to the victims of that evil," he said.

Walter Carter from St. John's West argued: "This is a disgrace to the Canadian public. A government which relaxes the regulations and curbs on drugs, that makes divorce easier, that permits abortion and homosexuality, is in the process of remaking our society. The question which we must ask is, in whose image and likeness?"

And Roland Godin from Portneuf posited: "I wonder, Mr. Speaker, if the present government, with its loathsome laws on divorce, abortion, on homosexuality, is not simply the tool of a dreadful plot against our civilization?"

Walter Dinsdale, MP for Brandon-Souris added: "Homosexuals prey on juveniles. It is something that spreads like a plague, for there is no more destructive drive than the sexual impulse running wild."

Even Turner's good friend John Diefenbaker, no longer the leader but a seventy-two-year-old opposition MP, insisted the bill "undermines the whole concept of a family as a unit." Dief predicted nothing less than the end of Canada. "The whole record of history has been nations that followed this course of gradually removing and debasing basic principles of life have not stood long."

David Lewis, an MP since 1962 and still a few years away from becoming NDP leader, called Dief's comments "nonsensical exaggeration," adding that a compassionate society ought not to label homosexuals as criminals. One can only imagine gay Canadians made of this debate, knowing that exposure would mean humiliation, job loss, and worse.

On abortion, the bill did not offer complete, unfettered choice to women. But it did decriminalize abortion and provided for circumstances under which a woman, in consultation with her doctor, would be permitted to have a therapeutic abortion, where the life or health of the mother was in jeopardy.

The law would stand for two decades until being overturned by the Supreme Court of Canada, which held that it violated Section 7 of the Charter, guaranteeing life, liberty, and the security of person. (There has been no federal law regulating abortions since that 1988 ruling.)

Turner's omnibus bill also brought an end to the highly restrictive circumstances around divorce. In the 1960s, divorce applicants had to obtain a private investigator's report establishing that adultery had taken place. Then, a bill granting the divorce would be introduced in the House of Commons and debated by a parliamentary committee. Only when that bill passed would a divorce be granted.

At one level, this was an extremely heavy lift for Turner personally. As a staunch Catholic and man of his generation, he was personally opposed to abortion, homosexuality, and divorce. One must also consider how truly ahead of his time Turner was in legislating these new rights. Homosexuality was still seen by much of the population as deviant behaviour bordering on criminal. New York's famous Stonewall riots were still six months away when the government introduced its bill at the end of 1967.

Easing restrictions on abortion also cost Turner the friendship of one of his closest associates: Dalton McGuinty Sr., whom he'd known since the two attended St. Patrick's College school in Ottawa. McGuinty was president of Turner's Ottawa–Carleton riding association and a serious Catholic (his ten children included a future premier of the same name and the MP David). McGuinty resigned his riding association position and ended the friendship.

"It was an unfortunate falling out," says Dalton McGuinty Jr., Ontario's twenty-fourth premier, who not only would become good friends with Turner, but arranged a gala in Turner's honour in 2008, while he was premier. The crowd of 550 people, at $225-a-plate, raised tens of thousands of dollars for two of Turner's favourite charities: the Canadian Museum for Human Rights and the World Wildlife Fund.

"But whenever JT referred to my dad, he only ever spoke kindly of him as 'one of my guys,'" McGuinty adds.

Turner explained his thinking decades later, telling his friend Arthur Milnes, the in-house historian at Kingston's Frontenac Club Hotel: "[For] a Roman Catholic, where the life or health of the mother is in danger, there is not a religious problem. I explained that to the Canadian Council on Catholic Bishops in 1968 and they accepted that, and they did not campaign against me on the abortion issue."

It helped that Turner had done his homework. He explained to both the Anglican and Catholic churches that the courts had increasingly been permitting abortions when the life of the mother was in danger. He told Milnes: "I showed them legal opinions from three leading Catholic lawyers from across the country, plus our own opinion from the Department of Justice."

And there was more in the 126-page, 120-clause package of Criminal Code amendments, which covered everything from regulations on drinking and driving, firearms possession, lotteries, harassing phone calls, misleading advertising, and cruelty to animals. It was the heaviest lift of criminal law reform since the code was adopted in 1892 and Canada's new justice minister was at the centre of it, calling it one of the great debates in recent years.

Turner's omnibus bill, technically Bill C-150, ultimately passed with plenty of votes to spare: 149 to 55. Twelve Progressive Conservative MPs supported it, including the party's leader, Bob Stanfield.

Turner also always had in the back of his mind the reforms first enunciated at the 1960 Kingston Conference that he was now in a position to implement. In a speech at Toronto's Osgoode Hall Law School, he told a class of future lawyers: "We must disabuse ourselves of the myth that poverty is somehow caused by the poor. We must recognize that the law often contributes to poverty." Turner's bail reform bill of June 1970 went on to receive praise for its humanitarian approach to making the law as fair for the poor as it was for the rich. His Kingston Conference legal aid review paper was now the law.

"If you look at the Just Society, the guy that put through the Just Society was John Turner," says Grafstein. "Trudeau couldn't get it through Parliament. John Turner was *great* in Parliament. He taught me a lot about how to deal with politics: principle and people. You've gotta get the principles right, but he was fantastic with people too."

Politically, John Turner was going places and lots of people were noticing. Around this time, Montreal lawyer and Canada's future United Nations ambassador Yves Fortier invited one of the city's most eligible bachelors, Brian Mulroney, to a dinner party. While standing in the kitchen with Fortier's wife, Carol, Mulroney offered, "John Turner has one ambition and that's to become prime minister. But there might be a couple of people who stand between him and that." When Carol asked who, Mulroney responded: "They're right here in this kitchen." Mulroney was barely thirty years old, but, as described by L. Ian Macdonald in his book *Mulroney: The Making of a Prime Minister*, he was already musing hard about Canada's top job in politics, and who he'd have to beat to get it.

Having said that, Turner and Mulroney remained solid acquaintances. After the 1968 election, Mulroney was in Vancouver on business when he ran into Turner, who was in town to speak to a Canadian Bar Association convention. Turner invited Mulroney up to his hotel room for a visit after the evening was over and the two drank for nearly four hours.

Turner's time as parliamentary secretary to the Minister of Northern Affairs and Natural Resources, more and more people were noticing Turner's rising star. In February 1970, he was invited to meet with the editorial board of the *Toronto Star*. The paper's editor-in-chief, Peter C. Newman, was so impressed, he sent Turner a private note after the meeting saying, "You convinced fifteen people that you should be the next Prime Minister of Canada."

Turner also had the great advantage of having people on his staff who were as good as he was. Besides Grafstein (whom Trudeau would appoint to the Senate in 1984), Turner had three future cabinet ministers on board: Lloyd Axworthy, David Smith (also a future senator), and Irwin Cotler.

The Montreal-born Cotler was a graduate of Yale Law School and a long-haired radical who had a poster of Che Guevara in his office. When Turner saw the Guevara poster, he told Cotler, "You know, he executed a lot of people in prison."

"So, I did some homework and took the poster down," Cotler now says, smiling.

At a meeting with America's Attorney-General John Mitchell (who'd eventually go to jail for Watergate-related crimes), Turner explained Cotler to Mitchell: "He's my one resident radical." Turner, in turn, became Cotler's role model.

"He was a due process radical," Cotler recalls of his former boss. In 2003, Cotler himself became justice minister. "John Turner taught me the importance of Parliament," he says. "Parliament was the lifeblood of democracy. I never forgot that." He remembers Turner reading Rachel Carson's hugely influential *Silent Spring*, the first book that put environmental degradation from pesticides on the public's radar screen. "He had a commitment even then to the environment," he says.

Despite the circles Turner grew up in, he never seemed to practice the overt (or even covert) anti-Semitism that was so prevalent in Canada during his time. He hired people with last names like Grafstein and Cotler and in 1970 appointed the country's first ever Jewish Supreme Court justice, Bora Laskin. In 1973, he made Laskin chief justice even though Laskin wasn't his first choice. Turner's preference was to follow tradition and give the job to Ronald Martland, the court's most experienced judge at the time, but Trudeau overruled him. Turner also leaned on McGill's first Jewish law professor, Maxwell Cohen, for advice.

"Turner respected brains, drive, ability, and concern for the less fortunate," Grafstein says. "He found those characteristics amongst his Jewish advisers."

Turner cared deeply about the integrity of his judicial appointments. He wanted judges of merit, not ones to whom the party owed a political favour. "He saw the courts as the pillar of constitutionalism," Cotler says. "Judicial appointments had to be both marked by the integrity of the process and the distinction of the appointees."

Having said that, Turner would appoint 130 judges during his tenure in Justice, of whom sixty-nine were known to be Liberal Party supporters. Only twelve were Progressive Conservatives, two were New Democrats (including the esteemed Thomas Berger as chief justice of the British Columbia Supreme Court), four were neutral, and thirty-four had unknown political leanings. However, Turner also cared about (and tracked) the ethnic makeup of the judges he appointed. His team kept a list of "Ethnic Appointments to the Bench," which included German, Czech, Hungarian, Polish, Greek, and Italian judges, as well as three Ukrainians.

Funnily enough, when Turner sought the advice of others in his office as to whether or not to hire Cotler, they all advised the justice minister against it. When Cotler asked why Turner ignored their advice, Turner said, "I knew you cared a lot about Bobby Kennedy. That was enough for me."

Ah, Bobby Kennedy.

Robert Francis Kennedy was the third-born son from America's most famous political dynasty. His oldest brother Joseph was killed in action during World War II. He served as attorney-general to his next oldest brother, President John F. Kennedy, who was assassinated on November 22, 1963. When President Lyndon Johnson shocked his country by announcing that he would not stand for re-election in 1968, RFK eventually entered the race for the Democratic presidential nomination.

Bobby Kennedy was three-and-a-half years older than Turner, who considered RFK a very close friend. Numerous times over the years, Turner regaled people with stories of "my friend Bobby. We were both attorneys-general." The fact that both men had the same position in their respective governments seemed a significant point of connection for Turner.

Bobby Kennedy was shot by Sirhan Sirhan on Wednesday, June 5, 1968, dying the next day. His death took place right in the middle of the 1968 Canadian election campaign and caused so much grief in Canada, there was some discussion of cancelling the leaders' debate scheduled for June 9, the same day as Kennedy's funeral. But the debate did go ahead as planned.

At his 79th birthday party at the Toronto home of his former political adviser Al Pace, Turner and I had a quiet moment together and I asked him about his relationship with RFK. In June of 1968, Turner said, Kennedy called him with a request.

"John, I don't know anything about Canada and I'm running for president," Turner says Kennedy told him. "Can you give me a briefing?"

According to Turner, the two arranged to meet in Madison, Wisconsin, after an RFK campaign event, at which time Turner gave him the briefing.

"Four days later," Turner told me, "he was dead."

Turner had no doubt told the story many times, but that didn't diminish its effect. We both sat silent and motionless for several seconds as I tried to take in the enormity of it.

It was only many years later that I realized the story is not completely accurate. To be clear, I'm not alleging any fabrication. But it's quite possible that Turner, having heard so many comparisons to being "Canada's Kennedy" and feeling deeply connected to RFK, simply bevelled the edges on some of the facts.

First and foremost, Bobby Kennedy didn't live long enough to see John Turner win the same job he had. Kennedy died on Thursday, June 6. Turner, of course, was not appointed minister of justice and attorney-general until the Trudeau government's swearing-in ceremony on Saturday, July 6, thirty days later. It was close, but RFK and JNT were never attorneys-general together. In fact, Kennedy had stopped being U.S. attorney-general in 1964, when he quit to successfully run for a Senate seat in New York, the position he held at his death.

Furthermore, Turner told the same story to former journalist and Queen's University archivist Arthur Milnes, but in that telling, the time between Kennedy's and Turner's Wisconsin meeting and RFK's death was two weeks, not four days.

Finally, Turner told Milnes the two men met in a steak house in Madison, after Kennedy wowed a crowd of 15,000 students with a speech at the field house at the University of Wisconsin. The only reference I could find on the internet to a Kennedy speaking at that university was RFK's brother, Massachusetts Sen. Edward Kennedy, on October 27, 1966, during which he was heckled to explain his position on the Vietnam War. When I asked the university's archivist to look into UW's records to see whether the Kennedy–Turner story could be confirmed, Troy Reeves emailed saying he examined "various sources I trust" but "found no reference to it. Personally, after his brother didn't receive the warmest of welcomes in 1966, I doubt he [Robert] would have spoken on campus. Doesn't mean he didn't speak somewhere in Wisconsin, just not, I'm pretty sure, at UW."

Turner did say the speech was at the university's field house. It seems inconceivable that Turner would simply make up such a story. However, would it not also be odd for a senior cabinet minister, in the middle of a new leader's first election campaign, to leave the country?

To be sure, Kennedy and Turner did know each other. During Turner's early days in Montreal, he and his sister Brenda were friends with the Timmins family, whose son Robert married Pamela Turnure. Turnure was Jacqueline Kennedy's press secretary (in fact, she was the first ever press secretary to a First Lady) and travelled to Dallas with Jackie when her husband was assassinated. Because of their friendship with the Timmins family, both Turner siblings were invited to the wedding and reception in the fall of 1966 in Jackie Kennedy's Manhattan apartment on Fifth Avenue. Turner would have been a minister without portfolio at the time, while Robert Kennedy would have been in his second year as the junior senator from New York.

"Someone snapped a picture of John and Bobby Kennedy there," Brenda says. "And that's where they first met."

Another story that has persisted through the years is that Turner was a pall-bearer at Kennedy's funeral. Numerous reports indicate there were 13 pallbearers who carried Kennedy's casket to Arlington National Cemetery. Names included former astronaut John Glenn, former Defense Secretary Robert McNamara, Gen. Maxwell Taylor, two sons Robert Jr., and Joe, and his brother Sen. Ted Kennedy. The name John Turner does not appear anywhere.

"He did embellish stories about his relationship with Bobby," Turner's sister Brenda now says. "I don't think they were close friends. He wasn't a pallbearer at the funeral."

But midway through Turner's tenure as justice minister, there *was* a significant funeral that he did attend. So did the prime minister, the leader of the opposition, the NDP leader, the Socred leader, about 100 MPs and senators, and almost every member of the Quebec National Assembly.

They were all at Notre Dame Church in Old Montreal to remember the first Canadian politician in a century to have been assassinated.

CHAPTER FIVE

The War Measures Act

WHEREAS NEARLY 10 PER CENT of American presidents have been killed on the job, assassination has thankfully not been part of the Canadian historical playbook. Throughout the first century of Canada's existence, only one politician had been assassinated, Thomas D'Arcy McGee in 1868.

That streak would end in 1970, while John Turner was justice minister. And Turner would find himself at the centre of one of the most excruciating debates in which any Canadian cabinet has ever engaged.

On October 5, 1970, British trade commissioner James Cross was kidnapped by a Quebec terrorist group called the Front de libération du Québec, or FLQ. Neither the federal nor provincial government knew much about the FLQ: the size of its membership, how well armed it was, how much sympathy it had among the Quebec populace, or specifically what it wanted beyond independence for Canada's predominantly Francophone province. Even though bombs had been blowing up in Quebec mailboxes for the past decade, the kidnapping shocked Canadians.

Prime Minister Pierre Trudeau's cabinet met on October 7 to consider its options. The FLQ had given the government until noon the next day to have its separatist manifesto read in full on CBC during prime time or they insisted Cross would be killed. As a result, the broadcast did happen on October 8.

Two days later, Quebec provincial cabinet minister Pierre Laporte was kidnapped while tossing a football with his nephew on the front lawn of his home.

Three days later, on October 13, Trudeau uttered the three most memorable words of all his time in public life. Reporter Tim Ralfe buttonholed the PM outdoors on Parliament Hill and asked him just how far he'd go to maintain order. Trudeau's reply: "Just watch me."

By this point, tanks were cruising the streets of Montreal. Armed soldiers in uniform became a familiar sight in Ottawa, including at the Turner household. Soldiers would hang out in the basement when not on duty.

"We'd go chat with them," recalls Elizabeth Turner, who was six years old at the time. "They came to the circus with us, the soldiers, and with me to school. Soldiers with a uniform and a gun. They'd escort us in and out."

Geills Turner noted, not particularly happily, that her children received a military escort to go to school and her husband enjoyed the same protection to go to work, but if she needed to go shopping, "the soldiers did not come." No satisfactory explanation was ever forthcoming. "The idea that they don't care about the little wife was an interesting one. If they kidnapped me, would anyone care? I don't know."

Meanwhile, her husband told her: "If I ever get kidnapped, don't let anyone pay the ransom."

On October 15, the city of Montreal asked Parliament to invoke the War Measures Act, a rarely used security measure that permitted law enforcement to arrest anyone sympathizing with or belonging to the FLQ. The provincial government echoed the request the following day. The War Measures Act was first enacted by Parliament after the outbreak of World War I, on the grounds that "by reason of the existence of real or apprehended war, invasion, or insurrection, it is deemed necessary or advisable for the security, defense, peace, order, and welfare of Canada." There was little doubt World War I met those criteria. But did the situation in Quebec in 1970?

The federal cabinet was told the FLQ reportedly had two tons of dynamite that could be blown up by remote radio frequency. Jean Marchand, a cabinet minister from Quebec who was close to Trudeau, called the FLQ "a state within a state that must be disorganized." Both anglophone and francophone cabinet ministers were urging the firmest possible response to what they called an "apprehended insurrection," although Trudeau acknowledged to cabinet that "You'll only know after the fact whether an insurrection was real or not."

But one former Quebec MP, now representing an Ontario riding, encouraged his prime minister to pump the brakes just a bit. John Turner argued Canada was a democracy and the cabinet ought not to forget that. He reminded his colleagues that invoking the War Measures Act was a potentially destructive move that could deprive thousands of Canadians of their rights and therefore needed to be justified before Parliament and Canadians.

Trudeau didn't explicitly disagree with Turner, but he did want an ultimatum given to the FLQ that night, with more members and sympathizers arrested.

"The longer we gave opinion makers in Quebec, the more we stood to lose," Trudeau told cabinet, recorded in documents available at Library and Archives Canada. Marchand feared that even with a big sweep, Cross and Laporte might not be saved—but if the FLQ were somewhat disorganized, an ultimatum might prove useful. He also suspected that Montreal's municipal police service had been infiltrated by FLQ sympathizers and worried he couldn't vouch for the Quebec Provincial Police, either. This was particularly problematic since no one knew whether FLQ membership was 200 or 2,000 strong.

Turner said allowing Premier Robert Bourassa's government to negotiate with the FLQ had immobilized the federal government, at a time when it was essential to mobilize public opinion behind it. He explained that a bill had been drafted with a wide enough mandate to cover everyone linked with FLQ activities; it would not cover censorship.

Cabinet eventually agreed that if the Quebec National Assembly made a written request for the War Measures Act to be invoked, it would do so as of 9 p.m. that night. The police would be granted extraordinary powers to search homes, arrest people without warrant, and detain people without bail. Furthermore, the two opposition leaders, Robert Stanfield of the PCs and Tommy Douglas of the NDP, would be informed and their agreement sought.

Cabinet took a break, during which time Trudeau sought and got Stanfield's concurrence. He also spoke to Ontario premier John Robarts who promised his province's support. Meanwhile, Turner received a confidential memo from Irwin Cotler, his current policy adviser and a future justice minister himself. "The issue is not liberty versus security," Cotler wrote. "The question is: are we going to have both greater liberty and greater security, or are we going to have neither liberty nor security?"

The House was informed just before 10 p.m. that the government would introduce special legislation, simultaneously activating police raids in Quebec. The next day, the Act would be proclaimed with Turner's desired guardrails in place: that the regulations be limited in time and scope, and no further regulations would be made without Parliament's consent. Cabinet documents show the Quebec-based ministers led the discussions. And even though he was the justice minister and a former Quebec MP, Turner did not overly insinuate himself into the conversation. Cabinet was convinced the public wanted action right away.

In his speech to the nation, Trudeau calmly excoriated the "self-styled revolutionaries" behind the kidnappings, who wanted seventeen convicted criminals released and charges against six more dropped. Noting one felon was serving life for bombing public installations and committing seventeen armed robberies, Trudeau wondered whether Canadians were actually being "asked to believe they're unjustly dealt with? Deserve freedom immediately?" Then, referring to Cross and Laporte, the PM added: "Should there be harm done to these men, the government promises unceasing pursuit of those responsible." Trudeau spoke slowly, calmly, but with eyes that seemed to blaze with fury. He wanted Canadians focused not on any potential overreaction by the government, but rather on the FLQ, which "chose to use bombing, murder, and kidnapping."

Two days later, Laporte was found murdered, his body discovered in the trunk of a car at Montreal's Saint-Hubert Longueil Airport. As far as the federal government was concerned, that was their evidence of the apprehended insurrection. Now, FLQ members wanted twenty-three of their imprisoned colleagues released with safe passage either to Cuba or Algeria in exchange for Cross' life to be spared.

On October 20, Turner received a letter addressed to "My dear Attorney" from his counterpart in New Zealand, expressing his condolences for the murder of Laporte.

"I'm full of admiration for the resolute action taken by Mr. Trudeau, in which, of course, you as Attorney-General must have been taking a most active part," wrote Daniel Riddiford. "I conclude by wishing that this crisis will soon be over and that a period of peace, which your great country deserves, will follow."

Turner responded on October 30, acknowledging the difficulty of imposing the War Measures Act. "But I believe events have shown that we were right," he wrote his New Zealand counterpart. "Our country is going through a very sad and difficult time. Speaking for myself and my colleagues, I'm grateful for your sympathetic understanding."

On November 6, police raided the hiding place of the FLQ cell responsible for Laporte's murder. After extensive negotiations, five FLQ kidnappers were eventually flown to Cuba on December 4, and Cross was released after sixty-two days in captivity. On December 28, three more FLQ leaders were discovered in a rural farming community, arrested, and charged with Laporte's murder, essentially bringing the crisis to an end. The prime minister and his justice minister had worked well together during the crisis. Trudeau presented a cool, forceful presence to the country, while Turner managed things well in Parliament, even introducing legislation to bring an end date to the Act and ensure the government's powers were eventually curtailed.

Turner did make one speech during the crisis that has left himself open to criticism more than half a century later.

"It is my hope that someday," he said, "the intelligence upon which the government acted can be made public, because until that day comes, the people of Canada will not be able to fully appraise the course of action which has been taken by the government."

It may have been Turner's hope, but it was wishful thinking. The evidence for the apprehended insurrection has still not been revealed to Canadians.

Four months later, Turner gave a speech at Yale University offering some personal reflections on the War Measures Act. He wanted to explain under what authority the government was acting, the justification for invoking the Act, and the impact on civil rights. To an American audience, the last point was a heavy lift for Turner, who explained that Canada's Bill of Rights was an ordinary act of Parliament, and not at all comparable to America's Bill of Rights, which was entrenched in the U.S. Constitution. (Canada's Charter of Rights and Freedoms was still more than a decade away from becoming part of the Constitution.)

The justice minister acknowledged the Act invoking martial law was "a drastic remedy. It essentially authorizes the government to do almost anything at all." Further, the cabinet wasn't required to disclose the reasons for invoking it. But Turner pointed out that both the governments of Montreal and Quebec had sought it, two public figures had been kidnapped, the possibility of remotely ignited explosions at power installations or public squares were genuine threats, and the government had concluded existing criminal legislation wasn't adequate to meet those threats.

The invocation of the Act worked. The FLQ was dismembered and half a century later still has not reappeared.

But Turner went further, putting some uncomfortable questions to his audience. In future circumstances, how could a potentially inappropriate invocation of the Act be avoided? Is there a role for the judiciary to enquire as to whether an actual apprehended insurrection might exist? Do Canadians care about civil liberties only during ordinary times or during emergency situations as well? And what future aftershocks of using the Act might arise? It would be more than half a century later before any Canadian government dared again to use the

Emergencies Act, passed in 1988 as the successor to the War Measures Act. On February 14, 2022, the Liberal government of Pierre Trudeau's son, Prime Minister Justin Trudeau, invoked the Emergencies Act to break up the so-called Freedom Convoy of truckers, which had virtually occupied downtown Ottawa for several weeks. However, unlike in 1970, the official opposition Conservatives opposed the measure, while the NDP supported the government.

"We have become very aware of the fragility of a democratic order," Turner said. Then, echoing the advice given to him by Cotler several months earlier, he added: "The very strengths of democracy are also its weaknesses. The very liberties we strive to enshrine can become by excess the license that can destroy. There is no freedom without order under the law, and there can be no order under the law without freedom."

CHAPTER SIX

The Finance Minister

O N JANUARY 28, 1972, PRIME Minister Trudeau shuffled his cabinet and made John Turner the youngest finance minister in the twentieth century. He was only forty-two, but with nearly a decade of experience in Parliament and a strong legal background, Turner was the obvious candidate for the job. He received a flood of congratulatory notes, although many were sorry to see him leave the justice portfolio. Arthur Maloney, the well-known Tory lawyer, wrote to Turner, "There is a universal feeling of regret among the legal profession, however, that you were moved from the post of Minister of Justice…. You discharged the duties of that office in a way that no one else before you or after you has been or will be able to match."

"I regret the loss of a Minister of Justice whose talents conferred dignity upon the office and the administration of justice," wrote Supreme Court of Ontario justice Lawrence Pennell.

John Owen Wilson, British Columbia's Supreme Court chief justice, wrote to say, "My personal feelings get the better of me and I feel a deep personal regret that you are leaving the Ministry of Justice where you did your job so well and were so very helpful to all of us."

Turner now had a little more than three months to pull together his first budget, which may have prompted humorous notes from two well-known businessmen.

"I don't know whether to offer congratulations or condolences," wrote Charles Bronfman, the Montreal magnate whose family owned Seagram's and who also owned the Montreal Expos. "On the other hand, I know that you know what you're doing."

"Some have suggested your assumption of the Finance Ministry deserves condolences," echoed Conrad Black. "I know that it is a demonstration of well-earned confidence in you that is shared in both official and financial circles."

"I don't envy you," wrote Peter C. Newman, "but I'm damn glad you're there."

Turner responded to Newman's note with one of his own: "I suppose I haven't learned how to say 'no' to a Prime Minister of Canada. In any event, I don't know of any greater challenge. The management of our economy will be the single most vital issue of the decade."

One message pleased Turner more than any other. It was from his former boss, Heward Stikeman, whose confidential letter was written on February 1 which, as he noted, was the twentieth anniversary of the creation of his law firm, where Turner had worked in his younger days. "We are rooting for you and collectively send you our very warmest congratulations," Stikeman wrote. "It will not be easy, but you were never one to duck a difficult task." Stikeman added that he had his letter typed because he figured Turner had forgotten how to read a handwritten note. Turner responded, "I am dictating my reply because, if anything, my writing is worse than yours."

One former federal cabinet minister, in private business at the time, referred to the elephant in the room in his note to Turner. "The journalists of course all say the unpopularity of being the nation's chief taxer means an end to leadership hopes," wrote James Sinclair. "I've never felt this to be true." It's hard to know what to make of the fact that the leadership issue was being raised by a man who less than a year earlier had become Pierre Trudeau's father-in-law.

In his reply, Turner allowed that he was feeling somewhat "chagrined when I read my political obituary in every newspaper in the country." In a personal and confidential note, Turner adviser Jerry Grafstein acknowledged that the new minister ought to proceed on the assumption that "Finance is a minefield. The unexpected must be prepared for."

Turner's budget intended to focus on economic growth and job creation. His deputy minister was Simon Reisman, a brilliant but temperamental mandarin with degrees from McGill and the London School of Economics. He was part of the Canadian delegation at the inaugural session of the General Agreement on Tariffs and Trade in the 1940s, was a significant player in negotiating the Auto Pact with the Americans, and would be the lead Canadian negotiator on the

Free Trade Agreement with the Reagan administration. Reisman was ten years Turner's senior and had a healthy ego, as evidenced by his quip that Turner was "the best finance minister I ever trained."

It should have been a good time to become finance minister. The previous year's budget had cut income taxes, prompting Canadians to spend more, particularly on housing, which saw record new home construction. Exports were up, especially iron and steel, lumber, wheat, oil and gas, and autos. There were 330,000 more Canadians working in March 1972 than there had been twelve months earlier. And the economy was expected to grow by 6 to 6.5 per cent that year.

"There is no question that the economy is advancing and gaining strength," Turner told the House in his first budget speech on May 8, 1972. "Confidence is contagious and I believe it is spreading."

But it was also a tumultuous time. The previous summer, President Nixon undertook several economic measures to beat back inflation, including wage and price freezes, and the unilateral decision to decouple the international convertibility of the U.S. dollar to gold. Markets worldwide were in shock.

Turner got along extremely well with his U.S. counterpart, George Shultz. He visited Washington every few months to play tennis and have dinner with the U.S. Treasury Secretary, to ensure both sides understood each other. While Turner said that Nixon "impressed me enormously with his intellect," he had no illusions about America's designs on Canada's water, its bully-boy trade harassment, or definitions of what constituted government subsidies. Those who may have thought that Turner was a Johnny-come-lately to the free trade debate in 1988 should remember how wary he was as finance minister to America's increasing desire for a continental approach to economic and fiscal policy. In fact, two months *before* he became finance minister, he told the Empire Club in Toronto: "I do not believe that Canadians would contemplate with favour a free trade area or customs union with the United States. The political consequences would be irreversible and would dilute or even destroy any claim we had to our own sovereignty."

Budget-making in Ottawa at this time was very different from today. Now, no "i" gets dotted or "t" crossed in a budget without massive oversight by the prime minister's advisers. But in Turner's day, Prime Minister Pierre Trudeau left budget-making entirely to the finance minister's discretion.

"When Turner was here, on all financial and fiscal matters the prime minister would not push John around," said Marc Lalonde, the health minister at the time and a future finance minister himself. "All the fiscal decisions were John's."

Crafting his budget was complicated by the fact that the Canadian dollar was worth more than the U.S. dollar. Turner's prescription to assist manufacturers create more jobs was to cut corporate taxes dramatically, from 49 to 40 per cent starting the following January. He also offered manufacturers more generous tax write-offs for their machinery and equipment. Turner wanted more and new manufacturing in Canada and the jobs he hoped would come with it.

He was foregoing $500 million in revenue for the government (more than $3.2 billion in today's funds). "But these measures should not be regarded so much as a cost to the federal treasury as a major investment by the nation that over time will more than repay itself in terms of increasing jobs for our workers and increasing prosperity for all Canadians," he said.

To encourage more research and development in Canada, manufacturers could purchase scientific equipment and be exempt from paying sales tax. For the nation's elderly, Turner proposed increasing the Old Age Security pension and the Guaranteed Income Supplement by the rate of inflation, effective the beginning of 1972. There were additional income tax exemptions for seniors and the disabled, and enhanced pensions for war veterans costing the treasury another $375 million.

There was a tax deduction for post-secondary students and if they couldn't use it, their parents could. For infirm people who needed full-time attendant care at home, there was a new provision to allow them to deduct part of that cost, and also the cost of transportation to hospitals or doctors' offices.

Altogether, Turner was proposing to spend $16.1 billion dollars (the equivalent of a $104 billion budget today; the actual estimate for Canadian budget expenditures for 2022–2023 is nearly $400 billion). Turner's operational deficit projection was about $1 billion (equivalent to a $6.5 billion deficit today; the actual estimated budget deficit for 2022–2023 is $52.8 billion).

The minister wrapped up his budget speech by acknowledging, "I wish I could do everything at once. I am sure that each member of this House, were he standing in my place, would have a long list of priorities of things he would want to change, of inequities he would want to cure. The bare fact of the matter is that we cannot do everything at once. I believe the measures that I have announced tonight will help to meet those demands which deserve the highest priority—the easing of some of the financial hardship of many individual Canadians and the creation of permanent, well-paying jobs." And with that, Turner tabled his first budget, which he knew could be the last one before the next federal election.

The most memorable reaction came from the new NDP leader David Lewis, who felt the tax breaks for business were too generous and the benefits for average Canadians too miserly. Lewis famously referred to big businesses as "corporate welfare bums" and the insult both resonated and stuck.

* * *

The 1972 general election took place the day before Hallowe'en and proved to be a suitably frightening experience for the Liberal government. Trudeaumania had given way to concerns about the economy and the PM's arrogance. Despite the government's attempts to paint a picture of a happy nation with campaign ads proclaiming "The Land is Strong," the Liberals barely eked out a minority government win. Trudeau dropped seven points from 1968 to 38.4 per cent of the total vote, good for only 109 seats, compared to the Tories' 107 seats on 35 per cent of the vote. The NDP and Social Credit held the balance of power with thirty-one and fifteen seats, respectively.

Yet somehow, Turner emerged from the near-death experience with an enhanced reputation. No less than Brian Mulroney said: "Turner's so smooth, he's never made a mistake anybody can pin on him. He's the Liberal dream in motion."

The Progressive Conservatives won most of the seats in eight out of ten provinces. The Liberals came third in British Columbia. If not for Trudeau's overwhelming stranglehold on Quebec, where his party won sixty out of seventy-eight seats, his career as prime minister might have ended after one term. As it stood now, the government had precious little room for error, and Turner's next budget, less than four months away, would give the opposition its best shot to defeat the Liberals.

On February 19, 1973, Turner introduced his second budget, and the big-ticket item was indexing the personal income tax system to ensure Canadians didn't pay more tax by virtue of getting kicked into a higher tax bracket. Once again, he sweetened some other income tax exemptions, and pensions for seniors and veterans. He took the federal sales tax off all children's clothing and shoes as well as food products, including chocolate bars and soft drinks. He abolished the 10 per cent luxury excise tax on toiletries and cosmetics as well as clocks and watches costing less than $50.

Turner also reported to the House that economic growth was off the charts: 10 to 10.5 per cent in 1972. A quarter of a million new jobs were created, 25 per cent more than the previous year. The unemployment rate was 5.5 per cent.

"Some of this achievement comes from good fortune," Turner admitted to the House. "Much of it comes from the enterprise of Canadian business and the efforts of working men and women. But a good deal is due to the sound economic management and budgetary policies of this government," he also crowed, in effect patting himself on the back.

However, inflation was running rampant all over the world, which led to several serious strikes. The deficit would remain roughly the same as the previous year.

Turner's political mission with the 1973 budget was to find the sweet spot between what the Conservatives and New Democrats were prepared to support, and he did. The Liberal government survived.

As 1973 gave way to 1974, inflation continued to worsen despite the efforts of the world's major economic powers. Economic growth rates had hit 7.1 per cent in 1973 (the best in seventeen years and the best in the industrialized world except for Japan) but the inflation rate (12.65 per cent in 1974) was eating it all up and more. Turner said it was *the* issue that disturbed him and the country the most.

"Until we have brought inflation under control, it is imperative that the burdens it inflicts be equitably shared and that those people who are most vulnerable be decently protected," he said during his budget speech of May 6, 1974.

Commodity prices had doubled over the past two years. Moreover, the Arab oil-producing nations had banded together to reduce supply, quadrupling gas prices. Canadians may not have felt the sting quite as much, thanks to an agreement between the feds and Alberta to keep the costs for central Canadian consumers to a little more than half the world price. But it still stung plenty.

Turner told MPs he could fight inflation by trying to induce a recession, but "in my judgment, such a cure would be worse than the disease." Then, in words that would come back to haunt him, he rejected the official opposition's recommendation to impose wage and price controls.

"This would be totally ineffective in overcoming the kind of inflationary problem we have been and are still facing," he said. Noting that controls hadn't worked significantly in the United States or Britain, he added, "in the present circumstances where the prime causes of inflation are shortages of supply, controls are no cure at all."

Instead, Turner proposed higher corporate taxes on mineral exploration, oil, and gas: two points for the rest of 1974, three points in 1975, and four points in 1976. Furthermore, with prices going through the roof, Turner proposed cutting back on federal tax incentives to these sectors. It was essentially a $40 million tax hike for miners (the equivalent of more than $200 million today) and a $410-million hike for the oil and gas sector (more than $2.2 billion today). Turner also announced he'd hit big corporations with a temporary 10 per cent surtax on federal income taxes for the ensuing year, while at the same time exempting manufacturers and small businesses.

In total, Canada's finance minister was proposing to raise taxes on businesses by $790 million (about $4.3 billion today). And that didn't include another $10 million excise tax increase on big cars, high-powered motorcycles, private planes, and large power boats. He also boosted sin taxes by 15 per cent on cigarettes, cigars, tobacco, and alcohol (not beer, however) to raise another $100 million of revenue.

Knowing that he needed the NDP's support for the budget's passage, Turner then announced the goodies: extra money for farm loans, removing the sales tax on all clothing and footwear and on rapid transit vehicles for municipalities, bicycles, and heavy machinery used for home construction. Turner also created the RHOSP, or registered homeownership savings plan, that would work like the retirement savings plans. He enhanced income tax reductions for lower income and disabled Canadians. He also planned further increases to veterans' pensions and orphans' allowances and kept the deficit essentially where it had been the previous year.

Summing up, Turner said: "I am gambling that Canadians are too smart to be taken in by gimmicks, slogans, or slick jargon—that they want to know the facts, pleasant or unpleasant, and they ask only for a man's best judgment in meeting them."

Finally, to the opposition members whose votes he needed to keep the Liberals in power, he added: "If this House can bring itself to judge my budget with the same common sense and open mind, then I am sure that the measures I have proposed will commend themselves to enough Members to ensure its passage."

It didn't.

For only the third time in our history, and the first time on a vote related to a budget, a minority government was defeated on a vote in the House: 137 to 123. Every Tory and New Democrat MP voted to bring the government down. The Socreds joined the Liberals but the government didn't have the votes. The Liberals had survived nineteen non-confidence votes, but not this one, and as a result, Parliament was dissolved and Canadians would head to the polls on July 8.

In a scrum with reporters after the vote, NDP leader David Lewis said: "To ask us to support a budget which gave the average worker 96 cents a week in a tax cut is just irresponsible. The government had to come down. They were becoming paralytic almost."

Meanwhile, CBC reporter Ron Collister buttonholed Turner, asking him whether he had "any trouble in selling this particular kind of budget which may have been economically sound but maybe wasn't quite as politically sexy as some of your supporters may have liked it?"

Turner kept a straight face in responding: "One always has to draw the limits between sex and discipline, and this is a budget that has a bit of both."

It may have been Turner's budget that sent Liberals back on to the hustings, but the finance minister didn't show an ounce of regret. Keith Davey, one of the Liberal campaign co-chairs, recalled in his memoir, "No one campaigned longer or more effectively in the 1974 election than John Turner. Next only to Trudeau, the younger John Turner was the speaker everyone wanted to hear. His aggressive, staccato style was exactly right for that time."

Only two cabinet ministers were allowed to speak outside of their home provinces: Agriculture Minister Eugene Whelan from Windsor and Turner. In his reportage on the 1974 election, the *Globe and Mail*'s Jeffrey Simpson noted: "Turner was a superstar in that campaign. He could go into a room of twenty people who'd introduce themselves. He'd then take questions then remember everyone's names."

Irwin Cotler told a similar story. "We were in Halifax and he bumped into a woman. She'd met him before. She said, 'You don't remember me, do you?' And he said, 'Of course I remember you.' He then named her three kids and asked about them. He cared and remembered their names."

The election results were a triumph for the Grits. Trudeau and Co. picked up thirty-two seats for a total of 141 on the strength of 43 per cent of the total vote. The Liberals had their majority back. And in Ottawa–Carleton, in what Simpson described as one of the greatest kamikaze acts of all time, PC candidate Bill Neville lost to Turner by almost 11,000 votes. The Liberals may have had their majority back, but the international forces hammering the Canadian economy did not let up. Conrad Black, in his memoir *A Life in Progress*, described the months after the 1974 election as "wasted," with the federal government doing nothing. Turner tried negotiating voluntary wage and price controls and yet inflation kept rising.

The government's chief problem was that its prime minister had ridiculed Robert Stanfield when the PC leader suggested wage and price controls were necessary. Trudeau, at his cerebral, sarcastic, and arrogant best, wondered aloud whether he should simply stare down inflation by saying "Zap, you're frozen." It got a great laugh and made Stanfield seem out of it. Turner's 1974 budget, too, expressly rejected controls as an option. But it now seemed the only option the government hadn't tried was the one it had made a point of ridiculing and rejecting.

Despite this, Turner's reputation as a solid economic steward remained intact. One day, he called twenty senior reporters into his office in the West Block for a chat on background. With no cameras or microphones present, he held court for two hours, not once referring to briefing notes, about the state of the economy and what he was trying to do. It was a bravura performance.

In the spring of 1975, hockey was the subject of one of the Liberals' caucus meetings. Based on the historic success of the 1972 Summit Series with the Soviets, Alan Eagleson was attempting to put together a successor tournament called the Canada Cup for 1976. Trudeau was helpful in getting foreign leaders to come to Canada for the event, even going so far as to extend handwritten invitations. Former Agriculture Minister (now Senator) Joe Greene intervened, urging the PM to marginalize Eagleson if possible.

"Alan Eagleson is a Tory," Greene said. "This'll all be to their advantage."

But Turner interceded on behalf of his friend. "First of all," he told caucus, "there's no one in the Liberal Party like Al Eagleson. He'll get the job done." In fact, the six-team tournament in September 1976 was a triumph as Canada defeated Czechoslovakia in the final. The Maple Leafs' Darryl Sittler scored the overtime winner with an iconic fake slap shot on goaltender Vladimir Dzurilla, while Bobby Orr was named the tournament's most valuable player.

* * *

On June 23, 1975, Turner rose in the House yet again to introduce another budget designed to whip inflation. He unveiled massive spending cuts totalling $1 billion on capital projects, foreign aid, crown corporations, and other programs. Public servants' salary increases would be held to 3.1 per cent. The rate of increase for health transfers to the provinces would be cut back. There would still be nearly half a billion dollars in job creation programs, but income taxes on better-off Canadians would go up, and a special excise tax of 10 cents a gallon would be imposed on producers and importers of gasoline. The deficit would hit nearly $5 billion ($24.7 billion in today's dollars). Conservatives told Turner it was his reckless public spending and skyrocketing deficits that were contributing to high inflation and unemployment. Meanwhile, there seemed to be increasing daylight between the prime minister and him. Turner complained to friends that Trudeau didn't seem to be supporting him as he once had. Furthermore, his deputy minister Simon Reisman had left earlier in the year. Things just weren't good.

So, the government's most important minister sat down one night and took out a stack of index cards. In one pile were the reasons for staying and finishing the job he'd started. In the other pile, the uncomfortable truth about why it might be time to leave.

CHAPTER SEVEN

The Move to Bay Street

N OT LONG AFTER THE 1974 election in which John Turner helped secure a third consecutive mandate for Pierre Trudeau, the finance minister and the Rainmaker had dinner. Turner was anxious to get Keith Davey's advice on what ultimately was the most important question of his political life: how long did Trudeau intend to stick around?

"You have to give it two years," Davey told him. "By then, we'll know if the PM is leaving and if he goes, you're it. If he looks like he's staying, then yes, maybe you should leave and get on with the rest of your life."

Not since Sir Wilfrid Laurier's fourth consecutive victory in 1908 had any Canadian prime minister served more than three consecutive terms. So, Davey's advice was reasonable. Turner should wait for the midway point in Trudeau's third mandate, then try to establish whether the PM intended to try to seek a fourth term or retire.

But as the summer of 1975 dragged on, Turner realized he wasn't prepared to leave his political fate in Trudeau's hands. Officials in the department of finance were urging him to bring in wage and price controls, something he himself had already forcefully rejected and Trudeau had ridiculed. Meanwhile, Turner's confidential post-budget briefings showed an economy continuing to contract and unemployment continuing to rise. And so, on September 10, Turner and Trudeau met at the Prime Minister's Centre Block office to try to figure out the road forward.

Only the two men know with absolute certainty what happened in that meeting and they are both deceased. Given that neither was very forthcoming with the media on the day and most of the available sources come to us second- and third-hand, we may never know categorically what transpired. Suffice to say, Turner was unhappy with what he thought was an increasing distance between his position and the prime minister's on economic matters. His friends were telling him he was in a no-win situation and he should get out. Others say Turner went into the meeting prepared to resign but hoping Trudeau would beg him to stay. In his memoir, Paul Martin Sr. described Trudeau as having a "curious mixture of aloofness and shyness" that prevented him from really laying it on the line to keep someone. After barely defeating Robert Winters at the 1968 leadership, Trudeau hadn't gone the extra mile to ensure party unity by asking Winters to stick around and so Winters quit. Martin speculated Trudeau probably made the same half-hearted effort with Turner.

In *Grits*, Christina McCall-Newman suggests Trudeau *should* have said, "C'mon John, I won't be here forever, stick around. Here's External Affairs. See the world. And soon, your time will come." Trudeau apparently did hint that Turner would likely be the next leader and should hang tight, but he couldn't say it with any conviction. That was a problem for Turner, who, despite his outward confidence, was the sort of politician who needed to be appreciated, particularly, as we've seen, by the older generation.

Perhaps the best account of this moment in Canadian political history comes from a book on Trudeau written by his former adviser George Radwanski, who spoke to the PM about it two years after the fact.

"He left because he had grown bored and frustrated working with a prime minister who didn't particularly like him, who seldom praised him, and who refused to make him feel special," Radwanski wrote.

Trudeau confirmed for Radwanski that he admired Turner and his political judgment. "When there was an important political decision to make and I'd bring in a few guys to make the end decision, Turner was always one of them," Trudeau said. "It wasn't because he had clout and a strong backing, it was because I thought he was a good politician."

Turner's friend from his Montreal law days, Donald Johnston, confirms in his memoir that the PM and his finance minister had a solid working relationship.

"Despite the media's repeated attempts to find evidence suggesting a bitter relationship between Trudeau and John Turner, Trudeau gave them nothing to support it," Johnston wrote in *Up the Hill*. "Never did I hear him utter a disparaging word about Turner."

However, in this case, Trudeau took Turner at his word and assumed he really meant to quit. He asked Turner why he'd want to leave, given that "You're likely to be the next leader." But when Turner said enough was enough, Trudeau accepted the decision, then offered Turner a place on the Supreme Court.

Turner's face froze. This wasn't some negotiation for a consolation prize, he thought. It was so much more than that. But Trudeau didn't realize it, and when Turner rejected the high court, Trudeau made him another offer: the Senate. That infuriated Turner even more, the notion that the government's best performing rising star and most important politician in English Canada would somehow be put out to pasture at age forty-six was crazy. How could Trudeau not see that?

Sharp words were exchanged, and as McCall-Newman described it: "Turner emerged facing a life crisis, Trudeau emerged facing an economic crisis." She argues Turner resigned "for what he publicly described as private reasons and privately described as public ones."

Turner left the meeting steamed, scrummed with reporters immediately thereafter, and announced he'd be leaving cabinet effective immediately; however, he'd stay on as the MP for Ottawa–Carleton a while longer. When asked whether the PM had asked Turner to reconsider and stay on, Turner said, "No, he didn't ask me to stay."

Nevertheless, Turner's resignation letter to the PM thanked Trudeau for the opportunity to serve in two of the government's most important ministries and portrayed the resignation as long in the making.

"After the last election, I made a commitment to you to see my budget, which had been defeated, reintroduced, and passed in the House of Commons and remain as minister of finance for one year. That commitment has now been fulfilled."

Trudeau was equally complimentary in his letter to Turner, expressing "deep regret" that Turner was leaving, and claiming he'd miss Turner's "firm hand and shrewd judgement in our private meetings and at the cabinet table." Trudeau allowed himself a bit of nostalgia, recalling how Turner had immediately left the bitterness of the 1968 leadership race behind them to ensure Liberals emerged from that contest united.

Then, Trudeau inserted one line that stands out because it is decidedly not personal, but rather clearly aimed at reporters looking for trouble. "Since you did not base your resignation on any policy disagreement, I will not hesitate in the months ahead to seek your good counsel."

Neither part of that sentence turned out to be accurate.

The two men understood their collective importance to the country and thus made efforts to socialize outside of office hours to strengthen their rapport. They actually met in Jamaica once, each inviting the other to dinner (Turner groused to me years later that even when Trudeau proffered the invitation, he never picked up the cheque; Turner always did).

"But I guess the problem is, it was always business, very rarely just pleasure," Trudeau told Radwanski. "And when John told me, I'm getting out because I want to have more time with my family and kids, to me it meant exactly that. I accepted that decision and I respected it."

Ultimately, according to Trudeau, the lack of personal connection between the two men may have led to the resignation. "I think what went wrong is that we both sensed it was too bad that there wasn't more than that to it, that we weren't also closer personal friends," he said.

Nearly four decades later, at a Canadian Media Hall of Fame dinner, Turner was in a talkative mood. He was schmoozing with three of the all-time greats in journalism: Lloyd Robertson, Peter Mansbridge, and Peter Kent, who at this point was the federal Minister of the Environment in a Conservative govern-ment. While Kent was overseas covering the fall of Cambodia to the Khmer Rouge, Robertson and Mansbridge recalled, they had been busy reporting on Turner's resignation as finance minister.

"I fought the 1974 election against wage and price controls," Turner told the group. "We got a majority government and then we did a 180-degree turn."

Turner said he couldn't abide that and told Trudeau so. "All I could do was leave," Turner, then eighty-three-years old, said. He stressed it wasn't personal with Trudeau; they simply had a fundamental policy disagreement that couldn't be resolved and, the fact was Trudeau also had no plans to leave the job.

"Turner's leaving was really a matter of two complicated souls… who never would and never could understand each other," wrote Keith Davey in his memoir.

Oddly enough, before the 1974 election, Davey had reminded Turner that his job was to do everything in his power to win a majority government for Trudeau. Did Turner understand that could mean Trudeau staying on as prime minister even longer, and Turner missing his chance altogether?

Davey wrote that Turner's answer was: "I understand that. Give it all you've got." Davey did, Trudeau regained his majority, and now Turner was dealing with the frustration of that reality.

All of the above is the somewhat official version of the events of that night. But the widow of the man who would replace Turner as finance minister has another interpretation of how things played out. Adrian Merchant Macdonald, who married Donald S. Macdonald in 1988, says a conversation she had with Trudeau recalled a quite different exchange.

Macdonald says Trudeau told her that when Turner said he'd be leaving, Trudeau responded: "I respect your right to do so, but I wish you wouldn't." When Turner reiterated his intention to leave, Trudeau came back with: "Can't you stay until after the Ontario election?" (The Ontario Liberals had Premier Bill Davis on the ropes. With only eight days to go before election day, the Liberals were leading, and Davis looked as if he'd be a one-term premier.)

But Turner rejected that request as well, saying he'd already sent out a press release announcing his departure, leaving Trudeau hurt and startled. (Turner had, in fact, already told his deputy minister, some colleagues, and a journalist he intended to quit that night.)

The Macdonalds and Turners would move in the same social circles in Toronto for years, and Adrian insists, "I'd sit at dining room tables with John Turner, and he'd tell stories that just weren't true. My husband would look at me, just roll his eyes, and urge me to say nothing."

Calgary lawyer Darryl Raymaker echoes Adrian Macdonald's version of events, based on a conversation he says he had with Turner when they were seatmates on a flight from Lethbridge to Calgary. With both men nursing a Scotch and apropos of nothing, Turner nudged Raymaker, a Liberal delegate at the 1968 convention, and said, "You know why I quit in '75, don't you?" Raymaker confessed he didn't. "Because," Turner said, "I couldn't work for the son of a bitch any longer."

It's a story, incidentally, that Turner's wife Geills simply doesn't buy.

"I don't believe that," she says. "There was some disagreement over fiscal policy. But that was the issue. Nothing to do with working for 'that son of a bitch.' I never heard John say that."

For his part, Trudeau told George Radwanski two years after the fact: "I probably should have made John feel more wanted, more necessary, more desired, more useful, and in the interview when he told me that he was leaving, I probably should have pressed him a hell of a lot more to stay on."

Turner's resignation not only shook Ottawa to the core, it may also have cost the Ontario Liberals their first sniff of power since 1943.

"The resignation put Liberals in a terrible mood," says Howard Brown, a Toronto-based communications and public affairs consultant, who was working for the provincial Grits in that campaign. "It's very depressing when your country's star finance minister resigns. It put a damper on everybody's mood."

Sean Conway was a twenty-four-year-old Queen's University student in 1975, running for the Liberals for the first time in eastern Ontario's Renfrew North riding. He'd go on to serve for twenty-eight years at Queen's Park. "There's no question it had an impact," he says. "It had a very destabilizing effect. When a finance minister resigns in the last two weeks of the campaign during the home stretch, and we hear he and the PM aren't getting along...?"

There was another first-time candidate seeking office for the Liberals in that 1975 election: thirty-one-year-old David Peterson from London, Ontario.

"I remember that very, very well," says Peterson. "This was going to be our big breakthrough. There's no question it was insensitive timing to beat the band. And it was a kick in the ass to Bob Nixon."

To the contrary, then-leader of the Ontario Liberals, Robert Nixon, ninety-three-years-old when I spoke to him about this, says: "I was not concerned about the impact. But others, particularly after the election, were sure it had damaged us." (Nixon said in his view, NDP leader Stephen Lewis' "creepy good" performance had more to do with declining Liberal fortunes in Ontario than Turner's resignation.) Whatever the cause, the Liberals came third in the seat count in that election, which took place September 18, 1975. Lewis' NDP became the official opposition, and Davis survived his second election as leader with a minority government, on his way to four consecutive wins and eventually becoming the second-longest serving premier in Ontario history.

One month after Turner left the finance portfolio, Donald Macdonald brought in the wage and price control regimen the Liberals insisted wouldn't work.

Turner told his Bay Street friends Trudeau was screwing up the economy and Trudeau probably didn't help himself when he gave year-end interviews suggesting the free market wasn't working anymore. It was a shocking thing for a Liberal prime minister to say. Forty-five years ago, Liberals may have campaigned from the left, but they often governed from the right. "Let the free market do its thing" is something you'd never hear from today's version of the party, but many Liberals would have been perfectly comfortable with that sentiment half a century ago.

After the resignation, Trudeau and Turner wouldn't speak for nine years. But despite the messiness of it all, Turner emerged with his reputation intact and, at age forty-six, was considered a huge catch for the private sector. Unemployment and inflation were rising, the energy crisis had taken hold, and yet Turner left politics with his star shining brightly.

* * *

Ninety-three-year-old W.A. "Bill" Macdonald sits in the living room of his condominium in midtown Toronto, surrounded by windows offering a gorgeous view of Ontario's capital city. He overlooks Toronto's oldest Catholic cemetery, St. Michael's, which opened in 1855 and is virtually invisible from the street, surrounded as it is by homes and stores.

Macdonald and I are seated very far apart because COVID-19 has descended and we are practicing "social distancing." Almost half a century ago, as one of the leading tax policy lawyers in the country with the Toronto law firm McMillan Binch, Macdonald had cause to meet occasionally with the then-Finance Minister John Turner.

"He may have been the only minister I've ever met who was on time," Macdonald laughs.

"How come?" I ask.

Macdonald goes on to tell a story about a teenaged Turner being asked by his stepfather whether he wanted to go on an outing one day. Young John asked if he could bring a friend and the answer was yes, with the proviso that his stepfather would be leaving the house at 2 p.m. When Turner arrived at 2:05 p.m., his stepfather had already left.

"That was his lesson to be on time," Macdonald concludes.

Macdonald freely acknowledges his meetings with Turner were designed to "push for things we wanted or try to block things the finance department was doing." The two men developed a good working relationship.

In the summer of 1975, Macdonald met with Gordon Osbaldeston, a future Clerk of the Privy Council (essentially, the prime minister's deputy minister) but at this moment, Secretary to the Treasury Board.

"I'm worried John Turner is going to resign," Osbaldeston told Macdonald. "We need him for another year to maintain some fiscal discipline." Macdonald left the meeting so concerned that as soon as he got back to his office, he called Turner.

"Don't worry," Turner told him. "I won't be resigning."

Six weeks later, Macdonald came home from work only to have his oldest son come downstairs asking whether his father had heard the news: "John Turner has resigned," he said.

CBC News played it big: "To Ottawa, the resignation of a cabinet minister is important. But the resignation of a John Turner is an event," one anchor intoned.

The next day, Macdonald called Turner. "John, that was a blockbuster," he told him, adding business was taking him to Paris and Moscow for three weeks. "Don't make any decisions!"

Turner assured him he had nothing lined up and was in no rush to decide on his next move. Upon Macdonald's return, he and Turner met for lunch at a golf club on the Quebec side of the National Capital Region and Macdonald made his pitch. "You're going to have a lot of requests," Macdonald told him. "But we need your help more than the others do, so you'll be more important to us than you will to the others."

Naturally, Turner checked in with his former Montreal mentors at Stikeman Elliott to see whether he could resume his career there. But Stikeman's wanted a guarantee that Turner would never leave to go back into politics, a commitment he simply couldn't give. Turner took a few weeks to consider his circumstances, then signed on with McMillan Binch on Valentine's Day 1976.

"He was very important to us," Macdonald now says. "He had a bigger presence than anybody we'd already had." Turner assured his new partners this was not a temporary landing spot until he could dive back into politics. He was on Bay Street to stay.

Turner was a great catch. After all, he knew pretty much everyone who could be helpful to the firm's bottom line. For example, his friend George Shultz, the former U.S. Treasury Secretary, was now at Bechtel, the seventy-year-old American construction and civil engineering company. They became clients. So did the Royal Bank, Massey Ferguson, and Sandoz Canada. When a Canadian mining company needed approval from the Australian cabinet on a particular project, they enlisted Turner's help.

"John Turner called the Australian prime minister and got it done," says Will McDowell, now a partner at Lenczner Slaght LLP and a former Associate Deputy Minister of Justice.

Before long, Turner had joined the boards of directors of Canadian Pacific, Crown Life Insurance, Seagram's, MacMillan Bloedel, Massey Ferguson, Bechtel Canada, and more. He also became one of Conrad Black's chief legal advisers. "John is sensitive to what'll fly" is how Black described Turner's talent. The families were connected by virtue of the fact that Turner's wife Geills was goddaughter of Black's father George. Turner was impressed with Black, fifteen years his junior, given his comments to Peter C. Newman in *The Estab-lishment Man:* "Conrad has a mind of genius proportions and more important he's got balls!"

In relatively short order, Turner had become well ensconced in his thirty-eighth-floor office of the Royal Bank Tower in the heart of Toronto's Bay Street district. Watched over by a portrait of Sir Wilfrid Laurier, he made a great living as a corporate lawyer and director and bided his time as the prince in waiting. With Liberal fortunes continuing to sag in Ottawa, Turner's friends constantly reminded him the party could only reclaim its former glory if he were at the helm. The compliments took on a truth of their own.

Turner figured he needed to join one of the exclusive clubs in downtown Toronto, where so much business gets done. So, he and his friend former Ontario premier John Robarts, who coincidentally was now a partner in Stike-man Elliott's new Toronto office, set their sights on the exclusive Toronto Club, the oldest club of its kind in Canada (having been founded in 1837) and a home away from home for the country's business elite.

Turner and Robarts wanted to join the club together, figuring the symmetry of their Liberal-Tory heavy-hitter status would help their chances of getting in. But John Angus "Bud" McDougald, perhaps the country's pre-eminent corporate executive as head of the Argus Corp. and then chairman of the Toronto Club, is reputed to have said: "I don't want any fucking politicians in my club." The pair were rejected.

"He was the pre-eminent lawyer and corporate director in town and they still wouldn't let him in," says former Ontario premier David Peterson, still incredulous at the snub.

Turner decided to go elsewhere instead. "Not great for my dad at the time," Turner's son Michael now says, "but it led him to the York Club, a wonderful club that my dad loved and where our family shared some pretty special moments."

The Turners' oldest child, Elizabeth, had her wedding reception at the York Club. Turner himself always held court at his corner table in the dining room there and never looked back. "He was never a holder of grudges," says Liz.

Turner's name also soon became synonymous with Winston's, the pre-eminent place in the financial district to see and be seen (named after the former British prime minister, it was located at 104 Adelaide Street West, between Bay and York Streets). Winston's had twenty-three tables, and Turner had permanent dibs on Number Twenty-Three, an intimate seating-for-three table in the left corner of the restaurant. The publisher of the Toronto Sun, Douglas Creighton, had table Number One in the right corner of the restaurant. These were reputedly the only two tables in the entire city with exclusive telephone lines directly connecting Turner and Creighton to their respective offices.

"Mr. Turner was a Liberal so he got the table in the left-hand corner, and Mr. Creighton was a Conservative so he got the table in the right-hand corner," says John Arena, Winston's most famous proprietor.

Winston's became Turner's second home. He went there for lunch almost every day to hold court with captains of industry, finance, politics, media, and friends. He always had the same meal: sirloin steak and a tomato salad with finely chopped onions.

"The staff just brought him his lunch—he never ordered," says David Goyette, a Turner guest at Winston's and a former top adviser to Toronto mayor Art Eggleton, some of whose election campaigns Turner co-chaired.

One time, Arena received a fax from Buckingham Palace informing him that Princess Margaret and her daughter Sarah Armstrong-Jones would be coming to Winston's as Turner's guests. Arena was informed that the princess only drank Mountain Grouse Whisky, so he jumped through hoops to procure it for the meal. Turner warned Arena: "If the princess' glass is empty, don't ask. Just bring her another."

"Mr. Turner was so easy to please," recalls Arena, in remarkably good shape for a man of 98. "He was a beautiful soul. He was the man of the hour. No one could replace John Turner for his demeanor and savoir faire."

* * *

By-elections are usually tough on the party in power since they provide the public with a harm-free means of sending the government a message. If anyone needed any evidence that the Liberals were in deep trouble, they got it on October 18, 1976, the date of the Ottawa–Carleton by-election to fill Turner's now vacant seat. In a riding which Turner had won by nearly 11,000 votes just two years earlier, Tory candidate Jean Piggott cruised to victory by more than 15,000 votes over the Liberals' Henri Rocque. (Turner's long-time Montreal friend, thirty-four-year-old Sharon Sholzberg-Gray, ran for the Liberal nomination but didn't get it.) The worse things got for the government, the more people speculated as to whether replacing Trudeau with Turner might turn around Liberal fortunes.

Meanwhile, Turner capitalized on his perch at McMillan Binch to do two things that captured a lot of attention. He used his connections to get A-list speakers to be special guests at luncheons at the firm (former U.S. cabinet secretaries Shultz and Elliott Richardson, and captains of Canadian industry such as Ian Sinclair and Adam Zimmerman come to mind). And he and Bill Macdonald created a newsletter for corporate clients, replete with the latest hard facts and juicy speculation from the intersection of politics and business.

As Turner's replacement in Finance, it had been left to Donald Macdonald to bring in the wage and price controls that Turner had rejected. But two years later, Macdonald had had enough of public life, so he quit politics to return to practicing law. Who would replace him in finance?

There was a francophone MP, elected for the first time in 1963, who spoke almost no English when he arrived on Parliament Hill. But fourteen years later, he was garnering a lot of attention, first as president of the treasury board, then as minister of industry, trade, and commerce.

"To me," wrote Charles Lynch, the dean of the parliamentary press gallery, "Jean Chrétien is the most appealing minister in the Trudeau cabinet." Douglas Fisher, the former NDP MP now columnist, added Chrétien "was the most effective French Canadian cabinet minister in twenty years." The *Montreal Star's* Peter Thomson wrote: "So far as the parliamentary press gallery is concerned, treasury board president Jean Chrétien wins hands down as everyone's most popular cabinet minister." Turner surely noticed he now had an emerging challenger for the Liberal leadership.

When they were both in Trudeau's cabinet, Turner and Chrétien got on well, Turner even at one point calling Chrétien one of the best ministers anywhere. But that relationship began to deteriorate in the fall of 1978 when Global News and *The Toronto Star* discovered the existence of the McMillan Binch newsletter, and in particular, some harshly worded criticism of the government.

Chrétien, the newsletter said, had "lost leverage" in Ottawa. Energy Minister Alastair Gillespie had lost the PM's confidence. Macdonald and Turner concluded the Liberals would probably lose the next election. Chrétien seethed when he read the reports. They may indeed have been accurate, but what was Turner, supposedly a loyal Liberal, doing by putting out that information in hard copy?

Keith Davey may have been a closer friend to Turner than to Chrétien, but he too was extremely unhappy with the way he was characterized in the newsletters.

Turner had lumped Davey in with Trudeau and his advisers Michael Pitfield and Jim Coutts as "anti-establishment social democrats." Future Davey–Turner meetings in Toronto were strained as a result.

To outside observers, Turner's politics may have looked more conservative now that he was raking it in on Bay Street. But at his core, he was still philosophically a liberal (and a Liberal), as evidenced by an argument he had with one of his best friends, the world-renowned Canadian tenor Jon Vickers, who was three years Turner's senior and a frequent tennis buddy. On one occasion after a robust tennis match, Vickers began complaining to his friend, the former finance minister, about how high his taxes were.

"John," he began, "I don't mind paying 40 per cent or even 50 per cent of my income in taxes. But 60 per cent or 70 per cent? That's getting pretty tough." Vickers went on to say he knew opera choristers that were taking home more pay than he was.

Turner expressed no sympathy for his friend. "Then move out!" he said. Turner always believed higher taxes were the price we should happily pay to live in a more civilized society. Vickers apparently took Turner's advice to heart. Since his wife was from Bermuda, the couple eventually moved there. He died in 2015, after having returned to Ontario.

*　*　*

The constitution dictates that majority governments are permitted to last for five years, but custom also holds that prime ministers traditionally seek to renew their mandates around the four-year mark. One doesn't want to be seen as clinging to power or afraid of the electorate. But the Liberals simply couldn't risk going to the polls in 1978. In October, there were fifteen by-elections in seven provinces and the government lost thirteen of them. Two months later, *The Toronto Star* published a poll saying if Turner rather than Trudeau were at the helm of the party, the government would be re-elected.

Trudeau may have had an earlier window within which victory was possible, but it was an opportunity he missed. In November 1976, the Parti Québécois had shocked the country by winning a majority government led by Premier René Lévesque. Despite the economic storm clouds, Trudeau was urged to call an early election in 1977 to stare down the separatist threat, but the PM thought it too risky. Now it was 1979 and Trudeau was up against a five-year wall within which he *had* to call an election.

Interestingly, Turner interpreted the PQ's victory quite differently than Trudeau did. He said, "We must contemplate giving more powers and responsibilities not solely to Quebec under some form of special status, but to all the provinces." Turner would stay true to that view, something that would cause him no end of grief with his fellow Liberals in years to come.

Early in 1979, the Liberals brought together all the living former finance ministers to attend a special speech by Chrétien, who then held the position. Ed Lumley, who was Chrétien's parliamentary secretary but also a friend of Turner's, brokered a post-speech get-together for the two men, who were increasingly now seen as rivals. Lumley sensed Turner was trying to make up for the newsletter comments, but Chrétien was unmoved.

Despite his apparent increasing estrangement from some federal Liberals, Turner actually retained considerable political influence in Ottawa. When Charles Dubin retired as chief justice of Ontario, the cabinet was urged to appoint Justice Bert MacKinnon in his place. "Turner got wind of this and to demonstrate his political clout to his colleagues at McMillan Binch, he got his old buddy Ron Basford (still in cabinet) to propose William Howland instead," says Ian Binnie, one of the few Supreme Court of Canada justices appointed directly from private practice. Howland had been the former senior partner at McMillan Binch, and, remarkably, cabinet appointed him to the chief justice's post instead, where he remained from 1977 to 1992.

In the spring of 1979 with time running out on his government, Trudeau called an election for May 22. Surprisingly, the Liberals managed to get significantly more votes than the PCs, now led by thirty-nine-year-old Joe Clark. Trudeau garnered 4.6 million votes, good for 40.1 per cent of the total votes cast. Conversely, Clark captured only 4.1 million votes or 36 per cent of the vote. Under normal circumstances, those numbers should have delivered a Liberal majority government, but the vote splits were highly unusual and as a result, it was the Progressive Conservatives who actually won more seats: 136 to 114. The result was a Tory minority government, with the NDP's twenty-six seats and Social Credit's six holding the balance of power.

After eleven years of Trudeau, Canada looked utterly divided. Quebec gave the Liberals sixty-seven seats and the Tories only two. Conversely, everything from Ontario to British Columbia was overwhelmingly Conservative, the Liberals winning only three seats west of Ontario.

Was this the moment the 195 Club had been waiting for? Given the defeat, would Liberals demand Trudeau's resignation, opening the door for Turner's political comeback? Turner certainly wanted to be courted but he was enjoying life and building up a nest egg for his family. He also thought it was unlikely that anyone could save the Liberals at this point.

On June 4, the day before his fortieth birthday, Charles Joseph Clark was sworn in as Canada's sixteenth and youngest-ever prime minister. Although nowadays a general election loss is often immediately followed by the leader's resignation, Trudeau stayed put. Those loyal to him implored him to remain, believing Clark and his team's inexperience would render the new government short-lived.

Trudeau moved into Stornoway, the Opposition Leader's official residence, showed up to Question Period, and assumed his new role. But it soon became clear his heart just wasn't in it. That, plus the strains of his private life (he and his wife Margaret had separated a couple of years earlier) meant Trudeau had simply had enough. He was sixty years old, facing a leadership review at the ensuing annual general meeting, with three sons who needed him. Why hang on?

And so, on November 21, Trudeau announced his intention to resign as Liberal leader and asked the party to hold a convention to pick his replacement in Winnipeg in March.

Given the Liberal tradition of alternating between anglophone and francophone leaders, all eyes were on Turner and Donald Macdonald, two former finance ministers now working on Bay Street. Macdonald struck first, indicating his willingness to run for leader. The 195 Club also got to work. David Smith, Jerry Grafstein, Jim and Heather Peterson, John Swift, John deB. Payne, Jeanne Sauvé, Andre Ouellet, Robert Kaplan, Mark MacGuigan, and the last three presidents of the party's Ontario wing all urged Turner to go for it.

On December 10, the day before the Clark government would introduce its first budget, Turner invited his innermost circle of advisers to his office at McMillan Binch to deliver the news they didn't want to hear. He told them he was out. He just wasn't prepared to turn his life upside down and put his family through the meat grinder of politics again. He held a news conference later that day to share the news.

On December 11, Finance Minister John Crosbie brought down a budget featuring an eighteen-cent-per-gallon gas tax increase plus spending restraint designed to cut the country's deficit in half during what the Tories assumed and hoped would be a four-year mandate. But in one of the most bizarre miscalculations in Canadian political history, two days later, the House voted no-confidence in Crosbie's budget. The Tories felt certain that only six months into their mandate, they could govern as if they had a majority. Further, they felt sure that opposition MPs wouldn't risk failing to qualify for their gold-plated pensions by forcing an early election. But those MPs did risk that by a vote of 139 to 133. For the second time that decade (the first being Turner's own 1974 budget), the government of the day had fallen on a budget vote. Ottawa was abuzz as Clark called an election for February 18, 1980.

What were the Liberals going to do now? An end of March leadership convention was now far too late. Could the party pick a new leader almost instantly, then send him or her right on to the hustings to face Clark and NDP leader Ed Broadbent?

Donald Macdonald was in, but what about Turner? Did the PC government's fall alter the calculation for him? The myriad questions made for a fantastic political story, but the new developments didn't change Turner's mind.

"Turner knew in his bones that Trudeau wanted to stay," Grafstein now says.

Turner's troops may have understood their would-be candidate's decision, but it didn't come without frustration. Ever since the 1968 leadership convention, they'd been waiting for Trudeau to exit stage left so their guy could take over. As *The Toronto Star's* Ottawa bureau chief Susan Delacourt put it in her book *Juggernaut,* "They were trained for one mission only and that was winning the Liberal leadership." Now that mission was over before it had even begun.

Meanwhile, Trudeau was playing hard to get. He met with one of his top advisers, Jim Coutts, at Stornoway. Trudeau was reluctant at first but as Coutts pressed and pressed some more, he relented. Trudeau called Macdonald, apologized for all the disruption he'd caused in his former finance minister's life, and said that, given the new political realities, he intended to withdraw his resignation and join the election campaign right away. Macdonald, a total class act, stood down, welcomed Trudeau back to the leadership, and remained in private life. Later, he would say he felt he didn't have the "royal jelly" for the top job anyway and had only run out of a sense of duty. His widow, Adrian Merchant Macdonald, today says, "I am absolutely positive he was not unhappy that 'this cup passed.' He was much more humble than one could imagine. I pressed him on this, and I am sure."

On December 17, Trudeau called a news conference saying he'd changed his mind, and that it was the most difficult decision he'd ever made.

"My duty," he added, "is to accept the draft of my party."

Prime Minister Clark watched the news conference from London, Ontario, and was thrilled with the turn of events. He was sure the Liberals had overreached, were unprepared, and now had a leader who didn't even want to be there. He was sure he'd be rewarded with a majority government this time.

Alas, no.

"Well, welcome to the 1980s," Trudeau said on election night, in a speech that prompted screams of delight from the Liberal faithful at the Château Laurier Hotel. With more than 44 per cent of the votes, Trudeau won a 147-seat majority government. Clark's Tories lost 33 seats for a total of 103, garnering less than a third of the total vote. Canada's fifteenth prime minister would get one last mandate. And the 195 Club would have to cool its heels for another four years.

CHAPTER EIGHT

The Adviser

EVEN MORE THAN HALF A century later, his story still has the ability to astonish.

In 1971, with only a handful of games left in their National Hockey League regular season, the Canadiens suffered what might have been a fatal blow to their playoff hopes. Their starting goaltender, Rogatien Vachon, sustained an injury and was unable to play. As a result, the Habs called up their goaltender from the AHL Voyageurs to backup Phil Myre, who everyone assumed would now become the starting goaltender.

But head coach Al MacNeil had other ideas. He put a twenty-three-year-old call-up in goal for his NHL debut on March 20, 1971, in the Montreal Forum. (Strangely enough, the starting goaltender for the opposition Buffalo Sabres that night was this rookie's brother, surely the only time that's happened in NHL history.)

The Canadiens' goaltender caught lightning in a bottle. He won all six games he started in the regular season, then faced the mighty Boston Bruins of Bobby Orr and Phil Esposito in the first round of the playoffs. The Bruins were the prohibitive Stanley Cup favourites in the 1971 playoffs and nearly everyone thought they'd make short work of the Habs and their rookie goalie. But the underdog Canadiens shocked the hockey world by defeating the Bruins in seven games, then the Minnesota North-Stars in six, and finally the Chicago Black Hawks in another seven-game series to win the Cup. Their goaltender, whom few people knew before the playoffs had begun, won the Conn Smythe Trophy as the most valuable player in the playoffs.

A star was born. And his name was Kenneth Wayne Dryden.

Dryden would go on to win five more Stanley Cups with the Habs, with teammates such as Guy Lafleur, Serge Savard, Yvon Cournoyer, Larry Robinson, Jacques Lemaire, Steve Shutt, and Bob Gainey, in what many hockey observers believe to be the greatest NHL dynasty ever. And then Dryden surprised everyone again by announcing his retirement from pro hockey in July 1979. He was only thirty-one years old.

Dryden was an iconoclastic figure from the get-go. Having earned his law degree at McGill University, he skipped the 1973–1974 season so he could serve as a law clerk at the Toronto firm of Osler, Hoskins & Harcourt. Dryden had no intention of practicing law (in fact, he hadn't written the bar exams yet). He had a hankering to write a book, but maybe not just yet. Following his departure from pro hockey in 1979, he landed on this idea: "I wanted to work for an interesting person in an interesting field as their assistant," he says. And then he thought: "I'll bet John Turner would be an approachable person to talk to about this. He'd be an interesting person to ask who that person might be."

Turner and Dryden had met a couple of times during Number 29's hockey career and Turner reserved his table at Winston's to treat Dryden to lunch (more than once) to help plot the former goaltender's career path.

"What I remember most was his energy," Dryden now says. "He had a kind of exuberant enthusiasm about him on whatever he was talking about. He was a great looking guy, and his eyes drew you to him." Turner and Dryden began to make a list of business contacts who would prove remarkably helpful over the next many decades of Dryden's life.

* * *

Of course, John Turner would want to sit down with Ken Dryden and discuss Dryden's future. Who wouldn't? But would he be as enthusiastic about meeting with Jeff Mores? Jeff who?

Exactly.

Mores is today in his late forties, but as a student he was a member of a fraternal organization at the University of Western Ontario in London. Turner had also been a frat house member during his time at the University of British Columbia. Mores also knew Turner's son David from their time at the University of Western Ontario together. The young Turner impressed Mores as much more than a chip off the old block.

"He was always interested in what you were doing," Mores says of Dave. "He knew everybody. We'd be sitting having a coffee in downtown Toronto and people were always approaching him, just like his dad. He carved out a space outside of his dad. He worked hard not to rely on the Turner name."

Mores intended to move to Alberta in 2001 even though he didn't know a soul. But he did remember once meeting Dave's father at a convention of fraternal organizations. So, he cold-called John Turner at his office and asked for a meeting.

He got it. Turner gave him names and contact information for three senior executives in Calgary and introduced him around. Mores was in business.

"I was in my twenties and barely knew him," he says, marvelling at the memory of it. But Turner helped Mores get his insurance business established out West and would see him at future fraternal organization dinners. Apparently, it never fussed John Turner that Jeff Mores chaired the Conservative Party of Canada's 2006 Beaches-East York election campaign.

* * *

Ken Dryden got access to one of this country's most impressive rolodexes through his lunches with Turner: Arden Haynes from Imperial Oil; Douglas Bassett from CTV; Conrad Black of Argus; Jack Gallagher from Dome Petroleum; Bill Daniels from Shell; and Maurice Strong of Petro-Canada.

"He gave me their phone numbers and I called all of them," Dryden says.

He talked about the future of television with Bassett and working for Ralph Nader (as he had) with the future Lord Black. He tried to reach Strong but realized about ten minutes into the call that the person he was talking to actually had the job Dryden himself wanted. That man's name was John Ralston Saul, future author, political philosopher, and viceregal consort of Canada from 1999 to 2005 through his marriage to Adrienne Clarkson.

Dryden stayed in touch with Turner, who urged him to pass the bar exams, even though Dryden reminded him he had no intention of practicing law.

"Bring your legal experience to the end," Turner told him. "Your interests may change. When you're in a work circumstance, things can go off the rails. You may need to get the attention of the person you're working with. It's useful to be able to say, 'I'm leaving to practice law.' It's a credible option. It gets their attention. It'll help put things back on the rails again."

Dryden took the advice. He wrote the bar exam and a year later, authored a book. It was called *The Game: A Reflective and Thought-Provoking Look at a Life in Hockey*. It just might be the best sports book ever written.

Dryden and Turner continued to stay in touch. In 1984, Turner urged Dryden to run for the Liberals in that year's election. But at age thirty-six, Dryden didn't feel ready.

"I always imagined politics was the ultimate career if you had the chance," Dryden now says. "But I thought the best training for politics was doing things, taking on different jobs, learning about the country and yourself. Once you're in politics, if you don't know who you are, you're at the mercy of being buffeted all over the place."

Turner and his adviser Richard Alway assured Dryden he could win a seat.

"Just because I *might* win doesn't mean I *should* win," Dryden recalls thinking. "I want to win for the right reasons."

His introduction to Arden Haynes turned out to be extremely useful. In 1990, Dryden wrote *Home Game: Hockey and Life in Canada* with Roy MacGregor. The CBC turned it into a hugely successful six-part mini-series.

"I wanted Imperial Oil to be the sponsor," Dryden says. "They'd dropped *Hockey Night in Canada* but they were so much a part of my life story. They bought 10,000 books and put one in every library in Canada."

Dryden thought about standing for Parliament when Jean Chrétien was prime minister in the 1990s. But then the Toronto Maple Leafs came calling, offering him the presidency. How could he turn down a chance to run one of the most important franchises in all of pro sports?

He couldn't. He stayed with the Leafs for seven years, but when an ownership change and subsequent corporate shakeup took place, Dryden left the hockey world and called Turner over the 2003 Christmas break. He thought: "I'm fifty-six. It's now or never. If I don't attempt it now, I probably never will."

Turner connected Dryden to David Herle and John Webster, two of the senior-most advisers to the new prime minister, Paul Martin, who eventually got Dryden to a "yes" just before the writs for the 2004 election were drawn up.

Dryden served as an MP for seven years (2004–2011), made Martin's cabinet as social development minister for two of them (2004–2006), and managed to sign agreements with every province to establish the country's first national child care system, until the subsequent Conservative government of Stephen Harper abolished the plan.

And John Turner proved to be very helpful along the way.

CHAPTER NINE

The Comeback

IT MIGHT HAVE BEEN THE worst time in John Turner's life. Pierre Trudeau, Lazarus-like, had returned and brought the Liberals back into power, and with a majority government no less. The next few years would be dominated by internecine leadership battles within the Progressive Conservative Party among supporters of Joe Clark and Brian Mulroney. For Trudeau, it was an opportunity to achieve the one major mission that had eluded him so far, repatriating the Constitution with an accompanying Charter of Rights and Freedoms.

Turner, meanwhile, kept a low profile, putting his head down to build a successful, lucrative life for his family and himself. In his memoir *The Washington Diaries 1981–1989*, Canada's ambassador to the United States, Allan Gotlieb, described a meeting he had with Turner on May 24, 1982, in the American capital: "Turner was in top form: warm, self-confident, insightful, incisive, ebullient, energetic in everything he said, including the banalities."

Five months later in Cleveland, the pair met up again: "The Turner network in the US is remarkable," Gotlieb wrote. "If I want some respect in Cleveland, all I have to do is pretend he is PM. He will be."

What would turn out to be one of the biggest threats to Turner's political future took place in 1983. In January, Progressive Conservatives met in Winnipeg to consider their leader Joe Clark's future. Delegates gave Clark a 66.9 per cent endorsement, but inexplicably, the leader found that number insufficient. He called for a new leadership race, to take place in June, in which he intended to participate.

Clark led on every ballot except the one that mattered. Brian Mulroney passed him on the fourth and final ballot, winning the PC leadership with 54.4 per cent of the delegates, who were impressed with the candidate's argument that the party would never be successful if it couldn't compete with the Liberals both in Quebec and other ridings with a substantial francophone population.

William McDowell, a politics and history major at Queen's University in Kingston, watched that convention very carefully. His support for the Liberals went way back: his grandfather Earl had run for the party in the Quebec riding of Pontiac in 1952 (he lost badly to the Union Nationale). But McDowell watched the 1983 Tory convention with great interest because he'd eventually help Queen's professor George Perlin on the definitive book on the subject, *Contenders: The Tory Quest for Power*, co-authored with pollster Allan Gregg and journalist Patrick Martin. What was his conclusion?

"I thought in 1983 that Mulroney was going to be a handful and we [Liberals] were going to be in the wilderness," McDowell says.

Less than a year later, McDowell was introduced to Turner and, reservations about the future notwithstanding, was on board to help him become the next Liberal leader. "My professors at Queen's thought Mulroney was a very effective labour mediator and lawyer," he recalls, "but John Turner was the real thing as a rainmaker and commercial lawyer."

But this wasn't the law or a court room. This was politics. Over the ensuing year, Trudeau laid numerous traps for Mulroney, but the PC leader skillfully avoided them all. For example, when Trudeau brought in the Canada Health Act, Mulroney managed to get right-wing conservatives to stay mum and keep their complaints to themselves. Mulroney was not about to have his party portrayed as being against Medicare.

Meanwhile throughout the early 1980s, Turner's friend Richard Alway, the warden at the University of Toronto's Hart House, put together frequent events with special guests designed to keep Turner connected to the Canadian political scene. Alway was a huge Turner fan and consistently tried to get his friend to commit to making a political comeback. Turner refused.

"But he never shut us down either," Alway now points out. "He never said, stop organizing those meetings."

Even after Mulroney's convention victory, when the Liberals were at 20 per cent in the polls, Trudeau gave no indication he was about to leave, and Turner kept reminding Alway of that. Nevertheless, Alway continued organizing his lunches, one with Lester Pearson's respected nationalist Finance Minister Walter Gordon, another with Trudeau's backroom adviser Keith Davey. While Alway didn't expect to get a future endorsement out of either man (Gordon thought Turner far too right-wing), at least he thought he'd neutralized both men as opponents.

"A group of us told John, 'You should be preparing,' but he declined," Alway says.

"He's not gonna leave," Turner would retort. He told Gotlieb the same thing in April. "Turner and I talked of his plans," Gotlieb wrote in his diary. "He was cautious and noncommittal. I know he wants to succeed Trudeau, but he is deeply skeptical about the likelihood of Trudeau stepping down soon."

Nevertheless, a group of Turner-for-Leader supporters met regularly at the Royal York Hotel in Toronto. They believed their guy was the obvious choice to replace Trudeau, but they needed to persuade Turner of that. They wanted to commission a poll proving their hunch but were paranoid about anything leaking out to Trudeau. That meant *not* using the Liberals' own pollster, Martin Goldfarb, so Alway flew to Washington to discuss the issue with Gallup's renowned pollster Peter Hart. Remarkably, it was long-time Tory supporter and future Ontario Lieutenant-Governor Hal Jackman who funded the trip and the poll. He liked Turner, even though the two were in opposite parties. Essentially, the Turner supporters wanted to know what would happen to Liberal Party fortunes if Trudeau left and Turner took over. The poll's answer: Liberal fortunes would skyrocket.

Turner attended these secret meetings once or twice but "he never gave us any encouragement," Alway recalls—even when the group showed him the very favourable poll.

Turner and his McMillan Binch partner Bill Macdonald had a practice of going to Montreal four times a year to check in with clients Charles and Edgar Bronfman, owners of Seagram, the world's largest producer and distributor of distilled spirits. "The Bronfmans paid us a handsome sum to spend half a day with them," Macdonald says. The group would meet at Charles' home, then take in a Montreal Expos baseball game (Charles owned the team).

In the summer of 1983, Turner told Macdonald on the flight to Montreal that he thought the pressure on him to return to politics would soon become more intense.

"John," Macdonald told him, "the Liberals have been in for a long time. You could lose."

Thirty-eight years later, Macdonald tells me Turner "may have been more hopeful about his chances than he should have been. He'd stayed away from politics for a long time."

In July 1983, adviser John Swift sent Turner a confidential note urging him to clarify in his own mind whether he ever intended to be a candidate to replace Trudeau. Swift thought it would reflect poorly on Turner if he announced he wasn't interested in the leadership *after* Trudeau's departure, so if he genuinely wasn't interested in the job, he should say so now.

However, if Turner *were* interested (as Swift hoped), then steps needed to be taken immediately. First and foremost, the potential candidate needed to understand that with Trudeau now deep into his mandate, Turner needed to be prepared to contest both a convention and subsequent election. Furthermore, the party was in rough shape. "The dry rot goes to its foundations," Swift wrote. "Loyalty from the party and support from the public will have to be earned."

Swift also told Turner he needed to think about where he intended to run and recommended Vancouver Quadra. He urged Turner to go to New York to get some much-needed media training. And he drew up an org chart listing the campaign's top advisers: Payne, Alway, Torrance Wylie, Bill Lee, and "Mrs. T."

Shortly thereafter, Energy Minister Jean Chrétien met with Keith Davey at his office. The subject was the Liberal Party leadership. Chrétien was already anticipating the day when Trudeau would step aside, and he wanted Davey's support in what he was sure would be a two-person race with Turner. But Davey left him disappointed. He believed in alternation and thought it was an anglophone's turn to be leader. Chrétien failed to get the Rainmaker's endorsement.

In August 1983, Turner had one of the most important conversations he'd ever had with his daughter Elizabeth, then nineteen. They were sitting on the screened-in veranda at the family's cottage at Lake of the Woods in northwestern Ontario when Turner raised an issue that was preoccupying him.

"I've got people giving me calls asking whether I'll run for the leadership of the party," he told Elizabeth. "What do you think, Dump?" (Liz's nickname originally was Pumpkin but this had somehow morphed into Dump.)

Elizabeth was candid with her father. "As much as you like the practice of law, I think you're a bit bored," she said. She saw a man who was missing the kinds of interactions with other people that are unique to politics, and the chance to affect public policy in Canada.

During this discussion, Geills Turner walked in, wanting to know what the two were talking about. She wasn't happy when she found out.

"She thought when he left before that would be the end of it," Elizabeth says. "She doesn't love the spotlight. She does very well at it. She's great at engaging with people and talking to people. She's very smart and understands policy issues and believed in the public service aspect of it, but it was hard on her. She didn't love politics."

Geills Turner had supported her husband's political life in the 1960s and '70s, but she wasn't disappointed when he quit in 1975. She liked their family's new, post-political life in Toronto.

"To jump back in? Well, she was kind of taken aback," Elizabeth recalls.

But Turner's daughter had a different view. "I said, 'I think you should,'" she told him. "He was good at practicing law and enjoyed some aspects of it, but he missed making a difference in policy work. It was a call to public service and that was important to him."

Later that year, Turner and his friend (and Trudeau cabinet minister) Donald Johnston met for a private dinner at George Bigliardi's steak house in Toronto. Johnston reports in his memoirs that Turner was keeping his options open on the leadership issue and was non-committal either way. However, Johnston told his long-time friend that *he* intended to run for the job whenever Trudeau vacated it and Turner accepted that. Then, in perhaps a strong hint at his eventual plans, Turner reminded Johnston of one of his favourite religious quotations: "If one has been given the benefits of a good education, health, and talent, and the ability to participate in public life, then I believe one has a duty to do it."

In November 1983, pollster Angus Reid informed Turner that he was the runaway choice to replace Trudeau as Liberal leader. When asked, fully 35 per cent of Canadians opted for Turner, compared to just 10 per cent for Chrétien. Reid also pointed out that there were nagging concerns about whether Turner had the "skills and abilities appropriate for the 1980s," but insisted there was a reservoir of goodwill for Turner, whose candidacy could generate considerable excitement.

On February 29, 1984, Pierre Trudeau announced he would be leaving politics after having enjoyed the most famous "walk in the snow" any Canadian politician had ever taken. Trudeau had tried everything to get his party's polling numbers up, including a much derided "Peace Mission" around the world. Trudeau thought he was doing his bit to lessen tensions among nuclear powers. Critics saw him enjoying an international farewell tour on the taxpayers' dime. Now the Liberals were a sinking ship with Trudeau at the helm. At fifteen years and 164 days, he was the third longest-serving PM in Canadian history behind

William Lyon Mackenzie King and Sir John A. Macdonald. And most Canadians thought, that was long enough.

The day Trudeau announced his resignation, twelve-year-old Andrew Turner got some good advice from one of his teachers at Upper Canada College. "I sort of cringed because the day Trudeau resigned, my teacher told me when I got home there might be some press there. And sure enough, the press was outside our driveway."

Turner and his wife Geills were on vacation in the Caribbean when Trudeau made his announcement. This was supposed to be the moment the 195 Club had been waiting for. It had been sixteen years since they'd stuck it out to the bitter end, when their young candidate had reminded delegates that he wasn't running for some "vague convention in 1984." And yet, here they were.

The inner circle gathered at the Royal York and began making phone calls to Liberal MPs and cabinet ministers. John deB. Payne wasn't enthusiastic. "Geills will have a lot to do with this," he said.

One of the first things the Turner supporters discovered was that the 195 Club didn't come close to numbering 195 anymore. Ex-Turner aide Lloyd Axworthy, now the Transport Minister, was considering a run of his own. Jerry Grafstein was now a Senator and part of Trudeau's inner circle. In fact, the whole 195 Club now seemed to be more myth than reality. Having said that, of the seven men that eventually would contest the Liberal leadership, Turner had one quality the others didn't have: he wasn't part of Trudeau's last cabinet and they all were. He had no connection to the previous four years. As the savior-in-waiting, he represented change *and* continuity; he had no ties to the now unloved Trudeau *and* was capable of building a new Liberal coalition for the mid-1980s: young people, Westerners, Quebecers who wanted more provincial power, and blue Grits who cared more about deficits than Trudeau ever did. Turner knew his chances of success weren't a slam dunk. The Liberals had been in for a long time and their polling numbers were a dumpster fire. But he was an old-fashioned guy who felt a duty to the country to offer himself up, if he felt he could contribute.

"I remember Dad saying, 'I think I'm going to take a run at this. Are you guys okay with it?'" recalls Andrew. For the two older Turner kids, the decision wasn't as life altering. Liz was already off at university in California and Michael would enroll at Princeton a few months later. But for David and Andrew, who were still in school in Toronto, the decision might have had a more significant impact. The Turner parents allayed their boys' fears by saying the pair could remain at Upper Canada College as boarders and continue at the school they knew and enjoyed.

"He didn't want to uproot us" is how Michael puts it. In fact, the two younger Turner kids enjoyed a good deal of independence during their high school years with their parents living in Ottawa, and their mother coming back to Toronto every few weekends to check in. It was also the case that having John Turner for a father did come with its challenges.

"Kids were sort of nasty at that age," Andrew says. "You'd be at parties and guys would be there with their PC signs. You sort of had to weed out guys who were nuzzling up to you because of who your dad was or who was a prick to you because of who your dad was. Everyone had an agenda."

When Turner told Bill Macdonald he'd be leaving McMillan Binch, his partner's reaction was uncompromising: "You son of a bitch!" Macdonald told him. "You know I think the Liberals will be out." But Turner was all in.

Well, not quite *all* in. Besides his responsibilities at McMillan Binch, he had directorships at seventeen blue chip companies, but declined to quit them unless and until he won the leadership. Today, trying to maintain those links would be almost disqualifying. But the desire by so many Liberals to have Turner in the race was overwhelming, and so it didn't cause much of a ripple.

The Liberals, as a party, had successfully managed leadership transitions for decades, in part because the outgoing leader quietly "laid hands" on his eventual successor, who either by coincidence or design, was not from the same founding demographic. It's how Wilfrid Laurier subtly put his thumb on the scale for William Lyon Mackenzie King, who did the same for Louis St. Laurent, who courted Lester Pearson into public life, who did likewise for Pierre Trudeau. At key steps along the way, the retiring leader orchestrated events to favour his preferred successor and it made a difference.

Pierre Trudeau did none of that. He certainly didn't have the relationship with Turner to justify helping his former finance minister. But he apparently didn't lift a finger to help any challengers to Turner, either. It may well have been the case that Trudeau thought no one was up to the task of replacing him. Regardless, the departing leader's apparent disinterest in who replaced him helped contribute to a negative dynamic that had not been present at the previous four leadership elections.

Six Trudeau cabinet ministers sought the Liberal leadership, but there was never any question about which one represented the biggest threat to Turner's potential comeback. Jean Chrétien, then fifty years old, had been an MP for more than two decades, had been deeply involved in the successful 1981 Constitutional negotiations with the provinces as justice minister, and just couldn't understand why the faithful were so gaga for a guy who'd been out of the mix for almost a decade.

"I always told them that Turner is a good man but he's not as good as you think he is," Chrétien told author Ron Graham for his classic 1986 book *One Eyed Kings*. "He's better than Mulroney but I thought I was better still, otherwise I wouldn't have run."

Chrétien became even more bewildered when Turner seemed to make a serious unforced error at his campaign kickoff news conference at the Château Laurier Hotel on March 16. When asked about whether Franco-Manitobans should enjoy linguistic equality with their anglophone counterparts, Turner declined to weigh in, saying it was an issue for provincial jurisdiction. In that one reply, Turner repudiated two decades' worth of Liberal policy and opened the door for Mulroney to become the country's new champion of francophone rights. Ironically, much of Mulroney's backbench agreed with Turner's position, but Mulroney knew his party's road to government went through improving the Tories' performance with francophones, and so he demanded they keep their mouths shut, and they did. It was the first sign that a Turner-led Liberal Party might not be exactly what the troops had in mind. André Clouthier, president of Association Canadienne Français de l'Ontario, sent Turner a telegram to tell him "Your recent stand on bilingualism in Canada has left us thoroughly bewildered."

Having said that, Turner returned to public life determined to be different from his predecessor. He had no problem separating himself from Trudeau's views on many issues, figuring those views had made the Liberal Party a non-starter in too much of Canada. He was content to move closer to the business community, thinking Trudeau had created too much antagonism between business and government. And he was happy to pussyfoot around language rights, concluding that would go a long way to attracting support for the party in the West.

"The problem was, he was in a bubble on Bay Street," says Darryl Raymaker, the Alberta Liberal who met Turner in the 1960s and ran for the party in the 1979, 1980, and 1984 federal elections. "He attacked official bilingualism off the bat. That created all kinds of problems for himself from day one. But he'd surrounded himself with people who belittled Trudeau and didn't value his experience."

Because Trudeau had been in power for so long, his inner circle was well established. It meant that many young Liberals desirous of a place at the table, needed to look past him and to the next generation of potential leaders.

Kaz Flinn was just such a Liberal. She fell in love with politics and went to Carleton University both to get a mass communications degree and to be near Parliament Hill. She was president of the Young Liberals at Carleton and served on the party's executive with other youngsters who would become a big deal in the party's future, people such as David Herle and Richard Mahoney.

One day, Heather Peterson approached her and asked if she wanted to meet candidate Turner. She did, and the two then spent half an hour, one-on-one, in the board room of the campaign office. Flinn was twenty-three and getting the classic VIP Turner treatment.

"He was very committed to young Liberals," says Flinn, who was so impressed, she agreed to be national youth chair for Turner's campaign. Her mission was to secure young delegate votes from Liberal university clubs and in ridings across the country.

Herle was a young Liberal from Saskatchewan, where the University of Regina's president Lloyd Barber was a friend of Turner's. As a result, the candidate came to the campus to give a speech and Herle was deeply impressed. Turner even surprised the crowd of 500 by criticizing Trudeau's National Energy Program, which had infuriated the Western provinces when the federal government used the windfall from Western oil and gas revenues to pursue national objectives, including cutting themselves in for billions. Herle was so taken aback by Turner's comments, he got up and asked: "Given what you've said today, are you still a member of the Liberal Party?"

Herle never forgot the candidate's reply: "The Liberal Party is a big tent," Turner said, and he meant it. He simply thought there was room in a big national party for plenty of disagreement.

University of Ottawa student Dan Donovan wrote a letter to Turner in early 1984 urging him to run for leader when the job became open. To Donovan's surprise, he heard back: "Thanks Dan, I'd love your help if I get in," Turner wrote.

"That was a big deal, a posted letter from John Turner," Donovan now says. "It's not like an email today. A real letter like that can be meaningful to a third-year university student, waiting on tables." When Turner did get in, Donovan agreed to organize delegates for the candidate at the University of Ottawa.

Donovan and a friend eventually met Turner at the Château Laurier, but for whatever reason, he loaned his friend his dress shoes and therefore wore white sneakers with his suit. When Turner arrived, he noted, "Hmmm... those are some shoes." Two months later, Donovan and Turner met again but this time, Donovan had no suit. So, he borrowed his friend's, which was too small. "I looked like an idiot," Donovan recalls. "The sleeves were up to my elbows."

Turner arrived with Geills, shook Donovan's hand, and a moment of recognition kicked in. "You're the shoe guy, right?" he said. "I see you got your shoes fixed. Now we've gotta work on the jacket."

In the leadup to the convention, Manitoba MP Lloyd Axworthy asked Donovan whether he could arrange a meeting between Turner and Donovan's boss, Peter Ittinuar, the MP for Nunatsiaq in Nunavut, and Canada's first ever Inuit MP. Ittinuar was already a committed Chrétien voter but agreed to the meeting anyway. Afterwards, he told Donovan: "I didn't know Turner knew so much about the North. He knows of people and places that I know and not too many others do. I see why you like this guy."

Sharon Sholzberg-Gray and her husband Herb, whom Turner had fixed up years earlier, both got elected as Turner delegates to the convention. "I thought he'd be a good PM because he was honorable," Sholzberg-Gray now says. "He had a good heart."

Maybe so, but one thing became abundantly clear, relatively quickly, as Turner began campaigning for the job. He was rusty. *Really* rusty. His near decade on the political sidelines meant he wasn't as up on current issues as he should have been. Nor did he have a bushelful of policy prescriptions waiting to roll out. And people were noticing.

"I felt Turner was running on 1975 issues," wrote his friend Donald Johnston in his memoirs. "His long absence from Ottawa had created a generation gap. In politics, nine years is a generation, especially during that period of oil shocks, stagflation, recession, and technological change." While Johnston agreed with Turner's instincts to get a firmer hand on public spending and managing public debt, he also couldn't help but notice Turner had disassociated himself from the National Energy Program, the Constitutional renewal process, and Trudeau's handling of the economy.

"It was obvious he was rusty," wrote Keith Davey in his memoir. "His successful stint on Bay Street had not been a political plus and meant that there would be nagging doubts about just how rusty he had become."

Then Davey asked the key question: "Could the ultimate politician of the 1960s make it happen in the 1980s?" Whether he could or not, he'd have to do it without Davey's help. The Rainmaker agreed it was an anglophone's turn to be leader, but he declined to endorse Turner and the candidate was equally fine with that. In fact, Turner once poked Davey during a speech, in which he pledged to open up the party beyond the tight inner circle that ran things during Trudeau's last term.

"No elites, no rainmakers!" Turner bellowed, and Liberals couldn't have been confused about the reference. Three months later, Turner would be begging Davey to end his Florida vacation early and come back and help rescue him, but at this moment, he wanted nothing to do with a man who was seen as the ultimate insider.

"He was expected to blow the roof off the place," recalls Sean Conway, who was a Turner delegate at the 1984 convention. "I thought he was heroic and gallant." But Conway adds had he been asked, he'd have recommended Turner *not* come back to public life. He remembers thinking at the time, "As they say in tennis, you're not tournament tough anymore."

And then there was the candidate's speaking style. "He had this staccato voice," Conway says. "I thought, is that a human voice or a gatling gun?"

The more animated Turner got, the stranger he sounded. While Trudeau always sounded smooth, confident, and under control, Turner had this rat-a-tat-tat way of barking out his speeches. He'd get bug-eyed and clear his throat awkwardly.

In his book *One Hundred Monkeys: The Triumph of Popular Wisdom in Canadian Politics*, Robert Mason Lee described Turner's speaking style thus: "Words danced out of him like spit out of a skillet; his gestures were the incoherent of a wrung chicken; his eyes were burning coal tips on the rail line from hell."

One man who seemed not to notice any of these problems was Allan Gotlieb, who saw Turner at Niagara-on-the-Lake in May, a couple of weeks before the convention. "John looked majestic," he wrote in his diary. "He was drawing people to him as if he were some powerful electromagnetic force. He was certainly radiating something—confidence, I believe. The confidence that he has the Liberal leadership in his pocket. He talks like a man who has, and knows he has, a rendezvous with history."

Gotlieb was clearly so smitten, he didn't realize his favourite candidate was on an emotional roller coaster. In his book *Reign of Error: The Inside Story of John Turner's Troubled Leadership*, Greg Weston quotes Turner's long-time friend and campaign manager Bill Lee as saying: "For the first time, I think, I saw him become a complete nervous wreck."

Even Turner's sister Brenda was taken aback on the campaign bus one day when her brother looked at her and asked, "Brenda, do you think I can do this?"

"Of course you can," she told him, startled that he'd ask such a question. It was more evidence that, while Turner always radiated a confident exterior, he frequently battled insecurity on the inside.

As Turner tried to shake off the rust, Chrétien was gaining steam. His campaign had an underdog's energy. Furthermore, he moved further to the ideological left to create a greater contrast with Turner. Davey thought Turner looked like a Louis St. Laurent throwback, the way he talked, the way his suits fit, the long ago references he'd use, while Chrétien was current and wore his heart on his sleeve to great effect. Nevertheless, the conventional wisdom continued: Turner looked like a winner, and Chrétien was too tied to Trudeau.

Wherever he went, Chrétien became increasingly frustrated that he couldn't secure endorsements from colleagues. When Ed Lumley had been mayor of Cornwall, Turner urged him to get into federal politics and as a result, the two shared a bond that stuck. So, even though Lumley was Chrétien's parliamentary secretary when Chrétien was finance minister, Lumley backed Turner, partially because of their history and partially because Lumley believed in alternation. Lumley broke the disappointing news to Chrétien, before attempting to mitigate the disappointment by assuring Chrétien that he wouldn't work that hard for Turner.

That scenario played out over and over for Chrétien. He and his fellow Quebec MP André Ouellet were great friends and so were their wives. With 850 voting delegates, Quebec had a significant say in who the next leader would be, and Ouellet had a lot of influence over those delegates. While initially backing Chrétien, Ouellet could also see which way the wind was blowing. A few weeks later, he urged Chrétien not to enter the race, assured him he'd be devastated by the process and the result, and then backed Turner.

It was the same experience with another fellow Quebecer, Finance Minister Marc Lalonde, who told Chrétien it was an anglophone's turn. London's Judd Buchanan was Chrétien's parliamentary secretary for four years at Indian Affairs. But seeing what a wreck the Liberal Party was in Western Canada, he too backed Turner as the only hope to rebuild the party there. Sixteen years in cabinet and Chrétien had been unable to secure a single senior minister's backing, only three unknowns.

"They don't love the man, they love power," Chrétien told a colleague, quoted in Lawrence Martin's book *Chrétien, Volume 1: The Will to Win.*

David MacNaughton, a future Canadian ambassador to the United States, agreed, telling journalist Greg Weston that cabinet ministers "flocked to his side because they couldn't stand the thought of losing their place at the trough. Frankly it was disgusting."

Regardless, when legendary journalist Richard Gwyn badgered Chrétien to name one policy from the Trudeau years he'd change, Chrétien couldn't. Most Liberals wanted change *and* continuity, but Chrétien could only give them the latter.

The Turner camp also cleverly used Chrétien's loyalty to the party against him. Everyone knew, or thought they knew, that if Turner won, Chrétien would stick around and serve in the Turner cabinet. They also knew if Chrétien won, Turner wasn't quitting his lucrative career in Toronto to return to public life. It became obvious: if Liberals wanted *both* men in government, Turner was the choice.

Meanwhile, one of Ontario premier Bill Davis' closest advisers weighed in. In a column in the *Toronto Star*, Hugh Segal told his fellow Tories not to worry because he was sure the Liberals would make the wrong choice.

"The Grits will go to a candidate with little or no heart and less humanity," he wrote, referring to Turner. "If today's Liberals had the courage to make the right choice, they would not be today's Liberals. They would be the kind of Liberals for whom cooperative federalism, regional conciliation, and social conscience once again meant something."

In early April, with still more than two months to go before convention day, Turner adviser John deB. Payne sent his candidate a confidential memo warning him of what lay ahead; in particular, what he saw as increasingly biased media coverage against his candidate. "Having built you up as a myth and a crown prince for eight years, without any urging or acquiescence from you, they now want to bring you down a peg or two or three," he wrote.

A month before convention day, Payne followed that up with a blunt assessment. "The dumbest thing you have done in the campaign is phone the Prime Minister," he wrote Turner, in reference to the candidate's following up on critical comments Trudeau made in *The Globe and Mail* about Turner. "Trudeau has been itching to strike out at you for a long time. I thought you were too damned servile in your conversation and too damned uncomfortable.... Your decisiveness was tarnished."

Having said all that, Payne wrote he believed the public was reassessing Mulroney: they had "twigged to his shallowness, and are tiring of his rhetoric and pulpit-like voice." And then, in a final line he would surely regret writing, Payne concluded: "I cannot wait for you to take him on in a televised debate."

Turner's awkward internal family dynamics reared their ugly head at this time as well. University of Toronto law professor Bill Graham, who'd announced his intention to become the Liberal candidate in Toronto Centre-Rosedale, received a letter from Turner's brother-in-law David Kilgour, at this time the Tory MP for Edmonton–Strathcona. Despite the fact that Kilgour's sister's husband was the front runner to assume the Liberal leadership the following month, Kilgour excoriated Graham for running for "a party which is both intellectually bankrupt and infected with corruption down to its socks…. What gives?"

Graham sent a copy of the note to Turner, and asked: "If he's like this to his 'friends,' what is he like to the family?"

With typical Turner magnanimity, he sent a letter back to Graham saying, "Just a note about David Kilgour. He's a nice guy!!!!"

But not all Tories gave Turner grief. His great friend in both politics and faith, Father Sean O'Sullivan, wrote candidate Turner a note to "cheer you on as you enter the final lap in such a gruelling campaign." O'Sullivan had been the PC MP for Hamilton–Wentworth from 1972 to 1977 but quit politics to become a priest, in effect, living Turner's values of the highest form of public service.

"You are the most able parliamentarian I have ever known," O'Sullivan wrote, "and you will be a noble Prime Minister…. Our country will be so much better because you care deeply enough to make this sacrifice."

With two weeks to go until convention day, Turner got an odd note from Allan Slaight, the media magnate, who informed the candidate that he'd contributed to his leadership campaign. "You are the only possible choice to lead the Liberal Party in the challenging and critical times ahead," Slaight wrote.

But in the next breath, Slaight added he'd be voting and supporting the Conservatives at election time "because of my conviction that your party deserved a session in opposition because of the shocking mismanagement and arrogance it has demonstrated over recent years."

Turner generously replied a week later saying: "I know and understand your position completely and respect it."

Thousands of Liberal delegates and party members gathered on June 15 at the Ottawa Civic Centre to hear the candidates' speeches. The buttons that Turner supporters wore said it all: "Win with Turner." With all due respect to the other five candidates, pretty much everyone in the hall that night wanted to hear and see the contrast between Turner and Chrétien. CBC-TV had a camera shooting Turner's private pre-speech briefing. When asked what he wanted to leave the delegates thinking about after his speech, Turner beamed and said: "Leadership. I have to convince the majority of the delegates that I'm the one to lead the Liberal Party, that I'm the one to rebuild the Liberal Party, and I'm the one to win that next election." When the reporter mischievously asked whether there "was any heart in the speech," because Chrétien was seen as the candidate Liberals connected with more at an emotional level, Turner gently shook his head and said: "I've got my share of heart; I've got my share of mind. I am what I am."

Since Turner's unique selling proposition was, I can win, the candidate had to look like a winner—and he did, in a dark blue suit, pale blue shirt, and maroon tie. Before he proceeded to the stage, his wife Geills fussed with his suit a bit, then sent him on his way. He entered the hall to a massive demonstration and a procession waving huge flags from every province. It was big in every way, and Turner delivered. His was a solid speech, in which he looked every bit the prime minister in waiting.

"We have always formed the coalitions that banded Canadians together, not pandered to the powerful and the privileged," he said. "We have always welcomed dissent. We are at our best when we find common ground among opposing views. And now our party must become more open, more accessible, more accountable."

Turner assured delegates he was the one who could rebuild the party in the West, maintain its representation in central Canada, and win more seats from coast to coast. He looked great. He sounded great. If it wasn't a home run, it was surely a triple.

"For Liberals in this great assembly and across Canada it is the beginning of an era of reform and renewal," he said. "For Canadians it will be the beginning of a new era where hope, confidence, and compassion will be the guiding aims. Let us all rejoice in these new beginnings."

Perhaps understanding he couldn't out-sis-boom-bah Turner, Chrétien walked into the hall by himself, no marching band, no army of supporters, just "*le petit gar de Shawinigan.*" If the knock on Turner was that he didn't have enough heart, the knock on Chrétien was he was *all* heart but didn't convey enough prime ministerial gravitas. So, Chrétien went for a more serious tone, punctuating it with his famous "Vive le Canada" at the end, his fist thrusting into the air. If you were scoring it, it was a solid double, but clearly not the home run the candidate needed to encourage hundreds of delegates to change their minds. While Chrétien insisted to the CBC that "the fun is on our side," the bigger question was: were the votes?

Even before delegates were invited to cast their first ballot the next day, there was a big development. One of the party's most influential and longest-serving cabinet ministers, the previously neutral Alan J. MacEachen, a few weeks away from turning sixty-three years old, walked into Turner's box and the candidate absolutely beamed. Elected for the first time in 1953, MacEachen was exactly the kind of *eminence gris* Turner wanted to impress and now he had him. Then, before the first ballot results were announced, Edmonton Mayor Laurence Decore joined the Turner box. In a delegated convention, these endorsements conveyed exactly the kind of big momentum Turner relished. They also made the Chrétien camp despondent.

The first ballot results came in alphabetical order from party president Iona Campagnolo and when Chrétien's 1,067 votes, only 31 per cent support, were announced, Turner's campaign chief Bill Lee knew it was all but over. Turner clocked in at 1,593 votes, a whopping 46 per cent, and the finish line was in sight. John Roberts (185 votes), John Munro (ninety-three votes), and Eugene Whelan (eighty-four votes) dropped off the ballot and all backed Chrétien. Mark McGuigan (135 votes) exited and moved straight past Herb Gray to hug Turner. Donald Johnston, the former Stikeman Elliott lawyer that Turner recruited to the firm during their Montreal days, pulled a page from Turner's own 1968 convention playbook. With 278 votes (8 per cent), Johnston knew he had no hope of winning and chose not to play kingmaker. He stayed on for the second ballot, which would formalize Turner's victory. Even when Chrétien marched over to Johnston's box and made a direct appeal, Johnston wasn't moved. He knew Turner would win, thought he could get along with Turner, and worried about what image would be conveyed if five of the seven candidates in the race lined up against the eventual winner.

Leadership conventions can be bruising affairs, even when the outcome isn't in doubt. David Herle liked and admired Turner, but he'd thought he'd get more responsibilities and a hands-on role with the Roberts campaign, and so he joined the employment and immigration minister's team.

"I was on the Young Liberal executive and we were all for Turner," Herle now says. "But I'm from Saskatchewan. I'd be a no one if I tried to get into the Turner organization. But with Roberts, I was a big player."

Herle was now going to learn first-hand about the heartbreaking nature of these conventions. He says Roberts promised him he wouldn't be going anywhere after the first ballot, but after taking a call either from someone on Chrétien's team or Chrétien himself, Roberts changed his mind and moved to Chrétien's box.

"It provoked a melee in our section as we tried to take people to Turner," says Herle, who never spoke to Roberts again. Other friendships ended at that moment as well. When Roberts' own executive assistant Ivan Fleischmann moved to Turner's camp, Jerry Grafstein was waiting to put a Turner vest on him. Fleischmann told him to forget it. He'd just broken with his candidate, was distraught about it, and told Roberts he thought he had made a grave mistake by going to Chrétien. But he wasn't about to rub it in by putting on Turner paraphernalia.

"It's fair game to go over there and get your guys in there now, but do it with dignity for Christ sakes," Fleischmann told Grafstein in an exchange picked up by a CBC-TV crew.

The second ballot results were a foregone conclusion but the aftermath threatened to bring down the entire Liberal house of cards. As expected, Turner captured the prize with 1,862 votes, good for 54 per cent support, a much stronger mandate than Trudeau had won at the 1968 convention. Chrétien's tally went up considerably, based on the support brought by the other candidates: 1,398 votes or 40 per cent support. When Chrétien saw the numbers, he turned to his wife Aline and said: "Well, it's over for a very long time."

True to his word, Johnston stayed on to the end, as Turner did 16 years earlier. In fact, he got almost the same number of votes as Turner did at the previous convention: 192, good for 6 per cent support. There were 1,000 ex-officio delegates at the convention and by a margin of three-to-one, they voted for Turner.

The results were again announced by Campagnolo, the Liberals' first female president, who interestingly enough, despite being wooed into politics by Turner when she was a radio host in British Columbia, actually voted for Whelan on the first ballot and Chrétien on the second. When she announced the numbers, Turner immediately shook Bill Lee's hand, then hugged his wife, who patted him repeatedly on the back. He gave his daughter Elizabeth a kiss then shook hands with his three sons. "The boys were raised to be manly," a family relative says. "He didn't want to embarrass them by kissing them, so he shook their hands."

Almost imperceptibly, something significant happened in Turner's box. The moment the results were announced, Turner was the prime minister in waiting. Four RCMP officers in his box suddenly tensed up and assumed the responsibilities for Turner's security. The candidate's advance team faded into the background. One of the security detail members immediately spoke to the Turner children to let them know what their new reality would be like. Andrew may have only been twelve-years-old, but he instantly grasped the enormity of the moment. As he was fighting his way through the crowds to get to the stage, his mind turned to the summer camp he was about to attend for the first time later that summer. He said to his mother, "I hope I can get through camp and make friends before anyone knows who I am."

"It was so sweet," Geills recalls, "because he knew this was going to be big. He knew this could be a big handicap, dragging this ball and chain behind you."

Today, Andrew says "I broke down in tears when he won the convention because I knew our lives would change quite a bit." Even though his father was about to become prime minister, Andrew's first thoughts focused on summer camp and whether he'd have to change schools because of an anticipated move to Ottawa. (Turns out, he didn't.)

Almost immediately, Campagnolo sensed she had a problem. The Chrétien forces were completely demoralized and heading for the exits. She considered the prospect of the live television coverage showing significant disaffection with Turner's victory. And so, she said the first thing that came into her head.

"What can you say in ten seconds that will stop people from fleeing the hall in the middle of the winner's victory speech?" she later explained.

Campagnolo then welcomed Chrétien to the stage by saying he was "second on the ballot, but first in our hearts."

"I thought it was the simple truth," she later said, insisting she was simply trying to help unify the party and keep the Chrétien folks in the room. It worked. But rankled many Turner supporters.

"Iona was well intentioned, but it did a tremendous disservice to the new leader," says Stephen Hastings, who had become a Turner supporter a few years earlier at the University of Toronto. "And it emboldened the Chrétien people. Mr. Turner may not have publicly criticized her for saying it, but he didn't think it was helpful."

In his memoirs, Donald Johnston echoed those views. "She probably expressed the sentiments of a majority of those present but, to an already divided audience, it did not seem an appropriate comment if unity was an objective."

But the most bizarre moment of the convention was still to come. There was an expectation in the hall that the beloved former leader would take to the microphone, congratulate his successor, and then urge all Liberals to unite under the new leader to defeat the Tories. Trudeau, iconoclastic to the end, did none of that. As he was invited to the podium, he took a single step forward and waved to the crowd, which roared its approval. But then, Trudeau did nothing, and the crowd noise dissipated.

What happened? Donald Johnston, who was there on the platform, thinks he knows.

"Our leader of sixteen years, by this simple non-action, legitimized the notion of holding back support from Turner," he wrote in his memoir. "In the critical months that followed, many other Liberals did the same." The moment called for Trudeau to set aside whatever issues he had with Turner for a bigger cause. But when the moment arrived, Trudeau refused to meet it.

Ironically, later that night, Turner received a congratulatory note from the leader of the opposition: "Mila and I have just watched your impressive victory. We want to convey to you, Geills, and the children our warm good wishes for health and happiness in the future. Sincerely, Brian." It was a classy gesture on Mulroney's part, but in truth, Mulroney was ecstatic at the outcome. He figured if his road to the prime minister's office was through Quebec, then Chrétien would have been a much bigger threat to that strategy than Turner.

Allan Gotlieb may have been one of Canada's finest public servants, but his political antennae weren't always so finely tuned. "I'm so excited, I couldn't sleep," he wrote in his diary after the convention, describing Turner as "strong, intelligent, principled, a Canadian nationalist, but pro-business, pro-American. He has the leadership qualities that can make us proud to be Canadian." Gotlieb also mentioned how pleased he was that Chrétien had lost. "He's an egotist, no man to lead a country," he wrote, in a line that would not stand the test of time too well.

The Liberals now had a leader who wanted nothing to do with his predecessor, and the feelings were mutual. The new leader wanted the party to be more fiscally responsible and less rigid about official bilingualism, figuring that was the way to winning more votes out West. He wanted a Louis St. Laurent party, whereas it was currently a Pierre Trudeau party. The key was to win. If he could keep the Liberals in power, these huge ideological chasms could be managed.

With Turner's victory, Canada's two main political parties now both had fluently bilingual leaders. That had never happened before in Canadian history. It also set up a scenario where, perhaps for the first time since Sir John A. Macdonald and Sir Wilfrid Laurier, both major parties could lay claim to being competitive for the hearts and minds of Quebecers. Liberals had every reason to feel bullish coming out of the convention. They'd been in government for 66 of the previous 88 years and with only five leaders. The Vatican had *nine* popes over the same period. Being Liberal leader was great job security—until it wasn't.

Turner's victory wasn't the beginning of the cleavages within the Liberal Party. The progressive and business wings had long been in conflict with one another, but they co-existed well in that big red tent as long as the Liberals were in power. Leadership transitions had also always gone relatively smoothly.

But as Turner would soon learn, things were about to change. Canada's natural governing party was about to begin a nearly three-decades-long very public family feud that wouldn't be resolved until another leader named Trudeau came along in 2013.

CHAPTER TEN

The Family

AFTER EIGHT YEARS IN TORONTO, the Turner family was moving back to Ottawa. First-born Elizabeth conveyed how she felt on the drive to the capital city.

"I threw up all the way to Ottawa in the car," she now recalls with a smile. "I had the flu."

As the oldest, Liz had the strongest memories of all the kids of the family's previous stint in Ottawa, when Turner was in Pierre Trudeau's cabinet. She remembered attending Rockwood Park Public School for kindergarten, then switching to Joan of Arc School in Hull, Quebec, for grades one to six. Liz enjoyed the neat privilege of riding in her father's government limousine and going to the governor-general's residence to pick up Claire Butler, whose father Esmond was the GG's secretary. The group would drop Turner off at the Parliament buildings, before taking Liz and Claire to school. All four Turner kids would learn French but only Liz went to a francophone school.

"Ottawa is truly a bilingual city and I love that about Ottawa," Liz says. "I remember speaking to Dad's staff, when you spoke to them, you didn't know if they were anglophone or francophone. No accent at all."

The Turners lived in Ottawa when the political temperature wasn't so toxic. The families of Liberal and Tory MPs knew each other. They ate in the parliamentary dining room together.

"We trick-or-treated at Diefenbaker's house," Liz says. "It was never suggested that 'They're Conservative, we can't hang out with them.'"

As finance minister, Turner had tried to include his older children in some of his public responsibilities, such as attending Remembrance Day ceremonies. The kids would also sit in the House of Commons public gallery to watch their father on significant occasions. Like most children, they didn't necessarily appreciate how important their father's job was to the public agenda of the country.

"I had no clue he was in politics," confesses Michael, who was just seven years old when his father became finance minister. Having said that, Turner didn't let the job consume him.

"He would leave cabinet meetings to come home for his kids' birthday parties," recalls Geills. "If there was a sporting event, he'd be present there. Family was very important to him. It came first."

When Turner resigned the finance portfolio in 1975 and the family moved from Ottawa to Toronto, it was again the oldest Turner offspring, Elizabeth, who was most affected.

"I was the eldest, facing going to high school in a new city, so I wasn't super thrilled to move from Ottawa," she says. "I was at an age when I had an opinion. I remember telling my father, 'I appreciate that you're getting a great new job, Dad, but I'm not really happy with this move.' So we had a couple of discussions, encouraging me on that front." Liz ended up at the independent Bishop Strachan School, just two blocks from the family's new home, which helped.

Turner was a man of his generation, meaning he was no helicopter parent enrolling his kids in myriad after-school programs and driving them all over hell's half acre to attend. But one thing he surely did take an interest in was how his kids did in school. Education was important to Turner and he was paying four independent school tuitions to ensure his kids were well educated.

In those days, the schools mailed students' report cards home. When Turner got hold of a report card with less than adequate grades, "He'd be in his den sitting in his chair and he'd say, 'Get down here,'" Michael recalls. "You had no clue what your report card was going to look like. He was very stern. There were some tense moments there." As the kids got older, they wised up and got to the mail before their parents did.

"By the end we were steaming open the envelopes to get a look at it to see what sort of conversation there'd be," Andrew laughs.

Turner, of course, grew up without his own father. His stepfather Frank Ross was a strict disciplinarian, and Turner adopted some of that manner into his own approach.

"He often said 'Children should be seen and not heard!'" says Michael. "And it wasn't a joke. He meant it. It was one of his favorite quotes. You had to know when to speak at dinner."

The Turners had regular Sunday dinners as a family and if guests were included, Turner wore a jacket and tie and expected his kids to be similarly attired. If he asked his kids whether they had all washed their hands before dinner and he suspected someone was fibbing, he was all over that. "Which washroom did you go to?" he'd ask, before marching down the hall to check to see whether the soap or sink were still dry.

"Dave often took some heat for that one," Michael smiles.

Church attendance was also mandatory.

"If he was away, he'd look me in the eye and say, 'Mike, make sure you get those other two boys to church,'" Michael recalls. Kids being kids, the boys figured out how to get out of church duty.

"We said we'd go to the 8 a.m. service on Sunday which was too early for him," Andrew confesses. "So instead, we'd go to UCC and shoot hoops." Turner would later ask his sons what the sermon was about "and you'd scramble to come up with an answer," Andrew says.

Andrew also notes how different his parenting style is from his father's. "We take more from our kids than he would ever take," he says, pointing out that when Turner saw the back-talk Andrew took from his kids, "Dad was biting his tongue. We'd have been sent to our room if that language was used."

While Michael says his father was "not touchy feely," Turner left little doubt about how much he loved his children. "His big thing was the five-way daddy hug," recalls Andrew. "All four kids and him in the big embrace."

"The Daddy Hug," Michael echoes. "That's a strong memory from my childhood. Or he'd give you a handshake and then tug you in with a big smile on his face."

Turner loved going to watch his sons play football on Saturdays at UCC. He'd stand on the sidelines, smoking a cigar, cheering on the boys. "He'd give you the hug and tell you you did great," Andrew says. "He didn't pump your tires too much but he'd never criticize either. Even though he was a fantastic athlete, he never pushed us to do anything athletically."

The Turners were not what you'd call a big TV family. They watched the news and maybe hockey and football games, "But I don't think he watched a TV show in his entire life," says Andrew. "He wasn't a TV guy. Or movies."

Those memories come from the Turners' Toronto years from 1976 to 1984. After their father's return to public life in 1984, life got quite different for the Turner kids.

"It didn't sink in until after first year university," Liz recalls. "Then it definitely sunk in." At that point, their father was prime minister and the kids were teenagers. The two eldest went to university in the United States, where they could enjoy an anonymity that surely would not have been possible in Canada. Liz went to Stanford University in California and Michael attended Princeton University in New Jersey. After her first year, Liz got a summer job in Lake Louise, Alberta, where, of course, everyone knew what her father did for a living. There was no doubt a built-in assumption that Liz thought she was better than everyone else because of that.

"At the pub after a shift, some of the kids came up to me and said, 'We've decided you're not so bad after all,'" Liz remembers, relieved at the time.

Unlike the two older Turner kids, the two younger children attended university in Canada: David at the University of Western Ontario in London and Andrew at Queen's University in Kingston. Neither had any interest in going to the United States, which suited the family's financial situation just as well, given the massive pay cut Turner had taken.

"Dave was a Western guy," recalls Michael. "He went to the right school for him. His grades weren't the best in high school so he wouldn't have got in [to an American university] anyway. But he was a pig in shit in Western. Loved it there."

"Queen's was perfect for me," adds Andrew. "I had no interest in going to the U.S." But Andrew says had he and David wanted to go to the States, their father would have figured out a way to make it happen, huge tuitions notwithstanding.

"He was willing to pay anything for [education]," Andrew says. "Outside of that we were on our own."

Despite being a big player on Bay Street, Turner was home for dinner most nights. When the kids were growing up, Sunday night was a "must attend" family dinner, which often included guests—particularly priests from the local church.

"My Dad used to say, 'It's nice for them to get invited to peoples' homes because they've got no family nearby,'" Liz says.

Liz often took advantage of those occasions to argue theology and a woman's place in the church with a clergyman. Her father would usually defend the church. "Oh well, Elizabeth, the Catholic Church has to incorporate views from other parts of the world where they're more conservative," Turner would say.

"He wasn't convincing me at all," Liz says.

Having said that, Turner himself was hardly a staunch, doctrinaire Catholic. As justice minister, he'd legalized abortion and homosexuality. He also, according to Liz, thought it was ridiculous that priests couldn't marry and that women couldn't have significant roles in the church. He once sent Liz a speech he'd given at St. Michael's College at the University of Toronto, noting how many significant Old Testament characters were female and that at one time, priests did marry and had families.

"He'd always say, 'I'm a Christian first, a Catholic second,'" recalls Rick Alway. "He was a liberal Catholic."

* * *

Another significant part of family life centred on the parents' love of the North. Turner became deeply connected to Canada's far north, while Geills adored the cottage she and her family visited in Lake of the Woods in Kenora, in northwestern Ontario. As Manitobans, the Kilgours would hop over the Manitoba–Ontario line to enjoy their cottage which Geills' parents purchased in 1947. Geills' maternal Uncle Jack had the place next door.

After Geills and John married and the couple began having children, Lake of the Woods remained close to the family's heart and part of its annual summer plans, even though it took two days to get there from southern or eastern Ontario.

"We kept it because my mom loved it but my dad loved it too," says Liz. "He'd sit and gaze at the lake. It was one of his favorite views—the Canadian shield, the pine trees. He loved it. He'd get in a canoe and go to Turtle Bay or canoe around the whole island. He'd read files from work or politics. He was more relaxed there."

Geills adds: "John was in the canoe all the time in Kenora. Then someone made him a handmade kayak, which he paddled in until he could barely get into it."

Sometimes the family would take the train to Sudbury, then switch trains to Kenora, followed by a five-minute boat ride to Coney Island, one of the closest big islands. Actually, it often took two boats to get all the family's luggage to the cottage. Turner took pride in organizing with military precision the logistics required to get the family and a summer's worth of "stuff" up north.

When Turner returned to politics in 1984, he still made it a point to get to Lake of the Woods every summer. Stephen Hastings, who worked in Turner's office, was occasionally responsible for loading up the family station wagon and driving it to the cottage. It was a twenty-two-hour drive from Ottawa to Kenora.

"One year, my dad was in town and Mr. Turner and I met him at Stornoway," Hastings says. "Mr. Turner asked my dad to come in for a drink. I said, 'Aren't you going to help me load up the car?' And Mr. Turner answered, 'No, you've got it.' He spent the next two hours drinking with my dad."

Hastings loaded the car, spent the next two days driving it up to Kenora, then spent a couple of days with the family. "He was very different up there," Hastings recalls of his former boss. "He was in his element. Plus, the place was almost always off limits to political people."

Turner was once a fiercely competitive athlete and that instinct never left him. He and his kids played a lot of tennis at the Royal Lake of the Woods Yacht Club, and Dad never mailed it in to let the kids beat him. Often, father and children would give each other the silent treatment for hours after a tough match.

"They'd be vicious games," Michael recalls. "We'd be trying *not* to pass the other but *drill* them. Someone after would be so pissed off, we wouldn't talk on the ride home. It was quite hilarious." Those matches notwithstanding, Lake of the Woods was the place where Turner had the most fun with his children, and where the kids had the most access to their dad.

Occasionally, Turner didn't mind hobnobbing with politicians when they were in his neck of the woods in the north. One time in the late 1990s, two of Ontario premier Mike Harris' cabinet ministers were at a fishing lodge in Lake of the Woods. Northern Development and Mines Minister Tim Hudak said to his friend John Baird, the community and social services minister, "I think that's John and Geills Turner over there." The pair walked over and offered apologies for interrupting, saying they just wanted to say hi.

"He made us sit down," Baird says. "He was a great raconteur. He regaled us with all sorts of stories."

The other major part of the Turners' relationship with the North were ten-to-twelve-day-long canoe trips the family would take in parts of Canada that few people had ever seen. From the time he was minister of justice, Turner befriended a bush pilot named Bob Engle, who was originally from Seattle but moved north and founded Northwest Territorial Airways in Yellowknife in 1962. As justice minister, Turner would use Engle's airline when he'd fly to the far north to visit remote communities or check in with northern outposts. But the Turner family would also use Engle's airline to get to some truly exotic northern locations. For example, the family would fly from Kenora to Plummer's Lodge on Great Slave Lake in the Northwest Territories, while a second pontoon plane would schlep the canoes and other equipment. Then from the lodge, the family would be flown yet again to another location, where their canoeing adventures would begin. The trips started in the mid-1970s and continued for several years, until the kids went off to university and Turner went back into politics. But they were incredibly ambitious. Turner himself would do the research required to find routes that were navigable by families.

"He'd look at notes of others who'd done the routes, find the good campsites, find the right routes to canoe, find sections of rivers that were interesting with white water," adds Liz. "We'd align the canoes and carry the packs and do portages." This was decades before GPS so Turner actually had to pore over maps to find the best routes, which mattered, because Mother Nature could be unforgiving. It was crucial not to miss an important direction. For example, the Burnside River in Nunavut finished off with a fifty-foot-high waterfall before emptying into Bathurst Inlet and the Arctic Ocean.

"There'd be times the adrenaline was pumping," says Michael, who did five of these trips between 1977 and 1981.

"One time, the wind came up as we were in the middle of a great expanse," Liz recalls. "The weather changes pretty fast up there. We were far from shore. That was a little nerve-racking. And paddling upwind to boot was very strenuous. The portages weren't short. I was carrying packs of forty to fifty pounds. You'd see black bears and caribou there."

Geills recalls sitting at the bottom of Pike's Portage, a trail leading from Great Slave Lake to Artillery Lake at the edge of the Barrens. She saw a couple of Indigenous people who'd landed at the portage site. "The woman was loaded up with all the gear, and the man walked behind with the gas can," she says. "That says it all right there."

Frequently, John paddled on his own in the stern because Geills, a talented photographer, had traded in her paddle for a camera. She took literally tens of thousands of pictures of some of the most exquisite parts of Canada on those trips. "John had to paddle for the two of us," she admits. "I was snapping pictures all the time. But all those canoe trips and tough rivers, my goodness, how much he enjoyed them all."

Some years, the blackflies and mosquitos were miserable, meaning they all had to wear nets to avoid being constantly attacked. Geills would have to make bread from scratch (as she always did) inside a tent; otherwise, the dough would be rife with bugs. John and Liz tended to do the cooking and the trick was to eat quickly, or they'd be eating a lot of flies with their meal.

"There were definitely complaints," Liz acknowledges.

"From a kids' standpoint, you'd ask, what the hell are we doing up here?" Michael admits.

"But," Liz adds, "my parents came from the 'suck it up' school. You were either a true Canadian or you were a tourist."

One year, as the family was paddling down the Burnside, Geills speculated the Turners may have been the first non-Indigenous family ever to make that trek by canoe. When the family finally got to the portage site, after conquering the intense Burnside rapids, third-born David said: "Now I can go back to just worrying about the bears."

As Andrew thinks back on those trips, he realizes his own youngest child is now roughly the same age he was when he went on his first trek. "Would I go today in the middle of nowhere? It was pretty ballsy," he now admits. "What if someone gets appendicitis? You're in deep shit. It's still a leap of faith with kids that young. If something goes wrong...."

On Andrew's first trip, the group decided at one point to cross a giant lake, taking the most direct route, right into the teeth of huge wind and waves. "We probably had a seven-to-eight-inch clearance on the gunwales," Michael recalls.

"Dave and I were freaking about it," adds Andrew. "We're thinking to ourselves, if we go over now, we're not getting to shore. That was one of our dumbest moves on any trip."

But Bob Engle and John Turner loved the challenge. "Big water out there, John," Engle would say. "Sure is, Bob," Turner would answer, smiling.

All these years later, the Turner kids can say they did something highly unusual. "Not a lot of people can say they swam in the Arctic," says Andrew. "We look back, it's very fresh. It was a highlight of our childhood for sure."

Turner once penned an article in which he wrote that he truly became a Canadian once he went north of the sixtieth parallel and paddled the Burnside.

"We had survived the test of the North. We had shared another unique family experience," Turner wrote. "Together we had escaped into the Northern frontier and we had survived... What a privilege it was to have run these waters alone.... I have never felt more Canadian than when alone in the remote northern vastness."

CHAPTER ELEVEN

The Prime Ministership

O N THE DAY OF ANY leadership convention, the winner is the most important person in the party. But on the day after the convention, one could argue the runner-up is the most important person, because it is the silver medalist who will ultimately decide whether the party comes together or continues the internecine leadership intrigue.

In 1983, before the results of the fourth and final ballot at the Progressive Conservative leadership convention were announced, Joe Clark took an impromptu walk out of his box, traversed the floor of the same Ottawa Civic Centre where Turner won his leadership contest, and made for Brian Mulroney's box. I was a twenty-three-year-old cub reporter covering that convention for CHFI and CFTR Radio in Toronto, constantly cruising the floor of the convention looking for interviews, and to my shock, suddenly found myself with an exclusive face-to-face encounter with Clark as he made his unscheduled walk. Since almost all the television crews offering live coverage of the event were moored to their locations around the hall, I had Clark literally all to myself for a good two minutes before they could get unmoored and make their way through the massive crowd towards him.

I had done the math and even though Clark was ahead on the three previous ballots, I knew the percentage of newly available delegates he'd need to win was almost certainly beyond his reach. So I stuck my microphone in his face, pushed the record button, and asked some cheeky but obvious questions.

"Mr. Clark, where are you going?" I asked.

"I'm going to speak to Mr. Mulroney," he responded.

"Are you going to concede?"

"Not at all," Clark assured me, still hopeful he could get a big enough chunk of John Crosbie's newly released delegates to win. "I'm going to tell Mr. Mulroney that whoever wins this convention, this party *has to be* unified when we leave this hall. We need unity if we're going to prevail in the next election."

Suddenly, the crowd around Clark picked up the significance of his message and began chanting "UN-I-TY! UN-I-TY! UN-I-TY!" Clark certainly knew all too well how impossible it was to lead a major national party that wasn't unified. If Mulroney won, Clark wanted a head start in assuring the new chieftain that he could count on the loyalty and support of him and his supporters.

Of course, Mulroney did win, Clark repeated his message of unity in his concession speech, and for the next year, practiced what he preached. Mulroney did enjoy leading a unified party and caucus, something Clark never did.

The question for Liberals now was, could Chrétien put the hurt feelings of the leadership contest behind him and contribute to handing Turner a unified party?

Naturally, the kind of olive branch Turner could offer Chrétien would go a long way in determining how committed Chrétien would be towards assuring party unity. Having come second, Chrétien was clearly the most important Quebecer in the party, and he wanted responsibilities that reflected that. But Turner also owed other Quebecers such as André Ouellet, Marc Lalonde, and former Quebec Finance Minister Raymond Garneau for his strong showing in La Belle Province.

It didn't help matters that the day after the convention, Turner kept Chrétien waiting on the phone for 20 minutes before taking his call. His people insisted no slight was intended—things were simply chaotic—but it augured poorly for resolving the Chrétien question and demonstrating the competence Turner had promised to bring to the job.

Negotiations continued with Chrétien over several meetings. The runner-up tried to impress upon Turner that he simply couldn't accept being the party's third or fourth man in Quebec if he was the party's number two man in the whole country.

"You owe me Quebec," Chrétien told him.

Eventually, a compromise was found that theoretically would save face all around: Chrétien would become external affairs minister, deputy prime minister, and the general overseer of a Quebec triumvirate of advisers. Turner hoped that would satisfy all concerned.

It was only the start of a tsunami of decision-making. Just a few months ago Turner had been enjoying a vacation on some Jamaican beach. Now he had adviser roles to fill in his PMO, a cabinet to appoint, and a farewell wish list from his predecessor, Pierre Trudeau, to consider. Turner also knew he'd have to make good on commitments he'd made to young Liberals who supported him, and he did. Kaz Flinn met with the new PM's chief-of-staff John Swift.

"What do you want to do?" Swift asked her.

"I dunno," she responded. "I'm from Atlantic Canada."

"Okay," Swift said. "You're the special assistant for Atlantic Canada."

Turner's office created five regional desks and staffed two of them with women, which was unusual at that time. Besides Flinn on the Atlantic desk, Elizabeth Coburn ran British Columbia; David Miller had the West; Marc Kealey oversaw Ontario; and Michel Savard was responsible for Quebec. The five's responsibilities included liaising with caucus members from their respective regions, finding out about their MPs' priorities, briefing the leader, and organizing trips to their regions. Will McDowell got a job in the Liberal caucus research bureau. Turner tried to get Jan Innes, who chaired his Toronto leadership campaign, to come back to Ottawa, where she'd worked for David Smith, but couldn't convince her to do so. "It's that filthy lucre from Bay Street, isn't it?" Turner teased her. Of course, he knew all about that.

As happy as McDowell was to be working in the PMO, he was also becoming increasingly concerned. Government may have been complex when Turner left public life in 1975, but it was exponentially more so now. McDowell noticed that while Turner may have been a corporate superstar on Bay Street, Ottawa was different.

"He had got soft," McDowell recalls thinking. "I wondered, maybe he wasn't going to meet expectations after all."

Nevertheless, Canadians were prepared to give him a chance. With Trudeau at the helm, the Liberals had been twenty points behind the PCs and going nowhere. Now, new polling with Turner in charge showed the Liberals back in first place, eleven points up on the Tories. It looked like a classic case of the party knowing when and how to rebrand itself with new leadership to remain in power.

"Since his triumph at the Liberal convention, he sounded more sure of himself," wrote journalist Michel Gratton, Mulroney's future press secretary, in his book *So, What Are The Boys Saying*. "He looked like a prime minister."

And then Turner did something truly inexplicable that jeopardized everything.

When power passes from one prime minister to a successor, and the two are from the same party, there's a tradition that the two will meet, and the successor will get briefed on what the outgoing PM thinks are the major issues of concern. Trudeau and Turner fulfilled that tradition, but this meeting was very different. For starters, the two hadn't really had a private conversation since their awful meeting in September 1975, when Turner resigned from Trudeau's cabinet, and even then, the two men maintained very different versions about what had transpired.

Trudeau called the meeting for June 20 in his Langevin Block office with a clear agenda in mind, namely, to ensure future employment for political types who'd been loyal to him. He'd made commitments to several politicians who'd run for him again in 1980 and now it was time to make good on those commitments. He wanted sinecures for twenty-six current Liberal MPs and, according to Trudeau's principal secretary Tom Axworthy, told Turner he was prepared to make those patronage appointments himself.

At that same moment, Trudeau adviser Jeff Shamie and Turner adviser Will McDowell happened to meet up. The two men had been roommates at Queen's University, and so Shamie asked his friend: "Do you know what's going on in there?" McDowell confessed he didn't. "*La patronage*," Shamie replied, using an exaggerated French accent.

What followed was a comedy of errors almost too bizarre to be true. According to Axworthy, who was in the meeting, it was Turner himself who offered to make the appointments for Trudeau. Here was the new leader's thinking: Trudeau had a bare majority in the House and if the Liberals lost twenty-six MPs to patronage appointments, that majority would vanish. Turner feared if he waited before calling an election, he'd be vulnerable to the vagaries of a minority Parliament. He had also been advised by the privy council office that, if he wanted Governor-General Jeanne Sauvé to dissolve Parliament and send Canadians to the polls immediately, Sauvé potentially could decline that request and offer opposition leader Brian Mulroney the right to try to form a government.

It was an insane explanation. But again, it appealed to Turner's love of parliamentary tradition. Did he, a brand new prime minister, really want to put Sauvé in such an awkward position? Having said that, more than four years into a five-year mandate, was it conceivable that any governor-general would deny a new prime minister the right to call an election?

"I pleaded with him to let Trudeau make the appointments," recalls Axworthy. "We knew there'd be a real fuss if Trudeau made the appointments.

But he [Trudeau] was prepared to do it and take the opprobrium. And John could distance himself from it all."

Turner's sister Brenda, who was a good friend of Trudeau's (they often had lunch together), confirms Axworthy's version of events.

"Trudeau told me *he* wanted to make those appointments," Brenda now says. "But John told Pierre, if you make those appointments, I won't have a majority in the House of Commons. Brian Mulroney might force an election. So, leave them to me and I'll do them."

Brenda says Trudeau's response was to point out that, yes, the appointments would put Turner into a potential minority Parliament, but, he added, "The polls are so high, Brian will never force an election." Brenda says she never told her brother about the conversation. Regardless, the patronage appointments became a huge scandal, affected how Canadians viewed Turner, and would come to play a decisive role in the ensuing election campaign.

"We emphasized he'd be taking a bigger risk carrying Trudeau's dirty linen," Axworthy says. "We argued it was better to have the break with Trudeau. Trudeau was quitting and immune to the criticism. I tried two or three times to convince him. But John went with one risk he thought was lesser than the other."

The other problem with Turner offering to make the appointments, besides carrying Trudeau's "dirty linen," was the fact that Trudeau didn't trust Turner to go through with it. Because their 1975 meeting had ended so badly, Trudeau this time insisted that Turner sign a document promising to make the appointments Trudeau wanted.

Yes, the request from Trudeau made Turner uncomfortable. But Turner came from a more civilized era when these kinds of appointments were a prime minister's prerogative. It was a generous but hugely naive take on the matter.

The more he thought about it, the less Turner liked what he'd agreed to. Graham Fraser, in his book *Playing for Keeps: The Making of the Prime Minister,* quotes Turner as telling an aide: "Turn away when I tell you this, because you're going to vomit."

There has been much analyzing and psychoanalyzing of this chapter of Turner's pre-prime ministership. Some have observed Turner's longstanding desire not to disappoint those from older generations and perhaps that was at play during his meeting with Trudeau. Others have insisted that the advice from the Clerk of the Privy Council, Gordon Osbaldeston, somehow got muddied up in a game of broken telephone. (Complicating matters, Osbaldeston later insisted he never offered such convoluted, ridiculous advice.)

When adviser Bill Lee found out about the agreement Turner had made, he exploded, convinced that Trudeau had just sabotaged his successor. Turner, again perhaps a touch too naive, was just as certain the appointments would be seen as Trudeau's and wouldn't scar his own image. That turned out to be a massive misjudgment.

In his book *Rise to Greatness*, author Conrad Black opines that Turner should simply have told Trudeau to make the appointments himself, and to heck with any concern about losing his majority in the House of Commons. "He didn't have to call the House and he could have won some byelections," Black theorized. "This made him appear to be bound hand and foot to Trudeau which was anything but the truth."

When the patronage agreement became public, the opposition and media had a field day with it, as everyone knew they would. John Crosbie, the MP from Newfoundland and Labrador, called it "The grossest orgy of pork-barreling the country had ever seen." Mulroney himself described "a gang dividing the loot after a heist. It's like an Edward G. Robinson movie with the boys in the back cutting up the cash."

Charles McMillan, researcher extraordinaire for the Tories, crunched the numbers and said the appointments would cost taxpayers $84 million in salaries and perks. The *Globe and Mail's* Jeffrey Simpson, in his book *Spoils of Power*, wrote: "The orgy confirmed what many Canadians already suspected: Liberals were pretty much of a piece, greedy, smug, more concerned with their own interests than with the national interest, oblivious to outrage, deaf to dissent."

If Turner was the man who could bring both change and continuity to government, all eyes were on his first cabinet to see how he would balance those competing priorities. The verdict was: not well. Chrétien, of course, went to bat for his people, wanting ten of his supporters in cabinet. He got three, in part because cabinet was much smaller: twenty-nine members instead of Trudeau's thirty-seven. But Turner disappointed many supporters when he appointed only a handful of new faces, and kept many of Trudeau's old gang, including Marc Lalonde in finance, even though he'd already indicated he wouldn't be running again. Turner loyalists such as Jim Peterson, Dennis Dawson, and Gilbert Parent were passed over.

The new cabinet was sworn in on Canada Day by Governor-General Jeanne Sauvé, then had its first meeting immediately thereafter. Health Minister Monique Bégin noted in her memoirs that the informal, buddy–buddy atmosphere was totally different from Trudeau's more disciplined tone. When she and her cabinet colleague Judy Erola escaped to women's washroom, they both noted what a "pussy cat" Turner was.

"Where was the powerful Bay Street lawyer, the outstanding finance minister, the big business candidate who would assure us a new lease on power?" Bégin wrote. "We were both amazed to discover a prime minister who needed to be loved and surrounded with comradeship, like one sees on television in a male locker room after a great game of hockey."

July 1 also happened to be the first day of Richard Mackie's new job with the PMO. Mackie was a reporter with the *Globe and Mail's* Report on Business, but he'd started in the Ottawa Press Gallery in 1969 with the *Toronto Telegram* and knew Turner from his days as a cabinet minister. When someone in Turner's office wondered if he was looking for a career change, Mackie decided to give it a whirl.

The first thing he noticed: "The office was totally disorganized," he says. "People were coming and going. People were never sure who they were reporting to."

Mackie's responsibilities involved communications and strategy, and "writing one-page briefing notes on things, because [Turner] hated longer notes." He also noticed the inner circles of advisers around Turner and was deeply concerned about what he saw.

Turner knew it was essential to send a strong signal of support to the civil service, something that would come easily given his mother's professional background. He invited all the senior bureaucrats to a meeting in the Langevin Block, shared the agenda he hoped to pursue as PM, and assured the public servants they'd be essential to achieving that agenda. Future Supreme Court Justice Ian Binnie was one of those at the meeting, then in his capacity as associate deputy minister of justice.

"As he was leaving, he reminded us that Mulroney had said that if the Tories won the next election, Mulroney would personally give us all 'pink slips and a pair of running shoes,'" Binnie recalls. It may have been one of Mulroney's best red meat lines for Tory partisans, but Turner "expressed distaste for the crudity of the remark, to a receptive audience of course," Binnie adds.

Canada's ambassador to the United States, Allan Gotlieb, expected his meeting with the new PM on July 5 to be glorious. He'd been predicting Turner's ascension to the PMO for years and he couldn't wait to brief Turner on the Reagan administration's plans to celebrate the twenty-fifth anniversary of the St. Lawrence Seaway, one of the most successful and important joint projects in both countries' histories. But Turner balked at participating and Gotlieb couldn't quite believe it.

"The White House is trying to be helpful to you," Gotlieb told Turner, whom Gotlieb feared was being held captive by the anti-American wing of the Liberal Party, which wanted him to keep his distance from a president who four months later would be re-elected in a forty-nine-state landslide.

Turner may have been preoccupied with what was evidently the biggest question in Ottawa at this time: when should he call the next election? Constitutionally, he didn't have to call it for another seven months. But he also had in the back of his mind Pierre Trudeau's experience from 1968, in which the new prime minister won his leadership convention, then moved almost instantly to take advantage of his party's newfound spike in popularity.

Turner consulted cabinet colleagues and senior advisers. He had a lot of conflicting currents to consider. For every good reason to go to the polls soon, there'd be an equally influential reason to hold off. Chrétien urged him to wait and insisted it would end disastrously for the Liberals if Turner were to go now, but Turner's people still viewed Chrétien with considerable mistrust and so that advice was considered suspect.

Queen Elizabeth II was supposed to make a royal visit to Canada in mid-August and there was also a visit from Pope John Paul II scheduled for September. "Can you think of two better tours to get your prime minister great publicity?" Mackie thought at the time. "Turner was a devout Catholic. There'd be lots of coverage with the Pope."

Maybe so, but officials in the Department of Finance told Turner a big increase in the deficit was coming, and the prime minister was hardly eager to cut spending or raise taxes on the eve of a campaign, particularly since part of his brand was as a successful economic steward from his own time in Finance. Liberal popularity was up massively, but many Canadians had never seen Turner in the House, performing the role of prime minister. He'd only been back in the public eye for a few months after having been out of it for eight and a half years. Many of Trudeau's MPs would be retiring and there'd been little effort to attract new, star candidates. The party machinery itself was exhausted after a bruising leadership campaign and the divisions between the Turner and Chrétien camps hadn't yet healed. In fact, they were worse as many Chrétienistas simply couldn't accept Turner's victory as legitimate.

Turner's sister Brenda Norris remembers a lunch shortly after the leadership convention at the prime ministerial residence at 24 Sussex Drive: "All the Liberal hotshots are saying 'We've gotta have an election,'" she recalls. "I said to John, 'You cannot. You are exhausted.'"

But Turner's old-school naivete also kicked in. Unlike Trudeau when he took over, Turner was a prime minister without a seat in the House of Commons and a huge part of him thought he needed his own mandate. Millions of Canadians had not had a chance to make John Turner the prime minister, only a few thousand Liberal partisans had. That didn't sit well with him.

"I can't serve on that guy's mandate," Turner would say, referring to Trudeau. "I was elected by the party, but not by the people," he told his daughter Elizabeth.

When he told his sister that a snap election call would necessitate cancelling both the Queen's and the Pope's visits, Brenda didn't hold back: "You're crazy," she told him. "You'll be seen with the Pope and the Queen. Don't do it."

Even Mulroney, as skilled a political strategist as ever inhabited the PMO, couldn't believe Turner was considering a snap election and so he gave his senior staff the summer off and actually looked into renting a cottage with his wife Mila. Speaking of this time more than three-and-a-half decades later, Mulroney expressed some sympathy for Turner.

"If you took Wayne Gretzky off the ice for eight years and brought him back, he'd be pretty rusty too," he says. Then the strategist in Mulroney comes out. "He should have taken the summer off and toured with the Pope and the Queen," then called an election for November, he says. "Any historian looking at it would see the damage was self-inflicted."

More than a week before Turner won the Liberal leadership, his adviser Bill Lee had written a paper outlining his options on election timing. A quick call could exploit whatever momentum might be created by a decisive convention win. Assuming a renewed majority government, that would let Turner and team hit the ground running to reconstruct the economy. It obviated the need to govern with "the same old gang" for a prolonged period and wouldn't require Turner to look for a riding in which he could get himself elected in a by-election.

However, the reasons *not* to call an election were equally, if not more, compelling. Turner needed the summer to reunite the party and let party members catch their breath after a bruising leadership campaign. He needed more distance from Trudeau and those patronage appointments. He needed to recruit candidates and raise money. And the party machinery was in dire shape and needed rebuilding.

"The Liberal Party was a skeleton," Mackie recalls. "Constituency associations had been neglected. Headquarters had been neglected. It took a couple of weeks before we even got phones into the headquarters. Nothing was organized. There was no campaign strategy."

Lee's memo also outlined the advantages of waiting until the spring of 1985 before going to the polls. Spring elections were "a time of hope." There'd be time to introduce legislation including a "Turner budget," and recruit new candidates.

But Turner rejected that advice and instead opted for a snap election call. He took two lengthy trips, just days into his prime ministership, that would keep him out of touch with his campaign team for dozens of critical hours. First, he insisted on going to Salt Spring Island in British Columbia to visit his mother. "I can't knock him for wanting to see his mother," Mackie now says. "But he should have been sitting down with senior advisers. He was away from Ottawa for too long." Making the British Columbia trip doubly sad: Turner's mother was deep in the throes of Alzheimer's disease. She didn't recognize her son anyway. (Turner's mother died April 18, 1988, at age eighty-three.)

Next, Turner flew to Windsor Castle to meet the Queen and personally asked her to postpone her visit. Why take himself out of Ottawa for so many hours when a phone call would have sufficed?

"Respect" is Mackie's one-word explanation. Turner admired the Queen and felt he owed it to her to deliver the news about cancelling her trip in person. But he also made the trip in a government jet rather than a military plane, necessitating a stopover in Newfoundland for refueling, adding even more time to the effort.

At one level, Turner's choices were honorable and consistent with his life-long practice of showing deference and respect to those who deserved it, particularly if they were older (the Queen was three years his senior). But in an age before cell phones, when so much of campaign communication still happened with fax machines, Turner's being out of touch for so long, that close to an election call, was beyond ill-advised.

On July 9, the prime minister asked the governor-general to dissolve Parliament and send Canadians to the polls for a general election on September 4. The polls were just too juicy. Of course, most of that polling had been done before the controversial patronage appointments were made. The landscape was shifting, but Turner and his advisers didn't yet know it. A still unhappy Chrétien told Mulroney "John Turner is just like Doug Wickenheiser," referring to the

Montreal Canadiens' 1980 first-round draft choice, who turned out to be a huge disappointment for Les Habitants. "He looks good until you put him on the ice."

Even one of Turner's best Toronto friends, Richard Alway, now says he had doubts at the time about whether Turner was adequately prepared for the job as prime minister. "There was no preparation for the leadership," he says. "He was in Jamaica one day and then back in the thick of it the next." Turner's personal belief that Trudeau intended to stay on the job led him to be inadequately prepared for the task ahead.

"He was always a person who prepared hard, as a student, and as a lawyer," says Alway. "He knew that he had to bone up on things to succeed. It didn't just automatically come to him. He's the bright young boy anxious to please, to impress. That's a large part of the personality. Do the right thing to receive approval and affirmation. He didn't have that."

Mackie puts it this way: "He trusted and listened to his friends but they weren't giving him astute, political advice. They were by far out of touch with politics."

Bill Lee was a notable exception and could see his leader was exhausted and making bad decisions. He had urged delaying any election until the following spring but was overruled.

"If we continue to operate in this manner, you'll be the prime minister with the shortest reign in Canada's history," he told Turner, in a top-secret memo.

Lee wasn't off by much.

CHAPTER TWELVE

The 1984 Election

O NE OF THE MORE INTRIGUING aspects of this election campaign was the fact that both major party leaders were running in ridings they had never contested before, and their decisions represented huge risks to each of them.

Despite being a Quebecer, Brian Mulroney entered the House after his 1983 convention victory by winning a by-election in a safe Nova Scotia riding, vacated by Peter MacKay's father Elmer, who was the MP for Central Nova. Mulroney really couldn't seek a seat in Quebec because the PC Party held only one seat in the entire province. But Mulroney's unique selling proposition was a promise to lead the Tories back to respectability in Quebec, and therefore for the general election, he chose to run in Manicouagan, which included his boyhood hometown of Baie Comeau. It was a gutsy move for two reasons. First, when Turner called the election, a Sorecom poll showed a 62 per cent to 28 per cent Liberal lead in Quebec. Mulroney would have to move an enormous amount of public opinion to be elected in his home province. Second, when he was the president of the Iron Ore Company of Canada, Mulroney closed down a mine in the riding in 1982, resulting in significant job losses. Would the voters remember that, or the generous layoff packages he negotiated at the time?

John Turner also had a hard call to make. He had entered Parliament in 1962 as a Quebec MP, then moved to Ontario when his first riding disappeared. But he too was trying to lead a renaissance for his party in a region of the country that had been beyond unfriendly to Liberals under Pierre Trudeau, the West. So, Turner, like Mulroney, went home. He picked Vancouver Quadra in British

Columbia, the first province he lived in after leaving England, despite the fact that the riding was represented by Bill Clarke, who'd won four consecutive elections there for the PCs. Like Mulroney, Turner chose the harder road, rather than trying for election in a safer seat.

Having said that, the disconnect between the presumed juggernaut behind Turner and the reality that there wasn't much organization there was about to become abundantly apparent. The Liberals should have had a big advantage inasmuch as they knew the timing of the election call. And yet, it was the Tories whose coffers were filled with money and whose campaign headquarters was bursting with more than 100 people, while the Grits were still trying to open theirs and find a plane.

One of Turner's great hopes was that many of the captains of industry whom he befriended during his interregnum on Bay Street would, like him, sacrifice some prime earning years for public service. Turner's campaign even drew up a secret list of "Possible Candidates of Cabinet Quality." Names included some of Canada's best-known board chairs, presidents, and chief executive officers, such as Trevor Eyton (Brascan), Douglas Bassett (Baton Broadcasting), George Cohon (McDonald's), Sonja Bata (Bata Shoes), Galen Weston (George Weston Ltd.), Allan Waters (CHUM Ltd.), J. Peter Gordon (Stelco), Richard Thompson (Toronto-Dominion Bank), and Thomas Kierans (MacLeod, Young, Weir), even though he was a well-known Progressive Conservative and loyalist to Ontario premier Bill Davis. As it turned out, no one joined the team, and it's unclear whether any of them were ever officially asked. (Kierans confirms he was not; his father Eric, incidentally, ran against Turner at the 1968 Liberal leadership convention.)

The Turner campaign had a second list of "Possible Candidates But Not of Cabinet Quality," and the names on that list are even more interesting. For example, North York Mayor Mel Lastman was apparently considered a big enough name to court to run as an MP, but not ready for cabinet. Lastman later proved good enough to become the first mayor of the Toronto megacity in 1997. The legendary Toronto retailer and theatre owner "Honest" Ed Mirvish made the list. So did former Montreal Canadiens' goaltender, now lawyer and author Ken Dryden, who actually *did* become a cabinet minister in Paul Martin's government in 2004, and negotiated Canada's first ever national child care program (before the Conservative government of Stephen Harper cancelled it).

Despite buoyant polling numbers, despite the Liberals being considered by many to be the natural governing party, and despite the public's apparent approval of Turner's replacing Trudeau, the new prime minister told his daughter Elizabeth he was under no illusions about the fight to come. "There was no expectation of winning," Elizabeth says her father told her. "Trudeau had pissed off so many people, particularly in the West. He knew he'd be in opposition and was looking to the next election. It was rebuilding time, that's the way he saw it. He fought the campaign with gusto but that was what he told me from the beginning."

Conrad Black noticed something else about Turner. "He appeared ready to take Trudeau's place at any time," he wrote in *A Life in Progress*. "But when the moment came, it became instantly clear that the years away had dulled his politician's desire, instincts, and sense of entitlement."

Turner had three things working against him from the get-go. First, from the time he marched back into public life in early 1984, he was constantly playing the expectations game and losing. The legendary silver haired knight-in-waiting was so deeply ingrained in the media (and therefore the public's) mind that when Turner showed himself to be much less than perfect, the verdict was swift and harsh. At his campaign kickoff news conference, reporters were far more aggressive than anything he'd remembered as finance minister. They wanted details about myriad things and they wanted them now. Trouble was, the PM's top advisers were trying to do six months' work in six days, were totally disorganized, and simply didn't have the answers.

"The campaign never came to grips with it," says Rick Mackie, who adds people weren't clear about who they reported to or what their specific tasks were.

Second, under Turner, the Liberals had made a significant ideological journey. Under Pearson and Trudeau, the party occupied the centre-left of the political spectrum and that's where its coalition now lived. But as a former finance minister, Turner had a much sharper eye on the state of the country's books and didn't like what he saw. He talked a lot more about fiscal probity than Trudeau ever had. In fact, on many issues, Brian Mulroney's Tories seemed to be the more progressive alternative.

"We did wonderful announcements," Mackie recalls. "But as a former finance minister, he always was worried about spending. That disconnect persisted throughout the campaign."

Combined with his position on official bilingualism and other Liberal sacred cows, the mismatch was becoming more apparent.

Liberals also noticed something else off-putting. Their party colours now included yellow, which Turner had used during his leadership campaign. The idea was to separate the leader and the party even further from Trudeau.

"The Turner signs were a big mistake, and I knew it right away," said twenty-one-year veteran MP Don Boudria to Brooke Jeffrey in her book *Divided Loyalties*. "They thought that would show change, but all it showed, in my view, was that we were lost."

Even a vacationing Keith Davey could sense it from Florida. He called his friend, Ontario MPP Sean Conway, and said: "As you know, the Hindenberg is on fire." Conway knew, because at one point he was summoned to accompany Turner on the campaign plane just to be with him, so Turner had a friendly face to relate to.

"He was a trooper," Conway recalls. "The stoicism... A month in, the campaign was in ruins. It's like going to a hockey game and you're behind 4–0 in the first five minutes and no matter what you do, it isn't going to change the result. How do you go on?" Conway concluded it was simply a mixture of Turner's sense of both Catholic and democratic duty.

Observers well remembered the line in Turner's run for the leadership about "no more rainmakers!" It was a clear signal that he wanted a new crew running the show, and so Keith and Dorothy Davey took note by booking a vacation to Florida, assuming they wouldn't be needed. Some assured Davey that, Turner's rhetoric notwithstanding, he'd ultimately be in charge. But Davey heard nothing, so off to Longboat Key the couple went. Bill Lee would reprise his role from the leadership campaign and run the general election effort.

Almost immediately, things went off the rails. The analytics Davey and company had come up with four years earlier were of little interest to Lee. "You're worried about old Liberals," Lee told one of the party's pollsters, Martin Goldfarb. "I want to reach new ones."

The problem was the Liberal campaign wasn't reaching anyone. Mixed messaging, no apparent strategy, a disconnect with the party's base, and a leader who looked uncomfortable all combined to torpedo everyone's efforts.

A great example of the left hand not knowing what the right hand was doing involved the appointing of campaign co-chairs. Lee asked Izzy Asper (former Manitoba Liberal leader), Doug Frith (rookie MP from Sudbury), and Lise St. Martin-Tremblay (a party vice-president from Quebec) to assume the co-chair roles. But unbeknownst to Lee, Turner had already picked Marc Lalonde for the Quebec role, despite the fact the finance minister wasn't seeking re-election. Then, after Frith had flown from Sudbury to Ottawa to assume his responsibilities, he emerged from the plane to be told he was being replaced by another Sudburian, rookie MP Judy Erola.

"The juxtaposition between the Turner we knew–the golden boy–and the guy who came back..." muses David Lockhart, Turner's future senior policy adviser. "What happened to that guy?"

* * *

And then there was the bum patting.

Turner had always been a jock and had a locker room way of relating to people, regardless of whether they were male or female. "I'm a very tactile politician," he told CITYtv reporter Colin Vaughan during a scrum in Toronto. "I slap a lotta shoulders. Hug a lotta people."

But less than a week after he called the election, Turner got caught by a CTV news camera in Edmonton patting party president Iona Campagnolo on the derrière. Campagnolo's reaction took him by surprise: she whacked him right back on *his* butt. Turner loved it and leaned over to whisper in her ear, laughing: "You've been waiting some time to do that, haven't you?" The cameras got it all and it became a huge issue.

Despite campaign advisers telling him to cease and desist, Turner did it again just days later to Liberal organizer and future MP Lucie Pépin. CBC News anchor Sheldon Turcott introduced the story by referring to the "touchy problem Prime Minister Turner had today."

If there's one thing campaign managers can never predict, it's the seemingly insignificant issue that comes out of nowhere and completely derails campaign planning. Such was the bum pat. It suddenly became the talk of the country, and more pointedly raised questions about Turner's propriety.

"I think people are losing their sense of humor," he said in a scrum in Toronto's Little Italy.

But broadcaster Colin Vaughan wasn't having it. "Women do find it offensive, and it does date you, John," he said, showing no compunction about calling the prime minister by his first name in public.

"I don't think they find it offensive at all," Turner shot back, then, playing to the crowd of supporters around him, shouted: "Lots of hugs and lots of pats on the bum!" One older Italian man took Turner at his word, grabbed the PM's face in his hands and kissed him on both cheeks.

The bum pat was one of those cultural touchstones that divided Canadians. Some found it offensive, demeaning, and old fashioned. Others thought people ought to relax more. First-time candidate Sheila Copps tried to diffuse the issue when asked about it: "Frankly, I'm shocked," she told reporters. "I thought I had a pretty good behind and he's never been near it."

Writing three years later in his memoir *What Are the Boys Saying?*, Mulroney's press secretary Michel Gratton said: "I still don't believe these incidents, important as they were to the campaign, reflected the respect John Turner holds for women. But this image of him patting ladies on the backside raised questions about what kind of person he really was."

Liberal organizer Jan Innes took a different view. While in her early twenties and at a meeting at MP David Smith's home, Turner gave her a tap on the tush because he was pleased with something the team had accomplished.

"I saw it as, we're all part of the team and that he was recognizing my part of the team effort," Innes now says. "It wasn't sexual. I didn't see it as pejorative. I just regarded it as a job well done."

In fact, Innes disagreed with Campagnolo "making a big deal of it. He was the leader. She was giving him a black eye in public. She should have taken him aside in private."

The bum patting tagged Turner as a politician of the 1960s and '70s, but maybe not the '80s. "Turner always seemed out of sync with the events and moods swirling around him" is how Peter C. Newman put it in his book *The Canadian Revolution, 1985–1995*.

"In the old days, he'd get together with the boys in the media after hours and have a few 'Scotcherinis,'" says Lockhart. "Now after his comeback, it was a whole new media landscape—with women. He was unfamiliar with the game. Iona was a symbol of that."

Turner thought the issue was a big nothing-burger but the media just wouldn't let it go. In fact, they nicknamed his campaign plane "Derri-Air." (Ed Broadbent's was dubbed "Ordin-Air" because of the NDP leader's constant references to "ordinary Canadians," while Brian Mulroney's jet was nicknamed "Million-Air," given the candidate's, and the party's, well-heeled status.)

The election calendar added fuel to the fire because August 15 heralded a leaders' debate focused on women's issues, organized by the National Action Committee on the Status of Women and moderated by future Ontario cabinet minister Chaviva Hosek. Liberals can't win elections if they don't carry the female vote, and the story was now lasting not days, but weeks.

"It took forever to get him to apologize," Mackie says. "He apologized, just before the NAC debate, but he never understood that women didn't appreciate it."

At a photo op just before the NAC debate, Turner confided in his two chief competitors about how he regarded public life in 1984.

"Jesus Christ, it's tough out there," he said to Mulroney and Broadbent. "It's goddamned brutal."

Mulroney knew whereof Turner spoke.

"I had a great deal of sympathy that campaign summer for John Turner, who is an intelligent, thoughtful, and principled man," Mulroney wrote in his memoir. "He was raised in the old parliamentary practice of respect and courtesy."

But Turner didn't help his "Yesterday's Man" problem during a campaign stop in Thunder Bay. "You know, when C.D. Howe died, I was the executor of that man's will," he told the crowd, referring to Canada's one-time "Minister of Everything" during World War II. It's true that Howe was first elected to represent a Thunder Bay riding in 1935. It's also true he'd been dead for nearly a quarter of a century. But he was a huge figure in Canadian history and in Turner's life, so why not mention that detail?

"It just seemed an odd thing to say in a riding that wasn't friendly to Liberals in 1984," says Will McDowell.

* * *

The two most important women in Turner's life, his wife and his daughter, were both committed to seeing him succeed. Elizabeth got permission from her employer, Richardson Greenshields in Winnipeg, to take a leave and move to Vancouver. She rented an apartment and dove into the local campaign in Quadra, organizing door-to-door canvasses, giving speeches, and often taking the campaign plane to two or three different events in a day. The three Turner sons, one of whom was in university while the other two were still at Upper Canada College, joined at one point as well.

Elizabeth was a frequent attendee at her dad's news conferences, where she'd stand at the back and listen to the media pummel her father. He was the prime minister, and if there was a groupthink among the media, it was that Turner wasn't going to sashay to victory. He'd have to earn it. It drove Elizabeth mad.

"Some of the questions were so over the top that I'd pipe up," she recalls. "But my dad took me aside and said, 'You gotta have patience because they're just doing their jobs. It's an important part of the process, challenging people who are running for important roles and decisions they make.'" Elizabeth got it, but that didn't mean she liked it.

Lockhart didn't like it either. "Some of the criticism was so unfair," he now says. "In the '60s and '70s, the clipped cadence with which he spoke was called Kennedyesque. By the '80s it was mocked. His flaws were magnified by the media."

"I grew frustrated that we were unable to lift him above the caricature he had become in the press, which exploited his nervous laugh and certain mannerisms that made him appear uncomfortable in his own skin," wrote former MP and Newfoundland and Labrador premier Brian Tobin in his memoir *All in Good Time.*

Much has already been written about Geills Turner's role in the two campaigns in which her husband was Liberal leader (and more will be said in Chapter 16). Suffice to say at this moment, Geills was buffeted by two conflicting emotions. On the one hand, she truly disliked the fishbowl that politics inflicted on her life and wasn't particularly happy to see her husband jump back into that world. On the other hand, she was fiercely devoted to seeing her husband succeed, couldn't abide sloppy staff work (and told them so in no uncertain terms), and was a smart, attractive woman, shoehorned into the often unappealing and undervalued role of political spouse.

"There was lots of tension all the time," says Mackie. "She wasn't happy being schlepped around the country as an appendage."

There were numerous boiling points on the hustings. Mrs. Turner's temper on the campaign plane became so legendary, the pilot told the campaign staff that if she was on the plane the next day, he wouldn't be.

Davey's solution (as described in his memoir) was to tell the first couple that the campaign wasn't going well, but if they could run two separate tours, one for the leader, another for his wife, it could double its effectiveness.

"We did that just to keep her off the leader's plane," Davey wrote.

Geills Turner was sent to the Northwest Territories. Mackie wrote a fifty-page speech for her. "She was terrific on the stump," he says. "And she was happy to get off the campaign plane."

* * *

Sergio Marchi loved Pierre Trudeau. As a York University graduate in urban planning and a Young Liberal to boot, Marchi didn't know a thing about Sault Ste. Marie (had never been there) or its mayor Ron Irwin (had never met him). But he knew he wanted to make Trudeau the prime minister again and when

Irwin's campaign called him in desperation looking for a campaign manager, Marchi signed on. Irwin won that 1980 election and Marchi went to Ottawa for two years as Irwin's executive assistant.

Marchi returned to Toronto in 1982 and became a municipal councillor in North York. But two days into the 1984 federal campaign, his local MP, former cabinet minister James Fleming, dropped out, creating a new nomination race for a very safe Liberal seat in York West (Fleming had won it in 1980 with 57 per cent of the vote). Marchi contested and won a brutal nomination battle over future MP Maria Minna and future Ontario MPP Laureano Leone on the third ballot at 2 a.m.

Marchi's first ever meeting with Turner took place at Harbourfront in Toronto at the leader's speech attended by all the Liberal nominated candidates in Ontario's capital city. "It was the first time I ever shook his hand," he says. "After the speech, I found him wanting. I went home and asked, what happened to the guy I'd read so much about? He had this nervous cough and laugh. He wasn't confident. He wasn't a disaster, but I'd created expectations that weren't met."

Marchi had to acknowledge that, despite his backing Chrétien for the leadership, Turner "didn't ignore me. There was no retribution. He was a gentleman and shook my hand. But on the way home I remember thinking, my chances of winning would be much worse than I'd hoped. This is going to be a steep, uphill climb."

Brian Tobin described one of the more unfortunate campaign events in his memoir. In 1984, Tobin was a rookie MP seeking re-election in his Newfoundland and Labrador riding. He organized a big, enthusiastic crowd to show up in Stephenville to welcome the prime minister. But Turner was having an off day.

"I'm delighted to be here in Stephenville with Brian Mu—, Brian Mu—, er…. Sorry," Turner stumbled out of the gate. He tried again. "I'm delighted to be here with Brian P—, Brian Peck—." No, it wasn't Brian Peckford either.

Tobin was fast on his feet and prevented the scene from becoming even more embarrassing. "The trouble with this country's politics is that there are too many Brians around. Two too many!" he crowed, referring to the opposition leader and the PC premier. The crowd ate it up, but it was a bad unforced error.

"It was a painful anticlimax to a painful campaign, made doubly agonizing because I liked John so much," Tobin wrote. "But he didn't have it."

More and more Liberals were coming to that conclusion. One day, PC organizers Norman Atkins and John Laschinger, both members of Ontario premier

Bill Davis' Big Blue Machine, were meeting, dealing with campaign matters. A Liberal friend showed up for a visit.

"We asked him whether Turner or Chrétien would have been the better choice," Laschinger says. "He said, 'Your tougher opponent would have been Jean Chrétien.' Turner just didn't seem to have the intuition anymore."

(As an example of how small a world Canadian politics is, Laschinger's father's second wife was a woman named Gwyn Swift. Her son John Swift was part of Turner's inner circle. The two stepbrothers were both influential advisers on opposite sides of the fence during the 1984 campaign.)

As difficult as the campaign was for the Liberals, the party had two opportunities in late July to try to reset the narrative. Turner performed well at the French language debate on July 24, even though eight years on Bay Street meant he couldn't be as impressive as Mulroney, whose French was flawless. The French debate just wasn't a game changer.

But the English language debate the next night sure was.

CHAPTER THIRTEEN

The 1984 Election Debate

I F THERE WAS ONE THING John Turner was confident of, it was besting Brian Mulroney in a debate. The two men had known each other for two decades. They liked and respected each other. But Turner thought his superior legal and analytical mind gave him a big advantage.

The Liberal campaign team's job was to prep Turner for the one remaining event that could turn things around: the leaders' debates. They got hold of President Jimmy Carter's handbook, which they thought offered good, standard advice. Carter had a strong debate in 1976 against President Gerald Ford (the first presidential debate since the original Kennedy–Nixon contest in 1960). But Carter was bested in 1980 by his Republican challenger, Ronald Reagan. Regardless, there was lots in the book to chew over.

The handbook talked about putting the candidate through short policy briefings, practicing mock debates, videotaping and reviewing those practice sessions later, and having the stand-ins for the other leaders ask far tougher, more belligerent questions than anything you'd see in a real debate. By going through that process, Turner ought to be ready for any curve ball Brian Mulroney or Ed Broadbent might throw.

John Swift presented that process to Turner, after which Turner proceeded to make his first miscalculation.

"I can beat Mulroney, debating the issues," he told his team.

What Turner didn't understand was that this wasn't a Hart House legal debate. It was a television spectacle, which millions of people would be watching and which could determine the outcome of the campaign. "Turner didn't get that it was a tennis match where the ball could explode at any minute," says Rick Mackie, who was part of the debate prep team.

As a result, Turner took a deep interest in things perhaps better left to his staff: the ground rules, length of responses, positioning of the lecterns, even the size of the water glasses. It didn't seem the best use of his time. Conversely, Mackie says, he didn't take seriously enough the training camp he needed to go through to be ready for this important confrontation. Turner also got contradictory advice from his advisers: Keith Davey wanted him to rough up Mulroney; Bill Lee said avoid personal attacks, look like a prime minister.

One of the night's big questions was, how would the leaders handle the campaign's biggest gaffe to date—not Turner's bum patting, but rather Mulroney's indelicate language in response to the prime minister's patronage appointments. Mulroney was on a late-night flight from Manicouagan to Montreal when he did what many politicians used to do in earlier, more innocent times, he walked into the plane's rear cabin and thought he'd let his hair down with reporters for what he assumed was an off-the-record chat. In public, Mulroney had zealously chastised Turner for the patronage appointments. But here, in private, the opposition leader let rip. Referring to former Liberal cabinet minister Bryce Mackasey (who'd been appointed ambassador to Portugal), Mulroney said: "There's no whore like an old whore," adding that were he in Mackasey's shoes, he would "have been right down there in the trough, too."

Mulroney's problem was that not all of the reporters had agreed to speak off the record and therefore didn't feel beholden to keep the conversation secret. With a week-and-a-half to go before the leaders' debates, Mulroney's "no whore like an old whore" comments were splayed all over the *Ottawa Citizen*.

It was a terrible, unforced error which unmasked Mulroney as a hypocrite on the patronage issue and threated a year's worth of efforts to make the PC leader a trustworthy alternative to the Liberals. Some Canadians already worried that Mulroney seemed too slick, too rich, and with a too-gorgeous wife in Mila. His campaign tried to remind everyone that Mulroney had grown up in poverty, while Turner was dancing with a princess. But this scandal threatened to undo all that work.

The Tories may have hoped the issue would go away, but it wouldn't, and so Mulroney eventually read a short statement, insisting he was just engaged in some casual banter, and that it had been a mistake to treat "so important a matter in a way which might be misunderstood, and [I] very much regret having done so."

Mulroney, as Turner before him, learned a lesson the hard way that the old rules of politics were gone and the candidate needed to be wary of everything he said and to whom he said it.

When the Liberal war room heard about the incident, Davey spoke to Turner immediately and gave him this warning: "John, the kind of language Mulroney was using tonight is offensive to a lot of people. Believe me, it will not play in small-town Ontario."

Turner's response: "You're fucking right!"

* * *

Turner's final English debate preparations went well. His advisers reminded him to avoid those habits that just looked odd, placing his hands on his hips, clearing his throat with that barking sound, squinting while listening, or clenching his jaw. Davey warned Turner *not* to raise Mulroney's bawdy comments about patronage, as they could boomerang back on the Liberal leader.

Turner seemed ready.

The format of the debate in 1984 was significantly different from today's debates. The first and obvious difference is that there were only three participants (there was no Reform Party, Canadian Alliance, Bloc Québécois, Green Party, or People's Party, yet). The three leaders would make opening statements and then the debate would be divided into four segments, each featuring a one-on-one with only two leaders.

The moderator for the English debate was an academic named David Johnston, who sixteen years later would be appointed Canada's twenty-eighth governor-general. Johnston had moderated the 1979 leaders' debate between Prime Minister Pierre Trudeau, Tory leader Joe Clark, and NDP leader Ed Broadbent. He was at his office at the University of Western Ontario in London, where he was dean of the law school, when the call came asking him to take that job.

"I got picked because the networks couldn't agree on a moderator," Johnston says. "They thought I'd be a sensible timekeeper."

Five years later, he was now principal at McGill University and asked to reprise his role. Johnston knew all three leaders reasonably well. Turner would occasionally phone him to share a celebratory call if McGill won a football title. Turner's sister Brenda Norris was also on McGill's board of governors while Johnston was principal. The Johnstons and Mulroneys lived fairly close to each other in Montreal's Westmount neighbourhood, so they travelled in some similar social circles. He also knew Broadbent through previous labour arbitrations.

"I had admiration and respect for all three," Johnston now says.

Early in the debate, the patronage issue came up, but only peripherally and it went away without anything memorable emerging.

"It didn't become a cause célèbre," Johnston recalls.

But then, in the debate's third segment, Turner inexplicably did what his advisers had urged him not to do: *he* raised the patronage question. Mulroney, who'd been improving his game over the past year by going up against Trudeau in the House of Commons, saw his moment and pounced. The next three minutes would change the course of Canadian history:

Turner: "I would say, Mr. Mulroney, that on the basis of what you have talked about, putting your nose in the public trough, that you wouldn't offer Canadians any newness in the style of government. The style that you have been preaching to your own party reminds me of the old Union Nationale. It reminds me of patronage at its best."

"When John said that, I counter-punched," Mulroney told me two decades ago for a previous book called *The Life: The Seductive Call of Politics*. The Tory leader decided to rag-the-puck with a bit of a filibuster. He gave a long response, and Turner let him go, uninterrupted:

Mulroney: "Mr. Turner, the only person who has ever appointed around here for the last twenty-odd years has been by your party, and 99% of them have been Liberals and you ought not to be proud of that, nor should you repeat something that I think you know to be inaccurate. You know full well that was a figure of speech that was used, and I do not deny it. In fact, I have gone so far, because I believe what you did was so bad, I have gone so far, sir, as to apologize for even kidding about it. The least you should do is apologize for having made these horrible appointments. I have had the decency, I think, to acknowledge that I was wrong in even kidding about it. I shouldn't have done that, and I said so. You sir at least owe the Canadian people a profound apology for doing it. May I say, respectfully, that if I felt I owed the Canadian people, and I did, an apology for bantering about the subject, you sir owe the Canadian people a deep apology for having indulged in that kind of practice with those kinds of appointments."

Turner, stammering: "Well, I have told you and told the Canadian people, Mr. Mulroney, that I had no option."

Those last four words, "I had no option," sparked something in Mulroney. Turner held his hands open and to his sides as he said it, conveying a further impression that he was a prisoner of his circumstances.

Johnston thought the exchange had run its course, and so he interceded in an attempt to move on to another issue by saying to one of the journalists on the panel, "Mr. Trueman, your next question." But those four words and Turner's look of resignation prompted Mulroney to ignore the moderator's request. The monitor on Johnston's desk lit up with a message in all caps from his producer: LET THEM GO AT IT!

"So, I didn't intervene," Johnston says.

Mulroney pounced.

Mulroney: "You had an option, sir! You could have said I am not going to do it! This is wrong for Canada and I'm not going to ask Canadians to pay the price. You had an option, sir, to say no, and you chose to say yes to the old attitudes and the old stories of the Liberal Party. That, sir, if I may say respectfully, that is not good enough for Canadians."

Mulroney and I discussed this moment of the debate more than two decades ago. "As soon as John Turner said, 'I had no option,' I came alive," he said. "It was a very rapid-fire exchange. I'm sure it didn't last any more than ten seconds. But it was a devastating ten seconds."

That could have been the end of it. But again, inexplicably, Turner tried a second time to make a nuanced constitutional argument Canadians weren't the slightest bit interested in hearing.

Turner: "I had no option. I was…"

Mulroney: "That is an avowal of failure! That is a confession of non-leadership and this country needs leadership! You had an option sir. You could have done better."

Turner was now completely on his heels. He looked like a beaten man. Then, Johnston invited him to respond further. And Turner wasn't ready for it.

Johnston: "Mr. Turner, your response please."

Turner: "I just said, Mr. Moderator, taking the Canadian people through the circumstances, Mr. Trudeau had every right to make those appointments before he resigned. In order to do so, yes, I had to make a commitment to him. Otherwise, I was advised that with serious consequences to the Canadian people, I could not have been granted the opportunity of forming a government."

In his own memoir, Mulroney described the moment thus: "He gave me my golden opportunity (why, I'll never know) and I seized it."

Interestingly, Johnston was so involved in watching the clock, reminding himself of who the next questioner was, and reading his monitor screen that he didn't fully appreciate at that moment the significance of the exchange.

"I thought, Brian Mulroney scored a point and John Turner was in the corner, but that's it," he says. (When he told that to BCTV host Jack Webster the next morning, the fiery Scotsman responded: "I don't know what you're smoking. It was a knockout.")

Indeed, it was, partly because it was so dramatic and partly because it was so spontaneous. So much of what's said at leaders' debates are canned, prepackaged lines. But this wasn't.

"That's why face-to-face confrontations are useful," Johnston says. "We want to see leaders react in an unscripted, emotional way. Handling that difficulty is part of leadership."

Last year, Geills Turner and I talked about that moment in the 1984 campaign. She acknowledged to herself that "what Brian said was probably true. John had a choice. And maybe his comeback wasn't as slick as it should have been and he looked like a loser. Maybe John could have had a different answer."

On the ride back to Stornoway after the debate, Mulroney's wife Mila told him: "I think you just hit it out of the park." Twenty-four hours later, that was confirmed. After a day of campaigning in Hamilton, Mulroney met with PC pollster Allan Gregg at 1 a.m.

"We've just looked at the overnights," Gregg told him. "You've just been responsible for the most radical change in modern Canadian political history."

David Herle watched the debate with his mother at her home in Regina. "I knew it was bad," he says. "I didn't know it was election-ending."

"It was a fucking disaster," says Will McDowell. "He was so flat-footed."

First-time candidate Sergio Marchi was too nervous to watch the debate. Instead, he went canvassing and got updates from the voters.

"Your guy is taking a shellacking," one said.

"Mulroney just hit your guy on the chin," said another.

Jan Innes was deeply upset after the debate. "He just wasn't savvy in communications," she says. "It was the new norm, and he wasn't there. He stumbled. There was no excuse, and he wasn't able to put a game face on to defend those appointments."

Author Greg Weston recounts an exchange between Turner and his campaign manager Bill Lee the day after the debate. "Gawd, Bill, I really blew it, didn't I?" Turner said.

Lee tried to sugar-coat it. "I wouldn't say it was your finest hour, no."

David Johnston and Turner would have many more casual encounters over the ensuing years. They never discussed that night again.

"It wasn't awkward," Johnston says. "John could manage these things in compartments. It never carried over to our rapport."

* * *

Technically, of course, the campaign wasn't over. There were still almost six weeks to go, which meant Turner had to continue to get out there and put on a brave face every day, despite the entire country knowing he was, politically anyway, a dead man walking.

One week after the leaders' debate, Bill Lee wrote Turner a "strictly personal and confidential" memo on where things stood in the campaign. Lee described circumstances that were nothing short of a horror show. When the election was called, the party had no apparatus or plan in place in English Canada. Liberal party headquarters was "a disaster area." Candidates, including cabinet ministers, still "do not see a focus to this campaign." Lee's most serious concern was the leader's tour, which he felt Turner was spending too much time trying to run himself, conveying an impression that the campaign was disorganized. There were also far too many people who had access to the leader. "Some of these people are consummate purveyors of doom and disaster," Lee wrote. "They were not helpful to your morale during the leadership. They could detract from your performance during the remaining month of this election." Lee well understood that many from Turner's large political circle wanted to be considered close advisers. "But we cannot afford to have you worn down or risk confusion in this crucial phase of the campaign."

Ontario MPP Sean Conway continued to accompany the leader on the campaign plane. He established the practice of introducing Turner at his speaking engagements and running a little interference "when the mayor of Punkeydoodles Corners wanted his moment with the candidate." He also had the job of trying to keep Turner's spirits up when journalists in the back of the plane were mimicking popular songs (such as The Beatles' "All we are saying, is give Chick a chance," using Turner's UBC nickname, and "Going down the toilet, on the Turner ship of state").

The situation became so dire for the Liberals that Turner did the one thing he swore he'd never do. He called "The Rainmaker," told him he was going to fire his long-time friend Bill Lee, and asked Davey to cut short his Florida vacation and come home to run the campaign. When Turner, Davey, and pollster Martin Goldfarb met for breakfast on August 4, the news was grim.

"We have twenty-five seats in English Canada," Goldfarb told the group.

Turner was incredulous. He'd known it was a much closer race, but no one had levelled with him on how disastrous things were.

"You're ten points behind and falling fast," Davey told him, as described in his memoir *The Rainmaker*. "Quebec is falling apart too."

"We wanted to be away [in Florida] so as to not be available for comment," says Dorothy Davey, Keith's widow. "When we came back, there wasn't much we could do."

Davey told Mackie the campaign's biggest problem was the leader himself.

"Keith," Turner told him, "I want you to know who is running this goddamned campaign. I am. That's who."

"John Turner wanted to be his own chief of staff," Mackie recalls Davey saying, before famously adding: "Turner's problem is he wants to be both the jockey and the horse."

Things continued to get worse. David Smith, the future senator but at this time the MP for Don Valley East, invited all the Metro Toronto candidates to his home to brainstorm. "We're nineteen points down," he told them. "How do we get back in this?" The consensus was to consolidate the Liberals' traditional base as much as possible: young, poor, women, minorities; talk about the environment; offer enhanced pensions and ideas for job creation; and focus on women's issues. Turner did that well at the NAC women's debate on August 15, but the game was almost over.

On Friday, August 24, Turner showed up to the Canadian Club in Toronto to give a luncheon speech. He went right into the heart of the country's financial district to announce a new tax policy which would impose a new minimum tax on the rich. The campaign had every expectation that the high-circulation Saturday newspapers would give the story big play.

The *Globe and Mail* certainly did. In an example of the dirty pool the Liberal campaign accused some in the media of playing, the *Globe* ran a closeup shot of Turner, mid-speech, with an angry look on his face, and the luncheon's logo on the backdrop behind him, emerging from his head. The logo consisted of two forks, which, when shot from the angle the photographer chose, made Turner look like the devil with horns protruding from the top of his head. Yes, you could blame Turner's staff for not catching a potential embarrassing image in the making. Or you could say the *Globe* probably had hundreds of other images to choose from, but for whatever reason, decided to embarrass the prime minister on the front page of its best-read edition of the week with just ten days to go. The picture was taken by Canadian Press photographer Andy Clark, who would go on to become the official photographer for Brian Mulroney.

Seeing their leader ridiculed on the front page of the country's national newspaper was a horrible way for the Liberal campaign to start the day. "I deeply regret seeing my old friend John Turner humiliated," Ambassador Allan Gotlieb wrote in his diary. "It's true he ran a poor campaign, but the Canadian media treated him disgracefully."

More than three-and-a-half decades later, Geills Turner's contempt for the newspaper hasn't abated much. "Why would someone set him up that way or take the picture that way?" she asks. "The Globe shouldn't have used it."

Turner's provincial colleague from his finance minister days, former Ontario treasurer Darcy McKeough, also couldn't believe what he was seeing.

"He was a great guy, badly treated," says McKeough, who also thought about returning to public life from the private sector after Bill Davis retired in 1985. But he didn't. "Turner's example was one of the reasons I didn't go back after Davis quit."

By the last week of the 1984 election campaign, everyone knew Mulroney's PCs were headed for a big victory—the only question was: how big? For the Liberals, the national campaign was over. For them, the question was: could Turner win Vancouver Quadra? Just before election day, Geills Turner appeared as a guest on Jack Webster's show to make a last-minute pitch to British Columbia voters. Webster brought his A-game, peppering her with questions on everything from capital punishment to her husband's pitiable campaign. But Geills took it all in stride and performed admirably. She came across as smart and likeable, and the more Webster attacked, the more she flirted with him. She was totally disarming.

On the patronage issue, Mrs. Turner insisted, "They were Mr. Trudeau's appointments, not my husband's. He shouldn't have been blamed for it."

Webster came back at her. "Actually, it was still awful, wasn't it?" he asked.

"I agree!" Mrs. Turner surprised the host. "It was awful! My husband wouldn't have made those appointments."

Webster tried to provoke Geills into saying something headline-inducing with his next attack. "You'd much rather have stayed in the kitchen, doing your baking and polishing John's shoes, than be on this campaign, right?"

"You really think that's what I'd rather be doing?" Mrs. Turner shot back smiling. "That's nonsense and you know it!" Webster was trying to get under her skin, but Geills just wouldn't permit it. Webster kept trying.

"I'm really sad to say your husband's going to be beaten on Tuesday," he said.

"Who says he's going to be beaten?" Mrs. Turner volleyed. "Joe Clark says we shouldn't count on anything yet and I think Mr. Clark's a very wise man. Life is full of challenges and you don't walk away from challenges just because of a potential downside."

She took calls from the public and gave as good as she got. When Webster cut off a caller who was too gentle ("Let's get to some nasty callers!"), Mrs. Turner replied: "I can handle them. I'm not afraid to come on your show, Jack." And they shared a laugh.

"What was your university degree in?" Webster asked.

"Math and physics," she responded. That actually shut Webster up for a few seconds. "Back to the phones," he said. Geills Turner may have hated what was happening in her family's life at that moment, but you'd never know it. She was a happy warrior on her husband's behalf and put on a memorable performance with one of the meanest (if entertaining) interviewers around.

When I reminded Geills about the Webster interview, you could tell the memory of it pleased her. "I think I gave him back, didn't I? I'm not a pushover. I wasn't going to lie down and play dead. I'm in this job, I've gotta do my best."

Geills Turner knocked on doors in Vancouver Quadra right to the last moment. She knew her husband was going to suffer a humiliating defeat on election night, but dammit, she didn't want him losing a riding he truly wanted to win. John Turner *never* lost his seat in Quebec or Ontario and she didn't want him losing in British Columbia either.

I put it to Geills that had her husband lost Quadra, he surely would have had to resign the Liberal leadership immediately, which would have allowed the couple to move back to Toronto to the life she preferred. Didn't she secretly wish John would suffer personal defeat in Quadra as well?

"I definitely didn't want to lose," Geills insists "I don't like to lose. Honestly. Honestly!"

One time, while campaigning in the riding, she knocked on the door of Barry Auger, whose father Fred had published the Winnipeg Tribune in the 1950s, and later the Vancouver Province. Geills hadn't seen him since the '50s.

"I hope you're going to vote Liberal," she told Auger.

"My parents always voted Conservative," he replied.

"Come on, Barry," Geills shot back. "I haven't seen you in a long time. But aren't you a little old to be voting Conservative just because your parents did?" The two continued to have an amicable conversation, but Geills wasn't sure she had his vote.

On the last night of the campaign, John Turner went to Hamilton to do an event with former Ontario MPP Sheila Copps. Earlier that year, Copps had disappointed Ontario Liberal leader David Peterson by being one of four members of his provincial caucus to quit and run federally. All four were convinced Peterson was going nowhere but Turner was going somewhere.

"You'd have thought they were going to win the election," Conway recalls of that night in Hamilton. "The room was packed. There was such energy. Sheila was singing in Italian and Portuguese."

Nine months later, Peterson became Ontario's twentieth premier. Two of the four MPPs that abandoned him would lose the following night, but Copps and Don Boudria would win their seats.

Sergio Marchi spent election night convinced he was about to lose one of the safest Liberal seats in the country. "Nothing was stopping the Mulroney tide," he recalls. "People were in the mood for a change. You could see it in their eyes and words."

The Liberals had been in power (with the exception of Joe Clark's nine months) for two straight decades. "It was a tragedy that Turner became prime minister when the country was hungry for a change of government," says future Supreme Court justice Ian Binnie.

Canadians got exactly what they seemed to want on September 4, change of historic proportions. The Tories garnered a smidgeon more than 50 per cent of the total votes cast, an astonishingly high number in a multi-party system. It was good for 211 seats, a number never before reached (Diefenbaker's sweep in 1958 captured 208 seats). As always, the results came in from Atlantic Canada first, and in a part of the country that's almost always kind to the Liberals, the Tories won twenty-five out of thirty-two seats.

Then Mulroney made good on his claim of being able to penetrate Fortress Quebec. The Liberals went from holding seventy-four of that province's seventy-five seats to just seventeen. The PCs took fifty-eight. In Ontario, Bill Davis' Big Blue Machine came through as Mulroney took sixty-seven seats. The Liberals won only fourteen. Marchi watched nervously as he dropped twelve points from his predecessor's total vote in York West. In future elections under Jean Chrétien, he'd take almost 80 per cent of the votes. Tonight, he was thrilled the election wasn't happening a week later or he felt certain he'd have lost. But he narrowly won.

The story was the same as results came in from the West. The PCs won nine of fourteen Manitoba seats, the same in Saskatchewan, and all twenty-one in Alberta. The only question remaining: would Turner be able to win any of British Columbia's twenty-eight seats, and, in particular, Vancouver Quadra?

Turner, ever the gentleman, called Mulroney to congratulate him and conceded the prime ministership. "I'm sure it was a very painful moment for him—once the golden boy of Canadian politics, now defeated after barely two months in office," Mulroney wrote in his memoir. "He was extremely gracious, congratulating me on a strong campaign, promising a smooth transition and wishing me well."

David Herle watched the election returns in Saskatoon with Doug Richardson, a future Turner chief of staff in the opposition leader's office. "Quite a few rum and Cokes went down that night," Herle jokes.

Nineteen-year-old Christy Clark, the future premier of British Columbia, spent the election campaign working in Turner's office in Quadra and wishing she'd known the PM a decade earlier when he was the Liberals' shining star. She watched the returns intently on election night from Turner's Quadra campaign headquarters.

"I thought he was a stately man, a lovely gracious man," she now says. "But by 1984, he'd waited too long."

Turner desperately wanted to bring the Liberal Party back in Western Canada, but it was unrequited love. The Tories won nineteen seats in British Columbia, and the NDP won eight. All of B.C.'s twenty-eight ridings turned their back on Turner, except for one: Vancouver Quadra, which he miraculously won by more than 3,000 votes.

"I was excited, amazed, and astounded he won his seat," Herle says. "And it's been Liberal ever since." Turner's win in Quadra was part sympathy vote, part thanks for making the effort out West, and part acknowledgement of his team's hard work. It also gave birth to the political term "The Quadra Effect," in which one riding inexplicably bucks a regional or national trend.

Turner won 21,794 votes in Quadra, and one of them belonged to Barry Auger, Geills Turner's old friend from Manitoba, whose door she knocked on by happenstance. She got a note after the election from Auger saying, "I wanted you to know I voted Liberal."

The Liberals took 28 per cent of the total votes on September 4, good for only forty seats, and Turner's was the fortieth. It was the worst showing by the

Liberal Party in a general election *ever*. And for those who still loved John Turner, it was a painful kick in the gut.

"We went into the 1984 election with such high hopes," remembers Herle, a Saskatchewan native. "People in the West were waiting for him as the leader. He had an agricultural policy, for goodness sakes. He gave a shit."

Turner was nothing if not classy in defeat. He reminded his supporters during his concession speech that "the people are always right." (Ontario Big Blue Machine member Hugh Segal, the former senator, would add, "occasionally they're excessive, but they're always right.")

Turner also gave a shout out to volunteers from all parties, saying "You are the heart and soul of the democratic system." He quoted Churchill in saying "our defeats are but the steppingstones to victory."

Conrad Black noted Turner's grace in defeat in his memoir *A Life in Progress*. "He was magnificently philosophical as the greatest enterprise of his life swiftly became a prison of self-humiliation," he wrote. "But God was testing him, and John passed magnificently." Having said that, Black voted for the Tories, mostly, he says, out of loyalty to his old school pal John Bosley, who won in Don Valley West, and because he heard Geills Turner on election morning urging some American tourists to vote for Walter Mondale for U.S. President. (Black helpfully pointed out that not many did, as Ronald Reagan won forty-nine states six weeks later.)

Jerry Grafstein sent Turner a post-election, handwritten note, opening with a flourish. "Never have I shared the traumatic experience of such a swift roller-coaster ride of raw emotion—running the gamut from exhilaration, dismay, frustration, anguish, yet finally fooling the fates," he wrote. Referring to Turner's win in Quadra, Grafstein wrote, "You fooled the Greek chorus wanting to chant a tragedy."

Hoping to pick up his friend's spirits, Grafstein added, "Traumatic it was— tragic it is not!" He reminded Turner he still had his health and spirit intact. "These will stand you in good stead in the days ahead. De Gaulle said that leadership could only be forged in a crucible that overcame adversity. Your character has been tested and you refused to succumb."

Grafstein went on to remind Turner that plenty of leaders lost the first time out—Churchill, De Gaulle, Lenin, Diefenbaker, and Pearson—only to prevail in the end: "Keep the faith… we'll come back!!!"

Three days after election day in Ottawa, Turner met with Keith Davey, who advised him to get a new party director, principal secretary, and above all, some media training. According to Davey's memoir, the two had a heartfelt chat about Turner's future.

"Keith, can I ever be prime minister?" Turner asked.

"Yeah, John," Davey responded. "I think it's possible."

Turner pursued the issue. "The morning we had breakfast when you took over the campaign, you told me I could win the election."

"John," Davey confessed, "I had everything crossed but my eyes. What on earth was I going to say to my leader in the middle of a campaign?"

"How do I know you're not lying to me now?" Turner asked.

"I don't have to kid anybody now, least of all you," Davey said. "Mike Pearson came back and so can you."

No doubt, Davey was telling his leader what he wanted and needed to hear, but the example he gave was instructive. Pearson too was considered a star catch as leader, having won the Nobel Peace Prize and been one of the country's finest diplomats and external affairs ministers. But his first election as leader was a debacle, collateral damage in the 1958 Dief sweep. However, five years later, he was prime minister. Would Mulroney self-destruct as Diefenbaker had? Turner wanted to stick around and find out, while at the same time continue rebuilding the Liberal Party as promised.

The Turner–Davey relationship had hit the rocks during the campaign and wouldn't improve as time went by. "Turner couldn't stand him at the end and Davey knifed him so much that Turner wouldn't even attend his funeral," says former Turner staffer Marc Kealey. "And Turner went to *everyone's* funeral."

It's true: Turner thought funerals were important and instructive. "They're the best places to see who really cares," he'd say. But he wouldn't attend Davey's. "If I went," he told Kealey, "I'd be play-acting."

A week after election day, the elite of Montreal society gathered at the Montreal Museum of Fine Arts for the wedding of Jackie Desmarais' daughter. Dinah Shore was there providing entertainment. Turner's sister Brenda Norris was there as well. On her way up to the second floor to use the powder room, who should be coming down those same stairs but her friend, Canada's next prime minister, Brian Mulroney.

"I congratulated him on the election victory," Brenda recalls. "I put my hands on his shoulders and told him he fought a wonderful campaign."

Mulroney, not missing a beat, told her he'd called his campaign manager on election night, asking: "How could you lose Quadra?" Mulroney said the answer came back: "It was that goddamned sister of his!"

"He made me feel like a million bucks," Brenda says. "He's got a big Irish heart."

Turner had run into a buzzsaw of problems, some of his making, but some not. He could never match the expectations that greeted his return from the private sector. Close confidantes were giving him conflicting advice far too often. The Liberal fortress in Quebec deserted him, starting immediately after the French debate, when Mulroney outflanked him on French-language rights. Fully a quarter of Quebecers no longer defined themselves as lifelong Liberals in the ten days after that debate. Once the polls started to fall, the narrative was set and there seemed to be nothing he could do to stanch the bleeding. The English language leaders' debate was a disaster. And in Brian Mulroney, he was going up against an opponent who was as formidable a leader as the country had seen in half a century, maybe more.

"His gracious and articulate nationally televised comments in accepting our party's defeat was a character lesson for losers," wrote Donald Johnston in *Up the Hill*.

Walter Gordon, who was finance minister during Turner's time as a Liberal backbencher in the 1960s, wrote to Turner to tell him "You showed great guts and that is what we need more of in this country." But Gordon didn't leave it there. "One day, I may say this to Pierre Trudeau. He is the one who is responsible for our eclipse."

Charles Baird, the Chairman and CEO of Inco, echoed that thought in his post-election letter to Turner. "The blame is not yours but falls on your arrogant predecessor who exacerbated your already difficult position by handing the Tories the patronage issue," Baird wrote.

But not all Liberals were mourning. In Ontario, the relatively new leader of the provincial Liberals, David Peterson, the same Peterson whose potential shot at government nine years earlier may have been foiled by Turner's resignation as finance minister, saw a silver lining.

"When Mulroney won in 1984, I knew we could win the next election," he says, despite the fact that the Tories had owned Queen's Park since 1943. "I just thought, if a sure winner could lose, then we could win. Things are in a state of flux. I felt very strongly about that."

Trudeau's unpopularity had helped contribute to a situation where there were no provincial Liberal governments anywhere in Canada. None. Peterson was adamant at the time that the Liberals' losing federally opened the door to possibilities for him and his fellow Ontario Liberals.

He turned out to be right. Nine months later, he ended the forty-two-year-long Progressive Conservative dynasty in Ontario and formed the country's only Liberal government. Turner sent personal letters to each of the members of Peterson's cabinet, congratulating them on their new responsibilities. Rookie minister Greg Sorbara was one of those who received a Turner note.

"How very nice of him," Sorbara now says recalling the gesture. "All the more so given I went with Mr. Chrétien in the 1984 leadership, my very first political convention."

The election results meant Turner would be starting a new chapter in his life, as leader of the opposition. And the kids who put their hearts and souls into backing him made a decision election night.

"We made a pact at what we'd do going forward," explains David Herle. "We wanted him to be successful. We were going to fight for him as leader. We'd have his back."

Turner would need that and more because the next four years would represent a non-stop roller coaster ride that would destroy any other mere mortal. However, immediately after losing the 1984 election, he first had a miserable responsibility to perform. The family's dog Misty was dying and needed to be put down. As soon as the election was over, Turner did what needed to be done.

"He told me that putting the dog down was worse than losing the election," Geills remembers. "That's a very telling statement."

CHAPTER FOURTEEN

The Leader of Her Majesty's Loyal Opposition

THANK GOODNESS FOR CHARLES TUPPER.

Bill Lee had warned John Turner that if things didn't change, he'd be the shortest-serving prime minister ever. Lee wasn't far off. When Brian Mulroney was sworn in as Canada's eighteenth prime minister on September 17, 1984, it brought an end to Turner's brief term as PM after just seventy-nine days. Only Tupper's sixty-nine days in 1896 was shorter.

Pope John Paul II came to Canada on September 9. Technically, Turner was still prime minister, as Mulroney's swearing-in date was still eight days away. But Turner invited his successor to join him at his side in greeting the Pope anyway. In his memoir, Mulroney confessed to being "touched by the gesture," but he declined. While describing Turner as "ever gracious," Mulroney added, "the country only has one prime minister at a time."

Five days after becoming prime minister, Mulroney met with Queen Elizabeth II in Moncton, New Brunswick. It could have, and maybe *should* have been Turner's meeting, but the snap election call ended that possibility. Mulroney revealed a snippet of his conversation with the Queen in his memoir. She apparently told him about her summer meeting at Windsor Castle with Turner, when he came to urge cancellation of her scheduled trip to Canada. The Queen said Turner told her he felt he had no mandate to govern, hence the fast election call. I don't know whether the Queen violated protocol by referring to a private conversation with one prime minister to his successor, nor do I know whether Mulroney violated protocol by describing his private conversation with the Queen in his book. Regardless, it confirms the oft-heard story about Turner that he simply felt illegitimate serving on Trudeau's mandate, and felt he needed to establish one of his own.

There's one thing about leading Canada's natural governing party: they love you win-or-tie. Losing is not tolerated. Turner once spoke of the internationally respected Lester Pearson facing his own cabinet mutiny when Pearson was able to win only two minority governments but never a majority. Pearson left the country's top political job after just five years. So when Turner became the man at the helm of the party's worst showing ever, it didn't take long for the knives to come out.

"Our party is very unforgiving," says John Webster, one of Turner's young advisers at the time.

Turner had another reality to deal with. Mulroney was successful in large part because the man he defeated for the PC leadership, Joe Clark, had put aside his personal ambition to help the bigger cause: party unity. However, the guy whom Turner had defeated for the leadership never stopped wanting to be the leader. Not only that, but Jean Chrétien was convinced that he could have defeated Mulroney and kept the Liberals in power, had delegates chosen him at the convention earlier that year.

Even though rookie MP Sergio Marchi had backed Chrétien at the leadership convention, he never believed that. He told Chrétien he was lucky to have lost the leadership, otherwise it would have been he, Chrétien, taking the historic pounding instead of Turner. Chrétien disagreed.

"I'd have beaten Mulroney," he told Marchi.

"Not a chance," Marchi insisted. "Maybe you'd have won more than forty seats, but you wouldn't have won. When the herd wants to change, you can spit loonies upside down and people won't be impressed."

Having said that, Marchi felt Canadians were deprived of a classic showdown: Mulroney vs. Chrétien, two Quebec heavyweights going toe-to-toe. It was never to be.

As far as Webster was concerned, the Turner–Chrétien competition never ended. "Whenever you're the losing ticket on a leadership, you don't go away, you just plan to overthrow the incumbent and that was certainly well in hand in '84," he said on The Herle Burly podcast in the summer of 2021.

In his memoir, Sen. Leo Kolber confirmed the only way Turner was going to keep the troops loyal was to win. "It was a naked power thing," he wrote. "When [Turner] didn't do that, they felt little loyalty to him. And he wasn't very good, so he didn't deserve it."

Having said that, Turner found generosity in unexpected places. His fellow British Columbia MP John Fraser, a Progressive Conservative from Vancouver South, sent Turner a lovely note after the election and Fraser's own appointment as fisheries minister. "I'm glad you won Quadra because I have always been fond of you and hold you in high regard," he wrote, signing off, "God bless, John."

But Turner never thought of himself as a quitter. Ever since his track and field days in the 1940s, he'd been determined and competitive. He'd also seen Pearson torn up in the 1958 election, only to become prime minister five years later. "The gold ring slipped through his fingers and he was determined to get it back" is how Eleanor McMahon, one of Turner's communications advisers and a future Ontario cabinet minister, put it. "He felt the burden of people's expectations and not living up to them."

It may have been a small caucus with not much loyalty to the leader, but Turner was determined to change that. He regularly took one-on-one meetings with caucus members, believing, as one of his advisers said, "that caucus members had the right to talk to their leader and caucus colleague." Turner wanted to bring the different factions of the party together and took risks to make it happen. He created a new role of general secretary and gave the job to one of Chrétien's closest colleagues, David Collenette.

"Collenette had roots in the party and a good policy mind," says one of Turner's former senior advisers. "John's thought was, he wanted to show he wasn't differentiating between his supporters and Chrétien's supporters. He saw mileage in trying to rebuild the Liberal Party and that it was a big tent."

One of the intriguing subplots of the thirty-third Parliament was that one of the Progressive Conservative MPs from Alberta was none other than Turner's wife's brother, David Kilgour, who'd been an MP since 1979. But perhaps not surprisingly, the two brothers-in-law saw very little of each other.

"There wasn't a lot of hanging out as MPs," says Kilgour. "Everyone misinterprets here. It's a very crazy spin town." (Kilgour eventually became disenchanted with the Tories, sat as an independent, then crossed the floor to the Liberals in 1990, but only after Turner was no longer leader, so it could never be said that his brother-in-law poached him.)

Mulroney said in his memoir that he consulted with Turner on potential nominees for Speaker of the House and that he put Kilgour's name forward. But Turner apparently wasn't comfortable with the idea, which Mulroney then dropped. Kilgour died in April 2022 at age 81.

As Leader of Her Majesty's loyal opposition, Turner had to say goodbye to numerous advisers and come up with shadow posts for his thirty-nine other MPs. He gave the House leader's job to his long-time friend Herb Gray, who had thought of quitting politics altogether. Gray left a legal career after only six months to go into politics, had now been an MP for twenty-four years and wondered whether there wasn't something better out there for him. But Turner convinced him to stay.

Moving from the prime minister's office to the opposition leader's office meant many lost jobs among the faithful. Those that stayed with Turner tended to be younger and determined to help him rebuild the party after its worst show-ing ever. Stephen Hastings got his start in Ontario Progressive Conservative pol-itics, as his mother worked for the legendary Bette Stephenson, a medical doctor who became the province's first ever female labour minister, colleges and uni-versities minister, and finance minister. But while on the University of Toronto student council in the early 1980s, Hastings met Turner through Hart House warden Richard Alway; by 1984 he was working on Turner's leadership cam-paign. He spent election night in Vancouver Quadra and on the way back east, was offered a spot on the Ontario desk in the opposition leader's office. Turner loved nothing more than being on the road with his young staffers and calling their parents. "He'd take the phone at a restaurant and say, 'I'm giving your boy a steak; I'm feeding your boy!'" Hastings recalls.

"My best memories of working for John Turner were the road trips," says Kaz Flinn, another of the twenty-somethings staffing the opposition leader's office. "He treated me like a daughter. He was protective and gentlemanly." Flinn ran the Atlantic Canada desk and was in that region every June when both she and Turner had birthdays. "We'd have a Scotch," she says. "In fact, I had my first ever one with him. He'd wish me happy birthday in the lobby of a cheap hotel in northern New Brunswick. It was so great."

Turner also liked to walk around his opposition leader's office, dressed cas-ually in an old cardigan and stocking feet. "He was stealth-like," Hastings laughs. "You wouldn't hear him coming. Then, boom, he was there."

One day at Stornoway, Turner hosted a lunch for members of the Young Liberals' executive. Saskatchewan native David Herle was at the far end of the table and Turner, trotting out his best jock routine, would shout at Herle: "Hey Dave, this is pâté. Guys from Saskatchewan don't eat that shit!" Turner's attempt to establish a camaraderie in the room brought the house down.

Because Turner never sat in the House as prime minister, he hadn't taken a question period briefing from his staff since he was finance minister in 1975. He soon discovered that he *really* didn't like that part of the parliamentary calendar from the opposition perspective. His preference for compromise over confrontation made him look less than decisive as the attacker-in-chief. He disapproved of personal attacks in general and given that he had personal friendships with some government ministers, he found it particularly difficult to go for the jugular against them.

For example, in September 1985, Fisheries and Oceans Minister John Fraser came under fire for overruling inspectors and urging that tuna ruled unfit for human consumption be sold to the public. Fraser feared a massive recall of a million tins of tuna could force one of Atlantic Canada's most important employers into bankruptcy. The opposition had a field day with "Tunagate," but Turner didn't like it and declined to demand the minister's head.

"John Fraser and I are very good friends," Turner would tell people, noting their Vancouver-based ridings both shared a boundary with the NDP's Ian Waddell, who died in March 2021.

Fraser eventually resigned and his economic fears were realized. StarKist took a major reputational hit despite no one finding evidence that the tuna had caused any harm. Six years later, the company pulled out of Canada, putting 400 New Brunswickers out of work. But by then the opposition already had its pound of flesh. Turner truly disliked the part of politics that seemed to require destroying a fellow MP's career. (Fraser was fortunate; perhaps because of the unfair price he paid during Tunagate, he became the first ever elected Speaker of the House of Commons, from 1986 to 1993.)

In caucus, Turner had a kindred spirit in Raymond Garneau. Like his leader, Garneau gave up a high-powered job as chair and CEO of the Montreal City and District Savings Bank and CEO of Crédit Foncier in favour of what he hoped would be a senior role in a Turner cabinet. Now he was an opposition MP, took a huge pay cut, and was constantly fighting other Quebec MPs to be that province's lead political figure. Turner, convinced future victory would come with improved relations with the provinces, wanted Garneau to stay close with Quebec premier Robert Bourassa. Of course, that ran the risk of angering Chrétien. But Turner and Chrétien were on an unavoidable collision course.

Chrétien constantly felt marginalized, even as Turner tried to bring his rival's colleagues inside the tent.

Yet amidst all the Sturm Und Drang of Ottawa, some elements of civility remained. One day, Mulroney and Turner were chatting when the prime minister told the opposition leader that his wife Mila was raising money for cystic fibrosis research. Kids with CF often died by their twelfth birthdays, but thanks to medical improvements many could now expect to live into their forties and fifties. Shortly after, Mila received a letter at 24 Sussex Drive from Turner, congratulating her on the events she was mounting to raise millions of dollars for the cause.

"I mentioned it to John and that's the kind of thing he'd write to Mila about," says Mulroney. That may seem quaint by today's standards, but for John Turner, three-and-a-half decades ago, it's simply what a member of Parliament did.

On April 17, 1985, Turner demonstrated that civility again when he wrote to his colleague and rival Chrétien to mark the coming into force of Section 15 of the Charter of Rights and Freedoms, which Chrétien helped birth when he was Trudeau's justice minister.

"Your incredible success in bringing the Charter to life will guarantee fairness for generation upon generation of Canadians to come," Turner wrote in a private letter. "That you have succeeded so brilliantly as father of the Constitution is evidenced by the fact that everyone else is now claiming to be the parent!"

* * *

One of the most anticipated nights on Ottawa's political calendar is the parliamentary press gallery dinner, in which the politicians and media agree to sheathe their swords for an evening and tell some jokes at each other's expense. Everyone was expecting Turner to display a self-deprecating sense of humour and he didn't disappoint.

"I've been told to be successful at this event, you just tell jokes about some of the unfortunate things that have happened to you over the past few months," he began. "Sit back. Relax. Get comfortable. We have a lot of ground to cover in the next three hours."

Turner concluded his monologue with: "This evening will be remembered as an historic occasion. My presence allows you to boast to your children and grandchildren, because if it is true that we learn from our mistakes, you have just dined with the smartest man in Canada."

The following year's dinner featured a Turner who felt more comfortable taking a few shots at Mulroney. "Prime Minister, you have often said you were going to slap a paternity suit on me as being the Father of the Deficit. Many people ask me, John, how do you respond? I just tell them, in questions of illegitimacy, don't look at me. I'm not the bastard who is raising your taxes—he is!" Another gag focused on his prime challenger to the Liberal throne: "It's not that some of my caucus wants to be led by Jesus Christ. They just want somebody with the same initials." Or this one referencing the next election: "The *Toronto Star* has already prepared its headline for the morning after the next election: Turner wins election majority; Liberal caucus demands recount."

However, it wasn't all fun and games. What happened next within the demoralized Liberal caucus was unexpected and unprecedented. The Mulroney government had its own scandals and a handful of Liberal MPs decided to stick the knife in and twist it in a way Canadians hadn't seen before. Brian Tobin, Sheila Copps, Don Boudria, and John Nunziata created a self-styled "Rat Pack," which used increasingly aggressive and outrageous techniques to attack Mulroney and his ministers. Copps even famously leapt across a table at a committee meeting to interrogate and badger a minister under investigation. At first, Turner kept his distance from the Rat Pack, no doubt because their tactics went far beyond anything he would normally have sanctioned. But the group's efforts caught on. They even had T-shirts made up and one day, Turner put one on. The prime minister took note.

"I watched Turner change from being clearly embarrassed by such misconduct to countenancing it to encouraging it to embracing it," Mulroney wrote in his memoir. "One day, he put on a Rat Pack T-shirt, thereby as leader of the opposition publicly condoning such grave misbehavior. The next day I told my caucus, John Turner had just forfeited any chance of ever again becoming prime minister–that eventually Canadians would scorn such grotesque unparliamentary behavior and all those associated with it."

Unfortunately for Mulroney, his own government's missteps provided plenty of fuel for the Rat Pack, whose popularity continued to grow. And Turner couldn't have been blind to the fact that the tactics seemed to perk up Liberal morale, which increased his confidence as well.

As 1985 came to an end, Liberals gathered in Halifax in November for a convention that would in effect begin a year-long process culminating with a vote on whether Turner should remain as leader. The 1984 election results, combined with doubts as to whether Turner had the ability to turn things around, contributed to a malaise in the party, which Turner's allies feared could see him jettisoned as leader in 1986. A strong performance by Turner in Halifax was crucial to getting the leadership review process off to a positive start.

"Everybody was there, including Jean Chrétien," recalls David Herle. Chrétien was happy to remind people that if Turner didn't have the goods, a ready-to-go alternative was waiting in the wings. But on that November evening in Halifax, Turner *did* have the goods.

"He gave such a great speech," Herle says. "It was a combination of the greatest speech and a relief that he'd given it so well. He had people standing on their chairs, waving napkins. It was the first thing worth cheering for in months."

The applause and the cheering went on, and on, and on.

Turner wasn't anti-American, as his close relationship with Richard Nixon and George Schultz proved. He was a guest speaker at Nixon's eightieth birthday party. But he was wary of the Americans and in particular, a recommendation from Donald S. Macdonald to take a "leap of faith" on negotiating a Free Trade Agreement with the United States Macdonald had been tasked by Mulroney to chair a royal commission on the economy and Turner's successor as finance minister surprised many when he urged free trade negotiations.

"We enjoy this special community called Canada," Turner said to increasing applause in Halifax. "And even though it costs us a little more money to remain as Canadians, the price of being Canadian is a price worth paying!"

Then, seizing on Macdonald's most famous quote associated with his report, Turner added: "Donald, you want us to take a leap of faith. That is too big a jump. Unless we know where we are going to land, that is too big a jump!"

When Schultz got wind of Turner's views, he was disappointed at his friend's "bizarre twist."

But in Halifax, the room was in a frenzy. Turner got a standing ovation that lasted more than half an hour. He was finally able to deliver with passion and sincerity, without the distracting lip smacking, nervous laugh, and throat clearing. And the party was desperate to show the country how unified it was. Even Chrétien had to walk over to the Liberal leader and acknowledge his triumph with a handshake, which caused even more bedlam.

It was a night for the ages. The question was: could Turner's allies keep the afterglow burning brightly enough to get him through next year's leadership review? Mulroney's problems were starting to make many Canadians wonder whether he was re-electable. But there was no doubt in the prime minister's mind about how he'd vote in a Liberal leadership review if he could.

"As for John Turner, God bless him, I hope they keep him," Mulroney wrote in his memoir. "He's our biggest ally."

As it turned out, the glow from Halifax didn't last. Turner and Chrétien continued on their collision course, eventually meeting at Stornoway on February 4, 1986. Chrétien had hoped Turner would offer him the Quebec lieutenant's role he so desired at that meeting, but it didn't happen. The two men thought they'd agreed on a compromise candidate for party president in former cabinet minister Francis Fox, who'd lost his Quebec seat in the 1984 election. But the day after the meeting, Turner called Fox and asked him to stand down; Chrétien only found out after the fact and not from the leader.

On February 27, all the goodwill generated only a few months earlier in Halifax officially evaporated. Chrétien personally handed his resignation letter to Turner, in effect, doing to Turner what Turner had done to Trudeau back in 1975. For Chrétien, it brought an end to a twenty-three-year-long career in federal politics, although few people believed Chrétien was truly done. The move had "strategic retreat" written all over it.

Later that day, Turner informed the House of the development, saying he was shocked, that the country, the party, and the leader still needed Chrétien in public life, and that he had tried to convince the MP for Saint-Maurice to stay. In a letter sent to Chrétien later that day, Turner fibbed big time but tried to put a positive spin on developments, saying his rival's "support, your loyalty, and advice were invaluable. Jean, I very much regret your decision."

Chrétien would now cool his heels, as Turner had, at a Bay Street law firm (Lang Michener) and consider his next moves towards capturing the Liberal leadership he still coveted.

CHAPTER FIFTEEN

The Marriage

FEW PRIME MINISTERIAL SPOUSES IN Canadian history have evinced such polarized and powerful reactions as Geills McCrae Kilgour Turner.

So, I confess to having felt a certain amount of trepidation when I got off the elevator at the Turner's midtown Toronto apartment building, only to find a black miniature poodle greeting me as the doors opened. Fortunately, Brodie was very friendly and led me around the corner to the apartment, where a now eighty-three-year-old Geills Turner was waiting for me.

I greeted Mrs. Turner with a piece of political trivia.

"You know what today is, eh?" I asked. She looked back at me, understandably not as fixated on facts and dates as I. It was September 10, 2021.

"It was forty-six years ago today that your husband resigned as Canada's finance minister," I told her.

"I'd forgotten," she responded. "I'm a factoid illiterate."

I've met Geills Turner a few times over the years, the first time during the 1984 federal election campaign, but we'd never had what you'd call a long chat. On this day, however, we had an almost three-hour, wide-ranging conversation about her background, how she met her husband, motherhood, her husband's political career, her controversial reputation, the horrifically tragic past twelve months of her life, and what occupied her time these days.

One of the most important things to know about Geills Turner that sets her apart from other prime ministerial spouses is that she was probably born a couple of decades too early. Despite being born a woman in Manitoba in 1937, she still somehow managed a post-secondary life that included McGill, Harvard/Radcliffe, the University of Toronto School of Architecture, and then three decades later, Toronto Metropolitan University (then known as Ryerson), where she spent four years pursuing her passion for photography and getting a degree in photo arts.

Had her time at IBM in her twenties taken place in the 1980s or 1990s instead of the 1950s and 1960s, she undoubtedly would have been on a corporate trajectory that would have looked immeasurably different from the life she ended up leading. Look at Jill Biden, the wife of U.S. President Joe Biden. Born only fourteen years after Geills, she continues to have her own independent career as an English professor, despite being married to a senator, vice-president, and now the forty-sixth president of the United States.

Such options were not available to Geills Kilgour. When she married John Turner in 1963, she was expected to set her career aspirations aside, be the primary caregiver to the couple's children, manage the family's home life, and accommodate her husband's career, wherever that took them. And that's what she did. Sometimes happily, sometimes not.

"She was born fifty years too early," says a family friend. "She gave up her career. She had four kids and did a great job raising them. But in today's world, she would not have been a stay-at-home mother, and I think she was frustrated with that."

Elizabeth Turner, her eldest child, says, "If not for politics, she might have considered going to work. She's an amazing photographer. She edits old photographs. She's got eight hard drives full of pictures. When she talks to Apple Tech Support, she has to escalate the conversation immediately because no one knows how to deal with this eighty-three-year-old who knows things they don't."

What is Geills Turner like? Christina McCall-Newman describes her this way in her landmark book *Grits:* "She was good looking, athletic, well connected, well educated, quick witted, post grad at Harvard. Financial analyst in Montreal. Four kids in short order. Perfect examples of the beautiful people of Rockcliffe."

In his book *A Life in Progress*, Conrad Black described Geills as his "courtesy cousin," because she was Black's father's goddaughter. "To the day he died," Black writes, "he had a photograph of her having a glass of Champagne on her twenty-first birthday on the bureau of his bedroom." Black knew both Turners from the time John was first elected in 1962, because he was a freshman at Carleton University in Ottawa. However, as the years went on, Black writes the relationship ended over Geills "frequently exasperating people with her peremptory manner. I always defended her against all comers until I suddenly became the victim of one of her neurotically ill-tempered outbursts when she effectively dis-invited me from John's sixtieth birthday party in 1989. My championship of her became rather more muted after that."

"She doesn't suffer fools gladly," acknowledges Elizabeth. "She's highly intelligent, well-read, informed about what's going on in the world. She has opinions that are clear cut and informed. She's an amazing conversationalist when she's engaged, and she's interested in many things. She often had to carry the conversations when my dad ran out of steam."

Liz is also candid enough to recognize another trait in her mother. "I'm not sure she enjoyed being a full-time mother," she says. "She's not the most maternal of people. She's an amazing grandmother. She'd hold babies and coo, but babysitting? Not particularly. My Dad at one point said, 'There's gonna be no goddamned babysitting here. This isn't a drop-off centre!'"

With John already an MP at the time of the couple's wedding, Geills says she and her husband had no pre-ordained plan or understanding of how long John intended to stay in politics. The reality of caring for young children and being a political wife left little time to ponder bigger, more existential questions. Having said that, Geills' ambition was evident when she asked the law school at the University of Ottawa to admit her as a student. "It would be following in the footsteps of various relatives," she points out. But with young children and her husband's career being very full-time responsibilities, Geills wondered whether she could be a part-time student. The answer came back: no, you cannot.

"That was game over," she says ruefully.

In 1968, when her husband ran for the Liberal leadership the first time, Geills was on board.

"Why not give it a go?" she remembers thinking at the time. "He had this incredible sense of service, he'd been a track star, he was very competitive, so if you're in there and have been minister of justice, why not?"

Turner came third at the convention but clearly established in delegates' minds the notion that he was Prime Minister Pierre Trudeau's heir apparent.

Despite the head-to-head competition at the convention, Trudeau and Turner actually got along well personally and professionally at this stage of the game. Trudeau was still single at this point and occasionally needed a helping hand with his social life. For example, every year, industrialist Charles Rathgeb would have a big Grey Cup party (Rathgeb owned Comstock International Ltd, a mechanical and electrical construction company). In 1970, with the big game in Toronto, Trudeau wanted to go to the party after performing the ceremonial opening kickoff but was too shy to ask.

"Any chance you can get me invited?" he asked Geills. And she did.

"I introduced him to people," she recalls. "John did too. It was very interesting to watch him operate. He was extremely intellectual and impatient." Geills shepherded Trudeau through the party and ran interference for him when the conversations got too boring.

Trudeau married Margaret Sinclair in 1971 and the couple, like the Turners before them, immediately started a family. The couple's first child, Justin, was born on Christmas Day.

In fact, the night before Justin's birth, Trudeau called Geills and asked whether John was going to midnight mass. Geills confirmed that he was. Trudeau said his very pregnant wife didn't want to go to a French church and so Trudeau wondered whether the couple could tag along with John?

"Yes, indeed," came the reply. John called his priest and gave him the heads-up that a special guest would be coming. "Put aside a couple of seats at the back for the Mounties, but don't make a fuss" were Turner's orders.

Geills stayed home that Christmas Eve organizing the presents for the next day, while the others went to church. After Justin was born on December 25, she called Pierre and asked whether he wanted to come for Christmas dinner.

"I've got a tortière in the fridge, so I think I'll be fine," came the response.

"We always got along well," Geills says of her friend. "I've got pictures of Justin Trudeau playing on our living room floor with Margaret and me when Andrew was less than a year old."

However, Turner's resignation as finance minister in 1975 put an end to the couples' friendship. As Turner began a new career as a Bay Street lawyer, it was left to Geills to organize the family's move to Toronto and get the kids enrolled in new schools. She confirms she always assumed her husband's time in public life was over.

The Toronto years from 1976 to 1984 were great ones for the Turners. John was earning extremely well from his work at McMillan Binch, plus all his directorships. The family had a wonderful home in Forest Hill, one of the city's most luxurious neighbourhoods. Turner became famous for holding court at Winston's restaurant. And the family enjoyed it all while not living under the relentless microscope of a life in politics.

It was at this time that the canoe trips to the far north began. Geills also went to the Arctic on her own on two occasions to an elders' conference in the

Northwest Territories. She took myriad pictures of the proceedings including wonderful portraits of the elders. She offered the pictures to Toronto Metropolitan University (then known as Ryerson) but "nobody wanted them." This was four decades ago, well before most Canadians were interested in learning more about Indigenous Canada.

But politics always knocked at the door. When Trudeau temporarily stepped aside after losing to Joe Clark's Progressive Conservatives in 1979, there were early attempts to get Turner back into public life. But Turner pushed back and declined to seek the Liberal leadership. Just as well, since Trudeau came out of retirement and won the ensuing election in 1980, after the Clark government's unexpected early fall.

But as the prime minister's popularity tanked, politics came knocking on the Turners' door again. As the pressure to return to public life became more and more intense, Geills remembers having many questions. For example, if her husband did return to politics, Turner would be taking something in the order of an 80 per cent pay cut. All the Turner children were either in or soon going to universities, a couple of them hugely expensive American ones.

"How was all that going to work?" Geills remembers thinking at the time. "My mind was going a million miles an hour."

Plus, there was Ottawa. Geills loved her life in Toronto: the variety, the friends, being out of the spotlight, the cultural attractions, all of it.

"Ottawa is a one industry town," she thought. "You're either in it or not. I had good friends there [in the 1960s and '70s]. But to go back again would not have been my first choice."

When Trudeau officially announced his departure in 1984, the Turners were on a beach in Jamaica on vacation.

"Suddenly there were press people on the beach, asking John whether he was going to run," Geills recalls.

And what was Geills thinking?

"What the fuck is this?" she says, still bewildered by the scene nearly four decades later. "That brought the matter right to a head."

All of Turner's advisers knew Geills would be hugely influential in getting John to "yes." Given that she wasn't thrilled with the notion of a return to public life, why did she eventually consent?

"Did I have a choice?" she now asks rhetorically. "I think I'm a good sport. I'll go along with whatever's going on. It's a challenge. If that's what he wanted, then who am I to stand in his way? I didn't try to convince him not to do it."

The Turners were back in. But Geills was not about to play the part of the stereotypical politician's wife. As Greg Weston noted in his book *Reign of Error*, Geills "had no plans to be the subservient wife, standing one step behind her man, smiling adoringly at the mic."

Robin Sears, a political backroom veteran of many decades, mostly for the NDP, always reminded the young political staffers he was advising: "Be sure to make 'the spouse' your ally early, or there will be certain tears later."

Geills says she didn't have to wait long to be reminded of the things she hated about politics. It started with Jean Chrétien's right-hand man.

"The most staggering moment of the whole '84 leadership campaign was when John [won], and I stepped off the stage [after his speech], and Eddie Goldenberg tapped me on the shoulder and said: 'We're going to get you.' Right off the stage! He would destabilize John at every step of the road."

(For the record, Goldenberg disputes everything about this account. "It's total bullshit," he says. "Totally made up." Goldenberg says he's had precisely one encounter with Geills his entire life. It was at the 2006 Liberal leadership convention which chose Stephane Dion. "I was walking on the convention floor when I tripped a little bit. Turns out, I tripped on her foot. She said to me, 'Eddie, you didn't have to kick me.' That's the extent of my interactions with her.")

Everybody had an opinion about Geills once the Turners were back in public life. There were no fence sitters. People either thought she was a strong, smart spouse, offering shrewd advice as she looked out for her husband's interests, or a complete nightmare who was impossible to manage. Sometimes people felt both of those things simultaneously.

"She was very vocal, which was hard for the staff," admits Liz. "It's not that she was difficult, but she couldn't stand to see some of the stuff going on behind the scenes. And she had better instincts about people than my dad. She was a good adviser. Sometimes adamant. My job was to try to calm my mom down when she got so pissed off at something going on with the political team."

"The role of a political spouse is a tough role," adds Stephen Hastings, who worked in Turner's office. "She had an opinion and expressed it in great form. She was massively frustrated at the beating he was taking. Ultimately, she was very protective of him."

Geills herself doesn't necessarily dispute the notion that she could be a handful for her husband's staff.

"You've gotta remember, I'm an anal systems-engineer," she begins. "I really want to get in and fix their problems. It's ridiculous but that's the way I'm wired.

So, if I'm on a campaign and I'm not stupid and I see things not going in my husband's best interests, then I probably was vocal about how it could have been improved."

Richard Mackie, who worked both in Turner's PMO and his opposition leader's office, recalls one of the awkward things Geills had to deal with.

"I don't think she was a nightmare or a nasty person at all," Mackie says. "When your husband is patting women on the ass on national TV and spending time with beautiful women… He was making big money at McMillan Binch and she was having a great time and suddenly they're back in a miserable house, 24 Sussex, and then Stornoway. The people I know who worked closely with Geills really liked her."

Another Turner political adviser says: "It's not fair to say she's not a nice person. But can she express her opinion in a very forceful way? Yes. Did it impact on John? Yeah, it did. But he got better at it."

Another Turner adviser from back in the day: "There are always challenges working with the spouse of a leader or cabinet minister," he says. "She has some strong ideas. And she's an incredibly intelligent woman. She wanted what was best for John. She also recognized that people were trying to do their best on his behalf. I respected her opinions."

Geills admits to having been worried about the timing of her husband's political comeback. "The Liberals had been in power way too long," she says. "If you looked at the writing on the wall, you'd think it'd take a magician to pull it off." But she adds, despite the odds against success, "That tells you a lot about John. That gives you the measure of the man. You suck it up. It won't be a life-defeating moment."

Geills says her husband spent a lifetime overcoming setbacks and disappointments, everything from the premature death of his father to an injury that kept him out of the Olympics. "His sense of public duty was profound and the idea of not winning the election wouldn't have been a deal breaker," she says. "If someone told him he stood a 30–70 chance of losing, those are bad odds, but he'd have said, if it's in the interests of the country, I'll do it. He was that kind of guy. He answered the call."

Having said all that, Geills' numerous displays of temper have been well documented in previous books. Jean Riley, who was Louis St. Laurent's granddaughter, has spoken of putting her own baggage tags on Geills' luggage during election campaigns, so that when airport workers saw the tags, they wouldn't "lose" or destroy Geills' luggage. It all stemmed from an episode when Geills dressed down some flight attendants during a campaign flight.

Turner apparently incurred the wrath of his staff because he taught his wife how to read the code on the bottom of small, six-ounce Coke bottles, so she could see how recently the beverages had been bottled. As a result, Geills insisted Turner's staff provide small, recently filled Coke bottles at each hotel stop. One time in Halifax, Geills entered her hotel room, saw the wrong sized bottles, and apparently demanded her husband's staff replace them with the size she preferred. Someone was dispatched to do so.

On another occasion, Turner was in Question Period, primed to ask the first question and begin the House of Commons' daily theatre. Suddenly, his chief of staff Peter Connolly grabbed someone in the office, telling him to get Turner out of the House immediately. What was the crisis? Geills Turner was out walking the dog when it got hit by a car. In the days before cell phones, it was logistically complicated getting that message to Turner, who was preparing to bear down on the Mulroney government. Geills kept calling the opposition leader's office, demanding updates on whether Turner was on his way home to help with the dog situation. Connolly was on the receiving end of the calls and held the phone far away from his ear as Geills repeatedly demanded to know what was happening. When the call ended, in a comment that doesn't reflect well on the leader's chief of staff, Connolly said: "You know, that car got the wrong bitch."

"I don't think I was very good at politics," Geills now says. "I'm a very private person. I could talk to a postal worker for two hours and do it well, but how would I feel after that? I'd have to go to bed for two days. It could become very fatiguing for me. But I did enjoy my own little tour."

Turner was suffering from constant, chronic back pain during the elections in which he led the Liberals, particularly the second one in 1988. That, plus the party's sinking fortunes, and managing tensions between the campaign team and his wife, was an enormous amount for the leader to juggle.

"He lived in fear of his wife" is how Will McDonough, who worked in the leader's office, put it. "His driver would pick him up and he'd ask, 'What kind of mood is she in?'"

Another prominent former politician from back in the day remembers being asked to introduce Turner at an event. As he prepared to mount the stage to do so, Turner leaned over and whispered, "Say something nice about Geills." Turner well understood his wife's unhappiness with politics and hoped a few kind words would help soften her up.

Something that no doubt contributed to Geills' dislike of John's second go-round in politics was the unprecedented lack of loyalty so many Liberals demonstrated to her husband.

"I have a lot of sadness over how badly he was treated by his own party," she says. "It was appalling, appalling, appalling. They were stabbing him in the back the whole time." When I ask whether she had any conversations with Chrétien about any of this, Geills shuts the door. "I'm not going to get into that."

Who knows how much of this contributed to Geills' foul mood at what was supposed to be a Liberal gathering billed as "An evening with John and Geills Turner"? But something happened in the couple's hotel room as they were set to go down for the event and Geills decided at the last minute not to attend. Everyone was disappointed. One of Turner's staffers later asked him, "Why don't you just divorce her?"

His answer: "Because marriage is for life." Turner's staunch Catholicity would permit no other considerations.

In fact, the "Geills problem" became so intense that several senior Liberals had a meeting about whether they could stage an intervention with Turner and urge him to divorce his wife. It was Keith Davey that was the impetus behind the idea, which emerged from his own marital experience. Davey told numerous people he was unhappily married the first time, "but I'm so much better off since I remarried."

By contrast, the more traditional marriage the Chrétiens had was ideal for politics. Jean's political career was the project and Aline did everything she could to support it. "They were rock solid," says a former Turner staffer. "Mr. Chrétien's body was a temple. Mr. Turner's was an amusement park." This adviser points out Aline provided a stable, loving environment for her husband and the result was "a supremely, self-confident leader when it came to decision-making." Conversely, this source says, "Mr. Turner's level of self-confidence was always in question. Someone who has self-confidence isn't swayed by the last person who comes through the door."

However, what Turner's allies who were urging divorce failed to understand was that, despite their travails, John and Geills Turner were devoted to each other in their own way. For Turner, marriage was a solemn contract you just didn't break under any circumstances. And yet, interestingly, Turner was not judgmental or doctrinaire when it came to his own children on this issue. Three of the four Turner kids married (Michael never did), and all three of their first marriages ended in divorce.

However, he was less accepting when his friend and former Liberal back-room pal Jan Innes informed him that she was getting a divorce. "It was fine with me, but he was so concerned and upset when I did," Innes says. "After all, he maintained his marriage."

* * *

There's an old expression: "Politics is show business for ugly people." But John Turner gave the lie to this. When those baby blue eyes locked in on someone, male or female, it was impossible not to notice how unusually handsome Turner was and especially so for someone in politics.

Combine that with the fact that Ottawa lives on gossip and you may have some additional sympathy for Geills Turner's position. Her husband's good looks meant that he was often talked about in sexual terms.

Citizenship court Judge Yvonne Kerr, who died in 2016, once told Turner associate Marc Kealey: "He was so good looking. If he ever tripped and fell, I'd be underneath him before he ever hit the ground."

Shaughnessy Cohen, a Liberal MP in the 1990s who had a wicked sense of humor, found Turner so attractive she joked: "I *would* kick John Turner out of bed for eating crackers, so I could screw him on the floor."

Turner didn't exactly shut down talk about himself and other women. Ever since his dance with Princess Margaret in 1958, Turner's private life was fodder for political and media gossip. One day, with Turner well into his eighties, his great friend Arthur Milnes decided to summon up the courage to ask him about that evening with the princess. Milnes actually used the "F-word" when asking the question.

"Yes, I was that direct," Milnes recalls. Turner's answer was classic.

"I can't believe that you, Arthur, asked me that question," the former prime minister began. "You're an asshole, but okay, I'll give you an answer. Write this down. While I am not a kiss and tell guy, I'll say this: sometimes, Arthur, as Nelson said at Trafalgar, England does expect every man to do his duty!"

Milnes howled with laughter. "I will always treasure the memory of that answer," he says.

There were two other Princess Margaret stories, both of which originated during a trip she took to Ontario in 1985. David Peterson was the new premier, and members of his staff organized events in both Niagara-on-the-Lake and at Seneca College in Toronto. They invited the federal opposition leader John

Turner as well. In Niagara-on-the-Lake, Turner's special assistant for Ontario, Marc Kealey, was selected to accompany the leader on the trip. Both the RCMP and MI5 were on hand to provide security for "Whitey and Queenie," using the principals' code names. Turner told Kealey he needed two bottles of wine, one red and one white, plus two cigars. "Make sure all that shit is in my room," Turner said. When the princess arrived, Whitey and Queenie hugged in the lobby of the stately Princess of Wales Hotel, then were whisked up the elevator by security to a private room to enjoy their visit, the details of which remained with Turner.

When the princess went to an event at Seneca College, Jan Innes, who worked in Premier Peterson's office, remembers what happened when Turner walked in.

"Oh boy, did she light up!" Innes says.

On other occasions, Innes tried to get Turner to tell stories about the old days with the Kennedys. She says she tried to convince Turner to write the stories down, but he always refused. He did acknowledge spending time with Robert F. Kennedy and Marilyn Monroe and Innes couldn't help but ask: "Does that mean you spent personal time with her?"

Apparently, Turner wouldn't go there. "He was very cagey with me in his reply," she recalls. "But he didn't shut it down so I thought he may have."

Richard Alway recalls Turner quoting Martin Luther: "Sin greatly but repent more greatly." (The actual quote is more like: "Be a sinner and let your sins be strong but let your trust in Christ be stronger.") Turner flirted with the priesthood into his twenties, but his desire to flirt with women won out. Having said that, he loved, admired, and respected the four most important women in his life: his mother, his sister, his wife, and his daughter.

* * *

Media accounts from three-and-a-half decades ago were frequently highly critical of Geills and the role she played during the two campaigns of the 1980s. Geills admits to reading those accounts at the time but insists she wasn't debilitated by them.

"That's politics," she now says. "I don't think they like independent, outspoken, reasonably intelligent people, so that becomes irritating, particularly if they don't have access to you."

Lisa Haley, who spent twenty-five years on and around Parliament Hill doing issues management, including in Turner's opposition leader's office, says "Geills

Turner has never said or done anything out of line in my presence. In fact, when I'd offer to get coffee for her, she'd say, 'For heaven's sake, Lisa, you work for my husband. Look after him.'"

Historian and author Arthur Milnes, who bonded with Turner in 1995 when he was a reporter in the Northwest Territories, insists he's heard all the horror stories about Geills Turner, "But I have never met that woman. I've never in twenty years witnessed anything like that. She's been nothing but unfailingly gracious to me over the years. I've always had a soft spot for her." Milnes says he received a handwritten note from Geills in Christmas 2020, a few months after John died, pointing out how much her late husband enjoyed his phone calls with Art. "I've never been able to square the Geills Turner of legend with the Geills Turner I know," Milnes says.

Turner's long-time pal Alan Eagleson says, "It's easy to knock Geills Turner. But she was the strong horse in that household. I can tell you she was the glue that kept that family together." As to the people who thought the Turners ought to divorce: "They don't understand John and Geills if they say that. People always looked for the negative and ignored the positive."

For example, Eagleson says, when Turner would have too much to drink, Geills would say: "John Turner, no more wine."

"She may have been tough and abrasive but you can't say she was a bad wife," Eagleson says. "It may be the person she was obnoxious to deserved it. And we all get off the rails once in a while. If her name weren't Geills Turner, you'd never hear about it."

Sharon Sholzberg-Gray concurs. "I think they were very devoted to each other," she says. "An old-fashioned devotion."

Jerry Grafstein adds: "I think it was a good marriage because it lasted. Longevity is one of the tests of a great marriage."

The Turners were married from 1963 to 2020, fifty-seven years and four months.

CHAPTER SIXTEEN

The F-Bomb and the Booze

FORMER ONTARIO PREMIER BILL DAVIS was born on July 30, 1929, just seven weeks after John Turner. As a reporter, I covered Mr. Davis' last mandate at Queen's Park in the early 1980s and knew the man for almost four decades. I never, and I mean *never*, heard him use profanity. I knew Mr. Turner not as well and for not quite as long, and I never knew him *not* to use profanity. They were great friends, both cabinet ministers and first ministers at the same time, both moderate, pragmatic, and not political ideologues, but utterly different when it came to using the F-bomb or booze. John Turner loved a good drink. Bill Davis, while not the abstainer he was portrayed to be, might pour himself half a glass of wine over dinner, but then leave two-thirds of it untouched by dinner's end.

It may be strange to devote an entire chapter of a biography to cuss words. But they were an integral part of who Turner was, and his use of blue language at unexpected moments was both hilarious and wildly inappropriate, which made them even funnier. And he didn't mellow with age.

"What did Mr. Turner think of Donald Trump?" I asked Stephen Hastings, his former executive assistant.

"He thought he was a fucking asshole and said so," Hastings says. "He thought he was the personification of the worst aspects of politics."

Hastings recalls another occasion when someone, in Turner's presence, made a disparaging comment about Alan Eagleson, the former head of the NHL Players' Association, who went to jail in 1998 for fraud and embezzlement. Turner immediately pivoted and publicly admonished the person making the comment.

"He's my fucking friend," Turner said. "He made a mistake and I won't fucking hear any more of this. I'm not going to listen to a fucking word. I just don't want to fucking hear it."

Turner was nothing if not loyal to his friends. After Eagleson's sentence was over, Turner called him to say, "Eagle, we're having a lunch for you at the Senator Restaurant." Twelve friends showed up and it became an annual event. They called it the Freedom Lunch and invitees included Bill Davis, Paul Godfrey, Hal Jackman, Roy McMurtry, David Smith, Bud Estey, and Darcy McKeough.

"Gentlemen," Turner said, "I'm happy to see you all here. Whatever debt Alan Eagleson owed to society, if any, it has been paid in full."

Turner's fellow Finance Minister Darcy McKeough, Ontario's treasurer in the 1970s, admits with a laugh, "John 'fucked' a lot of things in conversation."

But there was more to Turner's standing up for Eagleson than simply loyalty to a friend. In the midst of Eagleson's legal travails, Turner called him.

"I was minister of justice," he told The Eagle. "I've worked with the American department of justice. They are the worst bastards in the world. They will charge you, they will convict you, they will give you a heart attack, they will try to ruin you, they will try to get you to commit suicide. They've got unlimited time and resources. Stick that big chin of yours up front and defy them."

Eagleson says the call "boosted my morale in the toughest time of my life. His friendship meant all the world to me."

Turner never spared the F-bomb when it came to defending people he cared about. When Laura Miller was charged in 2015 with criminal offences concerning the deletion of computer files related to Ontario's gas plant scandal, Turner called her.

"We hadn't spoken in two or three years," says Miller, who was executive director of the British Columbia Liberals at the time of the charges. "But that was a moment. He said, 'Don't let those fucking bastards get you down.' You really remember the people who reached out and he did." (Miller was ultimately found not guilty.)

Turner's impatience often brought out the profanity. While he had ample time for royal motorcades and protocol, he couldn't stand it for himself. During the 1988 election campaign, when his popularity temporarily shot through the roof, Turner's team booked a room for 200 people, but 500 showed up. His security detail was deeply concerned when the candidate insisted on wading through the immense crowd to get to the stage to give his speech. They wanted him brought through the back door, a much safer route. Turner was unamused.

"Fuck this bullshit," he told the RCMP. "We're going." And in he went, through a sea of humanity.

After delivering a campaign speech, Turner loved to debrief with colleagues to see what they thought. Sometimes, that meant checking in with Ontario MPP Sean Conway, who rode the campaign plane with Turner in 1984 just to keep his spirits up. Conway knew *Globe and Mail* economics reporter Tom Walkom, who was covering that campaign. He also knew Turner didn't like Walkom after the columnist had written a piece using quotes from an informal chat Turner had with reporters on the campaign bus.

"On the bus, for God's sake!" Turner complained, not realizing that the old rules between politicians and journalists were gone.

Conway approached Walkom after one Turner speech.

"What name is on your birth certificate?" he asked the journalist.

"Thomas George Walkom," he responded.

That was at odds with how Conway was used to hearing Turner refer to him.

"I thought it was 'That Fucking Walkom,'" Conway told the reporter.

"It was hilarious," Conway remembers. "The words were coming out of Turner's mouth so rapidly and every fourth one was 'Fuck.'"

Former staffer Lisa Haley acknowledges, "There's a point where you just got numb to it." Turner would regularly say to Haley: "You're a fucking all-star," or "You look abso-fucking-lutely gorgeous." There wasn't an ounce of lewdness when he said it. It was just Turner being Turner, trying to create a relaxed atmosphere in the office.

David Herle's mother was seventy years old and her son suspects she'd never heard the F-bomb uttered in her presence. Ever. And certainly not by a former prime minister. But at the end of a tribute dinner to Davey Steuart, a long-time Saskatchewan Liberal, Turner met his former aide's mother and wanted her to know how much he valued him.

"Mrs. Herle," Turner said, "your son is a fucking legend."

Mrs. Herle admired the former PM's grace and dignity, but the incident was never spoken of between mother and son again.

Liberal stalwart Howard Brown became a Turner fan while still a high school student at Grand River Collegiate Institute in Kitchener, Ontario. His father Burke took him to the local Liberal MP's nomination meeting in advance of the 1972 federal election with the promise of meeting "the next prime minister of Canada." Turner was the guest speaker and Brown, being the precocious Grade Thirteen student he was, introduced himself to Pierre Trudeau's star finance minister after the speech. Turner asked Brown what his plans were and Brown mentioned he'd be going to Ryerson Polytechnical Institute (now Toronto Metropolitan University) for journalism. Turner wished him well.

The next year, Brown founded the Ryerson Student Liberal Club and invited Turner to come speak before 400 students in January 1974. Turner met with the student executive after the speech and asked them if there was something he ought to put into that year's budget that would be good for students. Brown and Company told him, yes, they'd love to see some more federal support for student loans and housing. Turner and Brown stayed in touch and a decade later, Brown was a Turner delegate-tracker and organizer at the candidate's successful leadership convention.

So, when the two men saw each other at Donald S. Macdonald's memorial reception at the York Club in Toronto in 2018, there was a lot of history behind the handshake when they greeted each other. When Brown saw Geills Turner there, he told her that every time he saw her husband, "I always tell him to pass along my best wishes to you. Is he doing that?"

Geills answered honestly: "No, Howard, he's not."

"Well," Brown came back, "he's going to hear about that from me."

Shortly thereafter at the same reception, Brown cornered Turner. "John, I'm mad at you. What are the two words I always tell you to say to your wife on my behalf?"

Turner didn't miss a beat: "Fuck you."

In 2009, two of Turner's best Kingston pals, Arthur Milnes and Tom Axworthy, mounted a full-day conference at Queen's University to examine Turner's political life. The night before the conference at dinner, Turner began to get cold feet and let Milnes know he particularly objected to one of his conference panelists.

"I can't fucking believe you got me out here in Kingston to hear this fucking egghead Tom Kent talk about me," Turner said, referring to the well-known economist, journalist, and public servant. But the conference proceeded and Kent actually spoke quite glowingly of Turner's record. A chastened Turner approached Milnes after the conference. "I always liked that Tom Kent," he said. "He knows what he's talking about."

I had my own F-bomb experience with Turner. At his eighty-fifth birthday party in Toronto, Turner gave a bravura performance, speaking as he often did on the importance of people standing for office and engaging in democracy. I confess to being deeply impressed that at age eighty-five, Turner hadn't lost an ounce of the passion that so moved him on this subject. So, I approached him afterwards and asked whether he'd care to do an interview on the TVO nightly current affairs program I host called *The Agenda*, about some of the themes raised in the speech.

Turner looked straight at me with those baby blue eyes and barked out, "No fucking way," then turned around and walked away. While I was a tad gobsmacked, I also found the whole episode quite funny. It was so John Turner.

Shortly thereafter, I was on a phone call with his wife about something unrelated and mentioned the incident, but assured her I wasn't the slightest bit offended and found the whole thing kind of endearing.

The next time I saw Turner, he said: "Geills gave me hell and told me to apologize to you, so sorry about that." Again, I assured him it was no sweat. But he didn't change his mind about doing the interview.

Geills seems to have a sense of humour about her husband's proclivity for the F-bomb. "I probably did it too," she confesses. "My grandson Robbie swore somewhere. He was asked, 'Where did you learn to talk that way?' He answered, "From my grandmother when I was five.'"

On much rarer occasions, Turner's blue language did indicate anger. After South African president Nelson Mandela's death in 2013, Prime Minister Stephen Harper invited every living former Canadian PM (and opposition leader Tom Mulcair, among others) to fly with him to Johannesburg for the funeral. Joe Clark was already in Africa at the time, but Brian Mulroney, Jean Chrétien, Kim Campbell, and Turner all agreed to come along on Harper's plane. It was a magnanimous gesture by Harper, particularly since his relationships with some of his invitees were strained to say the least.

Turner's long-time aide-de-camp Marc Kealey picked Turner up from his Toronto home at 4:30 a.m. in order to drive to Ottawa for the special 11 a.m. flight. As Kealey pulled up to the hangar, Turner saw his old nemesis, Chrétien, and became enraged.

"Fuck it, I'm not going," he told Kealey, who begged his former boss to reconsider, but without success. Kealey then went on to the plane to give Harper the news.

"Turner just shook uncontrollably with rage," Kealey says.

Frankly, there were plenty of awkward dynamics on the flight: Harper vs. Mulroney; Chrétien vs. Mulroney; Mulroney vs. Campbell. But as they are occasionally called upon to do, they put aside their past grievances and rose to the occasion. For whatever reason, this time Turner couldn't. He didn't go and later called Harper to thank him for the invitation anyway.

Other times, if Chrétien wasn't around, Turner would partake in ex-PM activities. In 2017, to mark the 150th anniversary of the first ever session of the House of Commons, Speaker Geoff Regan convened four former prime ministers for a celebratory lunch. As the photographer was fiddling with his equipment in search of the perfect lighting, everyone could hear Turner mutter under his breath: "Just take the fucking photo." They all started laughing and even today, Mulroney remembers the incident with delight.

"That's exactly what he said," Mulroney recalls. "It was one of his favorite words."

But Turner's sister Brenda didn't like her brother's profanity, especially when she heard it in her home. "I told him at our dining room table one day about ten years ago, 'We do not do that, and if you continue to do so, you're going to have to leave!'" she says. "Mom would be enraged. He was chastened and glared back at me with those eyes. But I've talked back to him since I was six."

Well into his eighties, Turner was in Arizona on business for the City of Surprise. Municipal officials took him out for dinner after their meetings were completed. They went to the State 48 Brewery and apparently caught them on a night when the service was off. "I'm sitting beside him," recalls Jeanine Jerkovic, the town's economic development director. "He didn't hold back. His filter wasn't as high."

What did Turner say? "The fucking service is terrible here! Why would you bring me here?"

"I guess he's now at a point in his life where he can say what he wants," says Jerkovic, who adds she also saw a charming Turner treated like a rock star by Arizona residents (many of them Canadian ex-pats), when he made a presentation to the town's council.

In November 2005, Turner went to Israel to represent Canada at the ceremonies marking the tenth anniversary of former Prime Minister Yitzhak Rabin's assassination. Sitting with Kealey on a massive hotel patio overlooking Jerusalem, the two men polished off three cigars and a whole bottle of Johnnie Walker Black with Perrier.

"Isn't this fucking great?" Turner asked his friend. "It's the greatest show on earth."

Turner was born into a generation of hard-living men, many of whom consumed a lot of alcohol. His Bay Street days were replete with the typical two-or three-martini lunches; wine flowed liberally over dinners; and of course, the day ended with a night cap or two or more. That was simply how successful men of his generation dealt with the stresses of the job.

When his children were young, Turner made it a point to be home for dinner—that was his key family time. The evening often started in his den, perhaps reading the papers, and daughter Elizabeth would get him a drink.

"I'd make him his Scotch," she recalls. "Once I had a little sip. I thought it was disgusting."

In later years, when Ontario's twenty-fourth premier Dalton McGuinty wanted to mount a tribute dinner for Turner in 2008 to thank him for his years of public service, Turner's affection for alcohol came up in the premier's monologue.

"I won't be roasting John, not only out of respect, but because Scotch is highly flammable," McGuinty quipped, getting a big laugh before 500 people at Toronto's Fairmont Royal York Hotel.

When Turner was on the verge of coming back into public life in 1984, there was plenty of speculation about whether he was an alcoholic (almost everyone seemed to think not) or alcohol dependent (almost everyone seemed to think yes).

The legendary *Toronto Star* political columnist Val Sears wrote a piece pointing out, "He could drink a lot. But I never from 1976-84 saw alcoholic impairment interfere with anything he did. Never." And yet the issue wouldn't go away for Turner. In the lead up to the 1988 election, journalist (and future senator) Pamela Wallin gave the Liberal leader the heads-up that she'd be asking about his alcohol consumption during their CTV interview. Turner admitted he enjoyed a good party, but "I keep my eye on the ball."

Turner's advisers constantly feared their leader's use of alcohol would become an election issue. In fact, among his personal files at Library and Archives Canada, there is a very thick file entitled "Drinking Issue" containing newspaper articles, transcripts of media interviews, and memos among staff members on the subject. His people were concerned. At the parliamentary press gallery dinner in 1988, Turner wanted to make fun of himself referencing the drinking issue. He wanted to say: "I made a resolution to have only one drink a day. This one is for July 12, 1996," and then he'd pretend to knock one back. "The drinking one is funny," his adviser Michael Langill wrote him, "But I think it goes a little too far." The joke didn't make the cut.

The drinking issue certainly became fodder for radio talk shows, which prompted questions of how much personal information the electorate was entitled to about their leaders.

"He could drink more than anyone," recalls Jan Innes. "He'd be overly refreshed but could deliver a coherent passionate speech. It was amazing. I thought he was overdoing it, but he did it partially for his back pain or when he was unhappy personally."

One of Turner's former political associates, whose father was an alcoholic ("so I know something about this") insists Turner was never "over the top scary. Glassy-eyed maybe. But I could never believe how much he could consume."

Keith Davey's widow Dorothy once saw Turner, post-political life, walk into a restaurant in Toronto's Forest Hill Village at lunch time. As she waited for a friend to arrive, Davey watched Turner "walk straight to the bar, sit down, and order a double. He drank it in one gulp and walked out. I didn't say anything, but it was very sad," she says. However, Davey, who knew Turner for decades, adds: "I never saw him weaving or head-on-the-table drunk or inarticulate."

Whether or why Turner abused alcohol may remain a subject of considerable debate. What seems beyond debate is that many of those who loved him worried about how much he drank and thought he drank to excess. When I asked Turner's sister Brenda Norris about this subject, there was a long exhale that preceded her answer. She told a story of a time her brother stayed with her at her summer home in Saint Andrews, New Brunswick. Brenda was hosting a big cocktail party for her brother when one of her friends approached her.

"Brenda," the friend said, "he's belting back the Scotches. Is he an alcoholic?"

As Brenda looks back, she puts much of the blame for her brother's drinking on politics, particularly after his return in 1984. "I don't think he drank to excess before becoming opposition leader," she says, adding one of her favourite admonitions from her late mother.

"My mother advised me: don't drink 'til you're thirty because by then you're going to really need it."

Kealey, who probably spent more time with Turner in social situations than anyone else in Turner's latter years, says there was one intervention related to Turner's drinking and it was conducted by some members of the law firm Miller Thomson in 2010. "It was prompted by a few of the younger partners who took exception to JNT's drinking during work hours and returning to the office drunk and 'dis-orderly,'" Kealey emails. "That effort and JNT's reaction to it, in and of itself, was the catalyst to his departure from the firm. There was NEVER, repeat NEVER, any intervention with family or friends."

Turner's executive assistant at Miller Thomson, Jill Hamblin, admits to being concerned about her boss's drinking, "But I never thought it was my place to tell him to lay off."

Elizabeth Turner confirms there was never a family intervention per se, but there was concern, especially from her mother. "She'd give him shit all the time," Liz smiles.

"I've never seen my husband drunk," insists Geills. "He liked his wine. In the end he didn't drink hard liquor at all. The kids would be on him about 'Dad you've had enough.' But I never saw him drink after dinner. That was the end of the evening."

The family's bigger concern was Turner's inability to move if he indulged too much. In his mid-eighties, Turner was supposed to have a three-hour operation to deal with calcium buildup deposits on his spine. The procedure took nearly twice as long as expected and the surgeon called it one of the most difficult he'd ever done. Turner needed months of rehab to strengthen his legs again. While he may have gained a few more years of mobility thanks to the operation, it was high risk all the way.

"The problem was, he couldn't feel his lower legs," Elizabeth explains. "So, the drinking didn't help."

One time, Michael Turner had to come over to his parents' home to help him upstairs because his father had fallen, and no one could move him. "But the next morning, he had a board meeting and was downstairs on a conference call," Elizabeth says. "He was down there and totally fine. But that's one of the reasons Mom would give him shit. If he fell on the floor at home, she couldn't get him up."

That happened to Turner at least once at the York Club, one of his favourite downtown Toronto hang outs. Former Ontario premier Mike Harris found Turner in the bathroom, unable to move.

"He couldn't stand up," Harris says, "He asked me for help, and I carried him outside to his ride."

"He just collapsed," Elizabeth adds. "It was a temporary paralysis. It wasn't that he was too drunk. He couldn't put weight on his legs. That was very scary."

Even into his late eighties and early nineties, when his health truly declined and mobility became infinitely more difficult, John Turner was still a presence when he walked into a room. It's understandable that in social settings, friends or colleagues would have felt powerless to suggest to a former prime minister that he cut back on his drinking. It's also the case, as I witnessed, that the more Turner drank, the more comfortable he felt telling old war stories, which were endlessly fascinating. While others may have, I never saw Turner drink to excess or behave poorly because of an overindulgence of alcohol, and I saw him in social settings dozens of times.

Having said that, Brenda's point is extremely well taken. The body blows Turner took as leader of the opposition were unprecedentedly vicious and may have been enough to make an enthusiastic social drinker cross the line to more self-destructive behaviour.

CHAPTER SEVENTEEN

The 1986 Leadership Review

T HE YEAR 1986 REPRESENTED THE midpoint of Brian Mulroney's administration and the ship of state had accumulated myriad
barnacles. Too many scandals and ministerial resignations gave too
many Canadians a negative impression of the country's largest ever majority
government. But Mulroney had one important thing going for him: the Liberal
Party of Canada's constitution. That document required the Liberals to stage
a referendum on their leader at their November 1986 convention and determine whether they wanted him to stay or to go. As a result, for essentially the
entire year, Turner and his allies were utterly focused on that date with destiny.
Their mission was to emerge from the leadership review with an unambiguously
solid level of support, which they hoped would settle the question of whether
Turner was the right person at the right time for the job of Liberal leader, once
and for all.

Throughout 1986, it became pretty clear that the supporters of Jean Chrétien
and Pierre Trudeau were going to try to torpedo Turner's efforts. As a result, the
young Turks whom Turner had come to rely on made a pact. The Richard
Mahoneys, David Herles, John Websters, Terrie O'Learys, and Terry Popowychs
all resolved to do whatever it took to get Turner the support he needed. Furthermore, they wanted to assure their place in the party and take power away from
the old guard. Webster's slogan was: "Take no prisoners."

Turner's friend, the Bay Street auto dealer John Addison, agreed to put a fund together to help get youth delegates to the convention in Ottawa. (When the party's official fundraising chair Leo Kolber found out about that, he was not amused.)

While Alberta's Darryl Raymaker may have differed with Turner on various issues, he appreciated the leader's efforts to try to rebuild the Liberal Party in Western Canada, and so he and his wife organized delegates to go to the convention. "We were totally committed to Turner," says Raymaker, now eighty. "But we weren't so naive not to see his defects as a candidate."

As the year began, Keith Davey wrote Turner congratulating him on his perseverance and hard work and assured Turner of his "continuing friendship and support. I will do all I can to assist you."

Liberals were genuinely split on the question of Turner's future. For some, Turner's getting blown out of the water in the 1984 election was reason enough to dump him. They had seen little progress since then. There was still too much chaos.

However, others noted that Lester Pearson had suffered the same fate as Turner, at the hands of John Diefenbaker in 1958. Pearson actually lost a second election, before finally winning back-to-back minority governments, which history has regarded as some of the most impactful in Canadian history. The argument was: use this time to rebuild the party and get the leader's confidence level up.

Although a leadership review result of 50 per cent plus one counts as a win, conventional wisdom says no leader can survive having half of the party against them. The most significant precedent was in Winnipeg in 1983, when Joe Clark determined that 66.9 per cent support from Tory delegates wasn't a solid enough vote of confidence in him to continue. He called for a new leadership convention, assuming he'd win it and eventually get his detractors to put up or shut up. But Clark lost to Mulroney on the fourth ballot at the ensuing June 1983 convention. While no one knew what Turner's magic number would be ("he has to do well" was a familiar refrain), the assumption was that the number had to start with a seven. Herle merely wanted Turner to get a higher number than Clark.

The young Turks knew their party's constitution well and set out to exploit every nuance of the rules. As president of the Young Liberals, Herle ensured a unanimous endorsement from that group for his leader. The group organized numerous university campus clubs, knowing those club members could be chosen as delegates and sent to the convention to vote for Turner. The leader's sister Brenda and his wife Geills both got elected as delegates so they could go to Ottawa and vote "no" to review.

"All of 1986 was taken up with the leadership review," says Kaz Flinn, who worked in the opposition leader's office. "We were more political than we should have been because we were always looking over our shoulders and watching his back."

And yet, in the midst of all the drama, there were moments of civility. In September, Progressive Conservative MP John McDermid sent a handwritten note to Turner, reminding him that he had seen Joe Clark go through the same experience, and "I know the pressure you, your family, friends and supporters are under." McDermid, the MP for Brampton-Georgetown, added: "Although I sit across, I just wanted you to know you have my understanding & prayers for strength. Stick to your guns."

Davey wrote Turner a note at the end of August, telling him he'd just taken a trip to the United Kingdom, where he saw the musical *Chess*. Apparently, the male lead in that show was named John Turner. A billboard outside the theatre proclaimed: "John Turner dominates the stage whenever he is on it." Davey finished the note with: "Now that's what I call a positive omen."

A total of 2,626 delegates were chosen to attend the leadership review convention and every single one of them seemed to have a passionate stake in its outcome. One voter of whom that could not be said was a young political keener from Ottawa named John Baird, who held a job on Parliament Hill as a volunteer messenger. His gig had expired but his ID badge was good until the end of the year. He decided he wanted to meet the recently defeated prime minister, who was now leader of the opposition. "So, I moseyed up to him," Baird now says. "Even though I was a young Conservative, I liked him."

Baird was exactly the kind of young political nerd who would go to the Liberal review convention even though he wasn't a Liberal, just because it was in his hometown. "It was a fun thing to do," he says. "I was sixteen." A decade later, Baird would be elected as the Ontario MPP for Nepean–Carleton, serve in Premier Mike Harris' cabinet, then become the MP for Ottawa West–Nepean, and serve in Prime Minister Stephen Harper's cabinet. He stayed connected to Turner after both of their political careers were over, having the occasional lunch and shooting the breeze. Baird even replaced Turner on the board of Canadian Pacific.

One of the rites of passage for political people in Canada back in the 1980s was to appear on British Columbia broadcaster Jack Webster's eponymously named television program. Webster was a bombastic, shoot from the lip, equal opportunity insulter with a thick Scottish accent. He was nicknamed the "King of the Vancouver Airwaves" during his career, which lasted from 1953 to 1988. On September 19, 1986, Turner appeared on Webster's show to make the case for why Liberals ought to give him a chance to finish what he started. Turner stayed calm as Webster peppered him with aggressive questions, such as why his former friend and Liberal Rainmaker Keith Davey had written so many nasty things about him in a recently published memoir.

"Davey's trying to sell a book, I guess," Turner said, adding, "He's not being too helpful."

That was an understatement. Turner's disappointment with Davey was better manifested in his next response. "If there's one thing I remember Keith Davey for, and I like him for, it's his #1 rule: loyalty to the party, loyalty to the leader." None of which Turner was now enjoying.

Turner had been given some talking points by his staff the day before the Webster interview and those comments were much more pointed than what the leader ultimately said on the air. Advisers called Davey's book "inexcusable and hypocritical," but urged Turner to express more sadness and disappointment than anger. The memo urged Turner to accuse Davey of being unable to cede centre-stage to a new generation, and to stress that Liberals "can't return to the good old days when a few boys in the back rooms called all the shots."

Still, the opposition leader reminded Webster that he'd spent more time in Western Canada (and British Columbia in particular) than any major party leader since John Diefenbaker. Webster taunted him, insisting Turner would soon be out of a job because powerful eastern interests would take him down.

Turner pushed back.

"Sure, you want a media event out of this," he chided Webster. "But I think I understand the party, better than I did two years ago, that is for sure, but better than any other living Canadian. I never expected unanimity, but if you come to the convention in November, and I hope you do, there'll be substantial support for John Turner, the Member of Parliament for Quadra." That last bit was not only good fodder for local Vancouver viewers, but also gave some insight into the essential John Turner. He was a Member of Parliament.

A week-and-a-half later, with still a month to go before the convention, Keith Davey showed up on Webster's show plugging his book. He insisted he wasn't leading a crusade to dump Turner, just urging delegates to "think it through. It's not disloyal to want to dump the leader. As long as the review is there, it's your prerogative to use it."

Davey claimed he could make a case for both sides of the vote but wasn't yet saying which way he'd go.

Interestingly, it wasn't Webster who was Davey's toughest interrogator on this show. The legendary journalist Charles Lynch excoriated him on live TV for kissing and telling in his memoir about private conversations with Turner. "You're killing him slowly. You're going to drip him to death over the next two years," Lynch said. It was a rough ride for Davey, who ultimately came out against Turner continuing as leader. He told Liberal MP Roland de Corneille it was the biggest mistake of his career to back Turner at the 1984 leadership convention. Edison Stewart from Canadian Press described Davey as "the Ferdinand Marcos of the Liberal Party. Some people just don't know when to leave."

It was becoming a nasty, bitter, intra-family feud. For Turner loyalists, Davey's book was the last straw. Alfred Apps, who in 1979 became executive vice-president of the Liberals at just age twenty-two, referred to Davey as "the cancer in the Liberal Party." He wrote Davey a fourteen-page, single-spaced letter on September 29, sort of apologizing for using the term, acknowledging, "I have had my concerns about John Turner too. For too long, he did look like yesterday's man… The general impression was of a man unsure of why he was where he was, much less of where he wanted to go with the Liberal Party. The patronage flood at the outset of the last campaign broke my heart, and having to carry that albatross on my back during the campaign ran contrary to everything I had expected from him." Apps had been a Liberal candidate in Oxford riding in Ontario in the 1984 election.

But Apps went on to say he'd been impressed by Turner's growth, then accused Davey of having one shortcoming: "You have never held elected office either in the House or in the party. Your lack of democratic legitimacy has impaired the capacity of your leadership in the party and has tilted your own understanding of how a healthy party works away from democratic principles." He asked Davey to be chair of the platform committee and support Turner, and then he sent copies of his letter to nearly a dozen prominent Liberal officials and journalists.

The focus on the leadership review was actually interrupted on October 13 by a historic vote. For the first time ever, the Speaker of the House of Commons would be elected by MPs, rather than simply chosen by the prime minister.

The winner was Turner's fellow Vancouver MP John Fraser. Turner had the House in stitches describing his vote for his friend as Speaker.

"For some of us, it was an extremely difficult experience," he explained. "It was the first time in my life that I ever voted for a Tory."

As the calendar turned to November, it was truly crunch time for Turner and company. They continued to line up endorsements and, knowing they'd never get Pierre Trudeau or Jean Chrétien, they decided to chase another Big Kahuna from Quebec: former Trudeau (and Turner) cabinet minister Marc Lalonde. Lalonde had surprised many by backing Turner over his fellow Quebecer Chrétien at the 1984 leadership convention. Now, Turner invited Lalonde to dinner at Stornoway in hopes of getting his former finance minister to give him a public endorsement. But when Turner asked, Lalonde would only say, "I'll think about it."

On November 11, Lalonde issued a four-page letter to delegates that was absolutely cutting. He accused Turner of failing to win the support of Canadians and insisted there was no hope for improvement. "Loyalty doesn't mean you have to be dumb," he argued. The former minister cited bad fundraising, bad polls, and unsupportable expenses (the party was helping to pay for the Turners' maintaining an apartment in Toronto). "A popular leader will not cost the party money. Popular leaders generate revenue," Lalonde offered.

The effect of the Lalonde missive was to drop a bomb on the Liberal Party, ultimately ending lifelong friendships. For example, Herb Metcalfe was one of David Herle and Richard Mahoney's mentors in the party. Metcalfe had brought the young Liberals into cabinet minister John Roberts' leadership organization in 1984, where they learned valuable lessons about how to do politics. Metcalfe assured the pair he was pro-Turner and so they looked to getting him elected as a delegate to the convention as part of the slate in Ottawa Centre. But when Lalonde's letter was released, the Turnerites did some sleuthing. They discovered the Purolator package delivering copies of the letter originated with Metcalfe.

"It was the end of Rick's and my relationship with Herb," Herle now says. "It wasn't about Turner. It was about him lying to us. That's a personal betrayal." (Metcalfe would later be sentenced to house arrest and fined nearly $400,000 for tax evasion in 2015.)

As Lalonde's pronouncement made the rounds, Herle got out there to rebut it. He scrummed with reporters and appeared on *This Week in Parliament* with Don Newman. He was so furious, he broke off all ties with Lalonde for twenty years, after which time he tried to get Lalonde to chair Prime Minister Paul Martin's campaign in Quebec. ("He put me through an hour before saying yes," Herle recalls.) Ironically, the Lalonde letter seemed to have the opposite effect. Many Canadians saw it as an unnecessary pile-on and Turner's popularity actually enjoyed a five to eight per cent bump.

On the last weekend in November, Liberals gathered at the Ottawa Convention Centre to do their business. One of the highlights would be Turner's address to youth delegates. As Herle prepared to open the huge doors ushering Turner into the banquet hall, Turner shared some news he'd just received from the party's pollster, Martin Goldfarb.

"Goldfarb says we're doing badly with young Liberals," Turner said, concerned.

Then Herle opened the doors. More than a thousand young Liberals got to their feet and cheered madly for their leader. Turner looked at Herle and said: "Fuck Marty Goldfarb."

The speech Turner would give to those delegates had not gone through the normal channels. It was written by David Lockhart, who started as a volunteer in the opposition leader's correspondence office. Lockhart wrote the odd speech for Turner, who eventually said to him: "You've got a good pen, Lockhart."

Normally, all of Turner's speeches would go through chief-of-staff Doug Richardson, but this time Lockhart bypassed the gatekeeper, going straight to the leader.

"I put the draft on his desk, directly," Lockhart says. "And he loved it. It started my career. Sometimes it's the orders that you disobey that make you famous. I'm not famous but I'll always be grateful to Mr. Turner for accepting that speech." (Lockhart eventually made a name for himself as one of Ottawa's best writers, penning speeches for several cabinet ministers, including three budget speeches and multiple fiscal updates for Paul Martin and two budget speeches for Ralph Goodale when they were both finance ministers.)

On the eve of the convention, Turner received a handwritten note from his principal secretary. "Dear Sir," Douglas Richardson began rather formally, but quickly moved to a more intimate tone. "Often it is difficult to say how we really feel. At times like this, it is doubly so. The challenges you have faced have been more than any human should have to endure. Your grace under trying and difficult circumstances has inspired all. You have earned the victory that will be yours on Sunday. Our nation will be a better place, with a brighter future—because of your work, because of this Convention." He signed off simply with: "Good luck–Take care, Doug." Richardson's next note of significance to his leader, five months later, would be quite different but for now, it set just the right tone.

The suspense heading into the convention was intense. Nobody was saying (at least not publicly) what number they thought Turner would get or needed to survive. The public opinion polls were buoyant. The Liberals under Turner had an eight-point lead over Mulroney's Progressive Conservatives. But the government was so scandal-plagued, many Liberals thought the gap should have been twice as big.

Enter Jean Chrétien.

Turner's chief rival, now out of politics, arrived at the convention and as he tried to register as a delegate, the ensuing bedlam was something to behold. He was given the complete rock star treatment by many Liberal delegates. It was understandable at one level; Chrétien was coming off a triumphant book tour, having turned *Straight From the Heart* into a massive best-seller. When he launched the book the previous year in Montreal, both Trudeau and Turner showed up. Chrétien signed Turner's book: "Thank you for having won the convention because if you had not won, I wouldn't have had the time to write this book."

The inscription may have been cute, but there was nothing cute about what Chrétien's appearance now represented. Although Chrétien insisted he'd done nothing to organize the forces that wanted Turner out, it's also true that he didn't have to do anything. His mere presence energized the anti-Turner elements. It also infuriated the pro-Turner side when the party's allegedly neutral general secretary, David Collenette, escorted Chrétien through the hall.

"Sorry, but he shouldn't have been doing that," says Stephen Hastings, who recalls Geills Turner being so furious when she saw that, "she expected me to tackle Chrétien." Hastings didn't.

MP Sergio Marchi showed up at the convention ready to vote for review but insists he wasn't particularly active in his efforts. "A lot of Turner people thought I was a Jean Chrétien puppet," he says. "But Jean Chrétien never said a thing to me. No one made me do or say anything."

The lineups to vote on Turner's leadership were extremely long and at one point, a friend of John Baird's decided he'd simply had enough. He left without voting but gave his ID badge to Baird, the sixteen-year-old Tory, who hung around and did vote.

"There was no picture on the badge," Baird laughs at the memory of his chutzpah.

As party officials supervised the voting, a big split developed between Turner's camp and the conference chair, Sudbury MP Doug Frith. Turner's people argued the leader should be given the results of the vote before any public announcement was made. It was a courtesy they felt anyone in that position should be granted. (The NDP convention in Edmonton in 2016 when Tom Mulcair's leadership was reviewed is a good illustration of why Turner's people wanted this. Mulcair did *not* get a heads-up on that vote and learned at the same time as everyone else that only 48 per cent of delegates wanted him to stay on. Mulcair's expression conveyed complete and utter defeat. It seemed cruel and unusual punishment.)

But Frith's position was that everyone should learn the results at the same time. Team Turner persisted and eventually, Frith moderated his stance somewhat. Turner would see the result while in his seat just before the public announcement was made. But the standoff irreparably damaged Frith's and Turner's relationship and the Sudburian would soon pay a price for it.

At 1:38 p.m. on Sunday, November 30, the Leader of Her Majesty's loyal opposition and of the Liberal Party of Canada learned his fate. He was handed an envelope with the final count just before the actual announcement. Turner allowed himself a tiny smile, then he looked at Frith on the convention stage and winked at him. Of the 2,626 votes cast, Turner managed to get 2,001 party members to support his continuing leadership. It was a 76.3 per cent endorsement, nearly ten points better than Joe Clark's number, and an unambiguous signal from Liberals that they wanted Turner to stay. Then, hearkening back to Iona Campagnolo's controversial statement at the 1984 leadership convention, Frith said: "I've been waiting a long time to say this to you John, but you're first in our hearts."

Turner would refer to this moment as one of the most rewarding of his life.

The crowd went bananas, and John Baird smiled when he saw the final count of 2,001 pro-Turner votes. "I was the one!" he says. When I asked him whether he thought it was appropriate for a Tory to pass himself off as a Liberal to vote at a Liberal leadership review, Baird responded, "Nowadays this would be scandalous, but back then, we'd call it a youthful indiscretion."

What did Herle think of the results?

"We were ecstatic," he says. "It was astounding given the efforts we'd faced from the other side."

Turner did so much better than conventional wisdom suggested he would, and media accounts reflected that. Journalist Hugh Winsor wrote: "The convention showed [Turner] could stride instead of stagger, speak instead of stutter. It provided some tangible evidence of his victory boast that he is now ready to fight the Tories."

Even Sergio Marchi, who voted against his leader, came away from the experience prepared to give Turner a second chance. "I didn't think the number would be that high," Marchi admits. "I found some new respect for him."

Ironically, Turner's number was also buoyed by the fact that some delegates voted for him not because they loved him, but because the candidates they preferred to see lead the party weren't yet ready. They figured the Liberals would lose the next election anyway, so why waste a new and promising leader on a hopeless mission?

For Chrétien, there was now nowhere to go but back to his law firm. The result was decisive, even if it had been achieved by Turner's troops twisting arms, playing hardball, and stacking the convention in any way they could. Ironically, Chrétien lost the leadership to Turner two-and-a-half years earlier because the Liberal establishment hadn't been with him. Now, Chrétien lost again because the establishment *was* with him.

Turner's performance got him the immediate bump his team had hoped for. A month later, the Angus Reid polling outfit had the Liberals at 41 per cent support, with the PCs far back at 31 per cent, only three points up on the New Democratic Party. Gallup showed an even more favourable distribution: Liberals 45 per cent, Tories 30 per cent, and NDP 25 per cent. Shortly thereafter, Deputy Prime Minister Don Mazankowski sent Turner a note across the floor of the House: "It's really good to see you back in your old form again. Must have something to do with the polls!"

Turner gained political currency with his review victory and now he intended to spend it. Doug Frith was out as caucus chair. Herb Metcalfe and Leo Kolber both resigned from their party roles. Collenette was out as general secretary. He may have served in Turner's short-lived cabinet, but he was a Chrétien guy and that was that.

But even as Turner looked as though he was taking control of the party, his next big pronouncement undid a lot of the good feeling produced by his review victory. While running as a champion of the grassroots and bringing power back to individual party members, Turner announced that convention resolutions, approved by the membership, would *not* be binding on him or the caucus. He called those resolutions "highly persuasive and they set the general direction of the party," but that didn't mean they'd make the party platform in the lead-up to the next election.

John Turner ended 1986 on such a high note. But the resolutions decision, along with myriad other landmines to come, meant he'd be right back in the soup in 1987. A year's worth of organizational effort and pulling out all the stops resulted in an era of good feeling that lasted all of a month.

CHAPTER EIGHTEEN

The Two Accords

TWO HISTORIC AGREEMENTS SUCCESSFULLY negotiated by Brian Mulroney's Progressive Conservative government made 1987 an enormously consequential year for Canada. Whether they were net positive developments for the country is still being debated three-and-a-half decades later.

The first came on October 4, 1987, when the governments of Canada and the United States announced that they had reached a bilateral accord henceforth known as the Free Trade Agreement (FTA). Mulroney and President Ronald Reagan would affix their signatures to the deal the day after New Year's in 1988.

The Liberal party leader was immediately skeptical.

"I love it here," he told his fellow members in the House of Commons. "I love what we have built as a nation. I love what we stand for and above all, I love that it is ours. We have made a conscious choice to build this country against the odds, against the weather, against geography, and against the unceasing pressures coming from south of the border."

Turner understood the economic and political significance of the FTA. Generally speaking, he had always been in favour of liberalized trade with America, provided the United States was equally open to our business and that appropriate safeguards for Canada's unique institutions were in place. But he was convinced the agreement would raise issues around Canadian sovereignty that could affect the country for decades. He couldn't wait to get his hands on the text itself. The lawyer in him wanted to go clause-by-clause through the pact and find every shortcoming.

The fine print was made public in December 1987, after which Turner and his family took a two-week Christmas ski vacation in Collingwood, Ontario. Turner didn't do much skiing. When he returned to Ottawa, he brought with him his dog-eared copy of the FTA, replete with notes in the margins.

"He knew that thing stem to stern," says a former Turner adviser. "He constructed the case you saw play out for the following year from that period of study. One of the most intense periods of research I've ever seen from any leader. He was a first-year lawyer doing his thing."

Turner had a ton of questions and he wanted answers. How much access to our water had the Mulroney government given to the Americans? Would our unique universal health care system be maintained? What about our labour standards and jobs?

"There were economic benefits portrayed by government, but he was worried about what people couldn't see under the hood," that same adviser says. "He saw things and could analyze things so quickly. Nobody else was in the same league."

Turner had begun speaking out against the agreement, most memorably before a huge crowd at the Liberals' annual Confederation Dinner, in late 1987. He tried to take care not to come across as anti-American, but rather, as against this deal. Ontario cabinet minister John Sweeney, who saw the speech, sent Turner a note afterwards saying: "I know the difficult period you have just come through but on that evening many of us saw a new John Turner with the fire to lead. Your position is just right. Keep it up & give 'em hell!"

On December 18, Turner rose in the House to speak about the trade agreement. (Mulroney had sent him a letter earlier that day to apologize for not being in the House to hear him speak, citing a longstanding engagement he couldn't break. "As you know, I always try to be present on such occasions," Mulroney wrote in another example of the behind-the-scenes civility between the two men.)

Turner pulled out his 5×8 cards and blasted international trade minister John Crosbie, who'd called the Liberal leader "criminally negligent" in his speech just the day before. "Mr. Speaker," Turner began, "if it is a crime to care about this country, I plead guilty!" He added: "And as for negligence, I am not the minister of international trade who admitted that he had not even read the deal he is trying to pass off to Canadians." That was accurate. Crosbie fessed up in a scrum with reporters on June 28, 1988, that he hadn't, in fact, read the agreement.

With Turner's 1986 leadership review out of the way, the Liberals got down to the business of preparing for an election, which everyone assumed would take place in 1988. They struck a strategy committee, installed Sen. Michael Kirby as chair, and began mapping out a potential tour for the leader, thinking about what the campaign ads would need to say, and of course, putting together a platform. They also made the most important decision of all: what the election should be about. The Free Trade Agreement was the obvious choice.

Turner also made a controversial call related to his caucus. He resolved that no MPs would be protected from challengers, that they all had to go out and, if necessary, compete for their nominations again. Turner thought that was the way to ensure his MPs stayed close to the ground in their constituencies. It may have been respectful of local politics, but it certainly didn't endear the leader to his caucus mates, some of whom knew they'd have a tough time getting re-nominated.

One MP, Roland de Corneille from Eglinton–Lawrence, had private meetings with Turner twice about this. De Corneille was an ordained Anglican priest who wore his collar in the House and made a name for himself by working to bring disparate religious and community groups together. But his organizational abilities paled in comparison to a younger activist named Joe Volpe, who also wanted the nomination. Despite being a three-term MP, de Corneille simply couldn't compete with Volpe, who steamrolled over him at a bitterly contested nomination meeting. Albina Guarnieri won the nomination in Mississauga East, but only after police were called in to restore order. Things got so chaotic and so many irregularities in voting took place, the party's executive ordered a second nomination meeting, which Guarnieri also won. Turner wanted one of his social policy advisers, Patrick Johnston, to win the nomination in Scarborough West, but he wouldn't put his thumb on the scale for his friend. As a result, Tom Wappel, supported by Liberals for Life, brought in busloads of anti-abortion/pro-life supporters and snatched the nomination from Johnston. The respected nationalist Maude Barlow won a nomination in the nation's capital. But then the riding boundaries changed requiring a new nomination meeting to be called. Chrétien supporter Mac Harb won that second battle, costing Turner a potential caucus ally. Turner was no doubt standing on democratic principle, but it all had the effect of conveying an image of the Liberal party, in some constituencies, at war with itself, rather than with the Tories.

As much as the Free Trade Agreement gave Turner a mission as opposition leader, the other historic accord the federal government negotiated that year would prove to be a significant part of the Liberal leader's undoing.

In June 1987, Mulroney and Canada's ten premiers reached an agreement to accommodate five principles the province of Quebec wanted, in order to affix its signature to the constitution. Back in 1981, Pierre Trudeau reached a constitutional agreement with nine premiers, but not Quebec premier René Lévesque. While the agreement was ratified by Parliament and signed by Queen Elizabeth II, it was an irritant among many that, although bound by the deal, technically, Quebec hadn't signed it (despite seventy-three of seventy-five Quebec MPs backing it).

Now, with *his* unanimous agreement, Mulroney would have bragging rights that he was able to achieve something Trudeau couldn't (admittedly, Mulroney had it easier in that he was able to work with a Liberal, mostly federalist premier of Quebec in Robert Bourassa, rather than the separatist Lévesque).

For Mulroney, the Meech Lake Accord was a singular achievement. The question was: how would the Liberals react? Turner's initial reaction was to say it was an important day for Quebec. He walked across the floor of the House and shook the prime minister's hand. Mulroney later referred to that as his greatest memory ever in the House of Commons. Many Liberal MPs, conversely, wondered what in heaven's name their leader was doing.

The accord recognized Quebec as a "distinct society," a phrase that appeared in the body of the text, not just in the preamble. In other words, the phrase would have legal heft when courts interpreted future laws. The agreement also committed future prime ministers to select judges from lists submitted by the provinces and would give provinces compensation if they opted out of national cost-sharing programs. All provinces would get a veto on future constitutional changes, and the phrase "minimum national standards" would be replaced with "consistent with national objectives." These were all federal compromises offered to Quebec and the other provinces, designed to get Quebec to sign on. And it worked.

Meech Lake had two immediate effects: it burnished Mulroney's reputation as a leader who moved the yardsticks on national unity; and it dropped a bomb on the Liberal Party of Canada.

For Turner, Meech Lake was consistent with views he'd expressed for three decades. "In commending the prime minister and his colleagues, and the first ministers of the provinces," Turner said in the House, "I want to say to him that the work accomplished yesterday was encouraging and constructive for the country. Bringing Quebec into our constitutional fabric, fully into the Canadian family was an effort worth his time and worth the time of the first ministers."

It was a classy thing for Turner to have said, and exactly *not* what much of his caucus wanted to hear.

Meech Lake flew in the face of everything Liberals had believed when Pierre Trudeau was their leader. Many saw the "distinct society" label for Quebec as "special status" which Trudeau could never abide. Never mind that two of the most popular Liberal premiers in the country, Ontario's David Peterson and Quebec's Bourassa, were architects of the agreement. Too much of the Liberal caucus still adhered to the Trudeauvian vision of Canada. But three months after signing the agreement, Peterson won the biggest majority government in Ontario history. The prevailing political winds seemed to be *with* the new accord, even without the support of a significant chunk of the Liberal caucus and party.

How could Turner support this agreement when so much of his party didn't? Probably because the accord was consistent with what he'd been saying about Quebec publicly for two decades. When he ran for leader in 1968, Turner said: "Any discussion of Canadian unity must begin with the realistic acceptance of one basic fact, that the province of Quebec is different from all the other provinces of Canada. This must be recognized. A refusal to do so, a denial of this situation, could lead to the separation of Quebec from Canada. And politicians must face the facts."

It didn't help Turner persuade Liberals that he was, as he said, "on the right side of history" when the first ministers insisted that the accord was "a seamless web." Would the House of Commons or any of the country's ten other legislatures have a chance to review the agreement and propose amendments? Well, no, actually. Turner could sense a caucus revolt was about to burst forth and so he invited a dozen senior caucus members to a meeting. They were almost unanimous in their condemnation of the accord. Only Turner ally Raymond Garneau was onside. Don Johnston called it a "complete disaster," after which Garneau went for the jugular. Harkening back to when former Quebec premier René Lévesque likened the wealthy Montreal suburb of Westmount to "White Rhodesia," Garneau called Johnston a "Westmount Rhodesian." Critics insisted Liberals could oppose a bad deal without looking anti-Quebec, but Turner wasn't so sure. He'd worked with Johnston since their days as Stikeman Elliott lawyers in Montreal in the 1960s, but this profound disagreement over Meech ruptured their friendship. Johnston quit as external affairs critic, after which Turner made his next move.

"For some time," he wrote his old friend, "it has been clear that you have not been comfortable with a range of caucus positions. I regret that you are not willing to accept my efforts to accommodate you. In view of the circumstances, I have asked the whip to make appropriate arrangements with the Speaker."

That's a polite way of saying you're about to lose your front row seat in the House. Johnston eventually left the caucus altogether, sitting as an "Independent Liberal."

"Party members aren't, as a rule, looking for a fight with their leaders," wrote one of this generation's best Parliament Hill journalists, Paul Wells in *Maclean's* in 2021. "But, at a minimum, they want to feel that they're led by one of their own. If they don't, it saps motivation."

Turner clearly understood this was an issue for his party. At the parliamentary press gallery dinner in May 1987, he joked that "Some of you have complained that our caucus has a dozen different [positions] on every single issue. That simply is not true. We only have two, mine and everybody else's."

Then things got worse for Turner. Trudeau decided to break his silence and on May 27 (less than a week before agreement was actually reached), had a vicious anti-Meech op-ed published in both Montreal and Toronto newspapers. In a fashion that only Trudeau could pull off, he complimented Mulroney for giving away the store to the provinces in order to get unanimity. With Turner already on the record as saying he'd vote for Meech, amended or not, Mulroney was the prime target, but Turner suffered collateral damage.

On June 22, 1987, Turner wrote an open letter to all Liberals entitled "Why I support the Accord." He sniped back at Trudeau by referring to the "incomplete process of 1981–82," a reference to the lack of ratification by Quebec.

"The process needed to be completed, politically emotionally and psychologically... in a united nonpartisan way," Turner wrote, believing in his bones that the country needed Quebec to sign on, even if it were already effectively "in."

However, the pact's ratification by all the first ministers didn't end the debate. It merely started a three-year clock within which all the country's legislatures needed to ratify what the first ministers had agreed to. "Is the price too high?" Turner asked. "I don't believe it is." But it was becoming too high for too many Liberals. Toronto lawyer Timothy Danson, whose father Barney was a World War II hero who lost an eye in the Battle of Normandy and was a cabinet colleague of Turner's in the Trudeau government, challenged the Liberal leader straight on.

"I believe the Meech Lake Constitutional Accord is bad for Canada," Danson wrote to Turner. "It is contrary to everything I believe in. It has shaken me to the bone. If you are bitter towards me... I am prepared to face the consequences of my actions." Danson went on to say, "I know you have a long memory… but I am motivated by my opposition to Meech Lake, not my opposition to you," adding he would still work to get Turner returned to the PMO in the next election.

Danson misjudged Turner if he thought retribution was coming. "As I told your father, I respect your views," Turner replied, "and in no way do I confuse your position with opposition to me. There is indeed a difference."

The following month, Canadians voted in three by-elections. The NDP won them all. And now the Liberals were having a hard time attracting candidates to run for them in the following year's election.

"It was a real dark moment," says Dennis Mills. "So, I reached out."

Mills had worked on Trudeau's staff during the former PM's final majority government years. He told Turner he'd be prepared to seek the nomination in Toronto's Broadview–Greenwood riding, which had been solidly NDP for a decade, having been represented by Bob Rae and Lynn McDonald.

"But you and I have one problem," Mills told Turner. "I'm anti-Meech Lake and you're pro-Meech Lake. But I'm willing to do this."

The Liberal leader's response was classic Turner. "Goddammit," he said to Mills, "just don't give me too much trouble and you can be my goddamned fucking candidate."

True to his word, Turner opened Mills' campaign headquarters, bringing plenty of national attention to this local race. When they asked Turner why he would boost the prospects of an anti-Meech candidate, as he knew they would, he said: "I believe in parliamentary democracy where you can have other points of view."

"We walked along the Danforth," Mills recalls, referring to the riding's most famous street in Greektown. "He even spoke Greek."

Mills actually managed to help secure another candidate for Turner. At that time, he was working in corporate relations at the auto parts giant Magna International. Its owner, Frank Stronach, chaired a massive dinner at the Metro Toronto Convention Centre for the party and decided he would run for the Liberals as well. But first, he wanted to meet Trudeau. Mills called his former boss at Heenan Blaikie, the law firm where Trudeau now worked, and told him, "It would be helpful to me if we could all have lunch together." Trudeau said, sure, and two days later, the three men spent three hours over lunch at the Ritz-Carlton in Montreal. Stronach became the Liberal candidate in York-Simcoe, just north of Toronto. Magna had tens of thousands of employees in countries all over the world, but a lot of them lived in York Region and owed their livelihoods to Stronach. The Liberals had every reason to think they'd just scored a major catch.

But as so often happened during Turner's tenure, success seemed inevitably to be followed by crisis. On August 10, 1987, Turner's principal secretary resigned. "For some months, you and I have failed to agree on major policy decisions," Douglas Richardson wrote in his departure letter. While Richardson commended Turner for leading the party "with courage, much grace, and I believe history will record, with distinction," he nevertheless chastised Turner for the way he restructured the political and strategic inner workings of the party. He also seemed to chafe at the desire by some to replace loyal members of "The Leader's Team" in the opposition leader's office. However, Richardson added in blue felt tip pen in his own hand at the end: "Thank you for the opportunity to serve and good luck. As I said in my note prior to this November's convention—you are destined to succeed."

It was a generous closing, but Richardson's departure started an exodus as others also quit the opposition leader's office. Turner's former executive assistant Stuart Langford kept his powder dry for a year, but no longer.

"John Turner doesn't have a vision, that's the problem," he said. "He had nothing in mind of what he wanted to do if he became prime minister. He just wants to be prime minister... He doesn't have a clue. It's too bad. He's not an evil man. John Turner is a good guy, but he's got to go."

Even the Liberal Party president Michel Robert, in a scrum with reporters, allowed that: "There are caucus members who are questioning, more or less openly, Mr. Turner's leadership. And if measures are not taken within a certain number of weeks or months, there is a possibility of an open rebellion on this question."

On August 30, 1987, several dozen Liberals were called to a meeting at the west block on Parliament Hill for what David Herle calls "the most remarkable meeting in politics I've ever been in." The Liberal caucus was there, but so were some other special invitees from the leader's office and party headquarters. The idea was to have a three-hour-long, full-throated venting session, then see if people could emerge more united.

They couldn't. Sen. Pietro Rizzuto, a Trudeau appointee, made clear his opposition to Turner and that he'd had it. His fellow Trudeau-appointed senator, Davey Steuart, quipped: "Typical. The war hasn't started yet, and the Italians have given up already."

A few days earlier, Michael Kirby had sent Turner a memo which he "agonized" about whether to submit. But as chair of the Liberals' strategy committee, he decided to bite the bullet and send the leader a blunt assessment of things.

Kirby told Turner fundraising was becoming increasingly difficult, that the Royal Bank was refusing to further extend a line of credit to the party, necessitating a 20 per cent cut to the party's budget, and that upcoming polls would likely show the Liberals below 30 per cent support, an historically low number. He told Turner he was coming across to Canadians as "cold, nervous, unemotional, and remote," and was "indecisive, frequently changing his positions on major issues." Kirby described the mood of caucus members as "very worried they will lose their seats in the next election," and that they felt "irrelevant and unloved" by Turner. He added few in caucus felt close to Turner or that they had any influence with him.

It was a blisteringly tough report card. But it also offered a way forward. Kirby urged that Turner release his suggested amendments to the Meech Lake Accord ("this should have been done weeks ago"), oppose whatever trade deal the government made with the United States, spend time with caucus ("show that you will listen to them and like them as friends"), cultivate key media people, and "start appearing in public looking relaxed. Wear casual clothes. Look like you are having fun."

Kirby said most Liberals acknowledged Turner was trying his best and didn't want to see him hurt. But there was this ominous conclusion: "people are now deeply and genuinely concerned about the survival of the institution of the federal Liberal Party. This is the major issue which needs to be confronted and answered effectively."

When governments are unpopular, it's almost always the case that the official opposition benefits. But these were exceptional times. On August 29, 1987, as Kirby predicted, polls showed an unpopular Progressive Conservative government, but an even more unpopular official opposition. For the first time ever, the New Democratic Party led by Ed Broadbent was in first place. Some Liberals were utterly shocked. Others said, what do you expect? Our leader is no good.

Amidst the maelstrom, there were voices trying to buck up Turner's spirits. Sen. Andrew Thompson, a former Ontario Liberal leader, sent Turner a personal note on September 2, saying "My heart goes out to you at the arrogant pettiness which you are having to endure from some loud mouthed dissidents." Thompson urged Turner to hang in there, writing. "Like the champion runner which you were, there is the last lap before victory in sight, and I am completely confident that you will have the spunk and drive to achieve it."

Bill Lee, whom Turner had fired as his campaign manager in 1984 but whose friendship he maintained, wrote to say: "My greatest wish and expectation is [to] have you back in the prime minister's chair. I know you will give great leadership to the country."

Some Tories tried to buoy Turner's spirits. Conrad Black assured him regarding the media coverage of his travails that "a majority of people will eventually be offended by this sort of sniping and intrigue... Your perseverance will eventually suitably be rewarded."

Even the mother of a future Ontario PC Party leader and Toronto mayor, John Tory, added her encouragement. "I hope your family understands politics well enough to hold up," Liz Tory wrote him. "I want you to hang tough and get tough."

On September 26, 1987, the House of Commons held its first vote on the Meech Lake Constitutional Accord. Fully eleven of forty Liberal MPs did not vote with their leader. Nine months later at another vote on the accord, only fourteen of Turner's thirty-eight caucus mates were in the House when he spoke on the issue. Now, fifteen Liberal MPs formally opposed the accord. In an effort to avoid a public confrontation with their leader, Sergio Marchi and Doug Frith abstained. Eight others didn't show up to vote.

* * *

There were no fixed election date laws in Canada at this time, so no one knew exactly when the next federal election would take place. Since most majority governments last four years, the betting was sometime in the fall of 1988, and so in February, Turner appointed British Columbia senator Jack Austin to chair his transition team. But by March 1988, the notion that Turner could lead the Liberals to victory later that year was too absurd to ponder. Panic was setting in. The Gallup poll had the party in a very unfamiliar third place, fundraising was too hard, and the candidate search wasn't going well either. Pietro Rizzuto, the first Italian-Canadian ever to be appointed to the Senate (in 1976 by Pierre Trudeau) was Jean Chrétien's Quebec organizer at the 1984 leadership convention. Rizzuto was now convinced the Liberals were going nowhere under Turner and so he hatched a plot to get rid of his party's leader.

In April, Rizzuto secretly began personally circulating a letter among the thirty-eight Liberal MPs demanding Turner's resignation. He sought a meeting with Nova Scotia MP David Dingwall, who asked his legislative assistant Dan Donovan to tag along. Dingwall figured it would be easier to have his twenty-five-year-old assistant play the heavy and ask the tough questions, so he could keep his relationship with a fellow Chrétien ally solid. But Donovan had been loyal to Turner since his days at the University of Ottawa.

The pair walked into Rizzuto's office and all Donovan could think was "It's dark in here. There are red velvet couches and drapes. It looks like a suite for the Papal Nuncio." In between bites of his sandwich, Rizzuto told the two that Turner simply had to go. He said he'd talked to riding association presidents and caucus members and easily half believed Turner was already toast.

Donovan asked where Rizzuto's fellow Quebecer, former cabinet minister André Ouellet, stood. Rizzuto said Ouellet was in France but would be faxing in his signature for the petition demanding Turner's resignation. Donovan didn't like the sound of that.

Then, suddenly, Newfoundland MP and Rat Packer Brian Tobin walked in and signed the petition right in front of everyone.

Donovan and Dingwall continued their good cop-bad cop routine. "What if you present this petition and he doesn't leave?" Donovan asked. Rizzuto didn't take kindly to the question. "Who the fuck is this guy?" the senator asked, looking at Dingwall.

Donovan pointed out the obvious: Turner had won a solid endorsement from party members less than a year and a half ago. "I know Mr. Turner," he told Rizzuto. "He's not a guy who folds."

Dingwall signed the document anyway.

One by one, Rizzuto approached caucus members with the same speech and then presented his petition for signing. Remarkably, his plan never leaked, probably because there were no copies of the documents, just Rizzuto's originals. And he didn't allow potential signatories to see who else had signed on, while claiming he had more than half the caucus on board for this coup d'état.

Rizzuto brought the letter to Toronto MP Sergio Marchi, a rookie who was barely thirty-two years old. "I told him if he wanted an immediate answer, it's 'no,'" Marchi recalls. "But it's a big step. Do you demonstrate loyalty to the leader or the country first?"

"I'll let you reflect on it," Rizzuto told him.

Marchi spent several restless nights pondering the guilt he'd feel if he signed the document, while at the same time worrying the Liberals were dead in the water with Turner as leader. Rizzuto pushed him. "Sergio, I need an answer," he told him. "You're the last guy."

Marchi signed it. So did twenty-one other MPs in a caucus of thirty-eight members. And then Rizzuto called Turner saying they needed to meet.

On April 24, 1988, Rizzuto showed up at Stornoway and told Turner that he had letters signed by twenty-two of his MPs asking him to resign. Rizzuto did not bring the letters with him, but Turner's camp didn't doubt their existence. (Having said that, Turner's deputy principal secretary Doug Kirkpatrick went to Rizzuto's suite at the Château Laurier later that night and did verify the threat: he saw each of the twenty-two signed letters.)

After the meeting, Rizzuto debriefed Marchi on how it all went. "Pietro said [Turner's] first words were: 'I can't go on. I can't lead the party with so many people offside,'" says Marchi, recalling their conversation. Rizzuto urged Turner to resign for health reasons, which given Turner's wonky back wouldn't have been a stretch. Rizzuto also added one more detail: "I think John is going to leave," he told Marchi. He couldn't have been more wrong.

"Every time John Turner was challenged, and this is a thread throughout his life, he fought harder," says an adviser who was with Turner during some of his toughest times. Still, Turner was devastated and dumfounded to learn of the plot and was shocked when he eventually found out who had signed the letters. So many signatures belonged to MPs that he thought were loyal to him.

Turner convened his senior most advisers, telling them: "I've just been hit over the head." But the advice he got from his team was unanimous. "You can't let these guys stare you down," they told him. Then Turner's principal secretary Peter Connelly did something that would ensure his leader couldn't leave: he leaked the story, figuring if it's in the public domain, there goes the nicely choreographed departure Rizzuto promised.

Turner met one-on-one with each of the document's signatories. When Marchi came in for his meeting, Turner was incredulous.

"I can't believe you signed it," he told Marchi. "How could you sign that goddamned fucking letter? You've got such a bright career ahead."

Turner was convinced Chrétien was behind the powerplay and had probably forced the young MP to sign, but Marchi insisted that wasn't the case. "Blame me," he told him. "Don't blame Rizzuto or Chrétien. Jean Chrétien never called me, and Pietro did nothing to convince me." Marchi told Turner in the final analysis, he'd simply done what he thought was the right thing to do. "The country and party are bigger than you or me," he told him, "so I signed it."

Turner, of course, had to meet the caucus after this debacle. He had to try to do whatever he could to win them back, given that more than half wanted him out. As members of Parliament arrived in the west block for the meeting, members of the media were lying in wait to pounce.

"Did you sign the letter?" one asked Dingwall.

"No comment," he replied.

"Did you sign the letter?" they asked Tobin.

"What letter?" he responded.

Donovan was standing side-by-side with Turner's communications guy Bob Jackson at a urinal when former Toronto cabinet minister Charles Cacchia burst in.

"I thought he was going to take the two huge oak doors off their hinges," Donovan says. "He was just livid, swearing at Bob Jackson."

"You betrayed us. You assured us he was leaving," Donovan remembers Cacchia screaming.

"Mr. Turner is not leaving," Jackson responded. Cacchia stormed out, slamming the doors behind him.

(In spite of all this, Turner sent Cacchia a note in June 1988 to congratulate him on celebrating his twentieth anniversary in Parliament. "Your tireless work on behalf of your constituents, your commitment to the underprivileged in our society, to the protection of our environment, and to furthering the cause of world peace all serve to do you credit," he wrote.)

"It was a coup d'état, really," Donovan says. "By Jean Chrétien's people. And it all left a real deep wound," although Donovan adds he never saw anything that suggested Chrétien was directly behind the effort.

The caucus meeting consisted of what Marchi described as "several hours of passionate, honest discussion." The last to speak was Ouellet, who said he'd encouraged people to sign the letter but didn't himself. Then he closed the discussion by saying, "In the end, a leader needs to do what a leader needs to do," and sat down.

"Classic André Ouellet!" Marchi laughs, referring to the former cabinet minister's proclivity to sound definitive and authoritative, while actually saying nothing, but doing it with an air of self-importance.

"Ouellet was always stirring the pot," says Donovan. "He was playing both ends against the middle."

With all the MP's who wanted to speak having done so, it was now incumbent upon the leader to summarize what he had heard in a way that conveyed to the members that he would take their advice seriously. As Turner got up, he made what almost everyone in that caucus thought was a terrible mistake. Turner reached inside his suit pocket and took out a speech.

"Obviously, he and his staff had written this before the meeting even took place," Marchi recalls. "I thought, in one ear, out the other. It was a downer. I wasn't convinced he'd listened at all. It was noticeable to everyone. That would have been an occasion to acknowledge his deficiencies."

Turner always maintained the "pre-written speech in the pocket" story was a bum rap. He claims he always went into caucus meetings with notes that he would update during the meeting. In his book *A Deal Undone*, Andrew Cohen suggests it's possible the whole thing was a misunderstanding, but "it sure looked bad."

During calmer times, Cacchia told Cohen: "I felt sorry for the man because he was trying to build bridges. I would have liked to reciprocate, but ideologically it was impossible." Turner never bought that. He thought Meech Lake gave his opponents "intellectual legitimacy" to take him down. But Turner may not have appreciated the extent to which anti-Meech MPs saw Turner and other pro-Meech MPs as being Mulroney's accomplices. Regardless, Cohen says the bridge Turner was trying to build simply could not extend over such an "ideological chasm."

Years later, Marchi would frequently think about that letter he signed and how Turner fought back from it. "I respected his resilience," he now says. "I've had pangs of guilt because I made his political life harder, not easier."

* * *

May 1988 started with typical difficulty for Turner. On May 2, he fired Sen. Rizzuto as co-chair of the Liberals' national election campaign effort. Despite everything Rizzuto had put Turner through, the leader described him as "a man of honour, integrity and commitment to the Liberal Party." Turner said, "We disagree on only one issue: my capacity to lead the party to victory in the next election." Even Turner, who was prepared to put up with a considerable amount of insubordination, couldn't abide having a campaign co-chair who was convinced he couldn't win.

Then on May 11, Turner received a letter from Royce Frith, urging him to "replace me as your deputy leader in the Senate." While Frith assured Turner he wasn't out to have him replaced as leader, he bluntly told him his positions on Meech Lake and free trade were wrong, "so on the constant 'Big Two' of Canadian politics, I am against you," he wrote, adding Turner shouldn't be saddled with "a Senate deputy leader who is so opposed to your essential policies… I hope our friendship will survive this serious political difference."

Frith had been a Liberal activist since 1949 and had politely but firmly insisted on Turner replacing him. But Turner wouldn't. The pair met six days after the leader read the letter, told Frith he didn't want to replace him, and that was the end of it. Turner simply didn't demand the kinds of loyalty tests most leaders did. He told Frith to continue on, but to keep their exchange private.

On June 11, 1988, Turner received a confidential memo from advisers Michel Robert, Michael Kirby, and Gerry Schwartz billed as a "frank assessment" of where the leader and party currently stood. The memo started with the problems Meech Lake was causing, then added that Trudeau's continuing interventions weren't helping, and that polls would continue to show a drop in Liberal support, with both the Tories and NDP the beneficiaries. The trio noted the PM had made some changes to his office which had improved his position, and that Ed Broadbent was considered the "strongest, most compassionate, and likeable national party leader."

But later that month, Turner gave one of his most memorable speeches ever in Parliament.

"Mr. Speaker, we are here today to discuss one of the most devastating pieces of legislation ever brought before the House of Commons. We are here to debate a bill which will finish Canada as we know it and replace it with a Canada that will become nothing more than a colony of the United States," he said, just getting warmed up.

"So urgent and compelling is the impatience of the prime minister to pack up this country and ship it south that we are going to debate this bill for only a few hours. It took 121 years for Canadians to build this confederation. The government is proposing to undo that in less than half that number of hours."

At last, Turner had found the issue that pretty much *all* Liberals could embrace, although with some notable exceptions. Despite Turner's constant efforts to court him to his side of the debate, Robert Bourassa was with Mulroney on the FTA. But David Peterson was with Turner in opposing the deal.

Then Turner made one of the most important decisions of his entire time in public life. In July 1988, Turner pointed out that because Mulroney actually ran for PC Party leader in 1983 opposing free trade and had not included free trade in the PCs' 1984 election platform, Turner would instruct the Liberal majority in the Senate to refuse to pass any legislation giving effect to the FTA, until the people had a chance to render their verdict on the deal in an election.

"Let the people decide," he said.

In a caucus meeting on July 20, Turner told his fellow MPs: "Brian Mulroney wants to be governor of the fifty-first state. I want to be prime minister of Canada." For once, Turner had found an important issue on which the caucus almost unanimously backed him. (Once again, his old friend Don Johnston opposed him and decided not to run again.) So did the majority of Canadians in the ensuing public opinion surveys. The FTA proved to be one of those issues that simply overtook the country. Everyone was talking about it.

(I worked for CBC-TV in Toronto at the time and remember going into the "Cameraman's Lounge," where the subject of conversation was always one of two things: how bad CBC's management was, and what kind of lens are you using on that shoot? But at this time, I heard one shooter say to another: "Do you think water is or isn't in the deal?" Right then, I knew the issue had hit main street.)

The polls reflected it. Angus Reid had the Liberals and Tories tied at 40 per cent apiece, with the NDP falling back to its traditional third place position with 20 per cent.

Free trade had been a third rail issue in Canada for almost a century. In 1891, Sir John A. Macdonald opposed it and won. In 1911, Sir Wilfrid Laurier proposed it and lost. In 1947, William Lyon Mackenzie King snuggled up to it, but ultimately backed away. And even Mulroney himself warned against it when he campaigned to be Tory leader. "It affects Canadian sovereignty and we'll have none of it," he said in 1983.

But when the PCs came to power in 1984, they looked south and saw an America becoming increasingly protectionist. Mulroney thought, without a very detailed, new agreement on trade, Canada could be left behind. So, he changed his mind about free trade and negotiated an agreement.

Turner may have gone through every clause of the deal with a fine-tooth comb, but that didn't stop the government's most bombastic minister from taking him on. John Crosbie called the opposition's reaction "vacuous—they distorted and misrepresented its provisions." Then he used the "L" word (which everyone uses today, but generally wasn't used by honorable members back then).

"A simple lie, a simple exaggeration, or a simple allegation was far easier for ordinary people to follow than a complicated response explaining the truth," Crosbie went on. "CBC-type snivellers in Toronto were spreading alarm about the loss of Canada's cultural identity." However, after Crosbie's confession that he hadn't read the document became public, Turner had a field day with it.

"He has not read the document! What hypocrisy! What incompetence!" Turner offered with indignation. Crosbie shot back: "I've sold encyclopedias without reading every word in them and sold vacuums without ever vacuuming a house."

Stephen Hastings saw what the FTA was doing for his leader's spirits. When he and Turner travelled together in the summer of 1988, Turner saw a sign for Avis Rent-a-Car and its world-famous slogan: "We try harder."

"You see that?" Turner said to Hastings. "That's us. And don't ever fucking forget it."

In September 1988, Turner invited former Liberal fundraising chief Senator Leo Kolber to Stornoway for lunch. "Whaddya think?" he asked him. Kolber didn't hold back. Perhaps he was still miffed at being bypassed during the 1986 leadership review. Maybe, because he was pro-free trade, he simply thought Turner was barking up the wrong tree.

"You are going to get your ass handed to you in a sling," Kolber told him. "We might do better than the last time, but we have no hope of winning."

Turner countered he thought the Liberals could win a minority government if he could make the election about free trade. But Kolber said, "If I am right, you are going to hurt the country, you are going to hurt the party, and most of all, you are going to hurt yourself. Because if you lose two elections, your currency is going to be so badly debased you will never get it back in business."

The Liberal Party, as Turner often said, was a big tent. It had MPs and members who were on both sides of business versus labour; both sides of capital punishment; both sides of the question of gay rights; both sides of the abortion issue; and both sides of Quebec's place in confederation. How could the party possibly paper over all those cleavages?

By winning.

But once the Liberals were out of power, the ability of the leader to deal with those differences was dramatically diminished. Patronage appointments, cabinet jobs, foreign trips, and parliamentary secretariats simply didn't exist. And so Turner was often powerless to handle these profound differences.

On September 28, the Liberals held a special caucus meeting for MPs and nominated candidates at which time Turner rolled out the Liberals' election platform. He wanted to restore the cuts to environmental programs, push for a clean air treaty with the United States, eliminate leaded gasoline within two years, get more affordable housing built, give full-time homemakers a pension, and create child care for all who needed it. He wanted more opportunities for the disabled, apprenticeship training programs, a national year of service plan for youth, more post-secondary scholarships, a literacy campaign, and hospice care for people living with AIDS. He allocated $5 billion for infrastructure renewal, made a commitment to aboriginal self-government, and promised a law to clean up unethical behaviour in government.

And, of course, to top it all off: the Liberals would run hard against the Free Trade Agreement, which coincidentally, President Reagan signed that same day.

Everyone left the meeting excited. Morale, for once, seemed good. The Liberal slogan would be: "This is more than an election. It's your future."

Three days later, on October 1, 1988, Mulroney visited Governor-General (and former Liberal MP) Jeanne Sauvé and asked her to call Canada's thirty-fourth general election for November 21. "The key question for the electorate will be who can best manage change in the years ahead?" Mulroney posited to voters. (Crosbie confessed in his memoirs that he didn't much like "Managing Change" as the Tories' slogan, saying it was as limp as Trudeau's "The Land is Strong" in 1972.)

David Herle says he looked at the polls "felt horrible about our prospects." The PCs were entering the campaign at 43 per cent, almost surely enough for a second consecutive majority government.

But Michael Kirby was encouraged. He compared the 1984 to the '88 Liberal campaign as akin to moving "from the stone age to the space age." An October 4 affordable housing announcement in Toronto went well. I covered that announcement for CBC-TV News. Turner was on his game, and my post-event interviews with housing advocates all returned positive reviews. "He has heard our groaning" was the way one advocate put it.

But the next day, disaster struck, the first of many.

Montreal MP Lucie Pépin was tasked with coming up with the party's child care plans, which she costed at between four and eight billion dollars. Turner got his first look at the proposal just a few hours before he was set to meet the media on October 5, and when he saw the price tag, the former finance minister in him emerged. He was mortified. Journalists would no doubt ask about the cost of the program and the advice given to him was to respond by saying: "If the NDP can create 200,000 spaces in half the time of the Conservatives, at less than half the cost, then cost should not be an issue." But cost *was* an issue for Turner, who resolved not to talk about it during the upcoming news conference. When Pépin did begin to go there after reporters inquired, Turner literally put his hand over the microphone and whispered, "You cannot give a precise amount." Then his chief of staff Peter Connolly added fuel to the fire by saying the total cost "could be $8 billion, it could be $10 billion. Whatever."

The idea was to create 400,000 new spaces in seven years and encourage the provinces to create child care spots in schools and workplaces, enrich parental leave benefits, and recognize those women who don't work outside the home by converting the existing child care expense deduction into a credit, in effect, to create a refundable homemaker's credit.

Once a reporter asked Turner whether it was really the case that he could create twice as many child care spaces as the Conservatives but for less money, the Liberal leader was in trouble. Aides were sent in to help explain the policy but nothing seemed to help. Lost in the shuffle was the fact that Turner's Liberals were trying to do something that actually wouldn't be achieved for another twenty years (by Social Development Minister Ken Dryden), namely, putting a major commitment to a national child care plan into action. Instead, the reviews focused on a team that didn't seem to have its story straight.

David Vienneau of the *Toronto Star* wrote: "One of the bright spots of the Liberal election platform—a national day-care policy—turned into a publicity nightmare for party leader John Turner, who could not explain how it would work, or what it would cost."

The fact is no one could actually say what it would cost or who would be eligible for it. The daycare debacle reinforced the image that Turner wasn't ready for prime time and undermined his confidence.

"Turner never had the confidence to put another policy out," said his pollster Martin Goldfarb.

Every now and then, Turner would reveal hints of what so many saw in him. On October 7, on a Vancouver radio show, he went back to free trade and complained that "We surrendered our energy, we surrendered our capital markets, we surrendered our investment policy, we surrendered the supply management of agriculture. I think, and believe sincerely, that we've surrendered the economic levers of this country, that political servitude is inevitable as a colony of the United States." That was the Turner anti-free traders wanted to hear.

But then, on October 12 at the Liberals' flagship Confederation Dinner, Turner had a minor slip of the tongue. He wanted to refer to our "birth right" as Canadians, but the words came out "birth rate." It set off a round of taunting that in a social media age would have gone nuclear.

There was also the problem of Turner's back. His long-time affliction flared up at the beginning of the campaign and just got worse and worse. He started limping again and was in constant pain. How he powered through the agony was a testament to his guts and commitment, but it surely left him in a weakened state. The *Globe and Mail*'s Ian Brown wrote that Turner's walk reminded him of the family dog whose hips had been crushed by a passing car.

And yet, in a campaign replete with mistakes and seemingly going nowhere, Turner transformed into Captain Canada. Because he was a business Liberal, he had the credibility to oppose the FTA and people listened. I'm not opposed to free trade, he would say; I'm opposed to *this* flawed agreement. His star rookie candidate in Quebec, Paul Martin Jr., supported the deal, saying it was the best we could get. But Martin had to admit that position wasn't gaining any traction in his constituency. However, when Turner's anti-deal fury caught on, Martin's campaign suddenly blasted off.

John Gray described the phenomenon well in his book *Paul Martin: The Power of Ambition*. "What nobody was ready for was the emergence of John Turner as the voice of the last defiant cry of Canadian nationalism," Gray wrote. "Quite suddenly, the golden boy of business Liberalism was leading the charge against continentalism."

"I'm not going to let Mr. Mulroney destroy a great 120-year-old dream called Canada," Turner said with fire in his eyes.

There was a time when author, playwright, and newspaper columnist Rick Salutin would have had no time for a Bay Street lawyer such as Turner. But the 1988 election campaign forced Salutin, who was aligned with an anti-free trade coalition, to take a second look.

"I had a lot of affection for him, based entirely on some liaising during the free trade election," Salutin now says. "He had a wonderful moment then, for which his own class never ceased to punish him."

Salutin met with both John and Geills Turner late one night at the University of Toronto's Trinity College. Turner was steadfast in his belief that, given twenty minutes, one-on-one with any of his former Bay Street colleagues, he could convince them the FTA was wrong for Canada.

"I told him that was a waste of time, that he should focus on real people instead," Salutin recalls. "Geills, who I liked a lot, said, 'Listen to him John, he's right.'" Turner did listen.

In 1984, everyone knew the combination of Turner being too rusty and the Liberals being in power for too long was a toxic one. In 1988, things were different. "I'm ready now," he told Stephen Hastings.

Turner's experience in his first go-round in politics was minority government more often than not: in 1962, 1963, 1965, and 1972. So it was hardly irrational for him to think that, if he couldn't win outright, perhaps he could hold Mulroney to a minority this time around. After all, no Tory leader had won back-to-back majorities since Sir John A. Macdonald. None of the PC leaders in Turner's era, Diefenbaker, Stanfield, or Clark, had come close to winning consecutive majorities.

But Mulroney, his friend since the 1960s, was different, as Turner would discover for himself soon enough.

CHAPTER NINETEEN

The Attempted Coup

MOST LEADERS OF MOST POLITICAL parties have had to stare down opponents who wanted them out and someone else in. Losing a lot tends to exacerbate the problem. Just ask Conservative Party leaders John Diefenbaker, Robert Stanfield, Joe Clark, Kim Campbell, Andrew Scheer, and Erin O'Toole, all of whom lost too many elections for their supporters to abide. In some cases, one election loss was enough to incur the wrath of Tories with high expectations.

Stabbing the leader in the back hasn't been as regular a feature in the Liberal Party because the Liberals have done a lot more winning. In fact, from Confederation until John Turner, every leader of the Liberal Party of Canada, save for one (Edward Blake in the nineteenth century) became prime minister. However, no leader in Canadian political history can rival Turner as a target of out-and-out coup plotting, disloyalty, chicanery, and internecine warfare. They didn't stab Turner in the back. They came at him in full view, right from the front, as we saw in the last chapter with Sen. Rizzuto's letters imploring the leader to quit.

"Whenever you're the losing ticket on a leadership, you don't go away, you just plan to overthrow the incumbent and that was certainly well in hand," said John Webster, one of Turner's senior advisers, on the Herle Burly podcast last year. "So, there was a lot of blood on the rug by the time we got to the election call in 1988."

Turner did have his occasional shining moments during the campaign. On October 12, he spoke to the party's flagship Confederation Dinner in front of a massive crowd of more than 4,000 people in Toronto. Dennis Mills and Frank Stronach organized it. Turner was in awful pain but fought on, tossed his speech away, and just winged it.

"Any country that is willing to surrender its economic levers inevitably yields levers politically and surrenders a large chunk of its ability to remain a sovereign nation," he said. "I don't believe our future depends on our yielding those economic levers of sovereignty to become a junior partner in Fortress North America to the United States."

But part of the reason there was so much blood on the rug was that so many Liberals had lost faith in Turner's abilities. So, too, had much of the country. Two days later on Friday, October 14, some of the Liberals' senior brass, including Michael Kirby, André Ouellet, Alastair Graham, Michael Robinson, and Webster, met at party headquarters to consider the following question: should the leader be told how absolutely godawful his polling numbers were? Environics had the PCs in front at 42 per cent, the NDP in second at 29 per cent, and the Liberals trailing with 25 per cent. If those numbers persisted, it pointed to another massive PC majority government of 205 seats, the NDP at sixty-one, and the Liberals even worse off than in 1984 with just twenty-nine. Grits across the country have always feared the British scenario, where the once powerful Liberal Party virtually disappeared, as the United Kingdom became more polarized between Conservatives and Labour. Was that about to happen in Canada?

When asked who would make the best prime minister, John Turner was the choice of 8 per cent of Canadians. Eight per cent. In other words, more people believed Elvis was still alive than thought Turner would be a good PM. The advisers asked themselves another question: should the leader be asked to step aside for the good of his and the party's health?

In his book *Playing for Keeps*, Graham Fraser describes Webster asking Tom Axworthy, "How would we do if we replaced Turner with Chrétien?" Axworthy thought about it and postulated that Toronto would go Liberal, and the party would do better in Quebec.

Kirby was already concerned that images of Turner labouring with his bad back conveyed the impression of a weak leader. But then Turner during his speeches could be too emotional, too over-the-top for television as well. It was an odd combination. So, Kirby wrote a memo, a very detailed memo, in which he included some "what if" polling numbers projecting what would happen to Liberal fortunes if someone *not* named John Turner were the leader.

How that memo got to the opposition leader's official residence has been something of a mystery over the years. But Stornoway's household coordinator said that former cabinet minister André Ouellet personally delivered it.

"He was postmaster-general so maybe he took his job very seriously," one senior Turner adviser jokes.

Turner had been in Toronto that day, shooting campaign ads. He took a commercial flight back to Ottawa then hung out with senior adviser Doug Kirkpatrick at Stornoway. Kirkpatrick was about to leave the residence when Turner asked him to hang around a little longer and see what was in the envelope. The two men checked it out over beers in the kitchen.

Unlike the Rizzuto letters, this attempted coup did not demand Turner's resignation. But it did spend four to five pages setting out the utterly desperate circumstances in which the Liberal Party currently found itself. It asked whether it was in the leader's or the party's interests for Turner to continue. And it included polling showing the Liberals would be atop the polls if only Chrétien were the leader. How that was supposed to happen five weeks before election day wasn't clear. The memo was unsigned.

Turner's immediate reaction was to dismiss the inexorable conclusion to which the memo pointed. He wasn't about to resign and let Chrétien take over. Even if he wanted to quit, how exactly was the party supposed to hold a leadership convention so close to election day? The party constitution apparently did provide for the caucus and nominated candidates to select a new leader in the event of the leader's death during a campaign. Turner may have been politically dead at this moment, but as a person, he was certainly very much alive. The constitution had nothing to say about an unloved leader during the writ period. It was simply uncharted territory.

Kirkpatrick took the memo and put it into a safe in the centre block on Parliament Hill. Then he decided to shred it. He never wanted to see it again.

Meanwhile, Ouellet told chief of staff Peter Connolly to go to Stornoway and tell Turner his party wanted him out. Ouellet said all the Liberal nominated candidates would come to Ottawa in a couple of days, name Chrétien as the new leader, then spend the week prepping *him* for the leaders' debate. It was audacious. Kinda crazy, actually.

And then, CBC News got a whiff of all this. The craziness had only just begun.

On that same Friday, October 14, CBC television's chief correspondent Peter Mansbridge flew to Ottawa for a lunch date with Kirby, who'd confirmed the appointment that very morning. Mansbridge showed up but Kirby didn't. The CBC anchor sensed that something was up. The CBC's parliamentary bureau, led by bureau chief Elly Alboim, reporter/anchor Don Newman, and Mansbridge sussed out what was going on behind the scenes at Liberal HQ. Then the journalists had to debate: did they have the goods to go to air with this story? Could they destroy the Liberals with a story that may not have had every "i" dotted or "t" crossed? On the other hand, could they really cover the campaign as if everything was normal, when it obviously wasn't?

The following Tuesday night, CBC was ready to air its scoop, but sensing some loose ends, the brass pulled it ten minutes before airtime. The next night, however, it ran. Anchor Sheldon Turcott introduced the piece in the studio, throwing to Mansbridge who was in the field, reporting it.

"For the last several days," Turcott intoned, "there has been some astonishing maneuvering at the highest levels of the party. Some of the most senior people thought the unthinkable. Deep into this election campaign, they thought about putting pressure on John Turner to quit. But CBC News has learned they've pulled back and are now prepared to work to salvage the campaign. Our chief correspondent Peter Mansbridge has the story of a party in crisis." Mansbridge then told the tale.

There were some minor problems with the CBC's story. They said the key meeting in question among Turner's advisers happened the previous Thursday; it was actually on Friday. They named four of the campaign officials present but not Mike Robinson. Perhaps most problematically, the network used a graphic image of a memo flashing across the screen, suggesting they actually had the real memo, when they didn't.

Perhaps the oddest thing about the newscast that night was the placement of the story in the lineup. CBC News had an unprecedented story of a conspiracy to depose a major party leader in the middle of an election campaign, and yet the story ran *third* in that newscast's lineup, fully eight minutes after the newscast began. Why didn't the network lead with the story? It was bizarre. Columnist William Johnson wrote: "Television at its most allusive, most impressionistic, least precise, and most irresponsible."

Webster got a heads-up from Don Newman that the piece was going to air: "We watched in shock, horror, and disbelief."

Liberal stalwart Patrick Gossage went further: "The most flagrant political intervention by a major news organization in a national campaign in the modern life of Canada."

After he became aware of the report, Turner called it "the craziest thing I've heard in the last four years." The next morning, the brain-trust responsible for the memo tried to walk it back. They released a statement saying: "It is preposterous to conclude that because we meet, we are plotting against the leader. In fact, we are plotting with the leader to win the election."

Meanwhile, the latest polls in Quebec showed the Liberals would win five to eight seats. Eight years earlier, Pierre Trudeau had won seventy-four out of seventy-five Quebec seats. The Liberals were on the verge of a catastrophic election night result.

"There were a lot of people disaffected with Turner's leadership," Webster continued on The Herle Burly. "They felt he wasn't responding to what needed to be done. They all felt Chrétien could take over and win. I don't know whether anyone really thought through how you'd pull that off during a campaign with the whole voting public focusing to say we're going to dump this leader, put this one in, and win the election. Seems more than far-fetched."

Webster declined to label what happened a full-blown conspiracy. Yes, there were a lot of late-night phone calls happening in somewhat conspiratorial fashion. "It did have some momentum. And it looked like we could pull this off," he acknowledged.

According to Herle: "John Turner had people in senior ranks who had overtly supported other candidates or who were of dubious loyalty to him." Turner desperately wanted to bring outsiders into his "big red tent" to unify the party. Herle told Turner at the time he couldn't count on his opponents, that they would try to undermine him at every turn. But Turner kept trying.

"I found it very frustrating," Herle now says.

Ironically, what made Turner so susceptible to this disloyalty was one of his finer qualities. He gave his advisers multiple chances to make their case, even if the advice was bad. He declined to seek revenge on those who signed the Rizzuto letters and simply couldn't comprehend that people in his own party would go to such lengths to undermine him.

"I was young, and I lacked restraint," Webster told Herle, suggesting he was prepared to mete out Turner's revenge had the leader asked for it. "I wanted to do something about that. He was surrounded by people who kept betraying him."

Meanwhile, over at Mulroney campaign headquarters, the PCs considered their options. Hugh Segal, a future chief of staff for Mulroney, feared Turner might now be portrayed as a sympathetic tragic figure rather than an incompetent leader. (That insight wasn't so far-fetched. In the 2011 election, a stricken NDP leader Jack Layton campaigned with a cane, which he brandished as a badge of honour. Rather than seeing a weakened leader, Canadians saw a courageous man battling through significant health problems and rewarded him with his party's best showing ever. Layton died three months later.)

During his preparation for the 1988 election leaders' debate, Mulroney even practiced some lines he could potentially use on Chrétien, should the leader switcheroo actually happen. "How did *you* get here?" was one option considered. Another was much tougher, with Mulroney prepared to call Chrétien "an assassin."

Turner was all but a dead man walking at this point in the campaign. So, of course, politics being what it is, his greatest moments in public life were just around the corner.

CHAPTER TWENTY

The Defeat (Again)

WHEN JOHN TURNER SHOWED UP at the CJOH studios in Ottawa for the English-language leaders' debate on October 25, 1988, even Brian Mulroney had to acknowledge the gutsiness of his opponent. The Liberal leader was truly labouring as he entered the studio. His back was just killing him. In his memoir, Mulroney noted, "I found him very courageous to carry on."

Turner and his minions knew this was essentially the Liberal leader's last opportunity to save his party from a second consecutive annihilation at the hands of the Tories. A poor performance could doom the party forever. The French-language debate the previous night had gone well for Turner. NDP leader Ed Broadbent's mediocre French essentially sidelined him in that debate. But French debates don't normally decide elections. As the country saw in 1984, English debates can.

The day before the French debate, the Liberals had begun running a television ad that was the talk of the country. The commercial portrayed the free trade negotiations with the American negotiator eventually saying: "There's just one line that's getting in the way" of an agreement. Then, a hand entered the shot with an eraser and eliminated the Canadian–American border on the forty-ninth parallel.

The ad resonated because, of course, it played into every Canadian's insecurity about Americans wanting to erase everything that was distinctly Canadian in favour of an Americanized North American continent. Tories thought it was an outrageous scare tactic, but it worked. It put some wind in the Liberals' sails and made Conservatives play defense in the lead up to the debates.

Unlike in 1984, Turner now better understood the reality of election leaders' debates and committed to not being so flat-footed this time. He prepared in lawyerlike fashion, as if cramming for the trial of the century. His team even considered throwing a Hail Mary pass, unveiling a headline grabbing new policy at the debate. The idea was for Turner to announce his support for abortion on demand, up to the twenty-two-week mark of a pregnancy. This would have been a significant liberalization to the current arrangement, which Turner knew all too well, since he'd implemented it when he was Pierre Trudeau's justice minister. Ultimately, after careful consideration, the Liberals decided not to announce the change, fearing they'd lose a huge chunk of the party's traditional Catholic base.

One of the most significant adjustments the Liberals made to this election's debate preparation was the inclusion of André Morrow, a communications and advertising specialist from Montreal, with whom Turner got on well. The initial plan was to have Morrow help Turner with the French debate, then bring in advisers Henry Comor and Ray Heard for the English debate. Comor hardly fit the profile of a typical Canadian political adviser. British born, he was an actor and medical doctor, who eventually turned his talents to media training. His mission was to eliminate all artifice and let the real person emerge, not always an easy task on television and one with which Turner faced a huge learning curve. Meanwhile, Heard was a South African who'd run the news and current affairs division for Global Television, leaving that role in 1987 to become Turner's director of communications.

Both advisers expected to be deeply involved in Turner's debate-day preparations. But to their great surprise and chagrin, they weren't. After the French debate went so well, Turner's senior-most adviser Doug Kirkpatrick called Morrow and asked him to stick around Ottawa and spend the next day, the day of the English debate, with Turner as well. There was something about how Turner responded to Morrow that Kirkpatrick liked. The candidate seemed calmer and more focused. Morrow's messaging seemed more consistent.

One of the smartest decisions the PC team made during the 1988 campaign was to insist on the leaders' debates taking place almost a month before election day. Mulroney figured if for whatever reason the debates didn't go well, he'd still have plenty of time to recover. It turned out to be a hugely prescient decision.

As Mulroney and Turner prepared to do battle on the debate stage, Stephen Hastings couldn't help but scratch his head at the nature of their longstanding relationship. Friends since their Montreal days in the legal community, they'd often schmooze at parliamentary press gallery dinners or other events, asking each other about their families. "They had an incredible personal connection and fondness for each other," Hastings says. "Of course, that didn't mean they wouldn't go after each other."

That was clearly Turner's plan at the English debate. The Liberal leader took with him to his podium his handwritten notes, jotted down from his coaching sessions. While to the rest of the world Turner's left-handed writing was practically illegible, he wanted those notes at hand to remind him of what his priorities in this debate should be.

"Hope and fear. First hour important. Polite but on offensive. Modulate all the way through," the memo said. Turner reminded himself that his tone shouldn't be "too nasty," and that he needed to "talk to your opponent, do not address him."

The panel of journalists asking the questions at this debate was comprised of the CBC's David Halton, CTV's Pamela Wallin (the future senator), and Doug Small from Global. Ontario Judge Rosalie Silberman Abella (also chair of the Ontario Labour Relations Board) was the moderator.

The debate started underwhelmingly for all sides. The anticipated showdown between Mulroney and Turner wasn't materializing. Then, in the last fifteen minutes of the debate, Wallin brought up the topic of free trade, and that's where Turner put on what might have been the most impressive performance of his entire political life, and in the process, may have saved the Liberal Party from doom. As in the 1984 debate, when Mulroney eviscerated Turner over patronage, this exchange was also relatively brief. But Turner went for the jugular and Mulroney began to bleed at the hands of the one politician in the country who knew the Free Trade Agreement perhaps better than any other:

> Turner: "We gave away our energy. We gave away our investment. We sold out our supply management and agriculture. And we have left hundreds of thousands of workers vulnerable because of the social programs involved. I happen to believe you have sold us out. I happen to believe that, once you…"
>
> Mulroney: "Mr. Turner, just one second…"
>
> JT: "…Once any region…"

BM: "You do not have a monopoly on patriotism."

JT: "…Once…"

BM: "And I resent your implication that only you are a Canadian. I want to tell you that I come from a Canadian family and I love Canada and that is why I did it, to promote prosperity."

JT: "Once any country yields its economics levers…"

BM: "Don't you impugn my motives or any else's…"

JT: "Once a country yields its energy…"

BM: "We have not done it…"

JT: "Once a country yields its agriculture…"

BM: "Wrong again…"

JT: "Once a country yields itself to a subsidy war with the United States…"

BM: "Wrong again."

JT: "On terms of definition then, the political ability of this country to remain as an independent nation, that is lost forever and that is the issue of this election, Sir."

The transcript of the exchange can't possibly capture how hot it actually was. While both men weren't yelling at each other at the same time, there was the sense that it could explode at any second and turn into a shouting match. Turner was calm but intense. Mulroney definitely raised his voice as if affronted by Turner's allegations. Abella, as moderator, was faced with the same decision David Johnston had four years earlier.

"I remember thinking: do I cut them off or do I let them have the heated exchange that they wanted to have?" says Justice Abella, who retired from the Supreme Court in July 2021. "You don't know when you're in the middle of something how time or history will end up judging your call. Actually, this is what judges do all the time. We do our best and we hope that history will judge the decision to have been the right one at the time."

As far as viewers were concerned, Abella made the right call. She did not intervene. The drama continued.

Mulroney: "I today, Sir, as a Canadian believe genuinely in what I am doing. I believe it is right for Canada. I believe that in my own modest way I am nation-building because I believe this benefits Canada and I love Canada."

Turner: "We built a country east and west and north. We built it on an infra-structure that deliberately resisted the continental pressure of the United

States. For 120 years we've done that. With one signature of a pen, you've reversed that, thrown us into the north-south influence of the United States and will reduce us, I am sure, to a colony of the United States because when the economic levers go, the political independence is sure to follow."

BM: "Mr. Turner the document is cancellable on six-months' notice. Be serious. Be serious."

JT: "Cancellable? You are talking about our relationship with the United States."

BM: "A commercial document that is cancellable on six-months' notice."

JT: "Commercial document? That document relates to treaty. It relates to every facet of our lives. It's far more important to us than it is to the United States."

BM: "Mr. Turner…"

JT: "…far more important."

BM: "…please be serious."

JT: "Well, I'm serious and I've never been more serious in all my life."

As Turner continued to pummel Mulroney, his team of advisers began cheering him on from the trailers out behind the studios. They felt they were watching a prize fight, chanting "Go, John, Go!"

After the debate, Abella called her mother to get her view on how the event had gone. All Fanny Silberman could say was, "You kept interrupting the prime minister."

"I remember my stomach fell and I thought, well, okay, I had no plans for a career after this, anyway." Having said that, Abella adds, "It tells you a story about Prime Minister Mulroney too, because whatever his views were about how I moderated that debate, he appointed me to the court of appeal [in 1992]. Didn't have to."

After the debate, Turner returned to his trailer with a fair-sized smile on his face. The team then crashed an impromptu debate-watching party in the riding of Ottawa West–Nepean at a Liberal campaign headquarters, where Turner entered as the conquering hero.

The post-debate Tory spin team told Mulroney he'd given as good as he got during the exchange. They saw the debate as a win for the PM, or at the very least a draw. They thought their guy won on the substance of the debate, but that because expectations for Turner were "subterranean" (as Mulroney described them in his book), that became the story. Turner's blazing blue eyes connected with Canadians through the cameras.

"To have taken the abuse and disloyalty from his own party—after so many years of service—was a profoundly unfair thing for John Turner and his wife and family to have to endure," Mulroney wrote in his memoir. "And there he was in front of me in the studio, in great pain, but still soldiering on in spite of it all. He struck me as a gallant warrior and very worthy opponent."

In polls published after the debate, 59 per cent of Canadians thought Turner had won; only 16 per cent saw a Mulroney victory; 11 per cent opted for Ed Broadbent. Two days later, after Canadians heard further discussion and commentary in the news media, fully 72 per cent thought Turner had won.

In his memoir, PC cabinet minister John Crosbie sided with the vast majority of Canadians who saw it as a home run for the Liberal leader. "John Turner made a direct frontal attack on free trade," he wrote. "Mulroney looked evasive, unsure of himself and uncertain about his commitment to the Free Trade Agreement. Turner by comparison seemed genuine in his concerns about the evils of free trade, or so the pundits agreed."

The Liberals' insider tracking polls showed the party was poised to gain seventy seats thanks to Turner's performance. Sheila Copps, the rookie MP running for re-election in Hamilton East, thought Turner gave Liberals something to fight for.

"It was a breath of fresh air in a campaign that had a lot of stench in it," she said. Candidates who previously wanted no part of Turner in their campaign literature now wanted to be filmed with him and have him visit their ridings.

Twenty-five years later, Turner sat down with Catherine Clark on CPAC and told her, "In the last few minutes of that debate, I really got to Mulroney on it. That swung us. We did what we had to do. It changed the score in the election." And then he admitted, "It was one of the great moments of my life."

Suddenly, free trade shot to the top of the list of voters' concerns. The Liberals pulled even with the PCs in the polls, then moved ahead. The Tories were in trouble. Turner's numbers on trustworthiness jumped an astonishing 35 per cent. Mulroney tried to tell people that Turner was wrapping himself in the flag, "in the hope you won't notice he's naked underneath. It is easier to peddle fears and lies than to build a nation."

But Turner just kept at it, alleging "they'll check your wallet before they check your pulse."

At a certain point, the polls became so favourable for the Liberals, some actually mused about what a post-election cabinet might look like. Turner and David Herle went for drinks in Saskatchewan where the head of the Young Liberals asked his leader: "What will you do for a cabinet? Your caucus is so terrible. Where are your Marc Lalondes and Allan MacEachens?"

Turner responded about his former cabinet colleagues: "You didn't know those people. They weren't any good either!"

It was at this point that the Tories' campaign guru Allan Gregg informed his team what it would take to resurrect the PCs' flagging campaign: "The bridge between the fears of free trade and John Turner is John Turner's credibility. We have to bomb the bridge."

The bombs would come in the form of a full-out frontal assault on Turner's character. Cabinet minister after cabinet minister fanned out to give speeches and interviews to anyone who'd listen and the punch line was always the same: Turner is a liar who can't be trusted.

These were not the days of Donald Trump where politicians call each other liars at the drop of a hat. In Canada at this time, politicians *never* used that word to describe their opponents. It was unseemly; these were "honorable members," after all. But the mission to bomb the bridge changed all that and the L-word became common parlance for the rest of the campaign. The business community also got off the sidelines and spent $2 to 3 million in advertising in the last ten days of the campaign alone, extolling free trade's benefits and crucifying the Liberal leader who wanted to deprive Canadians of those benefits to save his own political skin.

Two ministers who had respected reputations with Canadians got into the act. "All they offer is fear," said Joe Clark, the former prime minister who was now the minister of foreign affairs. Finance Minister Michael Wilson wondered, "Does it take courage to lie to senior citizens about their Medicare, just to get a vote? Is this the type of man you would like to lead a crusade? No wonder half his caucus told him to quit."

Willard "Bud" Estey, who had retired from the Supreme Court earlier that year, also weighed in, calling the FTA a "good, sound, solid agreement." Emmett Hall, another former Supreme Court judge and one of the fathers of Medicare, went on record as saying free trade didn't jeopardize Canada's health care system. Simon Reisman, Turner's old deputy minister from his days in the finance department, called his old boss a "traitor" for deigning to criticize the agreement he'd negotiated

"He's reckless, he's betraying the country and he's playing with the future of our children and grandchildren," Reisman said. "I accuse him of being a traitor to Canada for saying the things he is saying."

Ronald Reagan and Margaret Thatcher seemed to violate a cardinal rule of politics by intervening in a foreign election campaign. Both made speeches backing the trade deal (although Turner got off a good line in response, saying Reagan was "a lame duck trying to rescue a dead duck").

A week before election day, Mulroney accused Turner of "fanning the fires of anti-Americanism. I think he is going to find out that negativism and destructiveness is not what Canadians want."

Turner shot back that he wasn't challenging Mulroney's patriotism, "just his bad judgement."

But it all served to put Turner on his heels. Where was the Liberals' counterpunch? Where was the campaign's second wind? When reporters asked Turner for a dollar amount on his spending promises, and he was unable to provide it, the polls began to shift. Even Turner's friend and former partner at McMillan Binch, Bill Macdonald, supported the Tories' position on trade. "But I voted for my partner," insists Macdonald, who adds Turner never held a grudge against him for publicly opposing him. "He wasn't that kind of guy," he says.

It's as if the 1988 election was three campaigns in one. Before the debate, the Liberals looked deader than dead. Immediately after the debate, they looked like they'd actually win the thing. But during the last ten days, the polls turned again. Partisan Liberal crowds remained enthused (200 people showed up at a Polynesian restaurant on a miserable, snowy night in Saskatoon). But the wheel had turned.

"Had the campaign been thirty-five days long instead of fifty-five, Turner would have been prime minister again," says David Herle.

"Had [election day] been one week earlier we'd have looked a lot smarter," adds John Webster.

As the Liberal campaign and members of the media landed in Vancouver, they gathered for a pre-election day party at the Hotel Vancouver. The campaign was over. The verdict was in the hands of Canadians. All that was left to do was party hardy and enjoy (or rue) the memories of the past two months.

With John and Geills Turner sitting in the front row, one of the leader's advisers, David Lockhart, decided this was the moment to display his remarkable ability to imitate both Turner and his favourite American president.

"[CBC reporter] Keith Boag got me five rum and cokes" is how Lockhart explains his temporary bravado.

Lockhart got to the front of the room, took the microphone, and, as Turner often described it, displayed "his full thespian talents." In a room of 200 people, he began to recite (by heart) John F. Kennedy's presidential inaugural address (and not just the easy part about "Ask not what your country can do for you," which everyone knows).

"Sometimes I did the inaugural and I'd see the tears welling up in his eyes," Lockhart recalls.

But not on this occasion. Everyone was too punchy and tipsy. And besides, Lockhart quickly transitioned into a mock news conference where he portrayed Turner as justice minister. Someone from the audience yelled: "What's your position on abortion, sir?"

It was Lockhart's cue to bring the house down with a perfect, staccato, big-voiced Turner impression.

"When I was minister of justice (pause), under Mr. Trudeau (pause), the prime minister of Canada (pause), the country in which we live (pause), it was an intense debate between the pro-lifers and the baby choppers. Ultimately (pause), I came down with the position of abortion, if necessary (pause), but not necessarily abortion."

Geills Turner was laughing hysterically, which was a good sign, and the Liberal leader told Lockhart afterwards, "You really got me down!" It was a much-needed way to end a campaign which the following night would not offer any laughs to the Liberal faithful.

On election day, November 21, 1988, Turner left the Hotel Vancouver and drove to Emily Carr School to vote. He chatted with some school kids about the Spanish naval officer Bodega y Quadra, after whom his riding was named. "I feel great, I feel first class. I dreamed we'd do well today," he told everyone.

Being in Vancouver gave the Turner team the advantage of learning about returns coming in from across the country from the late afternoon on. However, these being pre-internet days, there was no chance of hopping on a laptop to get results before they appeared on television. In fact, back then, there was no television coverage until the polls closed in each region, so the Turner campaign had to work the phones to find out what was happening in the rest of the country.

The results from Atlantic Canada briefly made the campaign wonder whether it had been too pessimistic. The Liberals took five of seven seats in Newfoundland, six of eleven in Nova Scotia, split evenly with the Tories (five each) in New Brunswick, and swept all four seats on Prince Edward Island.

But then came Quebec, which gave its native son Mulroney another huge margin of victory: sixty-three PC seats to just twelve for the Liberals, a loss of five seats and the party's worst showing in Quebec since confederation. (The NDP was shut out east of Ontario.) Canada's most populous province was more competitive this time, but still gave the Tories a narrow win: forty-six PC seats, forty-three Liberal seats, and ten for the NDP.

Despite Turner's herculean efforts to resuscitate the Liberal Party in Western Canada, it just didn't happen. The PCs may have lost 20 per cent of their seats in this election, but they had them to lose. In Manitoba, voters elected seven Tories, five Liberals, and two New Democrats. Saskatchewan back then was not the true-blue Saskatchewan of today: the NDP captured ten seats, the PCs four, and the Liberals zero. The results were particularly crushing for David Herle, who'd convinced Ralph Goodale to resign his seat in the provincial legislature and run for Turner. "I was convinced the only way the provincial party could gain some traction was if the federal party wasn't hated so fucking much," Herle explains.

Goodale captured almost a third of the votes in Regina–Wascana, but given the splits, it was good for only third place in the riding, where the top three candidates were all neck-in-neck. Goodale lost by 535 votes out of more than 45,000 votes cast. (Eventually, things worked out for Goodale, who would try again in 1993 and win the riding eight straight times, before finally losing in 2019. He was appointed Canada's high commissioner to the United Kingdom in 2021).

Alberta predictably gave twenty-five of twenty-six seats to the Tories with the NDP winning the other. And in British Columbia, the NDP took nineteen seats, the Tories twelve, and the Liberals just one: John Turner was re-elected in Vancouver Quadra.

All told, Mulroney won a second consecutive majority government with 169 seats to Turner's eighty-three and Ed Broadbent's forty-three for the NDP (the highest total ever for the NDP to date, but still only good for a third place showing). In terms of the total votes cast, the campaign essentially ended up where it began with the PCs taking 43 per cent of the votes, the Liberals 32 per cent, and the NDP 20 per cent. There was a hint of future trouble for the governing Tories. The fledgling Reform Party, led by the son of former Alberta premier Ernest Manning, took 2 per cent of the votes. (Who would have predicted that in the next election in 1993, Preston Manning would lead Reform to nearly 20 per cent of the votes and fifty-two seats?)

Even though Turner managed to more than double his party's seat count, the results may still have flattered the Liberals. The new Christian Heritage Party took 100,000 votes that might have otherwise gone to the PCs, helping the Liberals win Northumberland by twenty-eight votes, Hamilton Mountain by seventy-three, York North by seventy-seven, London East by 102, Haldimand–Norfolk by 209, and Hillsborough by 259. In other words, if just 374 votes had gone another way, the Liberals would have had six fewer seats and been stuck in the mid-seventies.

Despite a second consecutive loss, Turner could take some solace in a few things. First, voter turnout for the 1988 election was 75 per cent. The free trade issue did energize and engage Canadians and Turner surely gets a large amount of the credit for that. By comparison, in 2021, voter turnout was just 60 per cent.

Second, Turner made it through the campaign despite the debilitating return of his spinal stenosis.

"The '88 campaign was a profile in courage," says David Lockhart, echoing the title of JFK's book. "Every time he stood to give a speech or got in or out of a car or a plane, or stood for a long time shaking hands, you'd see it in his face. But he just kept pushing through the pain. And he never complained. He couldn't get into or out of a car without wincing."

Third, the Liberal Party did not mirror the British political experience as New Democrats fervently hoped it would. It more than survived to fight another day.

The Tories had won their second consecutive majority government, the first time this had happened since Sir John A. Macdonald's time, and Mulroney couldn't help but crow about it on election night.

"Sir John A would be proud of his pony tonight!" he said.

The effect of the Tories' victory was that Canadians were now about to embrace free trade with the Americans, after rejecting the notion numerous times throughout our history. Historian Jack Granatstein, in his book *Yankee Go Home?* saw it as a moment of Canadian maturation.

"However much John Turner and the FTA's critics on the left had tried to crank it up for one last hurrah, anti-Americanism ultimately proved not to have legs," he wrote. "Anti-Americanism had been marginalized, by-passed, and over-taken by events."

More than three decades later, Canadians are still debating whether the trade deal, and its two successor pacts (the North American Free Trade Agreement and the United States–Mexico–Canada Agreement) have been a net benefit to Canada. The enhanced economic expansion and job creation numbers are indisputable. In 2001, even former Liberal cabinet minister and Rat Packer Brian Tobin himself acknowledged that Mulroney was right and "I was wrong" when it came to the benefits of the FTA.

But with the benefit of more hindsight, it can be said that the FTA wasn't an unambiguous success. "I think Turner was right that the FTA would rip apart the east-west trade flows that had grown up behind the tariff wall and re-emphasize north-south supply chains, and that has led to a 'following out' of the C-suite in

Canada," says Mark Warner, a Toronto lawyer specializing in international business and regulatory law. Warner points out many multinationals that do business in Canada are now managed out of American regional profit centres, which admittedly might create more opportunities for Canadians in those centres. It has also led to Canadians' receiving cheaper goods and greater product choices, "but I think corporate sovereignty has been reduced inarguably. Turner got that right."

However, Warner also accepts that Canadian and American authorities in, for example, securities and competition law enforcement may work more collaboratively in a post-FTA era. "My guess is, Turner would not have liked that," Warner adds. "But is that harmonization a loss of sovereignty? I would say no because in most cases we converged to higher standards and regulators are less likely to be captured by domestic interests."

What about Turner's predictions of doom for Canada's pensions or health care system? Warner insists there's been no negative impact of the FTA on either. "If anything, FTA-inspired financial services liberalization have created more investment opportunities for our public pension funds and that has actually helped most of us a lot (so far)," he says.

On balance, Warner concludes labour and environmental standards haven't worsened because of free trade, our pensions aren't gone, and neither is Medicare. The independent dispute settlement mechanism has "mostly worked," according to Warner. "Did they seize our water? No. Are our wages lower? No. Our minimum wage is actually much higher."

After the election, many people observed that Turner seemed better off, even happier, in spite of the defeat. Perhaps it was the knowledge that he'd done his duty by returning to public life and the pressure was now off. There were also many new MPs who owed their election to what Turner called "the fight of my life" against free trade, and so there was a sense that the leader ought to be able to choose the time of his departure without a lot of internecine drama. But there was never any question he had to resign.

"I truly believe he's the best prime minister we never had," says one of Turner's advisers from this time. "We only had him for a cup of coffee. He had an innate sense of the country better than any other politician."

What would Liberals do now as they searched for a new leader? Once again, as they had with Turner, Trudeau, Pearson, and St. Laurent, party members would look for an outsider to rescue them from their predicament.

CHAPTER TWENTY-ONE

The Successor

LESTER PEARSON'S FIRST ELECTION AS Liberal leader in 1958 was a debacle. John Diefenbaker took him to the woodshed and in the process won the biggest majority government in Canadian history with 208 seats. But four years later, Dief lost eighty-nine seats, Pearson held him to a minority government and thus was allowed to contest a third election for the Liberals. And that one he won, in 1963.

There are some similarities to John Turner's circumstances. His first election as leader was similarly awful for the Liberals, as Brian Mulroney won the biggest majority government of all time in 1984 with 211 seats. Four years later, Mulroney did lose thirty-four seats, but maintained his majority.

"In the 1980s, you don't get two consecutive majority government losses and then get a third chance," says Conservative supporter Phil Lind, who could have been channelling Liberals' thoughts as well.

Stephen Hastings, who stayed with Turner as his executive assistant until June of 1989, says that remarkably, despite how it all turned out, he never once saw Turner feel sorry for himself or shake his head wondering why he left a lucrative job on Bay Street to suffer such abuse in politics. "He believed in the nobility of public service," Hastings says. "He thought he was doing really important work. It didn't work out. He was let down by lots of people. He was resentful of that."

It's doubtful Turner ever got over his hurt at what he saw as the shocking disloyalty he experienced from the Trudeau-Chrétien wing of the party. But his deep Catholicism allowed him to compartmentalize those feelings so they didn't destroy him. His religion taught him that life is about service and suffering. Turner did plenty of both.

"If it was hard on my dad, he never said anything to me about it," says his daughter Liz. "He never ever complained." Having said that, Liz does remember some comments about "the backstabbing that went on. He was not happy with Chrétien and his guys."

Turner's immediate task after the 1988 election was to create a shadow cabinet, knowing that the Free Trade Agreement would now be a fait accompli. In a demonstration of his reverence for the environment and Canada's natural riches, he gave the critic's role to a new MP everyone in Ottawa was talking about: Paul Martin Jr., whose father was a good friend of Turner's from the time they both contested the 1968 Liberal leadership.

A little more than five months after the last election, May 3, 1989, Turner announced his intention to resign his party's leadership. It was a bit of a clever move, inasmuch as leadership conventions must be called within twelve months of the leader's departure. However, the leader wasn't actually leaving, rather only indicating his "intention" to leave. It had the effect of shutting up the backbenchers who still wanted him out, while at the same time giving him a modicum of control on the actual timing of the next convention, since the twelve-month clock hadn't actually started.

Turner's address to the House of Commons on this day was truly one for the history books. When he was called upon by his friend and fellow Vancouver MP, Speaker John Fraser, the House shared a rare moment of unity as members offered sustained applause for the member for Vancouver Quadra. Deputy prime minister Don Mazankowski, NDP leader Ed Broadbent, and Turner's long-time friend Herb Gray had all previously spoken, extending warm words in his honour. Now it was Turner's turn to take in the applause and offer some wisdom to the House. As the ovation went on, Gray stood to Turner's left; his occasional ally and occasional foe André Ouellet was on his right; Rat Packers Don Boudria, Sheila Copps, and Brian Tobin were immediately behind him. Two rows back was a future deputy prime minister, John Manley.

Turner looked terrific: tanned, wearing a dark grey suit, white shirt, and bright red tie. He opened with a joke. "The goodbyes in this place are a lot more generous and spontaneous than the hellos," he said to laughs.

Next, he looked across the floor to his fellow British Columbia MP Frank Oberle Sr., who as a Progressive Conservative represented Prince George-Peace River, and without being too specific with details, began to tease Oberle, presumably about a fishing trip the two had taken. Turner began to ask Oberle, "Who had the matches? Who killed the salmon?" And then as the laughter began to rise, "Who had the bottle? Who saved whom?" The House was lapping up every bit of the performance. "Let it be a warning to any member who goes into the outdoors to go properly equipped," Turner added with a huge smile, as he reveled in the applause.

With the pleasantries out of the way, Turner now proceeded to make his point. First, as he looked up into the public gallery, he thanked "Geills and the family for all the support they've given me." It was just one line, but Turner had a hard time getting through it. As the applause mounted, Turner looked down, seemed to choke up, and sniffled as he composed himself. Other politicians might have (and have) gone on longer about their spouses and families in such circumstances, but that had never been Turner's way. Consistent with his admonition to others over the years to "keep it short," he did.

Next, Turner switched to French as he reminded MPs of the great privilege they all enjoyed representing Canadians in that chamber and why they must never forget the need to be respectful to one another. "Everyone here, each and every one of us, represents Canadians as a result of an election in a highly free country," he said, switching back to English to add, "This is and remains the forum of the nation. This is the place where finally issues must be decided."

Turner well understood the public's prevailing view of Parliament's irrelevance and tried to counter that. "People often wonder what we're doing here," he admitted. "Yes, it's a legislative workshop. There's business to be accomplished here on behalf of the people of Canada. But the word Parliament, taken from the Norman, was well chosen. Parliament. *Parler*—debate!" Turner's voice was rising, his passion increasing. He'd made this point thousands of times in the past, but these were different circumstances with an audience listening in a different way now that he'd announced his intention to leave.

"This is theatre. This is debate and it's the freest chamber in the free world!" Turner added to sustained applause. "It's unruly at times but it's untrammeled and uncensored and unpredictable."

Turner gave perhaps an unexpected view of television's influence in the chamber, saying it had converted the House into a town hall, "a forum for the people." He eschewed the opportunity to criticize TV, which many believe has led to a major uptick in showboating by MPs with a concomitant loss of gravitas.

He did regret that Question Period had become the dominant feature of parliamentary procedures. He hoped future parliaments might offer MPs more opportunities to speak on issues of their choice, and that their power be increased by having fewer whipped votes and more free votes. Turner noted that the House would be well attended for Question Period, but not for debates on government business, which he also regretted. "There must be ways that we can re-enhance the relevance of this place," he said, looking at Speaker Fraser.

Then, unsurprisingly, Turner quoted an old friend and rival, who at this point had been dead for a decade. "Mr. Diefenbaker used to say, 'Don't neglect this place. Spend your time here. It may take many years to build up a reputation in the House of Commons, but you can lose it in one day.'" Turner became wistful as he recalled the old Chief of the PC Party. As his voice softened, he said, "That is the importance of this place," and then looking directly at his friend, Speaker Fraser, as protocol requires, he concluded with, "and it's one place I'm really going to miss." With that, he sat down, looked up to the gallery once again to make eye contact with Geills, then felt the embrace of a heartfelt standing ovation.

"He had a reverential view of Parliament," says Irwin Cotler, whose father showed him the Parliament buildings and explained the meaning of "vox populi" when young Irwin was just eleven years old. "Today, that would be met with a mocking rejoinder. But Turner agreed."

Turner wanted one last trip to Washington as party leader and so he had his policy adviser David Lockhart organize it shortly after his retirement announcement. "The depth of his connections with the Washington and New York elite were so evident," Lockhart now says.

Turner visited the U.S. Department of State and met president George H.W. Bush's Deputy Secretary of State Lawrence Eagleburger. As Lockhart watched Turner move through the rococo colonnaded hallways, he paused by the portraits of past secretaries of state and told Lockhart a personal anecdote about each one from about 1950 onwards. "This is the milieu he's used to working in," says Lockhart, annoyed that Turner didn't get to be a big player at this level, rather than spending the past too many years dealing with "no-name backbenchers like Charles Cacchia who wanted to dethrone him."

Turner went on to meet the Speaker of the House Tom Foley, the Senate majority leader George Mitchell, and his old friend from long ago bygone days, Sen. Ted Kennedy, who brought him on to the floor of the U.S. Senate, then considered the world's most important deliberative body. Despite the bruising anti-free trade campaign Turner had just waged, he was introduced as "a great friend of the United States." It all combined to make for a spectacular political memory. As Turner came off the Senate floor, he looked at Lockhart, who as a long-time Kennedy admirer was also starry-eyed, and said: "You know Lockhart, it's all bullshit but it's fun isn't it?"

Next, Canada's ambassador to the United States, Derek Burney, took Turner on a night-time tour of the American capital. Burney had been Prime Minister Mulroney's chief of staff before being appointed to Washington, so he thought he might need an icebreaker in his back pocket when he met Turner. Turned out, when Turner was a track star at UBC, he once ran in competition with Burney's cousin Jack Burney, who went on to make the Canadian team and participate in the Helsinki Olympics in 1952. Turner and Burney might have been teammates had injuries not kept Turner from competing in the Olympics. Derek Burney also recalls joking "a bit nervously" about Turner's campaign stump speech in which he threatened to make Burney the next ambassador to North Korea if the Liberals won.

The pair saw the Washington Monument, the lights reflecting on the pool of the National Mall, and the Lincoln Memorial. As Turner read the excerpts of Lincoln's second inaugural address engraved on the walls of the memorial, he turned to Lockhart and said: "You know Lockhart, the power of words. The power of fucking words." Even in one of the most august, revered locations in the world, Turner still loved his F-bomb.

To this day, Burney maintains pleasant memories of the visit. "Despite not being able to convince him about the merits of the FTA, I had much respect for Turner since he was first elected to Parliament," he says. "He did not get a lot of support or credit from within his own party but he was a fine man. Certainly, it was a privilege for me to accompany him making the rounds in Washington."

Turner effortlessly blended into official Washington so well, it both thrilled and saddened Lockhart, who had a front row seat to all of it. "There was an obvious mismatch between his talent, reputation, and his circumstances," he recalls. "I thought he'd make a better prime minister than opposition leader. He wasn't used to operating on Level Two. He was used to running things."

A look through Turner's files in Library and Archives Canada reveals an astonishing amount of content produced during his two stints in public life. There were innumerable speeches to riding associations, service clubs, non-governmental organizations, churches, synagogues, business groups, women's luncheons, ethnic groups, policy seminars, breakfasts, lunches, dinners, university clubs, fraternity clubs, federal meetings, provincial meetings, municipal associations, picnics, Liberal party galas and annual general meetings, birthday parties, ribbon cuttings, fundraising events, tributes to fellow MPs, press gallery dinners, chambers of commerce, seniors' residences, labour groups, cultural events, embassies, and in every region of the country. And that doesn't include the hundreds of interviews, news conferences, or scrums he'd given to journalists as an MP, cabinet minister, prime minister, and opposition leader. Turner felt an obligation to be accessible to the public and in the days before social media, that meant being accessible to the fourth estate, bruising questions and all. Turner was happy to hang around for scrums in the parliamentary lobby when he was finance minister. He gave Pamela Wallin three one-on-one interviews in 1988 alone (for her eponymously named CBC Newsworld show) when he was opposition leader.

Even though Turner had announced his intention to vacate the Liberal leadership, there were still some special moments ahead. In February 1990, Canada's first ever female justice minister, Kim Campbell, was uncomfortable with the fact that Canada now had no law regulating abortion. In 1988, in its *Morgentaler* decision, the Supreme Court had overturned the existing law and tossed the responsibility for coming up with a new one back to Parliament. Those virulently opposed to abortion voted against Campbell's bill, because it did make abortion legal again. The trickier call was for pro-choice advocates, who were being asked to agree to some regulations around abortion. Only two Liberals voted in favour of Campbell's bill: Peter Milliken (the future longest-serving Speaker of the House of Commons in Canadian history) and Turner, who referred to the bill as "the best we could do under the Charter."

In her book *Time and Chance*, Campbell describes the moment when she walked across the floor to thank Turner for his vote, which was quite consequential, given that the bill passed by just seven votes. The moment had three points of significance: first, it was the current justice minister shaking hands with a former justice minister; second, it was one Vancouver MP thanking another; and third, although no one knew it at the time, it was a future prime minister expressing her gratitude towards a previous prime minister. (Later that year, the bill would die in the Senate on a tie vote.)

In June 1990, Liberals gathered in Calgary to choose Turner's successor as party leader. The race would go down in history as one of the least interesting, inasmuch as the outcome was a foregone conclusion. Jean Chrétien claimed victory on the first ballot with 57 per cent of the delegate support. Paul Martin Jr. placed second with 25 per cent, while Sheila Copps took third with 11 per cent.

But the convention's sub-plot was endlessly fascinating, as pro- and anti-Meech Lake Accord forces dominated the narrative, given that the deadline for all provinces to ratify the accord, June 23, 1990, was just two days away when the convention began. Some told Chrétien he was gambling with Canada's future if he sided with his mentor, Pierre Trudeau, and opposed Meech, against the wishes of two other powerful Quebec political figures in Mulroney and the province's premier Robert Bourassa. Chrétien tried to finesse the issue by saying the accord was salvageable, but only with amendments. At one point, some delegates chanted "*Vendu!*" at Chrétien ("*sell out!*"), one of the most hurtful epithets, Chrétien later admitted, ever hurled at him. When Chrétien hugged the anti-Meech premier of Newfoundland, Clyde Wells, after his victory, the optics for the pro-Meech side were terrible. MP Gilles Rocheleau quit the caucus the next day. MP Jean Lapierre proceeded to wear a black arm band, also left the caucus, sat with Lucien Bouchard, and helped create the sovereigntist Bloc Québécois.

But before all that drama, Liberals had to perform the somewhat awkward task of saying farewell and thank you to their outgoing leader, who had led them to two consecutive electoral defeats. And that meant listening to one final speech from Turner before choosing his replacement.

Turner's speech was a good one, but given the circumstances, it packed less of an emotional punch than his speech thirteen months earlier in the House. He told delegates that "nothing made my return to public life more worthwhile" than opposing the Free Trade Agreement. "I believe in this country," he said. "I believe that we are unique. I believe that we Canadians are different. I believe we have something worth preserving and worth fighting for. I believe that just as a majority of Canadians agreed with me then, an even greater majority agree with me now." Then, reaching a fever pitch, Turner erupted with volcanic passion, saying: "We must never give up on this country. Never! Never! Never! Never!" That brought the crowd to its collective feet.

Turner could have used the moment to revisit past internecine battles but didn't. There was a reference to how tough public life could be. "Goille and I ought to know," he admitted. "In public life there are no secrets. Your life becomes an open book, subject to a thousand different interpretations, speculation, and insinuation." But Turner wasn't complaining. "It comes with the territory."

And to no one's surprise, Turner reminded the audience of the thing that had motivated so much of his public life.

"One of the proudest moments in my life was the day I was first sworn in as a Member of Parliament," he said. "My proudest boast today is that I am the Member of Parliament for Vancouver Quadra!" And with that, Turner's time at the helm of the Grits was over, but not his time as an MP. Turner would complete the term to which he'd been elected, which would last until the summer of 1993.

For a man who experienced numerous highlights in the House over the course of four different decades, it could be said that Turner's finest hour as a parliamentarian was still to come, even though he was at the nadir of his political influence. On January 16, 1991, the day after the United Nations imposed a deadline for Iraq to withdraw from Kuwait, the House debated what Canada's response should be in light of Saddam Hussein's invasion of Kuwait five months earlier. Turner took the extraordinary position of repudiating his new leader's position and backing Prime Minister Mulroney's call for action.

"The whole history and tradition of commitment of the party to which I have belonged for thirty-five years has been in support of the UN," Turner began. "To do otherwise would repudiate the votes we have unfailingly cast in support of United Nations resolutions. It would also repudiate our commitment to internationalism and to the United Nations, the hallmarks of the Liberal Party and Canada's foreign policy for decades."

Chrétien listened to the speech, his face expressionless bordering on morose, as his predecessor urged Canada to join the coalition of allies and their military efforts as "a peacemaker."

"This is a crucial test for the United Nations, and Canada must support it," Turner added. Defense Minister Bill McKnight's office liked the speech so much, he had it broadcast overseas to Canadian Forces troops.

After Turner finished, Mulroney led his caucus in a standing ovation and then (as Turner had done for Mulroney after the 1987 Meech Lake Accord agreement) crossed the floor to shake the now Liberal backbencher's hand. It may have been Turner's most important moment, but those on Team Chrétien were deeply unhappy with it. MP John Nunziata, one of Turner's former Rat Packers, said rather ungenerously: "It's his revenge and he's trying to pave his way into certain boardrooms."

Chrétien sought his own revenge after the speech. He'd already had Turner locked out of his centre block office and moved to the less prestigious Confederation Building, west of the Hill, to join numerous other unknown MPs. But there were more petty consequences after the Persian Gulf speech to come.

Jean-Robert Gauthier, whom Turner had appointed party whip in 1984, gave his former prime minister the use of his centrally located office after Turner stepped down as leader. But Chrétien's people put an end to that. Once MP David Dingwall became the new whip, he brought that practice to an end. When a Canadian Press reporter asked Turner's aide Lisa Haley why, she responded: "I don't know. You'll have to ask protocol whether a former prime minister is outranked by a whip."

It got sillier. Apparently, there's a rule that MPs can't have staff members in the lobby outside the House, only party leaders can. After the Gulf speech, Haley saw Dingwall speaking to a security guard after the new whip noticed she was there assisting Turner. The guard approached Haley, apologized, but said she'd have to leave. Two other opposition MPs, Lucien Bouchard (BQ) and Nelson Riis (NDP), saw the kerfuffle, thought it was ridiculous that a former prime minister would be treated this way, and each issued Haley one of their party's opposition lobby passes, even though she wasn't with their party. That did the trick and Haley was permitted to stay thereafter, attending to Turner's administrative needs.

Turner gave one more speech of consequence in the House before his term as an MP expired. On September 10, 1992, he spoke about the PC government's second major attempt (after the failure of Meech Lake in June 1990) to achieve constitutional renewal, this time through the Charlottetown Accord. That arrangement was unanimously agreed to by the federal, provincial, and territorial governments, plus four additional Indigenous groups. It would enshrine aboriginal self-government in the Constitution; recognize Quebec as a distinct society within Canada; clarify the division of powers between the federal and provincial governments; significantly reform the Senate and how its members would be chosen; and offer Canadians, province by province by territory, a referendum on the entire package.

With the national plebiscite only six weeks away, Turner rose in the Commons to support the proposal. "If I were a Quebecer, I would say again: my homeland is Quebec, but my country is Canada," he said. And he evoked the same themes he'd begun advancing in the 1960s, as he talked about what was required to keep Canada united. "Those who opposed Meech Lake will bear the burden of history for the national disruption of the last three exasperating years," he said. "I have never in thirty years since being elected to the House of Commons had trouble as a Canadian with the concept of a distinct society. For me, it reflects reality. A different majority language, a different system of law, a different history, a different culture, different traditions, and a different sense of humor."

But regardless of whatever strengths this accord had, they couldn't overcome a nationwide antipathy to the man that led the negotiations. Mulroney's job approval rating stood at just 12 per cent. As a result, the Charlottetown Accord was voted down by Canadians, 55 per cent to 45 per cent, despite having had the support of the Progressive Conservative, Liberal, and New Democratic parties of Canada, not to mention unanimity among the premiers of the day. Pierre Trudeau, Preston Manning's new Reform Party and the two separatist parties in Quebec (the Bloc and Parti Québécois) all opposed it.

Mulroney's prime ministership came to an end in June 1993 and with it, one of the most turbulent and consequential decades in Canadian history. Progressive Conservatives replaced him with Kim Campbell at their leadership convention in Ottawa. Promising calmer times and a steady agenda, Jean Chrétien defeated Campbell in the ensuing election on October 25, capturing the first of three consecutive majority governments for the Liberals, and reducing the PCs to just two seats.

Turner's allies claim it was the seventeenth prime minister's labouring in the political vineyards for nearly a decade that helped create the conditions for Chrétien to become Canada's twentieth prime minister. And they saw consequences for the country in Turner's inability to get his old job back. For example, they believe Mulroney's time in the PMO hastened the intense centralization of power in that office, which has not diminished in subsequent years. Had Turner been able to remain PM, they argue, more ministers would have been empowered to run their departments, as Turner did during the Pearson and Trudeau years.

"What did we miss because of his short tenure?" asks former Turner aide Richard Mackie. "A prime minister with a great understanding of British Columbia and the Greater Toronto Area," he says. "Trudeau, Mulroney, Chrétien, and Martin were all Quebecers."

Stephen Hastings saw Turner's ability to find compromise as a strength. "He thought if you worked with the opposition and the provinces, you'd get a better bill in the end," he says. Turner also lamented the end of evening sittings, when members would go to dinner, play cards, and "deals got made." The House's schedule is more family friendly these days, but according to Hastings, Turner felt that came at a cost of MPs not having those opportunities to foster better relationships.

But Keith Davey's widow Dorothy offers a dissenting view.

"You need a lot of steel to be prime minister," she says. "Did he have it? I'm not sure. I don't know how you go through life being battered constantly and maintain your equilibrium. The young John Turner I heard had the royal jelly. But the guy who came back was broken." Dorothy Davey ran the 1974 election tour in Ontario for the Liberals and insists "he had the royal jelly then, I can tell ya." But by the late 1980s and 1990s? "I'm not sure he'd have been a good prime minister."

However, in his book *A Life in Progress*, Conrad Black writes that Turner simply couldn't endlessly resist the opposition of Trudeau and Chrétien. "He made his gracious exit, an admired and well-liked politician of the highest dedication and integrity who went, in a few weeks in 1984, from being the man of the future to a man of the past, but who yet retained and will always deserve the respect of the country," Black writes. "He was one of the outstanding justice and finance ministers and opposition leaders in Canada's history and it is a misfortune that he couldn't await another election which he certainly would have won."

CHAPTER TWENTY-TWO

The Post-Political Life

IN THE UNITED STATES, FORMER presidents are called "Mr. President" for the rest of their lives. They receive Secret Service protection until the end of their days. They have an annual pension of nearly a quarter of a million dollars. They're entitled to a furnished and staffed office anywhere in the United States. They have an annual travel allowance of $1 million. Even their spouses are entitled to $500,000 for security and travel. And when it comes time to meet their maker, they are guaranteed a ceremony with full honours and have the option of being buried in Arlington National Cemetery.

The tradition in Canada is to stop calling our heads of government by their titles as soon as they leave office. They go back to being "Mr. Turner" or "Mr. Mulroney" or "Ms. Campbell" right away. There is no RCMP security after they leave office. None. There is no particular pension that comes with being prime minister. If they served as MPs long enough, they're entitled to their MPs' pension. There is no budget for staff or office or travel, despite the fact they are surely called upon to attend numerous events, given their former jobs. And when they die, it is the discretion of the government of the day, in negotiations with the family, as to how "prime ministerial" the funeral service will be.

On the one hand, there's something levelling about holders of high office being treated more normally after their time in the spotlight is over. To a Canadian's sensibility, there's something bizarre about Sarah Palin, who served barely half a term as Alaska's chief executive, being called "Governor" for the rest of her life. But that's what they do in the United States.

Conversely, John Turner served 8,326 days as a member of Parliament, in two big chunks: 1962 to 1976, and then after his comeback from 1984 to 1993. That's twenty-two years, nine months, and seventeen days. He'd been a prime minister, opposition leader, finance minister, justice minister, and one-time Bay Street rainmaker. And yet, when it came time to resuming his life in the private sector after leaving politics for the second time, Turner not only encountered the financial realities of being an ex-prime minister, he also discovered the welcome mat on Bay Street was a lot smaller.

The fact was that much of corporate Canada was mad at Turner. His opposition to the 1989 Free Trade Agreement clearly signified to many in that world that he wasn't one of them anymore.

"He betrayed his earlier friendships by opposing free trade," says Phil Lind, Ted Rogers' top adviser at Rogers Cable TV. "Everyone cut him off after that. He got no decent boards. He knew it. And his friends knew that's what had happened to him."

Furthermore, Turner wasn't the prize-catch-former-finance-minister in his mid-forties anymore. He was now in his early sixties and much of Bay Street wondered whether he could still throw his fastball. He checked in with his former firm, McMillan Binch, but his old partner Bill Macdonald had retired and the younger guys had no connection to him and didn't want him back. Somehow, the word got back to Prime Minister Mulroney that Turner might be having difficulty in his job search. So, he asked their mutual friend, Conrad Black, to approach Turner with an idea. Offering an appointment to his former political foe might seem strange by today's standards of political toxicity, but it was actually nothing new for Mulroney. He'd appointed former federal NDP leader Ed Broadbent to chair a human rights commission in Montreal. He'd tapped former Ontario NDP leader Stephen Lewis to be Canada's ambassador to the United Nations.

"I knew the sacrifice John had made," Mulroney tells me, "[and] how difficult it would be to come back to Toronto and start all over again."

Mulroney didn't want a former prime minister embarrassed; he was also well aware of Turner's affection for the Catholic Church. So, he had Black approach Turner with an offer to become Canada's ambassador to Italy.

Mulroney explained to me his view that Turner "should take it easy and write his memoirs. The best place to do that is in Rome. I'd make him the ambassador where he could live like a king and write his memoirs and turn his life around."

Black delivered the message but reported back to Mulroney that Turner had graciously rejected the offer. The PM then enhanced it, offering to add The Vatican to a sort of double-posting. But again, Turner said no. He figured he had ten to fifteen years of significant earning power left and he simply felt the need to earn.

"He appreciated it enormously," Mulroney explains, "but he couldn't afford it. He had to try to make money in Toronto." While a diplomatic posting would pay Turner a six-figure salary, with any luck he could earn four or five times as much on Bay Street.

Enter Larry Bertuzzi. He wanted John Turner for his law firm.

Bertuzzi was gaining a reputation as one of the biggest names in sports labour relations, doing arbitration cases for various National Hockey League teams. He ran the mid-sized Toronto law firm Miller Thomson, which boasted about forty to fifty lawyers at the time.

"The story goes," explains Gerald Courage, a former chair of the firm, "they held a partners' meeting to let John in. He came into the room, worked the entire room and knew everyone's name before he'd even met the people."

Turner's arrival at the firm helped to grow Miller Thomson's client list and improve the quality of the clients.

"Certainly, from my standpoint, he gave us a great boost," says Douglas Best, a veteran lawyer at MT. "He was a real springboard."

"He was a larger-than-life individual who all of a sudden was walking the halls of our firm," recalls Steven Wesfield, a young lawyer at the time who had an office between Turner's and the coffee machine. "He'd drop by and we'd speak. Everywhere he went, people would turn their heads."

Within eight years, Turner had contributed to a tripling of Miller Thomson's size.

"It's not all John, but he was clearly a significant factor in our growth and credibility," says Courage.

Turner probably didn't docket a single hour during his time at MT, but no one expected him to. He worked his network of contacts, went for lunches and dinners to secure clients, and, of course, continued his tradition of calling people on their birthdays. "Every year on my birthday he'd give me a call and 'raise a glass to you Doug,'" says Best. "He was a great draw for the firm from a recruitment standpoint. He was a real ambassador both internally and externally."

Wesfield notes that Turner had serious street cred with huge corporate institutions and large family businesses, which in the past never would have taken their business to MT.

"He'd also tell me how there'd be disputes within those families," Wesfield says. "He'd be called in to help mediate issues that came up."

"He gave us this credibility and people loved meeting with him," says Best. "My clients were all over the idea of having John Turner come for lunch or dinner or a drink."

And what about the gossip that Turner wasn't successful enough to be signed by a bigger Bay Street firm?

"I never heard anyone say, 'Because he lost twice to Mulroney he was a second-tier guy,'" insists Wesfield. "He was first tier all the way."

There was a burgeoning issue of corporate directors' and officers' liabilities at this time, and so Turner and Wesfield teamed up with a major insurance broker. They mined Turner's corporate contact list and travelled all over Canada with a "road show." Turner would talk about his experiences as a corporate director, Wesfield would follow up on statutory liabilities, and then the broker would try to sell the company some insurance.

"We had very significant members of corporate Canada at meetings in board rooms," Wesfield says. "When John spoke, there was absolute silence. You could hear a pin drop."

Even though he was out of public life, Turner apparently never lost his zeal to turn young people on to politics. One time, Best mentioned during one of their regular lunches that his son Adam, who was in Grade 5, was doing a project on prime ministers. Next thing he knew, Turner had volunteered to come speak to Adam's class at Oriole Park Public School in midtown Toronto.

"He had many, many skills but one of his supreme skills was knowing his audience and tailoring his presentation accordingly," Best says. "The kids were gob struck. They were all pumped for it." Turner told the students there were three important things they could do with their lives: join the clergy, run for office, or be a teacher.

"So here he is, making their teacher out to be just short of God," Best says. "The teacher is awed, and the kids are all awed, and I felt like a Grade 5 in the back of the room gaining these insights."

Turner also preached the importance of honest, ethical, open relationships among the firm's partners. "He always said about law, 'This is a people business,'" Courage recalls. Turner emphasized the partners needed to be generous with each other and speak well of each other.

"I think it just was consistent with his view that individual human beings were important," Courage adds.

Turner told a twenty-nine-year-old Wesfield about the importance of being loyal to clients as well. "Steve," he'd say, "you run with the hounds or you run with the hares."

Wesfield interpreted those comments to mean, "If you had a client, stick with that client. Don't go to someone more attractive in that industry. Stay loyal to your contacts. They could count on John to be there, and John could trust me to be loyal to him."

Turner's assistant, Jill Hamblin, ran much of his life, given that her boss couldn't so much as send an email. He just was not a computer guy.

"He was so fascinating," says Hamblin, who came to Canada from the United Kingdom in 1974 and spent five years as Turner's assistant at Miller Thomson. "He was such a joy. He made me smile every day."

Turner was the first person Hamblin worked for that regularly took her to lunch. "He treated me with the utmost respect and courtesy," she says. "He talked to everyone, especially the wait staff, and remembered all their names." Hamblin also loved how when she brought her ten-year-old son Tristan to the office one day, Turner made time to "chat him up. He loved young people."

One day, the two were reminiscing about something and Hamblin got up the guts to ask the question she'd always wanted answered. "Mr. Turner, did you have a love affair with Princess Margaret?" she asked him. "He looked at me with a perfectly straight face, that twinkle in his eye and said: 'Every Englishman must do his duty!'"

Turner did love the Royal Family and once told Best a story that went back to his time as justice minister. During a visit to Canada, Turner asked the Queen Mother if she'd like a drink.

"What do you suggest?" she asked him.

"Let me make you a martini," Turner responded, and he did.

Three decades later, in August 2000, Turner wrote a letter congratulating the Queen Mother on celebrating her hundredth birthday. A few months after that, a reply came from Buckingham Palace and at the bottom of the note in the Queen Mother's handwriting was written: "To the man who made me the best martini I ever had."

Turner did pick up some directorships on boards such as Dominion of Canada, Empire Life, and Purolator. He also now had the time and desire to work on issues he was passionate about (such as the environment and conservation) for the World Wildlife Fund and Canadian Geographical Society. With the help of his friend, former MP Herb Gray, who now chaired the International Joint

Commission, he helped bring Lake of the Woods under the oversight of the IJC, saving the waterway from being decimated by algae blooms.

* * *

As a former prime minister, Turner respected people at all levels of government who had the guts to put their names on a ballot and get elected. That philosophy led him to volunteer to help his local city councillor in Toronto, Michael Walker, get re-elected. But Turner wasn't satisfied being a big name on Walker's letter-head. He got involved. He saw Walker canvassing the traditional way: a couple of advance people knocked on doors and if someone was home, they'd let them know the candidate was just down the street and ask if they would like to meet them. If so, then the advance people would make small talk until the candidate arrived.

When Turner saw this plan in action, he told the campaign, "That's a terrible idea. It's inefficient. Do what I do."

"He didn't go door-to-door, he stood in the middle of the street," says David Goyette, part of the campaign team for Walker, who served almost three straight decades on council. "If someone was home, they would come to meet him!"

Turner, always impeccably dressed, would accompany Walker, and yes, they would hold court in the middle of the street while their constituents came to them.

"It was much more efficient," Goyette acknowledges, "but the public relations side of it *is* a little precious."

Turner was always early for campaign meetings and so was Goyette. The two of them frequently talked for fifteen to twenty minutes before meetings got started. "I was always surprised how much respect he had for local government," says Goyette, who was also a senior adviser to Mayor Art Eggleton in the 1980s.

* * *

Even though he was now out of public life, Turner liked nothing more than to move an audience and continued to accept numerous speaking invitations. In 2001, he was the guest of honour in Orillia, Ontario for the annual Sir John A. Macdonald birthday dinner. Two decades ago, there were no debates as there are today about Macdonald's virtues. He was an unambiguously heroic figure in the history of Canada and Turner's choice as Canada's best ever prime minister. (Turner inscribed Jack Cahill's 1984 book about him, *The Long Run*, to his friend Arthur Milnes with: "To Arthur, Keep the faith and remember Sir John A".) Turner gave a great speech to a sold-out crowd in Orillia. Then, former PC Justice Minister Doug Lewis (who represented the area from 1979 to 1993) got up to ask a question.

"John Turner gave a warm, affectionate, relevant speech about Sir John A.," recalls Sean Conway, who was there. "Then the former ministers of justice went back and forth. It was so civilized and interesting. I thought, God, this is good. Politics at its absolute best."

Turner's affection for Sir John A prompted him to make history more than a decade later. He attended a ceremony at the foot of the statue of Macdonald in Kingston, marking the first time in seven decades that any prime minister had visited that site. Not since prime ministers William Lyon Mackenzie King and Arthur Meighen visited the site on the fiftieth anniversary of Macdonald's death in 1941 had any other PM gone there. The occasion also marked fifty years to the month of Turner's first election as an MP. Given that Kingston City Council has now removed the statue from its prominent place in the park, it seems likely that Turner will be the last prime minister ever to see it so prominently displayed.

* * *

All former prime ministers eventually return to Parliament Hill because all prime ministers have one post-political official duty they cannot shirk: being hanged. The unveiling of an official portrait always has subplots, and May 8, 2001 was no exception. Prime Minister Jean Chrétien was obliged to give a speech praising a man he couldn't stand, and Turner had to sit and politely listen to a man about whom he felt the same. When it came time for him to give his speech, Turner wasn't about to forego an opportunity with all of the nation's media in attendance. Four months later, author Jeffrey Simpson would release *The Friendly Dictatorship*, complete with cover photo of Chrétien photo-shopped to look like Muammar Gaddafi with a chest full of medals. Turner took aim, urging the friendly dictator to give ordinary MPs more of a voice. "I urge the members of this House from all sides to reclaim the dignity and independence that begat our system [and was] so much in evidence during the early years of our Confederation," he said, adding that except for throne speeches, budget votes, or critical national policy, the whip should be withdrawn.

"Parliament is the forum of our nation," he said. "It is not just a legislative machine."

Chrétien seemed decidedly unamused.

A year later, on June 18, 2002, another significant event brought Turner back to Ottawa. Peter Milliken, who would become the longest-serving Speaker in Canadian history, invited twenty former MPs from the "Class of '62" back to Parliament Hill for lunch, including the now seventy-three-year-old Turner. Forty years to the day after they'd all won their first election, the ex-MPs, including Herb Gray, Donald Macdonald, Edgar Benson, and "Red" Kelly, gathered to swap war stories and relive old glories. Milliken said the reunion was Turner's idea to honour Gray, whose tenure came up just five months short of forty years in the House.

"He was the dean of the House of Commons," Turner told Art Milnes at the time. "I didn't want it erased and I thought the best way to celebrate it, in a non-partisan way, was to gather the Class of '62."

* * *

If you want to see Turner at his best after he left politics, go online and find a speech he gave to Moses Znaimer's IdeaCity conference in Toronto in 2001. At seventy-two, Turner took to the stage and, without notes or a teleprompter, spoke from the heart about his concerns for Canada.

"There's no debate in Parliament. There's little debate in universities or academia. And the media aren't that hot either," he said, just getting warmed up. Then, referring to the mug in his hand and remembering that the owner of the satirical *Frank* magazine would be speaking later that day, he added: "I want to assure his editors this is a coffee, not a glass of Scotch," which, of course, got big laughs and applause.

Turner urged the audience to think about the big issues of the day: Where is our dollar going? Will it get so low that our country will be ripe for takeover? (It was worth $1.07 American when he was finance minister, he hastened to add, to applause.) Where are we going on energy? Who's going to help our softwood lumber sales into the United States? How many stories do you read about the environment? How's the air or water quality in Toronto? He assured the audience that despite campaigning against the 1989 Free Trade Agreement, he favoured free trade, it was *that* particular agreement he opposed. "Tell [President] Bush and [Vice-President] Cheney: if you want our energy, take our lumber," he said. "It's free trade, right? What a joke."

Turner wasn't talking like a typical former prime minister, smoothing out the rough edges into a more diplomatic presentation. He was on fire. He noted a poll he'd seen in the *National Post* which reported 50 per cent of Canadians felt they weren't going to have an independent country in ten years.

"Wow…" he responded, sounding deflated.

Having put the bait on the end of his hook, Turner now moved in to make the point that had animated his life for the past four decades.

"It's your generation that's going to have to rescue us," he told an overwhelmingly young audience. "We need a whole new generation for all the political parties."

Turner acknowledged how awful the media scrutiny into private lives had become. "It's a lot tougher today than it was in my day," he said, before adding under his breath, "thank God," to huge laughs.

"All the bright young people I know, including my three boys here and my daughter in New York, they're all making obscene amounts of money compared to what I made at their age," he continued. "They're on Bay Street, having a good time, living well, taking vacations, but at this stage, no one is putting anything back into Canada." There was a note of resignation in his voice.

Interestingly, none of the Turner kids has seen that speech in which they're referenced. Perhaps understandably, public life doesn't have much allure for them.

"If anything, especially with all the crap he was getting, the infighting, it deterred me from entering public life at all," says Andrew, who also acknowledges that his father told the Turner kids numerous times about "a duty to give back if you have talent."

"I don't really feel like having my closet looked into and seeing what skeletons people will find. I don't need my life scrutinized like that," Andrew admits.

Michael, who's a lawyer for a Toronto television production house, adds: "I truly have a great respect for those who do go into politics because it's a relentlessly unforgiving life. But people give you far more shit than you deserve for the effort you're making to try to help."

Turner revved up the energy again at IdeaCity, urged "the best and the brightest of your generation" to solve today's problems, and with his voice reaching a crescendo, looked offstage at Znaimer and said, "From time to time, Moses, someone's gotta remind us: let's not take this country for granted."

You could hear a pin drop. Then he brought his remarks to a conclusion.

"Okay, that's my message," he said quietly. "Use your influence. Every once in a while, some of us have to give something back!" The applause was thunderous and even the preternaturally cool Znaimer dashed on stage to hug Turner enthusiastically.

"People listened to him because he didn't have a political axe to grind," says Geills Turner. "He was speaking from his heart and that resonates. People understand that. John fundamentally believed in that. His beliefs suddenly seemed relevant today."

* * *

In 2003, Monte Hummel, president of WWF Canada, wrote what he acknowledged was a "barnburner of a letter, blunt to the point of rudeness" to Ernie Eves, who'd succeeded Mike Harris as premier of Ontario in 2002. Eves had represented the Parry Sound–Muskoka area for two decades, before retiring from politics in early 2001. But he was drawn back into public life the same year when Harris announced his surprise retirement. Eves had contributed to ringing alarm bells over acid rain, which was killing the lakes in his central Ontario constituency, so he was no stranger to environmentalism.

After Eves became premier, however, Hummel blasted him for doing "absolutely nothing" and asked him in the letter whether "he was prepared to do ANYthing" for the environment. Hummel then suggested Eves could use his good offices to unjam negotiations to create a national marine conservation area for Lake Superior, which would require that the province surrender the lakebed and parts of the shoreline and islands to facilitate an agreement.

"It frankly was a Hail-Mary [pass] that I hoped might insult/jar the Premier into action," Hummel now says.

The gambit worked and got the premier's attention. Hummel then decided to put one of his best-known board members to work: John Turner. "He had been a long-time champion of this site which, when protected, would be the largest freshwater reserve in the world," Hummel says. "So, I got John to request the meeting."

Eves and Turner had much in common. Turner had been prime minister, while Eves was now the premier. Both had been finance ministers. Both had left public life to work on Bay Street. Turner was a blue Grit, Eves a progressive conservative, so their ideological Venn diagram had lots of overlap. As a result, when Turner asked for a meeting, "I gave him the respect and time of day he deserved," Eves says.

"I'd already made up my mind before they arrived that I was going to do it," he continues. Nevertheless, the group met for half an hour, Hummel made the local pitch and Turner added that former U.S. interior secretary Bruce Babbitt (a member of the American WWF board) and Prince Philip had both championed the cause.

"I do remember he was extremely passionate about it," Eves recalls.

One of Eves' last acts as premier was to sign off on the documents, paving the way for the conservation area's creation by the government of Prime Minister Stephen Harper. Prince Philip later wrote Hummel a letter of congratulations on a job well done.

"Most important," Hummel concludes, "regardless of our puny human politics, egos, and lobbying strategies, one million magnificent hectares of the most beautiful, pristine freshwater in the world, and a cold wild coastline second to none, are now protected forever. Thank you, Ernie, Stephen, and John, whose respective contributions have gone pretty much unknown, unrecognized, and worse, not believed."

* * *

Even in his mid-seventies, Turner was called upon to try to fix problems within the Liberal family—and there were plenty as Jean Chrétien gave way to Paul Martin. In the leadup to the 2004 election, Chrétien's former Deputy Prime Minister Sheila Copps found herself fighting for a nomination against Tony Valeri, who was a Martin loyalist. Martin asked Turner to approach Beth Phinney, another Hamilton MP, in hopes of convincing her to stand down and let Copps run in her seat. Turner successfully convinced Phinney to do so, even though Phinney wanted to run again. But Copps declined the deal, determined to seek the nomination in her own riding instead. The result: Valeri beat Copps for the nomination, then became the MP in Hamilton East–Stoney Creek, Phinney won her Hamilton Mountain seat, and Copps' political career was over. But you can't say John Turner didn't try.

* * *

Because Turner was always happy to encourage young people to enter politics, he was a natural choice in 2005 as a judge for a televised contest called *Canada's Next Great Prime Minister*. Frank Stronach's Magna International put up $50,000 in prize money for the winning contestant who had to write an essay (or later, make a video) on what they'd do as prime minister. The five best contestants were invited to Toronto for a sumptuous dinner, followed by a question-and-answer session, with four former prime ministers and the audience in Roy Thomson Hall judging the outcome.

Turner arrived at the Intercontinental Hotel first (more than an hour early) and went straight to the bar, ordering a stiff Scotch. The elephant in the room was Peter C. Newman's new book *The Secret Mulroney Tapes: Unguarded Confessions of a Prime Minister*, in which Newman published the very raw musings of Canada's eighteenth prime minister, which he had on hours and hours of tape recordings. Mulroney had some indelicate things to say about many of his fellow PMs, including Kim Campbell's leading the PC Party to two seats in 1993. ("The most incompetent campaign I've seen in my life.") Mulroney felt betrayed by Newman's book but acknowledged he was reckless in talking to the author that way.

In any event, the revelations now had the potential to derail the TV show, as some PMs' noses were out of joint about the book. Joe Clark was particularly unhappy with comments made about his wife Maureen McTeer. Turner decided the scenario called for him to be his mischievous best. When Campbell arrived at the green room, he immediately said, "Kim, how are ya? I read the book!"

"John, come on now," Campbell responded.

"I'm just joking," Turner replied. "I'm sure Brian didn't mean it."

Mulroney showed up fifteen minutes later and immediately wanted to know whether Campbell had arrived. "Has she said anything about the book?" Mulroney inquired of Dan Donovan, the show's producer, and now the publisher of *Ottawa Life*.

Mulroney walked into the holding room and Turner immediately approached him.

"Great book!" he told his successor. Again, Campbell tried to be peacemaker. "Come on John, let it go," she said.

Despite the potential for hurt feelings and the whole program falling apart, the four ex-prime ministers, Clark, Turner, Mulroney, and Campbell, all got along just fine, and the show went on.

"Turner was great on the panel and with the contestants," says Donovan, who was an executive assistant on Parliament Hill when Turner was opposition leader. "And after the show, he'd go to the reception, talk to the families, talk about the importance of civility in public life, and that it was a high calling."

* * *

One of Turner's most important friendships began to blossom at this time in his life. Arthur Milnes once worked for an MPP in Ontario premier David Peterson's

Liberal government. He did the research for Brian Mulroney's memoir. He also worked in Stephen Harper's PMO as a speechwriter. That tells you a lot about Milnes. He couldn't care less about political partisanship, but rather seems to be able to find the good in all our leaders and is eager to help. He was a journalist for Northern News Services in Yellowknife and Fort Simpson for two years, a period during which he interviewed Turner for the first time. The two of them hit it off over their shared love of Canada's far north.

In 1999, Milnes was a reporter for his hometown Kingston Whig Standard and heard Turner would be making regular trips to the Limestone City for Empire Life board meetings. He contacted Turner and asked whether he might pick him up from the train station.

"Why?" Turner asked him.

"Because former prime ministers don't come to my town and take cabs," Milnes replied. And so, for the next seven or eight years, whenever Turner visited, Milnes would pick him up, take him out for drinks, and listen to the former PM's war stories. Both men came to love the tradition. One time, Milnes drove past the Kingston Penitentiary en route to Turner's destination.

"That used to be one of mine," Turner said, referring to his time as solicitor-general, when he was responsible for the nation's prison system.

Milnes still lives in Kingston and has established perhaps the most unusual political tradition ever. Somewhere in the back of his mind, he remembered President John F. Kennedy visiting Rideau Hall in Ottawa in 1961 and planting a tree alongside Canada's Governor-General Georges Vanier. It was a moment of wonderful symbolism, our two countries literally planting deep roots to further our relationship. So, on one of Turner's trips to Kingston, Milnes put in an unusual request.

"Could you do me a very important personal favour?" he asked Turner. "Could we stop by my house so you could plant a ceremonial tree?"

Turner was a little taken aback and asked, "Where?"

"In my backyard," Milnes responded, then pulled out a small plaque he'd had made in hopes of Turner's saying yes. He'd already bought the tree, some Canadian flags, and a special shovel, and dug the hole.

"Alright, let's do it!" Turner answered enthusiastically.

The pair arrived at Milnes' modest abode, where Turner met Milnes' wife Alison and gave her a big kiss. Next, the trio sat down with a bottle of Scotch as the Milneses listened to an hour of Turner's best tales.

"It was just the three of us and it was wonderful," Milnes recalls.

Milnes' home is a bit of a Canadian history museum, with pictures everywhere of former politicians. There's even a picture of Turner and Milnes when they first met, when Milnes was a Carleton University student. "We both look younger now," Turner joked upon seeing the picture. "At least, I do!"

Eventually, Milnes said, "Okay, want to do the tree?" And off to the backyard they went. It was pouring rain, so Milnes had a huge umbrella on standby to prevent Turner from getting drenched. The former prime minister grabbed the ceremonial shovel Milnes had purchased for the occasion, scooped a shovelful of soil from the wheelbarrow, and dropped it into the hole to support the tree.

"I haven't done that in a long time," Turner said. "I want to do another scoop."

After the deed was done, Milnes affixed the small plaque on the ground: "This tree was planted by the Right Honourable John N. Turner, seventeenth prime minister of Canada, June 27, 2006."

After the job was done, Turner asked Milnes: "Arthur, are you going to get Brian [Mulroney] to plant one of these?"

"Yeah, of course," Milnes admitted.

"Fine," Turner said. "But when he's at your house, don't let him piss on my tree!" The two burst out laughing.

Milnes takes pains to add that Turner was clearly joking. At the time, Milnes was in the midst of a five-year stint working with Mulroney on the former PM's memoirs. "I spent countless hours with Mr. Mulroney, and never once did he say a personally nasty thing about John Turner," he says. "He only spoke with the greatest admiration." Similarly, Milnes would get together two or three times a year with Turner, "And I never heard a bad personal thing about Mr. Mulroney," he adds. "He never asked me how he'd be portrayed in Mr. Mulroney's memoirs. I'm very sad we don't have more of that today in politics."

When Mulroney heard that Turner had planted a tree, he immediately agreed to do one as well. Since then, every living former prime minister (Clark, Turner, Mulroney, Campbell, Chrétien, Martin, and Harper) has also acceded to Milnes' charms and planted a tree. (He's still hoping to convince Justin Trudeau to do one.) Since then, the tradition has expanded. Milnes' backyard now features trees planted by President Jimmy and First Lady Rosalynn Carter, the first Canadian in space Marc Garneau, the first female Chief Justice of the Supreme Court Beverley McLachlin, Ontario's first NDP premier Bob Rae, and former Quebec premier Jean Charest. Each one has its own plaque.

* * *

259

In his mid-seventies, Turner's back increasingly acted up, causing him significant pain and adversely affecting his mobility. One day on Bay Street, former MP Sergio Marchi, who'd been a thorn in Turner's side during their days together in opposition, saw Turner dragging one leg quite noticeably while walking. Marchi crossed the street, approached Turner, and the two spoke amicably for several minutes. Turner invited Marchi to lunch, then added: "Sergio, I noticed you crossed the street to say hi. I appreciate your effort to approach me rather than pass me by."

"It occurred to me in that moment that he'd gone from the best table at Winston's to castaway in the business community," Marchi now says. The two had lunch three times at the York Club, one of Turner's favourite haunts, after that.

"We both had scars, but he was big enough to have lunch with me," Marchi adds. "I had immense respect for his ability to turn the page."

Turner always paid and refused to let Marchi treat.

"He'd say, 'I'm older than you. I used to be your boss,'" recalls Marchi, who says as a rule, he never drank alcohol over lunch.

"Well, you do today!" Turner smiled, and Marchi joined his former leader in a glass of red wine.

There was another example of Turner's mellowing towards Marchi. At a Toronto seminar focused on Lester Pearson's record, Turner was invited to give one of the keynote speeches. Organizers wanted Marchi to introduce Turner, despite their having crossed swords decades earlier. Marchi was happy to do it but wanted organizers to check with Turner first to make sure he was okay with it.

"At first, I thought he'd quietly say no," Marchi recalls. "But he had no problem. It was a great lesson in humanity. He was big enough to let me introduce him and I owed him the kind of introduction for the humanity he showed."

After Turner reached his seventy-seventh birthday, his health took the first of what would be several turns for the worse. His legs really started to go and his family bought him his first cane to help him walk. Despite his infirmity, he still loved going on canoe trips, although now, he needed Michael to accompany him.

"This is my seventieth year on the water," he'd say to Mike, who helped his dad in and out of the boat and pitched the tent. If Michael came along, "Dad could feel like he was pulling his weight."

On one occasion during a canoeing expedition in Algonquin Park, the group wanted to do a day trip, which would have been too exhausting for Turner. So, Michael set him up on a small chair with a sandwich, cooler, and view of the lake.

"We came back six hours later and he's still there, with a big smile on his face," Michael marvels. "He was so happy to be out there." Michael starts choking up at the memory of it. "I asked him, 'What did you do for those six hours?' And he'd say, 'I just looked around and reflected.' He could sit for hours. They're very fond memories. And very important to him."

* * *

In the lead up to the October 2008 federal election, David Herle found himself at CTV executive Ivan Fecan's reception before the Juno Awards. He spotted Brian Mulroney, went over to introduce himself, and thought he'd ingratiate himself with the former Progressive Conservative prime minister by taking a bit of a swipe at the current Liberal leader Stephane Dion, who wasn't setting Canadian politics ablaze with his performance.

"Christ," Herle told Mulroney, "Dion's going to do even worse than Turner."

Herle figured the comment would appeal to Mulroney's competitive side and ego. Instead, he caught an earful.

"You of all people should never mention those two people in the same sentence again," Mulroney scolded him. "John Turner was a great man and a victim of timing. This guy [Dion] hasn't got it."

Mulroney confirms the story. "There was no comparison between John Turner, who was flawlessly bilingual, a successful lawyer and businessman, a former justice minister, finance minister, and prime minister, and Stephane Dion," Mulroney says, sounding increasingly insulted on Turner's behalf as he tells the story. "I mean, come on!"

* * *

Turner may no longer have had positions on the best boards in the country at this stage of his career. But he was still a big name and managed to do fairly well. Former Ontario Lieutenant-Governor Hal Jackman appointed Turner to the board of one of his companies, Empire Life, from 2008 to 2014. CEO Les Herr would take Turner out for a meal once or twice a year and talk about life and Turner's favourite subject, the importance of democracy.

"He was smart as a whip," Herr says. "Sometimes he'd look like he was nodding off, but then a sharp question would come, and you'd realize he was resting his eyes but his ears were wide open."

Turner never missed a board meeting and Herr says: "Whatever the mandatory retirement age from the board was, they waived it for John."

* * *

In 2009, Arthur Milnes was teaching a continuing education course at St. Lawrence College in Kingston. There were only seven students in the class. Milnes told Turner about it and immediately Turner volunteered to take the train in to Kingston to speak to the class.

"He wowed that small group of students," Milnes recalls. "It's not too often a former prime minister of Canada comes to St. Lawrence College." Turner stayed for three hours, told stories, and took questions.

"He was totally committed to sparking an interest in public life among young people," Milnes says.

Further evidence of that could be found during Turner's last experience on the floor of the House of Commons. It was a truly special event. He was asked by political science students at Queen's University to be the Speaker at their sixty-fourth annual model Parliament in January 2011. Turner was eighty-one and his health had worsened. He needed a wheelchair to get into the chamber. But he dove into his responsibilities with gusto.

One of the organizers was Queen's student Andrew Lockhart, whose father David had worked for Turner during his opposition leader years. For Lockhart (the father) watching his son and his former boss from the gallery, it was what we used to call "a Kodak moment."

Model Parliament lasted for three days and it was a very thick agenda. Fully 308 students assumed their roles as would-be MPs, introducing bills, performing Question Period, and ultimately voting thumbs up or down on the government's Speech from the Throne, which was read by the real Speaker, Peter Milliken, assuming the governor-general's role.

"I want to do Question Period," Turner told Andrew Lockhart, and so he did, no doubt unaware of what was in store. One of the opposition MPs asked a question about the size of the prime minister's "member." Despite the normal prohibition on props, the MP held up a pineapple and a broccoli and inquired as to which one was more apt.

"Mr. Turner was howling in the chair," Lockhart says. "I was sweating buckets, but he thoroughly enjoyed it."

After the proceedings ended, Turner offered up his patented plea for more young people to get into politics and there never existed an audience more primed to hear that message.

"He made an impact on people," Lockhart says. "We were really impressed that a former prime minister would take the time."

Although he sat in the visitors' gallery in 2017, that was the last time Turner appeared on the floor of the House. It was a memorable experience for the quintessential House of Commons man.

* * *

Reaching one's eightieth birthday should be an occasion for celebration, but that may not have been the case for Turner. He was noticeably slowing down and, as it turned out, was professionally vulnerable. Most Bay Street law firms have a mandatory retirement policy which kicks in when lawyers hit their mid-sixties. Turner received an exemption from that policy as part of his deal with Miller Thomson, but his poor health was increasingly an issue. Carleton University professor Paul Litt's biography of Turner, *Elusive Destiny*, came out in October 2011 and Miller Thomson hosted a launch.

"There were nice speeches," Marc Kealey recalls, "particularly the managing partner who went on about John's enormous contribution to the firm. Three months later they kicked him out. I guess he was in his eighties and not much use to them anymore."

Turner's association with the law firm was now over after two decades. "You're big freight," Turner was told by someone at the firm, according to Kealey.

Art Milnes was working in Harper's PMO at the time and drove to Toronto to console Turner. "They're kicking me out," he told Milnes.

"I was very sad to see a former prime minister treated this way," Milnes says. "It was disgraceful. He gave that firm profile. It was pretty heartless."

Turner's assistant at the law firm, Jill Hamblin, concurs. "Miller Thomson did not treat him nicely," she says. "They could have given him an office for life. He loved coming into the office. I called Bennett Jones and they said they'd happily take him in. But he didn't want it to happen again, so he declined."

When I asked Geills Turner how the firm handled her husband's departure, her answer was succinct: "Not well."

"His mobility suffered a lot in those last years," Wesfield says. "It became a chore for him to come in. It was difficult to maintain the pace. To me it was kind of time." Courage says MT's mandatory retirement policy at age seventy is more generous than most firms. Turner stayed more than a decade beyond that. "Those facts speak for themselves," he says.

* * *

It's unusual for a former prime minister to insinuate himself into a party leadership battle, even more so at the provincial level. But in January 2013, Ontario Liberals gathered at the former Maple Leaf Gardens to pick a successor to Premier Dalton McGuinty, who was stepping down after three consecutive election wins and almost ten years in office. And Turner was determined to participate.

"Who are you supporting?" he asked his friend Marc Kealey.

"Charles Sousa," Kealey said, referring to the MPP for Mississauga South, where Kealey lived.

"He's the Harvey Kirck of politics," Turner shot back, referring to Lloyd Robertson's co-anchor on CTV News. "Big voice, second banana." Turner supported Eric Hoskins, who was *his* MPP in Toronto–St. Paul's. Both men knew their choices wouldn't make it to the finish line so when Turner asked Kealey where he was going on the second ballot, he indicated former Windsor MPP Sandra Pupatello would get his support.

"She's delicious," Turner smiled.

Turner's strongest memory of that convention was the fury he held for the candidate he had backed. Hoskins had allegedly promised to support Pupatello once he dropped off the ballot, but instead, made a decision on the convention floor to back Kathleen Wynne, who had all the momentum and victory in her sights. The move infuriated Turner, not because he disliked Wynne, but rather because he felt Hoskins had broken his word to Pupatello.

Pupatello made it to the third and final ballot, but lost to Wynne, who became Ontario's twenty-fifth premier.

* * *

With Turner no longer at Miller Thomson, Kealey decided to bring his now eighty-three-year-old friend and former boss into his own health care consulting company, putting him on a $20,000 a month retainer, and taking advantage of his still powerful connections. Turner could still open doors and did so for

Kealey & Associates in China, Mexico, Jamaica, Arizona, and, of course, all over Canada.

"He never slowed down," Kealey says. Even at age eighty-nine, Turner accompanied Kealey on a two-week business trip to Arizona, Vancouver, and Montreal. "It wasn't worth it financially, but I did it because he needed to be cared for. I wanted him back in the game."

Part of being back in the game meant speaking to young people, which Turner continued to do. Two to three times every month, Turner would make his pitch to school kids to water the garden that is Canadian democracy. In February 2019, he spoke to two high schools and two universities in Arizona, while on a business trip there. Turner was downright messianic in his devotion to speaking about democracy.

That trip was to the city of Surprise, Arizona, population 150,000, just west of Phoenix. (Legend has it the city was so named because its founder would be surprised if the town ever amounted to much.) Arizona gets a million visits from Canada every year, making it the eighth most popular state that Canadians visit. Most of those visitors come from west of Manitoba, but Surprise wanted to tap into Turner's expertise to see whether it could attract more people from central and eastern Canada. Could Surprise develop a program which would encourage Canadians to recover from significant health problems in their municipality? Could the city create a health facility there, to Canadian standards, that would be approved by the Canadian government and 80 per cent covered, for example, by Ontario's Health Insurance Plan? Turner was signed up to find answers to those questions and turn the proposal into a reality.

In February 2018, Turner went to Surprise to make a presentation to the city council. "We had groupies show up," says Jeanine Jerkovic, Surprise's economic development director. "We had twenty to twenty-five people in the hall of our lobby getting autographs and wanting to shake his hand."

* * *

In 2015, Marco Mendicino became the MP for Eglinton–Lawrence. A couple of years before that, he met Turner at a Liberal Party event. Despite Turner's being in his mid-eighties and frail, Mendicino was struck by one thing. "The spark was still in his eyes," he says.

Mendicino had watched Turner's last speech in the House of Commons on YouTube and it stayed with him. "His being able to stand up and articulate in an intelligent way, well, that resonated with me. He had a profound respect for oral advocacy in the chamber as a parliamentarian."

Mendicino was introduced to Turner by Flavio Volpe, head of the Automotive Parts Manufacturers' Association, whose father Joe represented the same riding as Mendicino during Turner's time as Liberal leader. Everything connects.

* * *

In April 2016, Liberals gathered in a Montreal church to remember Jean Lapierre, the former Quebec MP, whom Turner had appointed to the cabinet in 1984. Lapierre, his wife, sister, and two brothers were en route to their father's funeral when their plane crashed in Quebec's Magdalen Islands, killing all aboard. It was a horrific tragedy which shocked all of Quebec. After the funeral, David Herle approached Turner.

"You put him in cabinet when he was twenty-eight years old," Herle reminded his former boss. "He was the youngest minister ever at that time. What did you see in him at the time?"

Turner responded: "The same thing everybody else sees now." It was such a poignant line, Herle never forgot it.

* * *

In 2017, Milnes got a call from Turner.

"Arthur, can you get to Toronto tomorrow?" Turner asked. "You're buying me lunch."

Milnes immediately said yes.

"Aren't you going to ask me why?" Turner inquired.

"No," Milnes responded. The fact that Turner wanted him to make the trip from Kingston was enough.

"Fine," Turner said. "Get here quick before I change my mind."

Milnes arrived the next day to find Turner sitting on his walker in the lobby of his midtown Toronto apartment building. Beside him was the chair he sat in, in the House of Commons. Turner wanted Milnes to have it.

"That was one of the most meaningful, remarkable things ever done for me," Milnes says wistfully. "I tried to give it back, but he refused."

When asked why he was giving away such an important memento from his years in politics, Turner simply responded: "You'll value it." The plaque on the back of the chair reads:

The Right Honourable John N. Turner

A House of Commons Man

1962-76, 1984-93.

He also gave Milnes his picture of Wilfrid Laurier that he'd had since he was minister of justice.

"The chair is in my home office," Milnes says. "I'm sitting in it right now."

* * *

A couple of years after becoming Premier of British Columbia, Christy Clark found herself giving a speech about her province's economy to the Canadian Club in Toronto. Because Clark's father was a big Turner fan from way back, the former PM decided to take in the speech and sat front row centre.

As the premier made her way through the speech, Turner provided a mixture of heckling and support.

"I'd say something and he'd say, 'That's where economic growth needs to go, doesn't it Christy!'" Clark recalls. And it wasn't just the occasional "Hear, hear" Turner was contributing.

"We have to think about this too, right Christy?" Turner continued in full voice.

"I've never had a situation before where a supporter was editorializing on my speech as I was giving it," Clark laughs.

* * *

Precious few people ever heard Turner complain or feel sorry for himself, despite the enormous financial and personal sacrifice he made to return to public life in 1984. But Turner let that guard down just a bit when talking with former Ontario premier Mike Harris. The two were both members of Marsh Insurance's advisory board and despite their very different political stripes, Harris enjoyed their time together, calling Turner "friendly and fun."

One day, however, Turner must have felt comfortable confiding in a fellow first minister.

"All those bastards are going to forget you," he told Harris. "You won't get any help from them."

Harris concluded that despite Turner's yeoman efforts to rebuild the Liberals during six punishing years as opposition leader, "He felt abandoned by the Liberal Party. He was a little bitter."

* * *

There may be something to keeping former heads of government humble by not offering them lavish post-prime ministerial financial packages. But sometimes it feels wrong. One night, emerging from a Toronto Symphony Orchestra concert at Roy Thomson Hall, I saw Turner by himself, using his walker, and having no luck hailing a taxi to take him home. There was something sad about seeing a former prime minister, now in his eighties, so helpless. When I realized Turner was in trouble, I intervened and helped him get a cab home.

Numerous others have told me similar stories, including Brian Mulroney. One evening after Mulroney gave a speech at the York Club, his son Nicholas went outside, only to see Turner trying unsuccessfully to hail a cab. Nicholas urged Turner to come back inside, where he organized a taxi for him. "When I heard about that, I was angry," the older Mulroney says. "This is the way Canada treats its ex-prime ministers. We're a country heading towards forty million people and we throw our prime ministers out on the snowbank."

"What really bugged me was seeing him at the end," says Phil Lind, who'd known Turner since their days in Montreal. "We don't treat our prime ministers with any great deference."

* * *

Turner's relationship with Dalton McGuinty Sr. may have ended over a disagreement about abortion. But Turner always considered McGuinty "one of my guys." Strangely enough, Turner never had much of a relationship with McGuinty's son, the future Ontario premier. "Our political paths never crossed," McGuinty wrote in a *Toronto Star* op-ed, because Turner left the Liberal leadership in June 1990, and McGuinty was elected for the first time as an opposition MPP three months later.

But after becoming Ontario Liberal leader in 1996, McGuinty would walk the family dog in the park at the end of his Toronto neighbourhood street.

One time, he noticed an old man shuffling from his car to a park bench where he'd let his dog run loose while he lit up a cigar.

"Mr. Turner, is that you?" McGuinty asked the man.

"Well, who the hell else did you think it was?" Turner responded. McGuinty says that chance encounter actually "kindled a warm and lasting friendship."

One evening at a political event at the Metro Toronto Convention Centre, Turner and Kealey were leaving together. Turner used his good leg to step on to the escalator, but the other leg wouldn't follow. Turner was starting to do the splits and Kealey's attempts to lift him weren't working. Suddenly, a hand reached out from the step above, pulling Turner to safety. As he looked up, he saw Dalton McGuinty Jr.

"You carried me for a long time," McGuinty told him. "Now I'm carrying you."

CHAPTER TWENTY-THREE

The Ukrainian Election Observer

THERE WERE FEW THINGS MORE important in John Turner's life than spending Christmas with his family. Politics and business took him away from his family on myriad occasions, but Christmas to this serious Catholic was sacred. It would take something equally mammoth in importance to separate Turner from his family on December 25, 2004, and that was democracy.

The Canadian government has always taken a special interest in Ukraine, mostly because of the nearly 1.4 million people of Ukrainian background living in Canada. During the Cold War, Ukraine's struggle to maintain a semblance of independence, not to mention its own language and culture, in the face of Soviet aggression was always a story Canadians could appreciate. As a Liberal government staffer of Ukrainian background once said, "We have a lot in common starting with a large, overbearing neighbor."

Brian Mulroney well understood this when he was prime minister, and when the Soviet Union dissolved in 1991, he was the second head of a government anywhere in the world to offer official recognition to the newly independent Ukrainian state (only twelve minutes after Poland).

By Christmas week in 2004, Ukrainians were into a repeat of the second and final round of their fourth presidential election since independence, and delegations from around the world descended on the country to ensure a free and fair vote. The initial attempt at a runoff in November was widely repudiated as fraudulent, the country's high court agreed, and so Ukraine repeated the effort a month later.

The federal government's Canadian International Development Agency (CIDA) had created the "Canada Corps" for just such circumstances, and this would be its first mission. Four hundred election overseers would make up the Canadian delegation, ten times larger than anything Canada had previously assembled, with a view to providing an impartial assessment of whether the election was conducted in accordance with democratic standards. The group did two days of training in Ottawa and another day of orientation in Kyiv. There were twenty groups of twenty observers around the country. The Ukrainian Canadian Congress sent another 500 observers and the Organization for Security and Co-operation in Europe (OSCE) also had interested Canadian politicians as part of their delegation. In total, there were 8,300 monitors from around the world.

As it turns out, this was an issue about which Prime Minister Paul Martin cared a great deal. Growing up in Windsor, Ontario, he well remembered the influx of Ukrainians into his community after World War II. The fact that his father was also external affairs minister in the Pearson government meant "I really came to know the Ukrainian community in Windsor," Martin explains. "I had and have huge sympathy for, and personal interest in them." Martin wanted a high-profile person to head the Canadian delegation to Ukraine; someone whose democratic bona fides were beyond reproach, and who would be seen by both sides in the election as an impartial observer.

So, he called John Turner.

Martin recalled a time in 1988 when Turner was Canada's official opposition leader and he, Martin, was a rookie MP, that the two had discussed their mutual affection for the Ukrainian community. Furthermore, the PM knew that his father and Turner were great friends. "I had huge respect for John Turner, who was also very kind to my father after the [1968] leadership race." So, the current PM asked the former PM to go to Ukraine to represent Canada.

Turner initially wasn't thrilled with the idea of missing the first Christmas with his family in half a century. In fact, at the suggestion of Martin's wife Sheila, Martin's deputy chief of staff Karl Littler went to a Birks store at the ManuLife Centre in Toronto and bought Geills Turner a silver picture frame, put a picture of her husband in it, and gave it to her on behalf of the prime minister.

"It was a token of our appreciation that she'd given up John for Christmas," Littler says.

Turner understood he was being asked to play an important role, one for which he was uniquely qualified.

"This was a crusade for democracy," he said at the time. "It was an honour to be in Ukraine along with the other Canadians who sacrificed their Christmas because they felt that their presence would help ensure that democracy took hold in Ukraine."

Turner and a few staffers took a Challenger jet from Ottawa to Kyiv a few days before Christmas. Marc Kealey, Turner's long-time associate, says: "He took his responsibilities seriously and wasn't interested in being a figurehead."

Also on board were Littler and the then twenty-five-year-old Laura Miller, who'd never met Turner before and was delighted to have the opportunity.

"He told me stories about rescuing Dief from drowning and touch football with the Kennedys," she recalls. "I enjoyed those interactions."

As the Challenger was unloaded, Turner kept an eagle eye on the embassy officials unloading the group's luggage and loading it into a van. Prior experiences made him wary. "Bye bye, luggage," he deadpanned as the bags departed in a different vehicle.

The group also discovered why Kealey was so successful at understanding his former boss' needs when he asked: "Is anyone hungry?" Apparently, Kealey had insisted on keeping a second suitcase with the group.

"He opened the suitcase, and it was filled with groceries. That's Marc Kealey being the ultimate 'body man,'" Miller says, using the political term for someone who staffs political leaders on the road and ensures all their needs are met. Needless to say, there was plenty of alcohol in the second suitcase as well.

There was a method to Kealey's madness in bringing along the suitcase full of provisions. The Canadian delegation had been briefed about the potential for danger during the trip and it wasn't an idle threat. The presidential election featured a runoff between Prime Minister Viktor Yanukovych, considered Russia's candidate, and opposition leader Viktor Yushchenko, the more Western-oriented candidate. The atmosphere was supercharged with allegations of voter intimidation, fraud, not to mention an attempt to assassinate Yushchenko with dioxin poisoning. In fact, there was some discussion in the Canadian delegation about what to do if Yushchenko were to win, then be threatened with arrest or even imprisonment. Would Canada offer the opposition leader asylum? It was a tense time and bringing their own food just seemed like the smart thing to do.

As the trip progressed and people learned Turner was from Canada, they expressed their gratitude and often mentioned Mulroney by name, because of his early recognition of Ukrainian independence.

"Mr. Turner was quite generous about it, whenever Mr. Mulroney was mentioned," Miller says.

Paul Grod was vice-president of the Ukrainian Canadian Congress (UCC), part of that organization's delegation, and remembers Turner being a parade marshal at a Ukrainian festival. "He was always very interested in Ukraine," he says. Furthermore, Turner had served on the board of Northland Power, which was founded by Jim Temerty, a Ukrainian-born refugee who fled to Montreal as a young boy during World War II. "They became friends," Grod says, "and his story must have rubbed off on John."

On Christmas Eve, Turner, Grod, and Temerty had dinner in Kyiv at a traditional Ukrainian restaurant, then walked to the Maidan (independence square) to see hundreds of thousands of citizens gathered in the streets. "This is the greatest public display of democracy I've ever seen in my life," an awestruck Turner told Grod.

Turner also said that Grod needed to pass along some advice to the Ukrainian opposition leader. "He's gotta get rid of those fucking oligarchs," he said.

"Easier said than done," Grod replied.

"Tell Yushchenko he has to get rid of those fucking oligarchs," Turner repeated emphatically.

"I'll pass on the message, Mr. Turner," Grod said.

Even though Turner couldn't be with his family that Christmas Eve (he did speak to them every day by phone), he still wanted to attend a church service, which he did at a cathedral in Kyiv along with a handful of his advisers. At one moment in the service, he reached out to Taras Zalusky, a senior adviser to the minister responsible for CIDA and Turner's chief of staff on this mission, and said, "Taras: pax. That's Latin for peace." Turner was always at home in church.

Zalusky was a former CEO of the UCC and had worked for Liberal MPs and cabinet ministers since Turner was opposition leader. He'd already been in Ukraine for four to five weeks by the time Turner arrived and was amazed at how grounded the then seventy-five-year-old was.

"He was a marvel to behold," Zalusky recalls. "He'd say, 'This is about the actors, not the critics. It's about the people who are the electors. Monitor, but don't interfere.'"

At their first dinner together, Zalusky explained to their waitress that "a former prime minister of Canada was giving up his Christmas to ensure the integrity of your election." Turner strung together a few words in Ukrainian and the waitress apparently nearly fainted from joy.

Zalusky had Turner on what he describes as "a pretty happening schedule." There were meetings with international delegations and ambassadors, briefings, and the sharing of intelligence. "He had better intel than other ambassadors did," Zalusky says. "It elevated the status of our mission here and at home."

The night before voting day, Turner called all the group leaders to wish them well. He reminded them of the important work they were doing. "Democracy is critical to Canada and the world," he said.

On Christmas night, Turner's inner circle was having dinner at the hotel. Miller remembers it well because it was the first time she'd seen a full fish, not already fileted, on her plate. She called her parents and, of course, Turner insisted on talking to them and thanking them for letting their daughter come to Ukraine over Christmas.

"My parents were quite chuffed by that," Miller says.

Election day, December 26, 2004, started early for Turner. He attended when the polls opened in Kyiv at 8 a.m. and observed two other "oblasts" (regions) in rural Kyiv and a neighbouring province. He spoke to official delegates, local poll clerks, and then embassy-appointed translators to make sure he got the nuance of everything that was said. He met with the head of the election commission and civil society groups. Thanks to smartphones donated by BlackBerry, delegation members could "pin" one another, meaning they could maintain communications even if the government tried jamming or hacking cell service.

"People he met at polling stations were so happy that someone of his stature would come all the way from Canada to ensure their votes counted," Zalusky says.

Actually, there was some concern about the Canadian delegation. For example, third-generation Ukrainian–Canadian rookie MP Borys Wrzesnewskyj was one of twenty Canadian MPs who were part of the OSCE observer group and clearly favoured the opposition leader's campaign. During the first attempt at a runoff in November, Wrzesnewskyj went on stage during a rally and screamed fraud. It stuck in the craw of the outgoing oligarch-friendly Kuchma administration.

"We were very concerned that our people not be seen as a bunch of shills for Yushchenko," says Littler, "and Mr. Turner said so at the training session. He took an enormous amount of satisfaction that we conducted ourselves wholly appropriately with no confrontations with officials and with the right suspension of partisanship. He told people, 'Notwithstanding your feelings, you must conduct yourselves in an appropriate manner.'"

Turner reminded Canadian overseers: "This is for the Ukrainian people to decide. We may think one party is more democratic, but this isn't for us to decide."

In fact, Turner scheduled a meeting with the head of Yanukovych's campaign, but when the official failed to show up, even fifteen minutes past the scheduled time, Turner up and left.

"Those fucking assholes," he muttered to Zalusky. The lesson about punctuality Turner learned from his stepfather had stuck. He always hated it when people were late.

There was only one moment during Turner's trip where a potential public relations faux pas threatened the mission's credibility. Opposition leader Yushchenko gave Turner one of his trademark orange scarves, no doubt hoping Turner would wear it on camera, thereby giving a boost to the Orange Revolution's efforts.

"We made sure he didn't wear it," Zalusky says. "But for a moment, it didn't click with him that that was something he shouldn't be doing."

On the day of the vote, Littler wrote a first draft of the report that the Turner delegation would eventually present to Prime Minister Martin, and constantly revised the draft as voting information came in from the field. (Littler adds that Turner, the former lawyer, "eventually painstakingly went through the final version of the report and corrected my grammatical mistakes.") Turner's team found only minor violations of proper electoral procedure. Fully 90 per cent of polling stations had their returns properly reported in by 4 a.m. the next day, and Turner couldn't have been disappointed to report that the challenger Yushchenko prevailed 52 per cent to 44 per cent. The new president was sworn in on January 23, 2005.

Turner and almost the entire Canadian team gathered for a final dinner, as the hotel put on a generous buffet. He thanked the nearly 500 members present for their work. "The key to any democracy is a free and honest election," he said. "We were impartial observers. We remained impartial and neutral."

Turner seemed to be tearing up as he spoke. "He was very emotional," Zalusky recalls. "He had a glint in his eye. It touched him tremendously. We'd shone a light on the fact that this process reflected the will of the Ukrainian people."

Because the Challenger required refueling on the flight home, Turner's entourage stopped in Shannon, Ireland, where Laura Miller was sent into the terminal to purchase the "Famous Grouse" Scotch Whisky. "It was his Scotch of choice," she says. "And he was lovely. We did a little photo-op at the terminal."

Zalusky's enduring memory of the trip is how well Turner performed. "Better than most politicians I've seen in my thirty years," he now says. "There's a lot of cynical people running around Ottawa, but he was a true believer. He made people in Ukraine feel that they were part of something bigger than themselves."

Grod notes that even late into his eighties, Turner would continue to come to Toronto's Ukrainian festival. "He'd struggle to get on stage, but he came to show support for the Ukrainian cause," he says.

What was Turner's verdict of the mission? He told Kealey: "That was the best thing I ever did."

CHAPTER TWENTY-FOUR

The Birthday Parties

CANADA HAS HAD TWENTY-THREE PRIME ministers, but so far, only four have lived long enough to celebrate their ninetieth birthdays: Mackenzie Bowell, Charles Tupper, Louis St. Laurent, and John Turner. St. Laurent was the last PM to achieve that milestone, back in 1973. Jean Chrétien (eighty-seven), Paul Martin (eighty-three), and Brian Mulroney and Joe Clark (eighty-two) are the next in line with a shot at it. But it's been a rare occurrence in Canadian history, which is why Marc Kealey and Lisa Haley were anxious to plan something special for Turner. Left unsaid was that given Turner's increasingly poor health, this would almost certainly be the last chance to fete the man who meant so much to them.

The annual birthday parties had become a much bigger deal since the original celebration at Les Fougères in Quebec. And the guest list changed as well, depending on who was organizing the affair. For example, in 2004, David Herle and John Webster, two Turner stalwarts, got dropped from the invitation list. "That's because Gordon Ashworth organized it," Herle says. "I've been on the opposite side of every fight with Ashworth."

Turner was always "a birthday guy." It was often the first item on his agenda when he came into work in the mornings. He'd ask whatever assistant was working for him at the time whose birthdays were on that day and the phone calls would get done. Sometimes they were brief.

"Eagleson? Turner. Happy birthday. (Click)" was one of his favourites.

In the case of his eight grandchildren, he'd often call the night before, knowing they'd be at school in the morning.

Turner never failed to call his Kingston friend Art Milnes on his birthday, June 3. Conversely, Milnes didn't call Turner on his birthday, June 7, but rather arranged for others to call, thinking Turner would prefer that.

"He'd call me on June 8, the day after his birthday, wondering why I hadn't called," Milnes says. "I'd say, 'Sorry sir.'" Turner would blast him. "Art, you fucker, you didn't call me on my birthday, but Prime Minister Harper managed to find the time. Brian Mulroney found the time. Dalton McGuinty and Kathleen Wynne found the time."

What Turner never knew is that Milnes had arranged for all those calls to be made. "I'd call it Operation Birthday," he jokes. And it happened every year.

As Turner entered his eighties, the sparkle was still in his eyes, but his body was continuing to give up on him. Nevertheless, at his eighty-fifth birthday party, when a former female employee approached him to convey birthday greetings, Turner looked up from his wheelchair, grinned, and said: "Be careful. I'm still dangerous!"

Turner's ninetieth birthday offered an opportunity to truly reach new celebratory heights. There were two immediate challenges: where to have the event and whom to invite. Would old grudges be forgotten when making out the invitation list?

"No!" says Haley. "Mr. Turner thought it was hypocritical to invite them and hypocritical for them to attend. So, some weren't invited."

Turner did want every former finance minister and justice minister invited, given how much he had enjoyed those two portfolios. And yes, that included Jody Wilson-Raybould, despite the fact that only four months earlier, she'd embarrassed Prime Minister Justin Trudeau by resigning her post over the SNC Lavalin controversy. (She declined to attend.)

The organizers made clear this wasn't a Liberal Party event but rather a John Turner event, although Liberals certainly made up the majority of attendees. But Conservative Senators Pamela Wallin and Mike Duffy were there, as was Green Party leader Elizabeth May. Turner's wife Geills was not there, daughter Elizabeth suggesting she may not have realized what a big deal the event was going to be, was suffering from a bad back, and, besides, the family had just had a party three days earlier on Turner's actual ninetieth birthday.

"And she didn't want to see a lot of the people who were going to be there, to be truthful," adds Elizabeth, who was the only one of the Turners' four children who attended (so did her daughter Fiona: "It was great for Fiona to see her grandfather in his milieu," says Kealey).

Turner's sister Brenda had thought about going but begged off because of an arthritic knee. "Too much standing around listening to politicians' speeches!" she says. Paul Grod from Turner's Ukrainian election mission not only came, but Turner invited him to sit with him. "I was blown away being at his table," he says. Jim Temerty was at that table, too. Ukraine still mattered to the guest of honour.

Of course, the big question was whether Turner would invite Chrétien, and if he did, would Chrétien agree to show up. As it turned out, the answers were yes and yes. It was a great decision by both men, although Chrétien at first was miffed at having the last speaker's slot of the night. The organizers wanted it that way to let the mystery heighten of whether Turner's one-time nemesis would even speak at all.

"Why am I speaking last?" Chrétien asked them. "I won the most!" Chrétien was being accurate. His record (three consecutive majority governments, no losses) was better than Mulroney's two straight majorities, Harper's two minorities, one majority, and one defeat, Clark and Martin's one minority and one loss apiece, Campbell's one loss, and the current prime minister, Justin Trudeau's one majority.

Haley came up with a clever response. "Mr. Turner has known you the longest, so you're the grand finale," she said.

Chrétien attended and seemed to thoroughly enjoy himself. In fact, he bumped into Sharon Sholzberg-Gray and teased her with: "You only got your Order of Canada for criticizing me."

Physically, Turner was a far cry from the one-time fastest man in Canada. He needed a walker to enter the hall, and considerable assistance from both Kealey and Trudeau to mount the stage. The current prime minister reminded Turner that the two had once sat at the same cabinet table together. "Me?" Trudeau pointed out, "I was in a highchair."

Some of Turner's long-time friends in journalism took to the podium, including CTV's Lloyd Robertson and CBC's Peter Mansbridge. Former CBC anchor Don Newman said, "the measure of a man is when things are going poorly, and John showed class when things were at their toughest."

He then reminded the audience of one of Turner's favourite quotes: "My mother told me that hard times build character. And I've built a helluva lot of character."

When Turner took the microphone, he gave his speech seated, reading from file cards as had been his practice for more than half a century.

"As the oldest person in the room, I think I can say whatever the hell I want!" he opened, to laughs. He welcomed "both friends… and a few foes," then added, "Yes, I'm looking at you, Mansbridge," poking the former anchor of *The National*, who'd stepped down from that perch two years earlier.

Turner spent the next fifteen minutes taking people through some of the most meaningful parts of his life, starting with praise for his mother Phyllis, who "instilled in me a sense of democracy." He mentioned his favourite of St. Augustine's principles: "To whom God has given talent, let him or her give some back." Turner was a living manifestation of that principle.

Then he returned to the theme that animated his entire public life. "Men and women have to get involved in democracy more than they are now," he urged. "At the local level, provincially, federally. Help make things happen. Run for office if that becomes possible. Democracy doesn't happen by accident."

Switching back and forth between English and French, he reminded the audience of his time as parliamentary secretary to the minister of northern affairs. "I toured the North. I canoed it. I walked it. I rode it."

He expressed his dissatisfaction with the term "backbencher," saying it diminishes the role MPs are meant to play in Parliament. Then, with Justin Trudeau only a few feet away, he chided "prime ministers, who act in a manner that is, I'm afraid to say it, unilateral. We have to open up democracy again in Parliament. To disallow MPs to speak their minds compromises the very essence of democracy."

He ran through a few stories about the Kennedys, including the briefing that he supposedly gave Bobby (just two days before the assassination). He talked about the time Pierre Trudeau asked him to improve relations with Richard Nixon's administration "because they didn't get along." Turner embarked on a "Scotch and tennis" approach with his American counterpart George Shultz, going to Washington every few months. "We had a five-point agenda and we solved every point," he said.

When Nixon told him, "You're taking a big chance coming down here. You've got no witnesses. I've got George," Turner says he responded, "Mr. President, if I thought I needed a witness I wouldn't be here."

Shultz sent along a message for the occasion: "John Turner is still a promising young man from my perspective of 98 years," he wrote. "I say 'promising' because he has already accomplished so much in his life. We worked together closely and he provided ideas, interesting viewpoints, and drive. Above all, from my standpoint, is John's great capacity for friendship. It is a privilege to count him as a true friend. Congratulations and best wishes, John, as you celebrate your ninetieth birthday." (Shultz died on February 6, 2021, less than two months after turning 100.)

Turner concluded with Laurier's famous prediction that the twentieth century would belong to Canada: "With the talent I see around this room and the constant travel I see around this country, I'm more convinced the twenty-first century belongs to Canada." The room erupted with a standing ovation, after which Turner returned to his table to enjoy the rest of the show.

But the evening's great speeches were only beginning. One by one, every living former prime minister, some in person, some via video, contributed a memorable speech. Joe Clark may have been a charismatically challenged thirty-nine year old when he became prime minister in 1979. But now in his eighties, his self-deprecating humour has made him a fantastic dinner speaker and he did not disappoint.

"John Turner got along much better with John Diefenbaker than I ever did," said Clark, opening with a joke.

Clark went on to explain why he had so much respect for Turner. "In my early days as leader of the PCs, he would greet me with 'Mr. Leader,' as if that was the most incredible concept possible," he said. "Public service is about kisses and wins. But it's really about who you help and how you serve. And John Turner has done that well for 90 years."

Paul Martin told the story of how Turner invited his father for brunch the morning after the 1968 Liberal leadership convention, which was a crushing disappointment for Martin, Sr. "John Turner didn't have to do that, and it meant so much so my mother and dad," Martin, Jr. said. "John, I'll never forget it. That gesture was John Turner."

Kim Campbell, the only other prime minister to have represented a riding in British Columbia, appeared via video. She spoke of Turner's "principled pragmatism," and thanked him for supporting her bill on abortion when she was justice minister.

"We share a deep commitment to democracy and civility even though we don't agree on everything," Campbell said. "And those values are under strain today. It's important to have a touchstone and focus on trying to preserve these values." Turner could have spoken the exact same words himself.

Mulroney also appeared on video and opened with a joke. "I wanted to be there tonight, but I couldn't. I had no option," he said, referring to Turner's worst moment in the 1984 leaders' debate. Some of the room laughed. Some of the room didn't like it. The original moment may have happened 35 years earlier, but plenty of people were still unamused on Turner's behalf.

However, Mulroney got the crowd back onside by pointing out that his mother twice voted for Turner in Montreal, and that he referred to Turner in Christina McCall-Newman's book *Grits* as "the Liberal dream in motion." Then Mulroney paused before adding: "Jesus, did I really say that?" Laughs ensued.

Mulroney concluded with: "His attacks were without malice because he was a rare bird: a political leader without malice or vindictiveness. John was a gentleman in politics."

Harper also spoke via video and reminded Turner of a story he'd once shared: "John Turner once told me, 'I really became a Canadian when I saw Canada north of the sixtieth parallel.'" Harper added, "Thank you for your contribution to Northern Canada," which, of course, was also a passion of Canada's twenty-second prime minister.

As planned, organizers saved Chrétien for last as people in the hall wondered whether Turner's chief rival would speak at all. Chrétien did not disappoint. Whatever bitterness the two shared was ancient history on this night.

Chrétien started by pointing out how similar their political careers had been, with Turner always leading the way. Turner became a parliamentary secretary, and then Chrétien did. Turner became a cabinet minister, and then a year later, so did Chrétien. They both eventually became justice ministers, finance ministers, Liberal leaders, and prime ministers.

"And tonight, he is ninety, and I will have eventually ninety!" Chrétien added, using his own unique syntax to the crowd's delight.

Chrétien pointed out that thanks to Turner's longevity, the country was experiencing a unique moment in its history: never before, he said, has Canada had eight living prime ministers.

Then Chrétien added a line that seemed to put their fifty-six-year-long relationship into perspective. "We were good friends," he said, "But then life decided we should compete." It was a lovely way to describe what can happen when two well-meaning people want the same thing.

Chrétien's Deputy Prime Minister Sheila Copps attended the event and said, "When people get out of politics, the edges soften, and I think their political edges have softened a bit."

The evening was a complete success. Turner even had enough energy to hang around after the proceedings were done to pose for pictures. Even Chrétien approached Turner's daughter Liz asking if he might have a word with her father. When Liz looked at the long line of others waiting for a word, and not wanting Chrétien to have to wait, she offered to give his best wishes to her dad on his behalf. But no, Chrétien was content to wait, and eventually the two exchanged some gracious words, including Chrétien's amusing: "And John, we won't be taking names tonight."

Perhaps the most significant takeaway on the night was from Turner's granddaughter Fiona, who was born and raised in New York and is also attending university in the States. Well aware of the toxic nature of U.S. politics, Fiona was blown away at how people from different parties could be so civil to each other and in particular to her grandfather.

"It was such an eye-opener for her," says Elizabeth. "The U.S. political experience during her awareness has been awful."

"I'll never forgive myself for not going," says Turner's sister Brenda. "I've regretted it so much."

For one night in June in 2019, John Turner was a rock star in Ottawa again.

CHAPTER TWENTY-FIVE

The End

JOHN TURNER LOVED HIS LISTS. Throughout his entire life, he'd write reminders to himself on scraps of paper and stuff them into his jacket pocket. In his later years, Geills would take those scraps and type them up into something legible.

"His handwriting was notoriously unreadable," Geills says. "I would transcribe those notes and put them in his schedule." It was a big part of keeping Turner engaged with the rest of the world. "This is probably what kept John going," Geills adds. "I kept him going with an iPad and a cellphone and lists. It empowered him to do a lot more than he might have done had he been in a nursing home. He benefited from my eccentricities or whatever you want to call them. He went way past his due date. That's something I could do for him."

Turner's sister Brenda agrees. "Geills has been fantastic in the last few years taking care of John," she says. "She hasn't had a life of her own. She looked after John so well. I told her on the phone how much I admired her."

On September 17, 2020, Turner took a call from Arthur Milnes for a column Milnes was writing on John Diefenbaker, on the occasion of the 125th anniversary of Dief's birth. It would turn out to be the last interview of Turner's life. Milnes and Turner had done numerous interviews for columns over the years. Two decades earlier, Milnes had asked Turner how he wanted the history books to remember him, a question Turner frequently declined to answer for other journalists. But Milnes got this answer:

"That he put something back into the country," Turner began. "That he believed in public service, he believed in Canada, he stood up for Canada, never ducked, met the issues head on."

Turner said he and Dief "always enjoyed excellent personal relations because he saw me as a fellow House of Commons man who also believed in the importance of Parliament and the crucial role each MP, of all parties, should play in our system of government."

The next day, on September 18, Turner's physiotherapist arrived at the apartment after breakfast and put him through his paces. Turner then told his wife he was going back to bed and would have his lunch there, which was unusual, and gave Geills some concerns. But later that afternoon, he asked Geills whether he could have a glass of wine over dinner. Usually, she attentively watched his alcohol intake. When she agreed he could have a glass, "He practically ran down the hall to sit at the table for his wine," Geills says. She thought the moment was adorable and snapped a picture of her husband toasting her. At dinner, though, Turner didn't eat or drink much at all.

After breakfast the next morning, September 19, Turner wasn't speaking well. Something seemed amiss, so Geills FaceTimed a nurse practitioner who said she'd be over right away. Geills then spoke to her youngest son Andrew, who was en route to his cottage up north. He thought about turning the car around but then remembered his father had had several close calls over the past many weeks, only to rally and be fine. Andrew urged his mother to call 911.

"Daddy said never to call 911 again," Geills reminded her son, "because every time he ends up in hospital for a week and he's worse when he gets back home." Turner had told his family he never wanted to go back into a hospital. But Geills relented, called 911, and her son Michael as well.

However, before Michael, the paramedics, or nurse practitioner could arrive, Turner's on-site caregiver who was monitoring him suddenly said: "His heart has stopped beating."

Michael then arrived minutes later. "You could tell the lights had gone out a bit," he says, recalling his father's condition. "We got him back into bed. He gave one gasp in bed and that was the end."

John Napier Wyndham Turner died of congestive heart failure, with his wife and oldest son at his side, at around 12 noon. "He died exactly as he wanted," Geills says. "At home, without pain, having happily sat at the breakfast table."

Given the poor state of Turner's health, this moment was not a surprise for anyone. The family had held many discussions about what to do when the inevitable happened, and now that system kicked in. The paramedics left, and representatives from Humphrey Funeral Home arrived, placed a Canadian flag over the stretcher and assumed responsibility for Turner's body. When Michael saw his father's flag-draped body emerge, he was deeply moved.

"I didn't know they were going to do this," he says. "It's something I did not expect but it was beautiful."

Andrew, who was up north, got the news and began the solemn task of phoning and emailing family and friends. "I don't think I felt much shock, but it hits you," he says, fighting back tears. "I felt he deserved to get some peace at that point. He'd had a pretty shitty existence for the past couple of years. So, there was some relief there from my perspective." Andrew also admits he began second-guessing whether he should have gone north.

"You have that going through your brain," he says. "I was happy Mike got there just before he died. Mike and my Mom have really shouldered most of the burden, so I'm glad they were there to say goodbye."

Turner himself had left nothing to chance. He had organized every detail of his funeral, from the music that would be played, to the pallbearers who would be chosen; who would be honored with a speaking role (and perhaps more important, who wouldn't be); how religious the ceremony would be; and the list of invitees.

"He didn't want any of that to be a burden on the rest of us," says Michael, who reveals his father had a group of family and friends who had met every couple of years for a decade to review funeral arrangements. Michael met on many occasions with Monsignor Sam Bianco, Rick Alway, and Rev. Douglas Stoute and had a file at least three inches thick with details of what his father wanted.

Despite all that planning, there were aspects of the funeral that Turner simply couldn't have anticipated; first and foremost, who'd be allowed to attend. The world was six months into the worst global pandemic in a century and as a result, St. Michael's Cathedral Basilica, which can normally accommodate 1,600 mourners (which includes hundreds in the balcony), was restricted to fewer than 180. That gave rise to the family's first significant decision: should the funeral be held anyway, or delayed until more favourable circumstances would permit a larger crowd? Family members sought advice from good friends, including former Ontario premier Bob Rae, who only two months earlier had been appointed Canada's ambassador to the United Nations.

"You'll regret it if you don't go ahead with the funeral at the moment," Rae told Geills, "because *at the moment* is when the groundswell of support and interest is."

But there was one family member who was hoping for a postponement. It was the Turners' fifty-two-year-old son David, and not for reasons related to COVID-19. Two years earlier, David had been diagnosed with an endocrine tumor in his pancreas and liver. Complicating matters even further was that exactly a year before John Turner's death, David's ex-wife Deirdre faced a near-death health crisis of her own, requiring several months of hospitalization and rehabilitation. David parented the couple's two children, Dylan and Olivia, at this time.

"He was sick, but physically able" is how his mother describes it.

David participated in some clinical trials, improved his diet, and tried some holistic treatments as well. His doctors were initially impressed at his progress. But during the summer of 2020, his health took a turn for the worse. Even though he and Deirdre were technically separated, they still lived in the same home. Until now. Deirdre's health had improved, and so David moved into an apartment of his own and Dylan joined him there. Friends dropped in to keep him company, while his mother did a ton of research on the internet to see whether anything further could be done. His father was aware of all these goings-on.

David hoped that a delay in his father's funeral might provide an opportunity for his health to improve, thereby allowing him to attend. But his physical deterioration at the time of his father's death was significant. He not only didn't feel strong enough to attend the funeral, but he also didn't want to be seen in a wheelchair, a distraction from what that day should be about, namely, his father. So, he watched the funeral on television from his apartment with two friends.

John Turner's funeral took place on October 6, and considering the COVID-related protocols in place, it was still an impressive event. Nine RCMP officers in their traditional red serge carried the casket into the church as John McDermott, accompanied by Jason Fowler on guitar, sang *Amazing Grace*. There were fifteen honorary pallbearers as well, including Peter Cathcart, George Cooke, Alan Eagleson, Hal Jackman, Marc Kealey, Jim Temerty, and Steven Wesfield. The family had met up at the funeral home before the service, and Michael admonished all the children that "You're never going to experience anything like this ever again. Pay attention here. Don't be bored. Look around you, take it all in."

When the family arrived at St. Michael's, they followed the casket towards its place at the front of the church, beside Prime Minister Justin Trudeau and his wife Sophie. Mask-wearing was mandatory, and congregants were prohibited from singing. Those fortunate enough to have been asked to attend had to sit two metres apart, and had specific, staggered times at which they had to arrive. The gravitas was surely there, even if the crowd wasn't. As Arthur Milnes entered the church with his wife Alison Bogle, he thought to himself, I cannot believe that a kid from the wrong side of the tracks in Scarborough made the cut for this important event. "I'm still speechless over that," he says.

Turner had categorized the major aspects of his life and whom he wanted speaking about each. The prime minister would cover his political life; Richard Alway, the personal; Monte Hummel, his love of the environment and the North; his daughter Elizabeth would speak about her father's family side; and Monsignor Sam Bianco, the former rector at St. Michael's and a family friend, on Turner's religious side. There was only one imperative from the man they were eulogizing: keep it short!

Trudeau came forward, briefly touched the casket, then mounted the stage to speak. "I knew John my whole life," he began. "Today more than ever we need more people like John. His legacy calls on us not to wait for change to happen but to stand up and build a better country for everyone. John, you're a great Canadian. Your vision of a stronger, more just Canada lives on even now. Rest in peace." Trudeau descended, and bowed to Turner's family, his hand over his heart.

Next, Alway spoke of Turner's trinity of simple values: faith, family, and friends. Alway said Turner read from the Bible every day, and when he reached the end, he'd start over again. "Reconciling religious faith in a secular society was a constant theme in his political career," he said. Then, looking at Turner's widow and three children, he referred to the "full and equal partnership with Geills [that] is almost unique in modern political life. He depended on your, and your mother's, love and support."

Alway then described Turner as "essentially a happy man," with friendships lasting eight decades from his days at Camp Temagami in Northern Ontario. And "he was the leading English-Canadian politician of his generation, the George Brown of his political times. He deeply affected the debates of the country for a generation," Alway said. "Politics changed. He did not. Goodbye, old friend."

The next eulogy was supposed to have been given by Monte Hummel, president emeritus of the World Wildlife Fund, and with whom Turner shared a deep friendship rooted in their mutual love of the environment and the North. But Hummel was one of many who made the hard decision at the last minute not to attend over fears of contracting COVID-19. He and Turner had discussed the eulogy for years and "the only thing worse than giving a friend's eulogy at his request is not being able to give it," Hummel now says.

The eulogy Hummel couldn't give was entitled Sternsman for a Country, and told of a time when the Inuvialuit leader Nellie Cournoyea introduced Turner to the Northwest Territories legislature. She reminded all representatives present that "John Turner has probably canoed more of our lakes and rivers than anyone here today."

Hummel would have concluded his eulogy with: "John, you skillfully navigated the roiling rapids of our country's political life. I hope you have found calmer water. A quiet eddy, from which you can look back out into all that froth and current. Take satisfaction from where you've been, and how well you've paddled. Know that we appreciate your leadership, your extraordinary effort, and your safe passage. And now… rest, my friend. Rest."

It was a lovely eulogy, alas, never to be heard.

In Hummel's stead, it was left to Turner's then eighty-five-year-old friend Michael de Pencier, a past chair of WWF Canada, magazine publisher, and fellow canoeist with Turner, to talk of Turner's relationship with the environment. De Pencier's wife of nearly sixty years, Honor, was a lifelong friend of Geills', who snuck in the side door to watch her husband's eulogy. Because of her respiratory condition, the two slipped out immediately after.

"They were so kind to come and at personal risk," says Geills.

Of Turner's time on the WWF Canada Board, de Pencier said: "He opened doors and leaned on decision makers." Turner contributed to the protection of twenty-million hectares of Mackenzie River watershed, and western Lake Superior became the largest freshwater reserve in the world. "He experienced this country's wilderness in his muscle and bone," de Pencier said.

Elizabeth started by noting that her grandmother Phyllis "ran a soup kitchen out of her back door." That taught her father about giving back and about what strong women could accomplish. Had he not learned that lesson, Liz said, "He would not have married my mother, or got along with Aunt Brenda, both of whom were forces to be reckoned with."

Liz said her father was once "one of the fastest men in Canada, and later in life he became one of the slowest. But through it all, he was one of the most determined people I knew." She also described the Turners as a highly competitive family, in which the father thought nothing of warning his daughter that she'd be bumped out of the way if she didn't get her cross-country skis motoring more quickly. While playing tennis, "a double fault or missed shot provoked some colorful critique." And as always, when she saw her father gazing at the northern tundra at sunset, "It was in those moments he was truly happy and at peace."

The same was true at Lake of the Woods, where she saw her father sit for hours gazing at pine trees: "He never tired of the beauty of the Canadian shield."

Liz described her father as "game, right to the end." Then, she looked towards her mother and said: "Thank you for being feisty and persistent and cajoling him to eat healthy food right to the end." She complimented her brother Michael and other caregivers for their contributions and concluded with: "We've lost our northern star."

Andrew read a passage from the Book of Job, then Michael from the Book of Revelation. It occurred to me that, unlike the offspring of Pierre Trudeau, Brian Mulroney, or Stephen Harper, these children of a former prime minister are almost completely unknown to the Canadian people, either because they've chosen to live outside Canada or have shunned the limelight. David was the only Turner offspring to have considered going into politics, but ultimately decided against it.

Monsignor Bianco, the former rector at St. Michael's and friend of the family's, met Turner in 1976 and would have the most unusual conversations with him. "What concordance do you use?" Turner once asked the priest, a question unlikely to have been asked by any other former finance minister.

"He took sacred scriptures very seriously and expected priests to as well," Msgr. Bianco said.

The Very Reverend Douglas Stoute, another Turner family friend, led the intercessions. John McDermott and Jason Fowler performed *Ave Maria*. The carillon on Parliament Hill rang out Beethoven's *Ode to Joy*, a Turner favourite, and the attendees were warned about the serious protocols surrounding the taking of the eucharist.

For a former prime minister, one would have expected that the highest-ranking member of the Catholic church in Canada to give the final commendation, a series of prayers, at the front of the church, just before the end of the service. But in another unexpected move, Archbishop Thomas Cardinal Collins did *not* perform that function, and it was left to Msgr. Bianco, with an assist from Rev. Stoute, to do the honours, which included sprinkling holy water on the casket before it was escorted down the centre aisle and out of the cathedral.

Why would a former prime minister of Canada not want the church's senior-most representative to give the final commendation? Apparently, it goes back to Turner's somewhat complicated relationship with Archbishop Collins, who friends say was not totally enamored with Turner's more liberal Catholicism. Turner had been an honorary pallbearer at the funerals of two of Collins' predecessors: G. Emmett Carter and Aloysius Ambrozic. But his relationship with Collins was less close, partially because the two were from different generations. "By the time I got there, he was older and frail," Collins explains. "I simply didn't have as much to do with him."

Having said that, Turner did take Collins to lunch several times, which made me wonder what kinds of vigorous debates the two may have had about their different interpretations of Catholicism.

"When people have lunches, they're very discreet," Collins says, declining to bite on the question. "It's always good when priests are reticent about things."

The Archbishop says he never discussed funeral arrangements directly with Turner, but rather, with representatives from the funeral home, who well understood the family's preferences. For example, Catholic tradition suggests that when a casket enters the church, it should be draped with a white covering called a pall. But state funerals in Canada mandate the Canadian flag cover the casket, which is coincidentally what Turner wanted as well. And that's what he got.

"The pall represents the baptismal robes of the one at the end of their life," explains Collins. "Then the priest goes around the coffin with incense and holy water. This is a Christian going to meet the Lord."

When asked what he thought of the family's choice not to incorporate the pall in the ceremony, Collins exhales deeply and pauses for several seconds before responding.

"There are many different ways of looking at this," he says diplomatically. "They preferred another approach." To be clear, there was no snippiness or malice in Collins' tone. But by the same token, one could infer that the archbishop had wished the family might have made a different choice.

"He was a very charitable man," Collins emphasizes. "He had his views. But he was a great supporter."

The service concluded with a bilingual version of "O Canada."

"It sounds horrible to say I was enjoying a funeral," Michael says, "but I was pleased for Dad. I was so thankful we could put Dad's wishes into action."

Because of the small numbers at the church, the all-news television networks (which carried the service "live") intermixed post-service interviews from the site with other guests they'd lined up who were elsewhere. Kim Campbell was beamed in from Italy on CBC News Network and revealed the many connections she shared with Turner. She was an undergrad student at UBC in 1966 when Turner's mother was the chancellor there. Campbell's stepmother's mother was one of the die-hard 195 delegates to stay with Turner on his last ballot at the 1968 leadership convention. Campbell heard Turner speak on the Free Trade Agreement in 1988, and she quickly realized she disagreed with most of what he said.

"He may be responsible for my running in federal politics," she said.

Turner was the opposition leader when Campbell was a rookie parliamentarian. They both represented Vancouver ridings. "I always respected him," she said. "He had a pragmatic realism about what the parliamentary process could accomplish. There was a decency about him." Then, referring to where they came chronologically in the prime ministerial pecking order, Campbell offered: "He was seventeen, I was nineteen, both prime numbers but not prime ministers for as long as we'd like to be."

The eighteenth prime minister, who came between Turner and Campbell, remembered a man "who could attack us very vigorously and I have all the scars to prove it," said Brian Mulroney, "but there was no malice." And as for the fact that his prime ministership was so short? "There have been very few prime ministers in Canadian history and he was one of them," Mulroney noted. "That's a pretty good going by any standard."

Former Liberal cabinet minister Lloyd Axworthy, who'd known Turner for fifty-seven years, also avoided the funeral due to COVID-19. But in his television interview, he referred to Turner's truly believing that "Parliament was a crucible in which Canadians could be heard." Axworthy was with Turner during some of the former prime minister's biggest political moments. He was the leader's free trade critic while both were on the opposition side of the Commons. And two decades earlier, he worked with Turner in consumer and corporate affairs, trying to lower drug prices.

"Get a view on what's going on," Turner told Axworthy all those years ago. When Axworthy came back with a plan to get drug costs down, Turner told him: "We're going to go full steam ahead on this." More than half a century later, that moment stayed with the eighty-year-old Axworthy.

Former Governor-General David Johnston, who moderated the debate featuring the worst moment of Turner's political life, attended the funeral, then spoke to reporters after. "Three words," Johnston said. "Integrity, civility, and practicality. And a love of Canada."

In a separate interview with me, Johnston spoke of a man "with real principle. Friendships counted. That's a difficult thing for people in politics. They don't have friends. They have allies." Johnston described a Turner who was becoming increasingly concerned about political life, which he saw as a noble profession "and he feared it was becoming less noble."

The 1988 leaders' debate panelist, Pamela Wallin, who had a front row seat to Turner's finest moment in politics, recalled a speech in the House opposing capital punishment. "It was one of the most powerful pieces of oratory and moments of passion that I'd ever seen in a politician," Wallin said. "I sat there mesmerized for well over an hour."

Wallin recalled another moment when Mother Teresa visited Canada. Turner and Wallin sat beside each other at the event, as Turner had tears streaming down his face, so dazzled was he with the nun's commitment to people and the sacrifice it took.

Finally, the former journalist—now a senator—recalled a leader "who never took anything personally. He never walked out of a studio mad."

Another former Liberal finance minister, Ralph Goodale, flew in from Saskatchewan for the funeral, donning the souvenir scarf that Turner's campaign gave out to team members at the 1984 leadership convention. "I've kept it all these years," said Goodale. He spoke of "three M's: money, morale, and memberships," which were three of Turner's priorities as a party leader in opposition.

John Baird, the former Conservative cabinet minister, told me: "Had he not become leader when he did, he could have been a long-term prime minister. He was one of the most decent, honest Canadians I knew. If the Liberals had to be in power, I'd have preferred him over the first or second Trudeau."

Zainab Azim was interviewed on television and spoke of Turner's visit to Milton, where Azim was a high school volunteer. "He used his entire speech to speak to us, the young people in the room," Azim said. "He talked about public service as a way of life."

A week and a half after Turner's death, the Pearson Institute mounted a virtual discussion focused on the former PM's life. Former Justice Minister Irwin Cotler, who worked for the then Justice Minister Turner, said Turner "paved the way for the Liberal Party to come back to power, and Jean Chrétien was the beneficiary of that."

Dalton McGuinty penned an op-ed column on the John Turner he encountered. "He knew what life had in store for [young people]. He could imagine their inevitable triumphs and tragedies, and he believed that only a rich idealism could sustain them and keep a corrosive cynicism at bay," wrote McGuinty. "Turner believed the most important question young Canadians should ask of themselves is not what do I want from life? But rather, what does life want from me?"

McGuinty noted that Turner never took himself too seriously. "My son, Liam, impressed by the former PM's lifelong achievements, once said to him:

'Not only were you Canada's fastest runner, you were also our prime minister.' Turner replied: 'and I was fast at that, too.'"

David Herle suggests Turner would be appalled at the state of political discourse in Canada today, marred as it is by polarization and mutual disrespect. "He was old school but a good and better school of politics than we have now," Herle told me.

Turner was buried in a truly beautiful section of midtown Toronto's Mount Pleasant Cemetery. A tall flagpole, flying the Canadian flag Turner voted for as an MP, graces the gravesite. A modest-looking black marble headstone, engraved with white letters, notes his final resting place, his family name proudly stated in bold upper-case letters, with an engraved maple leaf on either side:

TURNER

RT. HON. JOHN NAPIER WYNDHAM TURNER

JUNE 7, 1929–SEPTEMBER 19, 2020

17TH PRIME MINISTER OF CANADA

BORN RICHMOND, ENGLAND

And below that, his wife's name, for when her time comes:

BELOVED HUSBAND OF

GEILLS McCRAE KILGOUR

DECEMBER 23, 1937

Two Canadian prime ministers are buried at Mount Pleasant Cemetery: Turner and William Lyon Mackenzie King. They share a distinctive feature: they are two of only three of Canada's prime ministers to have won personal election in three different provinces (King in Ontario, Prince Edward Island, and Saskatchewan; Turner in Quebec, Ontario, and British Columbia; and Wilfrid Laurier in Quebec, Saskatchewan, and Ontario).

Because so many of Turner's political friends couldn't be accommodated at St. Michael's Cathedral, former Ontario treasurer Darcy McKeough hosted a lunch after the funeral at the Toronto Club for some of that crowd, including yours truly. I followed up with Rick Alway on the part of his eulogy where he described Turner as "essentially" a happy man. Why the use of the adverb to qualify Turner's life, I wondered.

"Was he happy?" I asked Alway.

There was a long pause.

"He wasn't tortured," Alway insisted. "There was no sense of regret about how he lived life. He was happy enough. But he would have loved more grandchildren around him. Liz was in the U.S.; David's and Andrew's kids were around but not enough. But he wasn't that introspective, who'd have sat down at the end of his life to consider whether he was happy."

It was also at that lunch that I learned about David Turner's condition, which was not well known beyond his circle of immediate friends and family. I knew David a little, given that we had lived across the street from one another in midtown Toronto, and had seen each other at some of his father's birthday parties.

The day after the funeral, I called David, both to offer my condolences on his father's death and to inquire about his own circumstances.

"Dave, I have to tell you, I'm hearing some deeply concerning things about your health," I told him. "Are you okay?"

"Don't believe everything you hear," he insisted. "People shouldn't be gossiping about this. I'm fine."

Exactly three months after his father's funeral, David died at Toronto's Sunnybrook Health Sciences Centre on January 6, 2021. He was fifty-two. He was buried at the same gravesite as his father in Mount Pleasant Cemetery. The headstone's style echoes his father's white engraving on black marble, but lies flat in the ground, in front of his father's headstone and to the left. It simply says:

IN LOVING MEMORY
OF
DAVID RUSSELL TURNER

MAY 14, 1968
JANUARY 6, 2021

"DREAM BIG, NEVER GIVE UP"

The newspaper obituary described David as having had a "life well lived, but far too short." It noted his lifelong friendships which always resulted in phone calls on birthdays, "a trait perhaps inherited from his father." The obituary ended with David's hope that "a rowdy gathering be held to celebrate his life" once COVID protocols permitted.

As further evidence that everything connects, not only were John Turner and Brian Mulroney ultimately good friends, but some of their children and grandchildren were too. David Turner and Caroline Mulroney (who at this writing is a cabinet minister in the government of Ontario) became friends because their children Dylan Turner and Pierce Lapham played hockey together.

"It was so tragic," Caroline Mulroney says of David's premature death, adding emphatically, "He was a great dad, just a *great* dad."

COVID-19 made David's death even more agonizing for his family. Because of strict hospital protocols, he was allowed only two visitors and the list could not be changed. A best friend of thirty years and his brother Michael were chosen. Michael was apparently allowed to chaperone David's two children for a visit, but as Geills emailed Marc Kealey: "I, his mother, was not able to see him the entire time he was there. Cruelty was dished out to many during these troubled times and heartbreak was not just with Covid-impacted families."

As devastated as David's family was, they all agreed it was a good thing that he managed to live long enough to be predeceased by his father. "For John's sake, I wouldn't have wanted to put him through that," Geills says.

The two most important women in John Turner's life now had something terrible in common. Turner's mother and his wife had both lost husbands and sons in a relatively short space of time.

"It's hard particularly when you're surrounded by so much death and tragedy that your situation isn't that unusual," Geills says. "And you see others going through worse things. John's time had come. He'd had a good life. David Turner was a tragedy. He was much too young, with two young kids."

Geills' strength has truly had to come to the fore at this stage of her life. "How many people in my shoes, who've lost a husband and son and have to carry on... Fortunately, I have enough skillset and interests to keep me totally engaged. That's not to say I'm not unhappy and sad and all the things that one would be. But the idea of just sitting there watching Netflix is not something I'd ever do."

Geills also now shares the tragedy of losing a child with Alan Eagleson. "He has been an amazing friend through all," she says. "His own daughter died of cancer in the same time period, so we became fellow survivors."

On December 15, the Canadian Association of Former Parliamentarians held its annual special service to mark the passing of former MPs and senators. Given the times, it was done virtually. There were fifty-three former parliamentarians recognized during this service, including, of course, Turner, who was one of nineteen nonagenarians to have died since the last service in May 2019. Turner shared the ceremony with the likes of John Crosbie, "Red" Kelly, Leo Kolber, Aideen Nicholson, and Aileen Carroll.

"We are the poorer for their departure but the richer for their time on earth," said House Speaker Anthony Rota.

As a former prime minister, Turner was clearly the biggest name on the list. But emails between Geills Turner and Marc Kealey showed neither was particularly happy with the association's effort. While the story about Turner's saving Diefenbaker from drowning was mentioned in an accompanying video, the narrator said the incident took place in Barbados when in fact it was in Tobago. Kealey was also miffed at how few of Turner's accomplishments were mentioned, calling it "amateur hour."

"JNT got the same kind/type of accolade as one-term wonders (including Suzanne Tremblay—a BQ member who was elected to rip Canada apart)," he emailed Geills.

"I am so sorry that I alerted people to watch," Geills emailed back.

* * *

Turner's sister Brenda often wonders what kind of prime minister her brother would have been had he been able to keep the job longer. Now ninety, she's convinced he'd have been "fantastic. He had a sense of what's right and wrong. Being a lawyer, he could see both sides of an issue. But the end of his life was a Greek tragedy."

Brian Mulroney remembers former British Prime Minister Margaret Thatcher saying to him: "It's a funny old world. How surprised I was that John Turner wasn't a hugely successful prime minister."

Had he been able to win his first election in 1984, or come back to the PMO in 1988, Tom Axworthy is convinced the country would have benefited immensely. "He would have kept the good, traditional things about the Liberal Party while fixing the problems Trudeau left," he says.

For example, Axworthy points to Trudeau's downgrading of the importance of Parliament. "John loved Parliament," he notes, "and parliamentary affairs would have become a much-needed focus."

Not only that, Turner's international contacts from his days as finance minister would have served him well on the world stage. It also would have provided him with the experience to get Canada's fiscal house in order, something that Prime Minister Jean Chrétien and his Finance Minister Paul Martin did a decade later.

In addition, Axworthy believes Turner's being a British Columbia–based MP would have brought a "real Pacific perspective to issues, rather than have it be the last thing considered as it was then and is now. It would have been very interesting to have a Liberal focused on Western rapprochement. He might have been able to pull it off." But the war with Chrétien, the patronage appointments for Trudeau, and Turner's first cabinet filled with Trudeau retreads prevented all of that from happening.

One day, a Turner associate saw the former PM alone and frail on a Toronto subway car and thought to himself, "there goes the King Lear of Canadian politics," a far cry from the handsome, youthful candidate at the 1968 leadership convention. Turner seemed to want and need the love of the Liberal Party, which often didn't reciprocate. Fortunately, as Turner grew older, his stock did rise within the party, which pleased him immensely.

When Robert F. Kennedy's name came up, Turner never failed to be moved by RFK's 1968 speeches urging people to engage in the democratic process. "People who are willing to sacrifice something–family, time, money, opportunities, privacy, for the public life of our country," Turner would say. "We can't take this public process for granted. We can't leave it to someone else."

Turner also brought something to public life not often seen. "What's missing from politics today is people not feeling constantly used," says Turner friend Howard Brown. "John Turner took an interest when he met you. He sent you a letter thanking you for meeting with him. Most politicians today want to use you. Turner never made you feel he was doing that."

Turner didn't like to boast about his accomplishments, but in one of his many interviews with Arthur Milnes, he did make a bit of a list. He admitted to enjoying the free trade debate with Mulroney; being Pierre Trudeau's minister of justice and reforming the Criminal Code, the Bail Reform Act; setting up the Federal Court; and enhancing the rights of the citizen against the state under our court system. Then he allowed a rare boast from his time as finance minister: "I was the last guy before [Paul] Martin to have a surplus. By the way, when I was minister of finance, our dollar was $1.07," compared to the American dollar.

Actually, Turner had told others that "The only boast I've ever made is that I know more Canadians by their first names than any other Canadian alive." Even John Diefenbaker once said "John Turner was a person who could walk down the main street of most cities and towns in Canada and meet people he knew by name. That's a rare quality in today's world." He'd also met every prime minister since R.B. Bennett, which surely not too many, if any, other Canadians can say.

Of course, Turner's greatest joy in public life was speaking in the House of Commons. "Despite public criticism—much of it justified—Parliament is still our greatest forum of democracy," he said in 1968.

Turner once told his friend and fellow treasurer Darcy McKeough: "The greatest honour I have ever had was being a member of the House of Commons."

One of Turner's successors as Liberal leader, Michael Ignatieff, isn't the least bit surprised to hear that. "He was one of the last parliamentarians, someone who genuinely believed in the House and the ideal of debate," he says. "Boy, has that disappeared, in Canada and the United Kingdom. The heart of democracy is just empty these days."

In some respects, John Turner was cursed with his good looks. "He had everything going for him," wrote Dalton McGuinty. "The brains, the looks, the athleticism. He was a star. People were drawn to him and, perhaps because of that, a lot was expected of him. That expectation was a burden he carried throughout his public life."

Peter Herrndorf, who has run some of this country's best-known cultural institutions such as the National Arts Centre, Toronto Life magazine, TVO, and CBC News, wonders whether Turner was too attractive for his own good. "He was so handsome he raised the bar so high," Herrndorf says. "He couldn't meet those expectations."

No doubt, true. But if you're too young to have remembered John Turner in his prime, Canada Post has something of interest for you. On June 11, 2021, the post office created a stamp of Turner, depicting him behind the wheel of a boat, on open water, with a Canadian flag billowing in the background. Turner has an ear-to-ear grin on his face, looking movie-star-handsome and happy. Twitter had a mini-explosion when the stamp was released.

"I met this fine man on a few occasions," investor advocate John De Goey tweeted. "Had great admiration for him. This is a fine way to acknowledge his contribution to Canada."

Kristin Raworth, a self-described Joe Clark enthusiast, added: "I guess stamps CAN be sexy."

And Paul Martin adviser Scott Reid tweeted: "Mr. Turner was such a giant. I sat in the House of Commons gallery in 1989 as a lowly summer student to watch MPs acknowledge his sixtieth birthday. Just love this stamp of him. Looks like he was carved from twin slabs of granite and handsome."

If we're going to remember the King Lear of Canadian politics, we should remember this gloriously happy warrior as well.

Postscript

OVER THE DECADES, MANY MEMBERS of John Turner's staff did a good thing for history. They kept virtually every document that came through his political life: from opposition rookie MP, to cabinet minister, to prime minister, to opposition leader, and, once again, to opposition MP.

There are literally thousands upon thousands of documents at Library and Archives Canada, the guardians of our history. I've perused dozens of boxes filled with files of speeches, personal correspondence, policy papers, newspaper clippings, press releases, schedules, confidential political memos, transcripts of media interviews, and the list goes on. But perhaps the most meaningful documents are the 5×8 file cards on which Turner wrote bullet points for speeches in his own undecipherable left-handed handwriting.

One set of cards in particular caught my eye. Turner was speaking at one of his birthday parties and told the assembled crowd that he'd enjoyed every moment of his life, that he'd lived his life to the fullest, that he believed in the perfectibility of the human spirit. He wasn't getting older, just better.

He acknowledged he'd been given some good things in life. He listed his mother, his sister, his wife and children, health, friends, and luck. He made the interesting observation that he'd never been bored nor discouraged for too long. Like Frank Sinatra, he admitted to some regrets, but then again, too few to mention. "I don't know the Bible or Shakespeare as well as I should," he said.

And then, the man who grew up without a father concluded with: "I couldn't have asked for more; I deserved a good deal less."

You could be forgiven for thinking this was one of Turner's last birthday speeches, in which he gazed back philosophically at a life, much of it well lived. In fact, the speech was given on June 7, 1979, at what was only Turner's fiftieth birthday party. He had no idea that the most dramatic and consequential moments of his life were still to come.

Acknowledgements

WHILE IT'S TRUE THAT I wrote all the words in this book, it's even truer that completing this project in its current form would not have been possible without the contributions of several people whom I must now happily thank.

No one was more crucial to painting a more complete picture of John Napier Turner than his wife Geills. While she will not like every word I have written about her husband in these pages, I thank her for being extraordinarily giving of her time and energy. We had numerous interactions for this book including sit-down interviews, endless email exchanges, access to her collection of photographs which she, an extremely talented photographer, took herself, and very significantly, access to her husband's personal and confidential correspondence, lovingly cared for at Library and Archives Canada. All of these things contributed to making this book portray her husband's life more honestly and accurately. I'm also grateful to John and Geills Turner's offspring: Elizabeth, Michael, and Andrew, all of whom spoke to me for this book despite knowing me hardly at all. The fact that Turner's immediate family agreed to subject themselves to my questions at a time when they were still grieving the deaths of both their husband/father John, and their son/brother David was extraordinarily generous.

Michael MacDonald at Library and Archives Canada was extremely helpful in enabling me to see thousands of documents from Turner's time in public life. He and his team are responsible for protecting the documents that tell the story of our country, so I was not surprised at how they were all such sticklers for following the rules, particularly during a global pandemic which made getting access to things even trickier.

My friend of fifty years, Douglas Harrison, helped me navigate the way through Turner's early years at Stikeman Elliott. My friend of more than forty years, David Lockhart, provided wonderful insights into Turner's years as opposition leader. I'm lucky to count both of these guys as great pals all these years later.

Stacey Dunseath, executive producer extraordinaire at *The Agenda* at TVO, consented to allowing me to pursue this project, even though I sort of promised her I wouldn't take on another book after doing nearly 600 pages on Premier Bill Davis a few years ago. Khaleesi, I really meant it when I made that promise. But we both knew I'd probably break it. Thank you.

If not for John Turner, I'd never have met Arthur Milnes. It's one of the reasons this book is dedicated to him. Art and I share a passion for better understanding politics, politicians, and history, and I couldn't be more grateful to him for his advice on this project. Art, your love and respect for John Turner were always in my thoughts as I wrote this book. I hope what you have read accurately portrays the man you knew so well.

You can tell time is marching on when you start working with the children of your contemporaries. Such was the case with the talented Trilby Kent, herself an author, and the editor of this work. I admired her father Peter when he was both a journalist and MP. Her mother Cilla is a loyal viewer of the TVO program I host and frequently emails me her comments of said show. What a pleasure it now is to work with the other member of the family. Thank you Trilby, and I look forward to reading *your* next book.

Kudos also to Ken Whyte, all of whose books I have read and enjoyed. This was my first book for Sutherland House. I don't know why Ken green lit me, but I know I chose his imprint because of my enormous respect for his authorship and journalistic chops. Thanks Ken. I hope you think this partnership went as well as I do.

I won the lottery the day I was born to Marnie and Larry Paikin in Hamilton, Ontario sixty-two years ago. One could not ask for finer role models as parents and people. With both now well into their octogenarian years, I am incredibly blessed to still have both my parents with me, when so many of my contemporaries do not. I have never, not for one second, taken that fact for granted. I know my brother Jeff feels the same way. And speaking of Jeff, I could not admire him more, particularly how he has persevered through a year in which brain cancer took his wife Andrea, far too early.

My four kids continue to dazzle me with their accomplishments. Zachary, Henry, Teddy, and Giulia are turning into exactly the kinds of people I'd love to hang out with, and they inspire me to try to do my level best. Extra props for Zach for helping me translate French material into English for this book.

ACKNOWLEDGEMENTS

And finally, to Francesca, who has been a literary widow for nine books now. My writing nine books over our 20 years together (while holding down a very full-time job) would be impossible without your love and support. Nothing would work without your making it work. You have the most generous heart of anyone I know.

* * *

These books were very helpful references in the writing of this one:

All in Good Time, by Brian Tobin. Penguin Canada, 2002.

All the King's Horses: Politics Among the Ruins, by Ron Graham. Macfarlane, Walter, & Ross, 1995.

Bill Davis: Nation Builder, and Not So Bland After All, by Steve Paikin. Dundurn, A J. Patrick Boyer Book, 2016.

Brian Mulroney: Memoirs 1939-1993, by Brian Mulroney. McClelland & Stewart, Douglas Gibson Book, 2007.

Canada 1957-1967: The Years of Uncertainty and Innovation, by J.L. Granatstein. McClelland & Stewart, 1986.

The Canadian Revolution 1985-1995: From Deference to Defiance, by Peter C. Newman. Viking, 1995.

Chretien, Volume 1: The Will to Win, by Lawrence Martin. Lester Publishing, 1995.

Common Ground, by Justin Trudeau. Harper Collins, 2014.

A Deal Undone: The Making and Breaking of the Meech Lake Accord, by Andrew Cohen. Douglas & McIntyre, 1990.

Discipline of Power: The Conservative Interlude and the Liberal Restoration, by Jeffrey Simpson. Personal Library, Publishers Toronto, 1980.

Divided Loyalties: The Liberal Party of Canada, 1984-2008, by Brooke Jeffrey. University of Toronto Press, 2010.

Election: The Issues, the Strategies, the Aftermath, by Gerald Caplan, Michael Kirby, and Hugh Segal. Prentice-Hall Canada, 1989.

Elusive Destiny: The Political Vocation of John Napier Turner, by Paul Litt. UBC Press, 2011.

The Establishment Men: A Portrait of Power, by Peter C. Newman. McClelland & Stewart, 1982.

Friends in High Places: Politics and Patronage in the Mulroney Government, by Claire Hoy. Key Porter Books, 1987

Grits: An Intimate Portrait of the Liberal Party, by Christina McCall-Newman. Macmillan of Canada, 1982.

Hell or High Water: My Life in and out of Politics, by Paul Martin (Jr.). McClelland & Stewart, 2008.

Juggernaut: Paul Martin's Campaign for Chretien's Crown, by Susan Delacourt. McClelland & Stewart, 2003.

Ladies, Upstairs! My Life in Politics and After, by Monique Begin. McGill-Queen's University Press, 2018.

Leo: a Life, by Leo Kolber with L. Ian MacDonald. McGill-Queen's University Press, 2003.

A Life in Progress, by Conrad Black. Key Porter Books, 1993.

The Life: The Seductive Call of Politics, by Steve Paikin. Viking, 2001.

Losing Confidence: Power, Politics, and the Crisis in Canadian Democracy, by Elizabeth May. McClelland & Stewart, 2009.

My Years as Prime Minister, by Jean Chretien. Knopf Canada, 2007.

No Holds Barred: My Life in Politics, by John C. Crosbie. McClelland & Stewart, 1997.

One Eyed Kings: Promise and Illusion in Canadian Politics, by Ron Graham. Collins Publishers, 1986.

One Hundred Monkeys: The Triumph of Popular Wisdom in Canadian Politics, by Robert Mason Lee. Macfarlane Walter & Ross, 1989.

Paul Martin: The Power of Ambition, by John Gray. Key Porter Books, 2003.

The Player: The Life & Times of Dalton Camp, by Geoffrey Stevens. Key Porter Books, 2003.

Playing for Keeps: The Making of the Prime Minister, 1988, by Graham Fraser. McClelland & Stewart, 1989.

Politics of Purpose (40th Anniversary Edition): The Right Honourable John N. Turner, 17th Prime Minister of Canada, edited by Elizabeth McIninch and Arthur Milnes. McGill-Queen's University Press, 2009.

Power, Prime Ministers, and the Press: The Battle for Truth on Parliament Hill, by Robert Lewis. Dundurn, 2018.

The Rainmaker: A Passion for Politics, by Senator Keith Davey. Stoddart, 1986.

Reign of Error: The Inside Story of John Turner's Troubled Leadership, by Greg Weston. McGraw-Hill Ryerson, 1988.

Rise to Greatness: The History of Canada from the Vikings to the Present, by Conrad Black. McClelland & Stewart, 2014.

So, What Are The Boys Saying? An Inside Look at Brian Mulroney in Power, by Michel Gratton. McGraw-Hill Ryerson, 1987.

Spoils of Power: The Politics of Patronage, by Jeffrey Simpson. Collins Toronto, 1988.

Stikeman Elliot: Les cinquante premieres annees, by Richard W. Pound. Les Editions Transcontinental, 2003.

Time and Chance: The Political Memoirs of Canada's First Woman Prime Minister, by Kim Campbell. Doubleday, 1996.

Titans: How the New Canadian Establishment Seized Power, by Peter C. Newman. Viking, 1998.

Trudeau, by George Radwanski. Signet Publishing, 1978.

Trudeau and Our Times, Volume 1: The Magnificent Obsession, by Stephen Clarkson & Christina McCall. McClelland & Stewart, 1990.

A Very Public Life, Volume II: So Many Worlds, by Paul Martin (Sr.), Deneau, 1985.

The Washington Diaries 1981-1989 by Allan Gotlieb. McClelland & Stewart, 2006.

Why Canadians Get the Politicians & Governments They Don't Want, by Heward Grafftey. Stoddart Publishing Co., 1991.

Yankee Go Home? Canadians and Anti-Americanism, by J.L. Granatstein. Harper Collins Publishers Ltd., 1996.

Name Index

Former prime ministers (clockwise from top left) Paul Martin, Joe Clark, John Chretien and curr